Master Tax Examples and Q&As 2010–11

Master Tax Examples and Q&As 2010–11

a Wolters Kluwer business

Wolters Kluwer
145 London Road
Kingston upon Thames
KT2 6SR
Telephone: (0) 844 561 8166
Facsimile: +44 (0) 208 547 2638
Email: cch@wolterskluwer.co.uk
Website: www.cch.co.uk

This publication is sold with the understanding that neither the publisher nor the authors, with regard to this publication, are engaged in rendering legal or professional services. The material contained in this publication neither purports, nor is intended to be, advice on any particular matter.

Although this publication incorporates a considerable degree of standardisation, subjective judgment by the user, based on individual circumstances, is indispensable. This publication is an aid and cannot be expected to replace such judgment.

Neither the publisher nor the authors can accept any responsibility or liability to any person, whether a purchaser of this publication or not, in respect of anything done or omitted to be done by any such person in reliance, whether sole or partial, upon the whole or any part of the contents of this publication.

Legislative and other material

While copyright in all statutory and other materials resides in the Crown or other relevant body, copyright in the remaining material in this publication is vested in the publisher.

The publisher advises that any statutory or other materials issued by the Crown or other relevant bodies and reproduced and quoted in this publication are not the authorised official versions of those statutory or other materials. In the preparation, however, the greatest care has been taken to ensure exact conformity with the law as enacted or other material as issued.

Crown copyright legislation is reproduced under the terms of Crown Copyright Policy Guidance issued by HMSO. Other Crown copyright material is reproduced with the permission of the controller of HMSO. European Communities Copyright material is reproduced with permission.

Telephone Helpline Disclaimer Notice

Where purchasers of this publication also have access to any Telephone Helpline Service operated by Wolters Kluwer (UK), then Wolters Kluwer's total liability to contract, tort (including negligence, or breach of statutory duty) misrepresentation, restitution or otherwise with respect to any claim arising out of its acts or alleged omissions in the provision of the Helpline Service shall be limited to the yearly subscription fee paid by the Claimant.

ISBN 978-1-84798-295-7

No responsibility for loss occasioned to any person acting or refraining from action as a result of any material in this publication can be accepted by the author or publisher. Material is contained in this publication for which copyright is acknowledged. Permission to reproduce such material cannot be granted by the publisher and application must be made to the copyright holder.

British Library Cataloguing-in-Publication Data

A catalogue record for this book is available from the British Library.

Typeset in-house at Wolters Kluwer (UK) Ltd
Printed and bound in the UK by Hobbs the Printers Ltd

About the author

Sarah Laing is a Chartered Tax Adviser. She has been writing professionally since joining CCH Editions in 1998 as a Senior Technical Editor, contributing to a range of highly regarded publications including the *British Tax Reporter*, *Taxes – The Weekly Tax News*, the Red & Green legislation volumes, *Hardman's*, *International Tax Agreements* and many others. She became Publishing Manager for the tax and accounting portfolio in 2001 and later went on to help run CCH Seminars (including ABG Courses and Conferences).

Sarah originally worked for the Inland Revenue in Newbury and Swindon Tax Offices, before moving out into practice in 1991. She has worked for both small and Big Four firms. She now works as a freelance author providing technical writing services for the tax and accountancy profession.

Sarah is the News Editor of TaxationWeb Limited (www.taxationweb.co.uk) which provides free information and resources on UK taxes to taxpayers and professionals.

About the original author

Giles Mooney BSc (Hons) ACA CTA is a partner of The Professional Training Partnership (PTP). He is a Chartered Accountant and Chartered Tax Adviser, and has been involved in UK tax training for ten years. Giles started his career with a small firm of accountants and tax advisers, before working as a director of a large professional training company. He has written for a number of publications on various UK tax and business issues including writing PTP's own monthly publication *Professional Tax Update*. Giles entertains and educates professionals several days each week running tax seminars throughout the country.

Foreword

Master Tax Examples and Q&As is the fourth edition of this publication. It has been updated and expanded to include many more examples and questions posed by CCH customers using the CCH helpline service over the last year.

Learning tax from a book is something that concerns many people because the vast majority of books, while being technically very good, are lacking a practical edge. This book is therefore designed to be read alongside the *British Master Tax Guide* and similar books to bring the theory to life with some real-life (and some made-up) examples.

Each of the main taxes are considered individually and you can refer to the examples using the *British Master Tax Guide* paragraph references or by using the Legislation Finding List. This allows you to go straight from a tricky piece of legislation to a worked example.

Hopefully you will find *Master Tax Examples and Q&As* easy to navigate and more digestible than other technical tax books. You no longer have to read text books or tax legislation and then sit and wonder for a couple of hours about what it actually means – you can now read the theory and then use this book to understand the practical.

I hope you find the book interesting and useful.

Sarah Laing CTA

October 2010

Contents

About the author   vii
About the original author   vii
Foreword   ix
Abbreviations   xiii

Key Data   1

Income Tax   137

Corporation Tax   241

Capital Gains Tax   307

Inheritance Tax   371

Value Added Tax   427

National Insurance Contributions   471

Legislation Finding List   493
Index   499

Abbreviations

The following abbreviations are commonly used throughout this publication.

AIA	annual investment allowance
AIM	Alternative Investment Market
ABA	agricultural buildings allowance
ACT	advance corporation tax
AP	accounting period
APR	agricultural property relief
AQE	available qualifying expenditure
BATR	business asset taper relief
b/fwd	brought forward
BMTG	British Master Tax Guide
BPR	business property relief
BPRA	business premises renovation allowance
BTC	British Tax Cases (CCH) 1982-(current)
CAA 2001	Capital Allowances Act 2001
CASC	Community Amateur Sports Club
CCH	CCH, a Wolters Kluwer business
CFC	controlled foreign company
c/fwd	carried forward
CG	HMRC Capital Gains Manual
CGT	capital gains tax
Ch.	Chapter
CIS	Construction Industry Scheme
CLT	chargeable lifetime transfer
COMP	contracted-out money purchase
COSR	contracted-out salary-related
CPD	continuing professional development
CT	corporation tax
CTA 2009	Corporation Tax Act 2009
CTC	child tax credit
CTSA	corporation tax self-assessment
DIY	do-it-yourself
DTR	double tax relief
e.g.	(exempli gratia) for example
EIM	HMRC Employment Income Manual
EIS	Enterprise Investment Scheme
EMI	Enterprise Management Incentive
ESC	extra-statutory concession
ESM	HMRC Employment Status Manual
etc.	(et cetera) and so on
EWC	expected week of confinement
FA	Finance Act
FCO	Foreign and Commonwealth Office
F(No. 2)A	Finance (No. 2) Act
FY	financial year
FYA	first-year allowance
GAAP	generally accepted accounting practice
GWR	gift with reservation

HMRC	Her Majesty's Revenue and Customs
HP	hire purchase
IBA	industrial buildings allowance
ICTA 1988	Income and Corporation Taxes Act 1988
i.e.	(id est) that is
IHT	inheritance tax
IHTA 1984	Inheritance Tax Act 1984
IIP	interest in possession
INTM	HMRC International Manual
ITA 2007	Income Tax Act 2007
ITEPA 2003	Income Tax (Earnings and Pensions) Act 2003
ITM	HMRC Inheritance Tax Manual
ITTOIA 2005	Income Tax (Trading and Other Income) Act 2005
JSA	jobseeker's allowance
LEL	lower earnings limit
LLA	long life asset
LLP	limited liability partnership
m	million
MCA	married couple's allowance
MD	managing director
MIB	Motor Insurers Bureau
MV	market value
NACE	classification of economic activities in the European Community
NCO	not contracted-out
NIC	National Insurance contribution
NIM	HMRC National Insurance Manual
p.a.	per annum
p.; pp.	page; pages
PAYE	pay as you earn
PCTCT	profits chargeable to corporation tax
PET	potentially exempt transfer
PIM	HMRC Property Income Manual
plc	public limited company
POAT	pre-owned asset tax
PPR	principal private residence
PR	personal representative
PSA	PAYE settlement agreement
PSA 1993	Pension Schemes Act 1993
Pt.	Part(s)
PT	primary threshold
QCB	qualifying corporate bond
R&D	research and development
RAT	rate applicable to trusts
reg.	regulation(s)
s.	section(s)
SEE	small earnings exception
SERPS	state earnings-related pension scheme
SI	statutory instrument
SLA	short-life asset
SME	small or medium enterprise
SMP	statutory maternity pay
SSCBA 1992	Social Security Contributions and Benefits Act 1992
TDR	total disposal receipts
TMA 1970	Taxes Management Act 1970
TWDV	tax written-down value

UEL	upper earnings limit
UPIC	unquoted property investment company
UK	United Kingdom
USM	unlisted securites market
VAT	value added tax
VATA 1994	Value Added Tax Act 1994
WDA	writing-down allowance
WDV	written-down value
WTC	working tax credit
y/e	year ending/ended

Key Data

GENERAL

Finance Acts	3
Retail Prices Index	3
PAYE thresholds	5
PAYE returns	6
PAYE codes	10
Rates of interest on overdue tax	11
Plant and machinery – overview of allowances from April 2008	21
Interest factor tables	31
Foreign exchange rates	32

INCOME TAX

Income tax rates	52
Personal reliefs	55
Payment dates 2009–10	57
Time-limits for elections and claims	58
Car, fuel and van benefits	58
HMRC authorised mileage rates	63
Taxable state benefits	65
Non-taxable state benefits	66
Official rate of interest	68
Official rate of interest – foreign currency loans	69
Relocation allowance	69
Incidental overnight expenses	70

CORPORATION TAX

Corporation tax rates	71
Due dates	73
Time-limits for elections and claims	74

CAPITAL GAINS TAX

Rates, annual exemption, retirement relief, chattel exemption	76
Due dates	76
Time-limits for elections and claims	77
Entrepreneurs' relief (from 6 April 2008 onwards)	78
Exemptions and reliefs	78
Treatment of shares and other securities (after 5 April 1998)	80
Enterprise Investment Scheme	80
Roll-over relief	81

STAMP DUTIES

Rates, penalties and interest	82

INHERITANCE TAX

Inheritance tax rates: general	91
Lifetime transfers: 2002 onwards	91

Reliefs   95
Due dates for delivery of accounts   97
Due dates for payment of inheritance tax   99

VALUE ADDED TAX
VAT rates   100
Registration limits   100
De-registration limits   103
VAT on private fuel   105
Value added tax – 'blocked' input tax   118

NATIONAL INSURANCE CONTRIBUTIONS
NIC rates   119

INDIRECT TAXES
Insurance premium tax   133
Landfill tax   133
Aggregates levy   134

GENERAL

1-000 Finance Acts

Year	Budget		Royal Assent	
1982	9 March	1982	30 July	1982
1983	15 March	1983	13 May	1983
1983 (No. 2)	15 March	1983	26 July	1983
1984	13 March	1984	26 July	1984
1985	19 March	1985	25 July	1985
1986	18 March	1986	25 July	1986
1987	17 March	1987	15 May	1987
1987 (No. 2)	17 March	1987	23 July	1987
1988	15 March	1988	29 July	1988
1989	14 March	1989	27 July	1989
1990	20 March	1990	26 July	1990
1991	19 March	1991	26 July	1991
1992	10 March	1992	16 March	1992
1992 (No. 2)	10 March	1992	16 July	1992
1993	16 March	1993	27 July	1993
1994	30 November	1993	3 May	1994
1995	29 November	1994	1 May	1995
1996	28 November	1995	29 April	1996
1997	26 November	1996	19 March	1997
1997 (No. 2)	2 July	1997	31 July	1997
1998	17 March	1998	31 July	1998
1999	9 March	1999	27 July	1999
2000	21 March	2000	28 July	2000
2001	7 March	2001	11 May	2001
2002	17 April	2002	24 July	2002
2003	9 April	2003	10 July	2003
2004	17 March	2004	22 July	2004
2005	16 March	2005	7 April	2005
2005 (No. 2)	16 March	2005	20 July	2005
2006	22 March	2006	19 July	2006
2006	22 March	2006	19 July	2006
2007	21 March	2007	19 July	2007
2008	12 March	2008	21 July	2008
2009	22 April	2009	21 July	2009
2010	24 March	2010	8 April	2010
2010 (No. 2)	22 June	2010	27 July	2010

1-020 Retail Prices Index

The Retail Prices Index (RPI), issued by the Department of Employment, is used to calculate the indexation allowance for capital gains tax purposes. Certain personal and other reliefs are also linked to the RPI, subject to Parliament determining otherwise.

3

With effect from February 1987 the reference date to which the price level in each subsequent month is related was changed from 'January 1974 = 100' to 'January 1987 = 100'.

Movements in the RPI in the months after January 1987 are calculated with reference to January 1987 = 100. (With a base of January 1974 = 100, January 1987's RPI was 394.5). A new formula has been provided by the Department of Employment for calculating movements in the index over periods which span January 1987:

'The index for the later month (January 1987 = 100) is multiplied by the index for January 1987 (January 1974 = 100) and divided by the index for the earlier month (January 1974 = 100). 100 is subtracted to give the percentage change between the two months.'

CCH has prepared the following table in accordance with this formula:

	1982	1983	1984	1985	1986	1987	1988	1989	1990	1991
Jan.		82.61	86.84	91.20	96.25	100.0	103.3	111.0	119.5	130.2
Feb.		82.97	87.20	91.94	96.60	100.4	103.7	111.8	120.2	130.9
March	79.44	83.12	87.48	92.80	96.73	100.6	104.1	112.3	121.4	131.4
April	81.04	84.28	88.64	94.78	97.67	101.8	105.8	114.3	125.1	133.1
May	81.62	84.64	88.97	95.21	97.85	101.9	106.2	115.0	126.2	133.5
June	81.85	84.84	89.20	95.41	97.79	101.9	106.6	115.4	126.7	134.1
July	81.88	85.30	89.10	95.23	97.52	101.8	106.7	115.5	126.8	133.8
Aug.	81.90	85.68	89.94	95.49	97.82	102.1	107.9	115.8	128.1	134.1
Sept.	81.85	86.06	90.11	95.44	98.30	102.4	108.4	116.6	129.3	134.6
Oct.	82.26	86.36	90.67	95.59	98.45	102.9	109.5	117.5	130.3	135.1
Nov.	82.66	86.67	90.95	95.92	99.29	103.4	110.0	118.5	130.0	135.6
Dec.	82.51	86.89	90.87	96.05	99.62	103.3	110.3	118.8	129.9	135.7

	1992	1993	1994	1995	1996	1997	1998	1999	2000	2001
Jan.	135.6	137.9	141.3	146.0	150.2	154.4	159.5	163.4	166.6	171.1
Feb.	136.3	138.8	142.1	146.9	150.9	155.0	160.3	163.7	167.5	172.0
March	136.7	139.3	142.5	147.5	151.5	155.4	160.8	164.1	168.4	172.2
April	138.8	140.6	144.2	149.0	152.6	156.3	162.6	165.2	170.1	173.1
May	139.3	141.1	144.7	149.6	152.9	156.9	163.5	165.6	170.7	174.2
June	139.3	141.0	144.7	149.8	153.0	157.5	163.4	165.6	171.1	174.4
July	138.8	140.7	144.0	149.1	152.4	157.5	163.0	165.1	170.5	173.3
Aug.	138.9	141.3	144.7	149.9	153.1	158.5	163.7	165.5	170.5	174.0
Sept.	139.4	141.9	145.0	150.6	153.8	159.3	164.4	166.2	171.7	174.6
Oct.	139.9	141.8	145.2	149.8	153.8	159.5	164.5	166.5	171.6	174.3
Nov.	139.7	141.6	145.3	149.8	153.9	159.6	164.4	166.7	172.1	173.6
Dec.	139.2	141.9	146.0	150.7	154.4	160.0	164.4	167.3	172.2	173.4

	2002	2003	2004	2005	2006	2007	2008	2009	2010	2011
Jan.	173.3	178.4	183.1	188.9	193.4	201.6	209.8	210.1	217.9	
Feb.	173.8	179.3	183.8	189.6	194.2	203.1	211.4	211.4	219.2	
March	174.5	179.9	184.6	190.5	195.0	204.4	212.1	211.3	220.7	
April	175.7	181.2	185.7	191.6	196.5	205.4	214.0	211.5	222.8	
May	176.2	181.5	186.5	192.0	197.7	206.2	215.1	212.8	223.6	
June	176.2	181.3	186.8	192.2	198.5	207.3	216.8	213.4	224.1	
July	175.9	181.3	186.8	192.2	198.5	206.1	216.5	213.4	223.6	
Aug.	176.4	181.6	187.4	192.6	199.2	207.3	217.2	214.4	224.5	
Sept.	177.6	182.5	188.1	193.1	200.1	208.0	218.4	215.3		
Oct.	177.9	182.6	188.6	193.3	200.4	208.9	217.7	216.0		
Nov.	178.2	182.7	189.0	193.6	201.1	209.7	216.0	216.6		
Dec.	178.5	183.5	189.9	194.1	202.7	210.9	212.9	218.0		

1-040   PAYE thresholds

Tax year	Amount	
	Weekly £	**Monthly** £
2010–11	125.00	540.00
2009–10	125.00	540.00
2008–09	116.00	503.00
2007–08	100.00	435.00
2006–07	97.00	420.00
2005–06	94.00	408.00
2004–05	91.00	395.00
2003–04	89.00	385.00

Note

The figures for 2008–09 were increased from £105 (weekly) and £453 (monthly) from 7 September 2008 (as a result of the changes made during the year to the personal allowance). As a result, employers were required to add 60 to the previous tax code number for all L codes in time for the first payday on or after 7 September 2008 (e.g. 543L became 603L). The emergency tax code was 543L for paydays before 7 September 2008 but rose to 603L for paydays on or after that date.

Under normal circumstances, employers need not deduct tax for employees who earn less than the above amounts.

The PAYE monthly and weekly thresholds are calculated arithmetically from the personal allowance (SI 2003/2682, reg. 9(8)).

5

1-060   PAYE returns

PAYE returns: deadlines

Forms	Date	Provision	Penalty provisions
P14, P35, P38 and P38A	19 May following tax year	*Income Tax (Pay As You Earn) Regulations* 2003 (SI 2003/2682), reg. 73 and 74	TMA 1970, s. 98A
P60 (to employee)	31 May following tax year	*Income Tax (Pay As You Earn) Regulations* 2003 (SI 2003/2682), reg. 67	TMA 1970, s. 98A
P9D and P11D	6 July following tax year	*Income Tax (Pay As You Earn) Regulations* 2003 (SI 2003/2682), reg. 85–87	TMA 1970, s. 98
P46 (Car)	3 May, 2 August, 2 November, 2 February	*Income Tax (Pay As You Earn) Regulations* 2003 (SI 2003/2682), reg. 90	TMA 1970, s. 98

PAYE returns: penalties

Changes from April 2009

A new penalty regime has been introduced for returns for periods commencing on or after 1 April 2008 and where the return is due on or after 1 April 2009. Penalties are determined as a percentage of potential lost revenue. The percentage to be applied is determined according to whether the inaccuracy giving rise to the penalty was 'careless' (up to 30 per cent) 'deliberate but not concealed' (up to 70 per cent) or 'deliberate and concealed' (up to 100 per cent).

Earlier periods

Penalties (fixed, but see ESC B46) imposed for delays (TMA 1970, s. 98A)

Forms	First 12 months	Thereafter
P14, P35, P38 and P38A	£100 per 50 employees per month	Additional penalty not exceeding 100% of the tax and NIC payable for the year but remaining unpaid by 19 April following end of tax year

Penalties (mitigable) that may be imposed for delays (TMA 1970, s. 98)

Forms	Initial	Continuing
P9D and P11D	£300 per return	£60 per day

Penalties that may be imposed for incorrect returns

Forms	Provision TMA 1970	Penalty
P14, P35, P38 and P38A	s. 98A	Maximum of 100% of tax underpaid (s. 98A(4))
P9 and P11D	s. 98	Maximum penalty £3,000 (s. 98(2))

Interest on certain PAYE paid late

Where an employer has not paid the net tax deductible by him under PAYE to the collector within 14 days of the end of the tax year, the unpaid tax carries interest at the prescribed rate from the reckonable date until the date of payment. Certain repayments of tax also attract interest.

Interest on Class 1, 1A and 4 National Insurance contributions

From 19 April 1993 interest is charged on Class 1 contributions unpaid after the fourteenth day after the end of the tax year in which they were due. Interest is due on Class 1A contributions unpaid 14 days after the end of the tax year in which they were due to be paid.

For assessments issued after 18 April 1993 interest can be charged on overdue Class 4 contributions at the prescribed rate.

Law: SSCBA 1992, Sch. 1, para. 6(2), (3)

PAYE electronic communications: penalties (reg. 205 failures)

Penalties for tax year 2010–11 and later years
(SI 2003/2682, reg. 210AA)

Table 9ZA

Number of employees (note 1)	Penalty
1–5	£100
6–49	£300
50–249	£600
250–399	£900
400–499	£1,200
500–599	£1,500
600–699	£1,800
700–799	£2,100
800–899	£2,400

Number of employees (note 1)	Penalty
900–999	£2,700
1,000 or more	£3,000

Note

[1] Number of employees for whom particulars should have been included with the relevant annual return.

Penalties for tax year 2009–10
(SI 2003/2682, reg. 210A)

Table 9

Number of employees (note 1)	Penalty
1–5	£0
6–49	£100
50–249	£600
250–399	£900
400–499	£1,200
500–599	£1,500
600–699	£1,800
700–799	£2,100
800–899	£2,400
900–999	£2,700
1,000 or more	£3,000

Note

[1] Number of employees for whom particulars should have been included with the relevant annual return.

Penalties for tax year 2004–05 to 2008–09
(SI 2003/2682, reg. 210A)

Former table 9

Number of employees (note 1)	Penalty
1–49	£0
50–249	£600 (but see note 2)
250–399	£900

Number of employees (note 1)	Penalty
400–499	£1,200
500–599	£1,500
600–699	£1,800
700–799	£2,100
800–899	£2,400
900–999	£2,700
1,000 or more	£3,000

Note

[1] Number of employees for whom particulars should have been included with the specified information.

[2] But nil for tax year 2004–05 only (50–249 employees).

PAYE electronic communications: penalties (reg. 205A failures)

Penalties for tax quarter ending 5 April 2010 and for tax year 2010–11

(SI 2003/2682, reg. 210B)

Table 9A

Number of items (note 1)	Penalty
1–5	£0
6–49	£100
50–149	£300
150–299	£600
300–399	£900
400–499	£1,200
500–599	£1,500
600–699	£1,800
700–799	£2,100
800–899	£2,400
900–999	£2,700
1,000 or more	£3,000

Note

[1] Number of items of specified information the employer has failed to deliver in the tax quarter. (Each item mentioned in reg. 207(1) paras. (a) to (d) counts as a separate item of specified information.)

PAYE surcharges

(SI 2003/2682, reg. 203)

Specified percentage for each default in a surcharge period	
Default number (within the surcharge period)	**Specified percentage %**
1	0.00
2	0.00
3	0.17
4	0.17
5	0.17
6	0.33
7	0.33
8	0.33
9	0.58
10	0.58
11	0.58
12 and more defaults	0.83

1-080   PAYE codes

The PAYE code enables an employer or payer of pension to make any changes announced in the Budget. The codes are as follows:

L   tax code with basic personal allowance;
P   tax code with full personal allowance for those aged 65–74;
Y   tax code with full personal allowance for those aged 75 or over;
T   tax code used where HM Revenue & Customs reviewing other items in tax code. Also used where HM Revenue & Customs asked not to use other codes;
K   total allowances are less than total deductions.

Note

Codes A and H are no longer applicable for 2003–04 onwards. Code V is obsolete from April 2009 (as all individuals born before 6 April 1935 and qualifying for Married Couple's allowance (MCA) will be aged 75 and over during the tax year ended 5 April 2010. MCA is therefore due at the higher rate).

Other codes

The codes BR, DO, OT and NT are generally used where there is a second source of income and all allowances have been included in tax code which is applied to first or main source of income.

1-100   Rates of interest on overdue tax

The following tables give the rates of interest applicable under FA 1989, s. 178 and prescribed rates of interest (VATA 1994, s. 74 and former TMA 1970, s. 89). The rates apply to interest charged on overdue tax, with the exception of inheritance tax. From 6 February 1997 the rate for corporation tax diverges, see below.

Period of application		Rate %
From 29 September	2009	3
From 24 March	2009 to 28 September 2009	2.5
From 6 January	2009 to 26 January 2009	4.5
From 6 December	2008 to 5 January 2009	5.5
From 6 November	2008 to 5 December 2008	6.5
From 6 January	2008 to 5 November 2008	7.5
From 6 August	2007 to 5 January 2008	8.5
From 6 September	2006 to 5 August 2007	7.5
From 6 September	2005 to 5 September 2006	6.5
From 6 September	2004 to 5 September 2005	7.5
From 6 December	2003 to 5 September 2004	6.5
From 6 August	2003 to 5 December 2003	5.5
From 6 November	2001 to 5 August 2003	6.5
From 6 May	2001 to 5 November 2001	7.5
From 6 February	2000 to 5 May 2001	8.5
From 6 March	1999 to 5 February 2000	7.5
From 6 January	1999 to 5 March 1999	8.5
From 6 August	1997 to 5 January 1999	9.5
From 6 February	1997 to 5 August 1997	8.5
From 6 February	1996 to 5 February 1997	6.25
From 6 March	1995 to 5 February 1996	7
From 6 October	1994 to 5 March 1995	6.25
From 6 January	1994 to 5 October 1994	5.5
From 6 March	1993 to 5 January 1994	6.25
From 6 December	1992 to 5 March 1993	7
From 6 November	1992 to 5 December 1992	7.75
From 6 October	1991 to 5 November 1992	9.25
From 6 July	1991 to 5 October 1991	10
From 6 May	1991 to 5 July 1991	10.75
From 6 March	1991 to 5 May 1991	11.5

Notes

Fixed by Treasury order under SI 1989/1297.

Rates of interest on overdue corporation tax

With effect for **interest** periods commencing on 6 February 1997, the rates of interest for the purposes of late paid or unpaid corporation tax are different from those for other taxes. From

11

that date, the rate of interest on late paid or unpaid corporation tax will depend on the accounting period for which the tax is due and, under self-assessment, the nature of the tax due.

Self-assessment

For accounting periods within the self-assessment regime (or CTSA – APs ending on or after 1 July 1999), these rates are distinct from those for periods before the start of self-assessment because the interest is an allowable deduction for tax purposes (see below).

In addition, there are separate provisions for:

- overpaid instalments of corporation tax (which benefit from a more favourable rate – for details of payment by instalments, see below); and
- other liabilities such as the final liability due on the date specified in accordance with the table below.

Pre-self-assessment

For accounting periods before the start of self-assessment, there are two rates of interest applicable to all unpaid/late paid tax depending on whether the accounting period is within the Pay and File regime (APs ending after 30 September 1993) or note (i.e. periods ending before 1 October 1993).

CTSA (APs ending on or after 1.7.99)

1. Unpaid CT (other than underpaid instalments)

Period of application	Rate %
From 29 September 2009	3
24 March 2009 to 28 September 2009	2.5
27 January 2009 to 23 March 2009	3.5
6 January 2009 to 26 January 2009	4.5
6 December 2008 to 5 January 2009	5.5
6 November 2008 to 5 December 2008	6.5
6 January 2008 to 5 November 2008	7.5
6 August 2007 to 5 January 2008	8.5
6 September 2006 to 5 August 2007	7.5
6 September 2005 to 5 September 2006	6.5
6 September 2004 to 5 September 2005	7.5
6 December 2003 to 5 September 2004	6.5
6 August 2003 to 5 December 2003	5.5
6 November 2001 to 5 August 2003	6.5
6 May 2001 to 5 November 2001	7.5

Period of application	Rate %
6 February 2000 to 5 May 2001	8.5
6 March 1999 to 5 February 2000	7.5

2. Underpaid instalments

Period of application	Rate %
From 16 March 2009	1.50
16 February 2009 to 15 March 2009	2.00
19 January 2009 to 15 February 2009	2.50
15 December 2008 to 18 January 2009	3.00
17 November 2008 to 14 December 2008	4.00
20 October 2008 to 16 November 2008	5.50
21 April 2008 to 19 October 2008	6.00
18 February 2008 to 20 April 2008	6.25
17 December 2007 to 17 February 2008	6.50
16 July 2007 to 16 December 2007	6.75
21 May 2007 to 15 July 2007	6.50
22 January 2007 to 20 May 2007	6.25
20 November 2006 to 21 January 2007	6.00
14 August 2006 to 19 November 2006	5.75
15 August 2005 to 13 August 2006	5.50
16 August 2004 to 14 August 2005	5.75
21 June 2004 to 15 August 2004	5.50
17 May 2004 to 20 June 2004	5.25
16 February 2004 to 16 May 2004	5
17 November 2003 to 15 February 2004	4.75
21 July 2003 to 16 November 2003	4.5
17 February 2003 to 20 July 2003	4.75
19 November 2001 to 16 February 2003	5
15 October 2001 to 18 November 2001	5.5
1 October 2001 to 14 October 2001	5.75
13 August 2001 to 30 September 2001	6
21 May 2001 to 12 August 2001	6.25
16 April 2001 to 20 May 2001	6.5
19 February 2001 to 15 April 2001	6.75

Period of application	Rate %
20 April 2000 to 18 February 2001	7
21 February 2000 to 19 April 2000	8

Pre-CTSA

Period of application	Rate % pre-Pay and File	Rate % post-Pay and File
From 29 September 2009	3	3
24 March 2009 to 28 September 2009	2	1.75
27 January 2009 to 23 March 2009	2.75	2.75
6 January 2009 to 26 January 2009	3.5	3.5
6 December 2008 to 5 January 2009	4.25	4.25
6 November 2008 to 5 December 2008	5	5
6 January 2008 to 5 November 2008	5.75	6
6 August 2007 to 5 January 2008	6.5	6.75
6 September 2006 to 5 August 2007	5.75	6
6 September 2005 to 5 September 2006	5	5.25
6 September 2004 to 5 September 2005	5.75	6
6 December 2003 to 5 September 2004	5.25	5
6 August 2003 to 5 December 2003	4.25	4.25
6 November 2001 to 5 August 2003	5	5
6 May 2001 to 5 November 2001	5.75	6
6 February 2000 to 5 May 2001	6.5	6.75
6 March 1999 to 5 February 2000	5.75	5.75
6 January 1999 to 5 March 1999	6.5	6.5
6 August 1997 to 5 January 1999	7.25	7.5
6 February 1997 to 5 August 1997	6.25	6.25

Rates of interest on overpaid corporation tax

With effect for **interest** periods commencing on 6 February 1997, the rates of interest for the purposes of overpaid corporation tax are different from those for other taxes. The rate of interest on overpaid corporation tax will depend on the accounting period for which the tax is due and, under self-assessment, the nature of the tax repayable.

Self assessment

For accounting periods within the self-assessment regime (CTSA), i.e. APs on or after 1 July 1999, the rates of interest on repayments of overpaid corporation tax are distinct from those for pre-CTSA periods, because the interest is taxable (see below).

In addition, there are separate provisions for:

- overpaid instalments of corporation tax; and
- payments of corporation tax made after the normal due date.

Pay and File and earlier periods

For accounting periods within Pay and File (APs ending after 30 September 1993) and accounting periods before Pay and File, interest on overpaid corporation tax, repayments of income tax and payments of tax credits in respect of franked investment income received is given at the appropriate rate shown in the relevant table below.

CTSA (APs ending on or after 1 July 1999)

1. Overpaid CT (other than overpaid instalments and early payments of CT not due by instalments)

Period of application	Rate %
From 29 September 2009	0.5
27 January 2009 to 28 September 2009	0
6 December 2009 to 26 January 2009	1
6 December 2008 to 5 January 2009	2
6 November 2008 to 5 December 2008	3
6 January 2008 to 5 November 2008	4
6 August 2007 to 5 January 2008	5
6 September 2006 to 5 August 2007	4
6 September 2005 to 5 September 2006	3
6 September 2004 to 5 September 2005	4
6 December 2003 to 5 September 2004	3
6 August 2003 to 5 December 2003	2
6 November 2001 to 5 August 2003	3
6 May 2001 to 5 November 2001	4
6 February 2000 to 5 May 2001	5
6 March 1999 to 5 February 2000	4
6 January 1999 to 5 March 1999	5

2. Overpaid instalments and early payments of CT not due by instalments

Period of application	Rate %
From 21 September 2009	0.5
16 March 2009 to 20 September 2009	0.25
16 February 2009 to 15 March 2009	0.75
19 January 2009 to 15 February 2009	1.25
15 December 2008 to 18 January 2009	1.75
17 November 2008 to 14 December 2008	2.75
20 October 2008 to 16 November 2008	4.25
21 April 2008 to 19 October 2008	4.75
18 February 2008 to 20 April 2008	5.00
17 December 2007 to 17 February 2008	5.25
16 July 2007 to 16 December 2007	5.50
21 May 2007 to 15 July 2007	5.25
22 January 2007 to 20 May 2007	5.00
20 November 2006 to 21 January 2007	4.75
14 August 2006 to 19 November 2006	4.50
15 August 2005 to 13 August 2006	4.25
16 August 2004 to 14 August 2005	4.50
21 June 2004 to 15 August 2004	4.25
17 May 2004 to 20 June 2004	4.00
16 February 2004 to 16 May 2004	3.75
17 November 2003 to 15 February 2004	3.5
21 July 2003 to 16 November 2003	3.25
17 February 2003 to 20 July 2003	3.50
19 November 2001 to 16 February 2003	3.75
15 October 2001 to 18 November 2001	4.25
1 October 2001 to 14 October 2001	4.50
13 August 2001 to 30 September 2001	4.75
21 May 2001 to 12 August 2001	5.00
16 April 2001 to 20 May 2001	5.25
19 February 2001 to 15 April 2001	5.5

Period of application	Rate %
21 February 2000 to 18 February 2001	5.75
24 January 2000 to 20 February 2000	5.5
15 November 1999 to 23 January 2000	5.25
20 September 1999 to 14 November 1999	5.00
21 June 1999 to 19 September 1999	4.75
19 April 1999 to 20 June 1999	5.00
15 February 1999 to 18 April 1999	5.25
18 January 1999 to 14 February 1999	5.75
Before 18 January 1999	6.00

Pay and File

Period of application	Rate %
From 29 September 2009	0.5
27 January 2009 to 28 September 2009	0.00
6 January 2009 to 26 January 2009	0.5
6 December 2008 to 5 January 2009	1.25
From 6 November 2008 to 5 December 2008	2
From 6 January 2008 to 5 November 2008	2.75
6 August 2007 to 5 January 2008	3.50
6 September 2006 to 5 August 2007	2.75
6 September 2005 to 5 September 2006	2
6 September 2004 to 5 September 2005	2.75
6 December 2003 to 5 September 2004	2
6 August 2003 to 5 December 2003	1.25
6 November 2001 to 5 August 2003	2
6 May 2001 to 5 November 2001	2.75
6 February 2000 to 5 May 2001	3.5
6 March 1999 to 5 February 2000	2.75
6 January 1999 to 5 March 1999	3.25
6 August 1997 to 5 January 1999	4
6 February 1996 to 5 August 1997	3.25
6 March 1995 to 5 February 1996	4

Key Data

Period of application	Rate %
6 October 1994 to 5 March 1995	3.25
6 January 1994 to 5 October 1994	2.5
1 October 1993 to 5 January 1994	3.25

Pre-Pay and File

Period of application	Rate %
From 29 September 2009	0.5
24 March 2009 to 28 September 2009	2.00
27 January 2009 to 23 March 2009	2.75
6 January 2009 to 26 January 2009	3.5
6 December 2008 to 5 January 2009	4.25
From 6 November 2008 to 5 December 2008	5
From 6 January 2008 to 5 November 2008	5.75
6 August 2007 to 5 January 2008	6.5
6 September 2006 to 5 August 2007	5.75
6 September 2005 to 5 September 2006	5
6 September 2004 to 5 September 2005	5.75
6 December 2003 to 5 September 2004	5
6 August 2003 to 5 December 2003	4.25
6 November 2001 to 5 August 2003	5
6 May 2001 to 5 November 2001	5.75
6 February 2000 to 5 May 2001	6.5
6 March 1999 to 5 February 2000	5.75
6 January 1999 to 5 March 1999	6.5
6 August 1997 to 5 January 1999	7.25
6 February 1996 to 5 August 1997	6.25
6 March 1995 to 5 February 1996	7
6 October 1994 to 5 March 1995	6.25
6 January 1994 to 5 October 1994	5.5
6 March 1993 to 5 January 1994	6.25
6 December 1992 to 5 March 1993	7
6 November 1992 to 5 December 1992	7.75

Period of application	Rate %
6 October 1991 to 5 November 1992	9.25
6 July 1991 to 5 October 1991	10
6 May 1991 to 5 July 1991	10.75
6 March 1991 to 5 May 1991	11.5

Inheritance tax

Dates at which rates applicable	Chargeable transfers made on death %	Chargeable transfers not made on death %
From 29 September 2009	3	3
From 24 March 2009 to 28 September 2009	0	0
From 27 January 2009 to 23 March 2009	1	1
From 6 January 2009 to 26 January 2009	2	2
From 6 November 2008 to 5 January 2009	3	3
From 6 January 2008 to 5 November 2008	4	4
From 6 August 2007 to 5 January 2008	5	5
From 6 September 2006 to 5 August 2007	4	4
From 6 September 2005 to 5 September 2006	3	3
From 6 September 2004 to 5 September 2005	4	4
From 6 December 2003 to 5 September 2004	3	3
From 6 August 2003 to 5 December 2003	2	2
From 6 November 2001 to 5 August 2003	3	3
From 6 May 2001 to 5 November 2001	4	4
From 6 February 2000 to 5 May 2001	5	5
From 6 March 1999 to 5 February 2000	4	4
From 6 October 1994 to 5 March 1999	5	5
From 6 January 1994 to 5 October 1994	4	4
From 6 December 1992 to 5 January 1994	5	5

Key Data

19

Dates at which rates applicable	Chargeable transfers made on death %	Chargeable transfers not made on death %
From 6 November 1992 to 5 December 1992	6	6
From 6 July 1991 to 5 November 1992	8	8
From 6 May 1991 to 5 July 1991	9	9

Note

Rate change by order under the *Taxes (Interest Rate) Regulations* 1989 (SI 1989/1297).

From 16 December 1986 a single rate of interest has been prescribed in relation to all chargeable transfers, whether or not made on death.

Value added tax

Default interest on certain VAT recoverable by assessment is calculated at the following rates:

Date		Rate %
From 29 September	2009	3
From 24 March	2009 to 28 September 2009	2.5
From 27 January	2009 to 23 March 2009	3.5
From 6 January	2009 to 26 January 2009	4.5
From 6 December	2008 to 5 January 2009	5.5
From 6 November	2008 to 5 December 2008	6.5
From 6 September	2006 to 5 November 2008	7.5
From 6 September	2005 to 5 September 2006	6.5
From 6 September	2004 to 5 September 2005	7.5
From 6 December	2003 to 5 September 2004	6.5
From 6 September	2003 to 5 December 2003	5.5
From 6 November	2001 to 5 September 2003	6.5
From 6 May	2001 to 5 November 2001	7.5
From 6 February	2000 to 5 May 2001	8.5
From 6 March	1999 to 5 February 2000	7.5
From 6 January	1999 to 5 March 1999	8.5
From 6 July	1998 to 5 January 1999	9.5
From 6 February	1996 to 5 July 1998	6.25
From 6 March	1995 to 5 February 1996	7
From 6 October	1994 to 5 March 1995	6.25
From 6 January	1994 to 5 October 1994	5.5
From 6 March	1993 to 5 January 1994	6.25
From 6 December	1992 to 5 March 1993	7
From 6 November	1992 to 5 December 1992	7.75
From 6 October	1991 to 5 November 1992	9.25
From 6 July	1991 to 5 October 1991	10
From 6 May	1991 to 5 July 1991	10.75
From 6 March	1991 to 5 May 1991	11.5
From 6 November	1990 to 5 March 1991	12.25
From 1 April	1990 to 5 November 1990	13

For the default surcharge payable in respect of many non-payments or underpayments of VAT and for the serious misdeclaration penalty, see 8516 and 8528.

Interest on overpaid VAT arises under VATA 1994, s. 78 in certain cases of official error:

Period of application		Rate %
From 29 September 2009		0.5
From 27 January 2009 to	28 September 2009	0
From 6 January 2009 to	26 January 2009	1
From 6 December 2008 to	5 January 2009	2
From 6 November 2008 to	5 December 2008	3
From 6 September 2006 to	5 November 2008	4
From 6 September 2005 to	5 September 2006	3
From 6 September 2004 to	5 September 2005	4
From 6 December 2003 to	5 September 2004	3
From 6 September 2003 to	5 December 2003	2
From 6 November 2001 to	5 September 2003	3
From 6 May 2001 to	5 November 2001	4
From 6 February 2000 to	5 May 2001	5
From 6 March 1999 to	5 February 2000	4
From 6 January 1999 to	5 March 1999	5
From 1 April 1997 to	5 January 1999	6
From 6 February 1993 to	31 March 1997	8
From 16 October 1991 to	5 February 1993	10.25

Note

Generally, a repayment under VATA 1994, s. 78 in relation to any claim made after 18 July 1996 is not made for more than three years after the end of the applicable period to which it relates.

1-120   Plant and machinery – overview of allowances from April 2008

The following is a summary of the main plant and machinery allowances available from 6 April 2008. The cross references to commentary relate to the *British Master Tax Guide*.

Description	Detail	Notes	Commentary
Annual investment allowance	Full relief for first £50,000 (adjusted pro rata for shorter or longer periods).	1. Restricted relief for periods spanning 1 or 6 April 2008. 2. AIA can cover long-life asset and integral features, as well as standard P&M. 3. Groups and certain other related parties share a single amount.	2366ff.

Description	Detail	Notes	Commentary
First-year allowances (100%) for cars	Cars with CO_2 emissions not exceeding 110g/km.	Threshold reduced from 120g/km from 1 April 2008.	2368ff.
Other first-year allowances (100%)	Still available for certain energy-saving assets; environmentally beneficial assets; refuelling stations; plant used in ring-fence trades.	Payable tax credits available for company losses created by allowances re energy-saving or environmentally beneficial expenditure.	Energy-saving plant: 2376. Environmentally beneficial assets: 2378. Refuelling stations: 2380. Ring-fence trades: 2368.
Writing-down allowances (20%)	Standard rate of WDA for assets, including cars but excluding those assets attracting relief at just 10% as below.	1. Reduced from 25% for P&M only for expenditure incurred from 1 April or 6 April (CT or income tax). 2. £3,000 restriction for cars remains in place, but new system to apply from April 2009.	2324ff.
Writing-down allowances (10%)	Reduced rate of WDA applies to certain 'special rate' expenditure, covering long-life assets, integral features, thermal insulation.	1. Transitional provisions apply for periods spanning 1 or 6 April 2008. 2. AIAs (see above) are available for this expenditure. 3. Higher emission cars will have 10% WDAs from April 2009.	Long-life assets: 2324ff. Integral features: 2324ff. Thermal insulation: 2324. Cars: 2380ff.
Balancing allowances		No change from April 2008.	2324ff.
Balancing charges		No change from April 2008.	2324ff.

Plant and machinery: first-year allowances – from April 2008 (CAA 2001, s. 52)

Changes were made to first-year allowances from April 2008. Subject to the general exclusions listed below, full 100 per cent allowances are still available for the following types of expenditure incurred by a business of any size. If full FYAs are not claimed, WDA is normally available at 20 per cent on a reducing balance basis.

Nature of expenditure	Authority (CAA 2001)	Notes
Energy-saving plant or machinery	s. 45A–45C	Loss-making companies may claim tax rebate
Cars with very low CO$_2$ emissions	s. 45D	Threshold tightened from April 2008
Plant or machinery for certain refuelling stations	s. 45E	
Plant or machinery (other than a long life asset) for use by a company wholly in a ring fence trade	s. 45F	
Environmentally beneficial plant or machinery	s. 45H–45J	Loss-making companies may claim tax rebate

Key Data

Plant and machinery: first-year allowances – general

No first-year allowances are available, for a business of any size, for:

- expenditure incurred in the final chargeable period;
- cars (other than those with very low CO$_2$ emissions);
- certain ships and railway assets;
- long-life assets (other than plant or machinery for use by a company wholly in a ring fence trade, in which case a 24 per cent FYA is available if such expenditure is a LLA);
- plant or machinery for leasing;
- in certain anti-avoidance cases where the obtaining of a FYA is linked to a change in the nature or conduct of a trade;
- where an asset was initially acquired for purposes other than those of the qualifying activity;
- where an asset was acquired by way of a gift;
- where plant or machinery that was provided for long funding leasing starts to be used for other purposes.

Plant and machinery: first-year allowances – medium-sized enterprises (CAA 2001, s. 52)

Medium-sized enterprises are entitled to all the allowances listed in the table above. Until April 2008, they were also entitled to a 40 per cent FYA on any other plant and machinery. The removal of these other allowances means that the size distinction ceases to be relevant for capital allowance purposes.

All FYAs are subject to the general exclusions listed above.

Plant and machinery: first-year allowances – small enterprises (CAA 2001, s. 52)

Small enterprises are entitled to all the allowances listed in the table above. Until April 2008, they were also entitled to the additional allowances applicable to medium-sized enterprises (above). The first-year allowance rate of 40 per cent was, however, increased to 50 per cent for the years 2004–05, 2006–07 (but not 2005–06) and 2007–08 (and for financial years 2004, 2006 and 2008 (but not 2005)).

The removal of these other allowances from 2008 means that the size distinction ceases to be relevant for capital allowance purposes.

All FYAs are subject to the general exclusions listed above.

Plant and machinery: writing-down allowances (CAA 2001, s. 56)

	From April 2008	**Before April 2008**
Standard WDAs	20%	25%
Long-life assets	10%	6%
Overseas leasing	10%	10%
Integral features	10%	25% (i.e. treated as other P&M)
Cars over £12,000	Lower of £3,000 or 20%	Lower of £3,000 or 25%
Thermal insulation	10%	25% (but restricted to industrial buildings)

Integral features (CAA 2001, s. 33A)

The following assets are designated as integral features:

- electrical systems (including lighting systems);
- cold water systems;
- space or water heating systems, powered systems of ventilation, air cooling or air purification, and any floor or ceiling comprised in such systems;
- lifts, escalators and moving walkways; and
- external solar shading.

The draft legislation had proposed an additional category (active facades) but these were not in the event added to the list.

Expenditure on thermal insulation and long-life assets is also allocated to the 'special rate' pool.

Definition of small and medium-sized enterprises

This concept was relevant for capital allowances purposes up to 31 March or 5 April 2008 (respectively for corporation tax and income tax purposes).

A company or business is a *small enterprise* if:

- it qualifies (or is treated as qualifying) as small under the *Companies Act* 2006, s. 382, for the financial year of the company in which the expenditure is incurred; and
- it is not a member of a medium or large group (*Companies Act* 2006, s. 466) at the time the expenditure is incurred.

A company or business is a *small or medium-sized enterprise* if:

- it qualifies (or is treated as qualifying) as small or medium-sized under the *Companies Act* 2006, s. 382, for the financial year of the company in which the expenditure is incurred; and
- it is not a member of a large group (*Companies Act* 2006, s. 466) at the time the expenditure is incurred.

Under the *Companies Act* 2006, s. 382, a company qualifies as small or medium-sized for a financial year if two or more of the requirements shown below are met in that and the preceding financial year. A group is small or medium-sized under the *Companies Act* 2006, s. 466 in a year in which it satisfies two or more of the requirements per relevant category, as shown in the tables below.

There are two tables set out below. The first table is in respect of years ending on or after 30 January 2004 (but see exception below) and takes into account the changes made by the *Companies Act 1985 (Accounts of Small and Medium-Sized Enterprises and Audit Exemption) (Amendment) Regulations* 2004 (SI 2004/16). The second table is in respect of years ending before 30 January 2004. However, as an exception, the second table applies also to a financial year that only ends on or after 30 January 2004 by reason of an exercise of the power (conferred by the *Companies Act* 2006, s. 392) to alter the accounting reference date, by the giving of a notice (namely, Form 225, *Change of accounting reference date*) to the Registrar of Companies on or after 9 January 2004.

The first table is as follows:

Type of company	Requirements	
Small company	Turnover	Not more than £5.6m
	Balance sheet total	Not more than £2.8m
	Number of employees	Not more than 50
Medium-sized company	Turnover	Not more than £22.8m
	Balance sheet total	Not more than £11.4m
	Number of employees	Not more than 250

Key Data

Type of company	Requirements	
Small group	Aggregate turnover	Not more than £5.6m net (or £6.72m gross)
	Aggregate balance sheet total	Not more than £2.8m net (or £3.36m gross)
	Aggregate number of employees	Not more than 50
Medium-sized group	Aggregate turnover	Not more than £22.8m net (or £27.36m gross)
	Aggregate balance sheet total	Not more than £11.4m net (or £13.68m gross)
	Aggregate number of employees	Not more than 250

The second table is as follows:

Type of company	Requirements	
Small company	Turnover	Not more than £2.8m
	Balance sheet total	Not more than £1.4m
	Number of employees	Not more than 50
Medium-sized company	Turnover	Not more than £11.2m
	Balance sheet total	Not more than £5.6m
	Number of employees	Not more than 250
Small group	Aggregate turnover	Not more than £2.8m net (or £3.6m gross)
	Aggregate balance sheet total	Not more than £1.4m net (or £1.68m gross)
	Aggregate number of employees	Not more than 50
Medium-sized group	Aggregate turnover	Not more than £11.2m net (or £13.44m gross)
	Aggregate balance sheet total	Not more than £5.6m net (or £6.72m gross)
	Aggregate number of employees	Not more than 250

Expenditure unaffected by statutory restrictions re buildings

The restrictions in CAA 2001, s. 21 and 22 (buildings, structures and other assets) do not apply to expenditure in List C at CAA 2001, s. 23. List C, as amended at items 2, 3 and 6 by *Finance Act* 2008 with effect for expenditure incurred from 1 or 6 April 2008, is as follows:

(1) Machinery (including devices for providing motive power) not within any other item in this list.

(2) Gas and sewerage systems provided mainly

   (a) to meet the particular requirements of the qualifying activity;

   (b) to serve particular plant or machinery used for the purposes of the qualifying activity.

(3) [omitted by *Finance Act* 2008].

(4) Manufacturing or processing equipment; storage equipment (including cold rooms); display equipment; and counters, checkouts and similar equipment.

(5) Cookers, washing machines, dishwashers, refrigerators and similar equipment; washbasins, sinks, baths, showers, sanitary ware and similar equipment; and furniture and furnishings.

(6) Hoists.

(7) Sound insulation provided mainly to meet the particular requirements of the qualifying activity.

(8) Computer, telecommunication and surveillance systems (including their wiring or other links).

(9) Refrigeration or cooling equipment.

(10) Fire alarm systems; sprinkler and other equipment for extinguishing or containing fires.

(11) Burglar alarm systems.

(12) Strong rooms in bank or building society premises; safes.

(13) Partition walls, where moveable and intended to be moved in the course of the qualifying activity.

(14) Decorative assets provided for the enjoyment of the public in hotel, restaurant or similar trades.

(15) Advertising hoardings; signs, displays and similar assets.

(16) Swimming-pools (including diving boards, slides and structures on which such boards or slides are mounted).

(17) Any glasshouse constructed so that the required environment (namely, air, heat, light, irrigation and temperature) for the growing of plants is provided automatically by means of devices forming an integral part of its structure.

Key Data

(18) Cold stores.

(19) Caravans provided mainly for holiday lettings.

(20) Buildings provided for testing aircraft engines run within the buildings.

(21) Moveable buildings intended to be moved in the course of the qualifying activity.

(22) The alteration of land for the purpose only of installing plant or machinery.

(23) The provision of dry docks.

(24) The provision of any jetty or similar structure provided mainly to carry plant or machinery.

(25) The provision of pipelines or underground ducts or tunnels with a primary purpose of carrying utility conduits.

(26) The provision of towers to support floodlights.

(27) The provision of

(a) any reservoir incorporated into a water treatment works; or
(b) any service reservoir of treated water for supply within any housing estate or other particular locality.

(28) The provision of

(a) silos provided for temporary storage; or
(b) storage tanks.

(29) The provision of slurry pits or silage clamps.

(30) The provision of fish tanks or fish ponds.

(31) The provision of rails, sleepers and ballast for a railway or tramway.

(32) The provision of structures and other assets for providing the setting for any ride at an amusement park or exhibition.

(33) The provision of fixed zoo cages.

Items 1–16 of the above list do not, however, include any asset with the principal purpose of insulating or enclosing the interior of a building or of providing an interior wall, floor or ceiling that is intended to remain permanently in place.

Industrial buildings, hotels and sports pavilions; agricultural buildings and structures

These allowances are being phased out. To achieve this, the following percentages are applied to the writing-down allowances that would otherwise be available for industrial buildings, hotels and sports pavilions and agricultural buildings and structures.

Financial year beginning	Tax year	Percentage
1 April 2007 and earlier	2007–08 and earlier	100 per cent

Financial year beginning	Tax year	Percentage
1 April 2008	2008–09	75 per cent
1 April 2009	2009–10	50 per cent
1 April 2010	2010–11	25 per cent
1 April 2011 and later	2011–12 and later	0 per cent (ie no further allowances given)

Where a chargeable period straddles the financial or tax year, the WDA is to be apportioned on a strict time basis.

The restriction applies both to the standard four per cent WDA and to the higher WDA available for some used buildings.

No initial allowances are available.

Enterprise zones: industrial buildings, hotels, commercial buildings or structures

The following allowances are available for certain buildings in enterprise zones [1](industrial buildings; hotels and commercial buildings or structures[2]):

Date expenditure incurred	Initial allowance	Writing down allowance
Contract to be made within 10 years of site being included within the enterprise zone (but not expenditure incurred over 20 years after the date of the site being included)	100%	25%

Notes

[1] Areas designated by Orders made under the *Local Government, Planning and Land Act 1980* or equivalent Northern Ireland legislation (CAA 2001, s. 298(3)).

[2] Buildings or structures used for the purposes of a trade, profession or vocation (but not an industrial building or qualifying hotel) or used as offices; but not a dwelling-house (CAA 2001, s. 281).

Business premises renovation allowances (CAA 2001, s. 360Aff.)

Date expenditure incurred	Initial allowance	Writing down allowance
On or after 11 April 2007	100%	25%

Flat conversion allowances (CAA 2001, s. 393Aff.)

Date expenditure incurred	Initial allowance	Writing down allowance
On or after 11 May 2001	100%	25%

Dredging allowances (CAA 2001, s. 484ff.)

Date expenditure incurred	Initial allowance	Writing down allowance
On or after 1 April 1986	Nil	4%

Mineral extraction allowances (CAA 2001, s. 394ff.)

Date expenditure incurred	Initial allowance	Writing down allowance
On or after 1 April 1986	Nil	25%

Research and development allowances (CAA 2001, s. 437ff.)

Date expenditure incurred	Initial allowance	Writing down allowance
On or after 5 November 1962	100%	No provision for WDAs

Patent allowances (CAA 2001, s. 464ff.)

Date expenditure incurred	Initial allowance	Writing down allowance
On or after 1 April 1986	Nil	25%

Know-how allowances (CAA 2001, s. 452ff.)

Date expenditure incurred	Initial allowance	Writing down allowance
On or after 1 April 1986	Nil	25%

Assured tenancy allowances (CAA 2001, s. 490ff.)

Date expenditure incurred	Initial allowance	Writing down allowance
1 April 1986 to 31 March 1992	Nil	4%

Enterprise zones

Enterprise zones can be valid for up to 20 years in total. Those that still fall within that 20-year period are as follows:

Statutory instrument	Area	Start date
1989/145	Inverclyde	3 March 1989
1989/794	Sunderland (Castletown and Doxford Park)	27 April 1990
1989/795	Sunderland (Hylton Riverside and Southwick)	27 April 1990
1993/23	Lanarkshire (Hamilton)	1 February 1993
1993/24	Lanarkshire (Motherwell)	1 February 1993
1993/25	Lanarkshire (Monklands)	1 February 1993
1995/2624	Dearne Valley (Barnsley, Doncaster, Rotherham)	3 November 1995
1995/2625	Holmewood (North East Derbyshire)	3 November 1995
1995/2738	Bassetlaw	16 November 1995
1995/2758	Ashfield	21 November 1995
1995/2812	East Durham (No. 1 to No. 6)	29 November 1995
1996/106	Tyne Riverside (North Tyneside)	19 February 1996
1996/1981	Tyne Riverside (Silverlink North Scheme)	26 August 1996
1996/1981	Tyne Riverside (Silverlink Business Park Scheme)	26 August 1996
1996/1981	Tyne Riverside (Middle Engine Lane Scheme)	26 August 1996
1996/1981	Tyne Riverside (New York Industrial Park Scheme)	26 August 1996
1996/1981	Tyne Riverside (Balliol Business Park West Scheme)	26 August 1996
1996/2435	Tyne Riverside (Baltic Enterprise Park Scheme)	21 October 1996
1996/2435	Tyne Riverside (Viking Industrial Park – Wagonway West Scheme)	21 October 1996
1996/2435	Tyne Riverside (Viking Industrial Park – Blackett Street Scheme)	21 October 1996
1996/2435	Tyne Riverside (Viking Industrial Park – Western Road Scheme)	21 October 1996

1-140   Interest factor tables

Inland Revenue Press Release 72/99, issued 11 March 1999, states that 'legislative changes to the basis on which interest is calculated, and increased use of computers, have lead to disuse of the tables'. New interest factor tables are, therefore, no longer produced.

Repayment supplement

Repayment supplement was introduced in 1975. Until 5 February 1997, the relevant interest factors were identical to those applying in the case of investigation settlements (below). However, in the case of repayment supplement the tax month to which the interest factor applies ends on the fifth of that month and not on the first, as with investigation settlement interest. The table, which applies in relation to repayments made other than under Pay and File, incorporates the interest change to four per cent p.a. which came into operation on 6 January 1999.

Table of interest factors as at fifth of month

	5 Jan	5 Feb	5 Mar	5 Apr	5 May	5 Jun	5 Jul	5 Aug	5 Sept	5 Oct	5 Nov	5 Dec
1975	1.242	1.2495	1.257	1.2645	1.272	1.2795	1.287	1.2945	1.302	1.3095	1.317	1.3245
1976	1.332	1.3395	1.347	1.3545	1.362	1.3695	1.377	1.3845	1.392	1.3995	1.407	1.4145
1977	1.422	1.4295	1.437	1.4445	1.452	1.4595	1.467	1.4745	1.482	1.4895	1.497	1.5045
1978	1.512	1.5195	1.527	1.5345	1.542	1.5495	1.557	1.5645	1.572	1.5795	1.587	1.5945
1979	1.602	1.6095	1.617	1.6245	1.632	1.6395	1.647	1.6545	1.662	1.6695	1.677	1.6845
1980	1.692	1.702	1.712	1.722	1.732	1.742	1.752	1.762	1.772	1.782	1.792	1.802
1981	1.812	1.822	1.832	1.842	1.852	1.862	1.872	1.882	1.892	1.902	1.912	1.922
1982	1.932	1.942	1.952	1.962	1.972	1.982	1.992	2.002	2.012	2.022	2.032	2.042
1983	2.0487	2.0554	2.062	2.0687	2.0754	2.082	2.0887	2.0954	2.102	2.1087	2.1154	2.122
1984	2.1287	2.1354	2.142	2.1487	2.1554	2.162	2.1687	2.1754	2.182	2.1887	2.1954	2.202
1985	2.2087	2.2154	2.222	2.2287	2.2354	2.2445	2.2537	2.2628	2.2720	2.2812	2.2903	2.2995

	5 Jan	5 Feb	5 Mar	5 Apr	5 May	5 Jun	5 Jul	5 Aug	5 Sept	5 Oct	5 Nov	5 Dec
1986	2.3087	2.3178	2.3270	2.3362	2.3453	2.3545	2.3637	2.3728	2.3799	2.3870	2.3940	2.4019
1987	2.4098	2.4178	2.4257	2.4336	2.4411	2.4468	2.4555	2.4624	2.4693	2.4768	2.4843	2.4918
1988	2.4987	2.5056	2.5125	2.5193	2.5262	2.5327	2.5391	2.5456	2.5537	2.5618	2.5708	2.5797
1989	2.5887	2.5983	2.6079	2.6175	2.6271	2.6367	2.6462	2.6564	2.6666	2.6768	2.6871	2.6979
1990	2.7088	2.7196	2.7304	2.7413	2.7521	2.7629	2.7738	2.7846	2.7954	2.8063	2.8171	2.8273
1991	2.8375	2.8477	2.8579	2.8675	2.8771	2.8861	2.8950	2.9033	2.9116	2.9200	2.9277	2.9354
1992	2.9431	2.9508	2.9585	2.9663	2.9740	2.9817	2.9894	2.9971	3.0048	3.0125	3.0202	3.0267
1993	3.0326	3.0384	3.0442	3.0494	3.0546	3.0598	3.0650	3.0702	3.0755	3.0807	3.0859	3.0911
1994	3.0963	3.1009	3.1055	3.1101	3.1147	3.1193	3.1238	3.1284	3.1330	3.1376	3.1428	3.1480
1995	3.1532	3.1584	3.1636	3.1694	3.1753	3.1811	3.1869	3.1928	3.1986	3.2044	3.2103	3.2161
1996	3.2219	3.2278	3.2330	3.2382	3.2434	3.2486	3.2538	3.2591	3.2643	3.2695	3.2747	3.2799
1997	3.2851	3.2903	3.2937	3.2970	3.3003	3.3037	3.3070	3.3103	3.3143	3.3182	3.3222	3.3261
1998	3.3301	3.3340	3.3380	3.3419	3.3459	3.3498	3.3538	3.3578	3.3618	3.3657	3.3697	3.3736
1999	3.3776	3.3809	3.3842	3.3876	3.3909	3.3942	3.3976	3.4009	3.4042	3.4076	3.4109	3.4142
2000	3.4176	3.4209	3.4242	3.4276	3.4309	3.4342	3.4376	3.4409	3.4442	3.4476	3.4509	3.4542
2001	3.4576											

1-160 Foreign exchange rates

2009–10 Foreign exchange rates

		Average rates for the year to 31 December 2009 and the year to 31 March 2010			
		Average for the year to 31 December 2009		Average for the year to 31 March 2010	
Country	Unit of currency	Currency units per £1	Sterling value of currency unit £	Currency units per £1	Sterling value of currency unit £
Algeria	Algerian Dinar	113.373	0.0088204	115.670	0.0086453
Argentina	Peso	5.8426	0.17116	6.0580	0.16507
Australia	Australian Dollar	1.9923	0.50193	1.8829	0.5311
Bahrain	Dinar	0.5896	1.69607	0.6005	1.66528
Bangladesh	Taka	108.191	0.0092429	110.103	0.0090824
Barbados	Barbados Dollar	3.1280	0.31969	3.1853	0.31394
Bolivia	Boliviano	10.9794	0.09108	11.1804	0.089442
Botswana	Pula	11.0911	0.090163	10.8900	0.091827
Brazil	Real	3.1109	0.32145	2.9799	0.33558
Brunei	Brunei Dollar	2.2743	0.4397	2.2677	0.44098
Bulgaria	Lev	2.1974	0.45508	2.2063	0.45325
Burma	Kyat	10.0277	0.099724	10.2089	0.097954
Burundi	Burundi Franc	1929.10	0.00051838	1959.83	0.00051025
Canada	Canadian Dollar	1.7801	0.56177	1.7398	0.57478
Cayman Islands	C.I. Dollar	1.2851	0.77815	1.3067	0.76529
Chile	Chilean Peso	870.827	0.0011483	854.751	0.0011699
China	Yuan	10.7044	0.09342	10.8798	0.091913
Colombia	Colombia Peso	3358.97	0.00029771	3183.33	0.00031414
Congo (Dem Rep)	Congolese Franc	1263.11	0.0007917	1354.89	0.00073807
Costa Rica	Colon	898.802	0.0011126	906.539	0.0011031
Cuba	Cuban Peso	1.5673	0.63804	1.5935	0.62755
Czech Republic	Koruna	29.8025	0.033554	29.3613	0.034058
Denmark	Danish Krone	8.3581	0.11964	8.4083	0.11893

2009–10 Average foreign exchange rates (cont'd)

		Average rates for the year to 31 December 2009 and the year to 31 March 2010			
		Average for the year to 31 December 2009		Average for the year to 31 March 2010	
Country	Unit of currency	Currency units per £1	Sterling value of currency unit £	Currency units per £1	Sterling value of currency unit £
Egypt	Egyptian £	8.6820	0.11518	8.8012	0.11362
El Salvador	Colon	13.7107	0.072936	13.9391	0.071741
Ethiopia	Ethiopian Birr	18.7056	0.05346	19.7973	0.050512
European Union	Euro	1.1235	0.89008	1.1298	0.88511
Fiji Islands	Fiji Dollar	3.0833	0.32433	3.1723	0.31523
French Cty/Africa	CFA Franc	736.978	0.0013569	739.927	0.0013515
French Pacific Islands	CFP Franc	133.979	0.0074639	134.515	0.0074341
Gambia	Dalasi	41.6103	0.024033	42.4940	0.023533
Ghana	Cedi	2.2426	0.44591	2.3068	0.4335
Grenada/Wind. Isles	East Carib Dollar	4.2229	0.2368	4.3023	0.23243
Guyana	Guyana Dollar	316.241	0.0031621	322.95	0.0030965
Honduras	Lempira	29.6097	0.033773	30.1084	0.033213
Hong Kong	HK Dollar	12.1317	0.082429	12.3810	0.080769
Hungary	Forint	316.187	0.0031627	308.141	0.0032453
Iceland	Icelandic Krona	193.524	0.0051673	200.920	0.0049771
India	Indian Rupee	75.6294	0.013222	75.5588	0.013235
Indonesia	Rupiah	16175.8	0.000061821	15601.1	0.000064098
Iran	Rial	15443.8	0.000064751	15770.0	0.000063412
Iraq	New Iraqi Dinar	1802.03	0.00055493	1838.48	0.00054393
Israel	Shekel	6.1341	0.16302	6.1280	0.16319
Jamaica	Jamaican Dollar	137.646	0.007265	141.387	0.0070728
Japan	Yen	146.366	0.0068322	148.193	0.006748
Jordan	Jordanian Dinar	1.1077	0.90277	1.1278	0.88668
Kenya	Kenyan Shilling	120.848	0.0082749	121.942	0.0082006
Korea (South)	Won	1993.87	0.00050154	1924.48	0.00051962
Kuwait	Kuwaiti Dinar	0.4508	2.21828	0.4582	2.18245
Laos	New Kip	13295.8	0.000075212	13502.7	0.000074059
Latvia	Lats	0.7936	1.26008	0.7975	1.25392
Lebanon	Lebanese Pound	2348.60	0.00042579	2391.71	0.00041811
Libya	Libyan Dinar	1.9538	0.51182	1.9751	0.5063
Lithuania	Litas	3.8793	0.25778	3.8949	0.25675
Malawi	Kwacha	221.896	0.0045066	229.365	0.0043599
Malaysia	Ringgit	5.5051	0.18165	5.5113	0.18145
Mauritius	Mauritius Rupee	49.8915	0.020043	49.6959	0.020122
Mexico	Mexican Peso	21.0920	0.047411	20.8849	0.047881
Morocco	Dirham	12.6491	0.079057	12.7327	0.078538
Nepal	Nepalese Rupee	121.294	0.0082444	120.696	0.0082853
N'nd Antilles	Antilles Guilder	2.8053	0.35647	2.8523	0.35059
New Zealand	NZ Dollar	2.4870	0.40209	2.3637	0.42307
Nicaragua	Gold Cordoba	31.9532	0.031296	32.8596	0.030433
Nigeria	Naira	234.162	0.0042706	239.591	0.0041738
Norway	Nor Krone	9.8078	0.10196	9.6327	0.10381
Oman	Rial Omani	0.6022	1.66058	0.6132	1.63079
Pakistan	Pakistan Rupee	127.926	0.007817	132.082	0.0075711

2009–10 Average foreign exchange rates (cont'd)

		Average rates for the year to 31 December 2009 and the year to 31 March 2010			
		Average for the year to 31 December 2009		Average for the year to 31 March 2010	
Country	Unit of currency	Currency units per £1	Sterling value of currency unit £	Currency units per £1	Sterling value of currency unit £
Papua New Guinea	Kina	4.2283	0.2365	4.2584	0.23483
Paraguay	Guarani	7783.09	0.00012848	7779.04	0.00012855
Peru	New Sol	4.6983	0.21284	4.6586	0.21466
Philippines	Peso	74.5322	0.013417	75.1918	0.013299
Poland	Zloty	4.8775	0.20502	4.7177	0.21197
Qatar	Riyal	5.6946	0.1756	5.7982	0.17247
Romania	New Leu	4.7645	0.20989	4.7312	0.21136
Russia	Rouble	49.7386	0.020105	48.6544	0.020553
Rwanda	Franc	891.257	0.001122	908.223	0.0011011
Saudi Arabia	Riyal	5.8657	0.17048	5.9728	0.16743
Seychelles	Rupee	21.1657	0.047246	19.6567	0.050873
Sierra Leone	Leone	5314.64	0.00018816	5723.55	0.00017472
Singapore	Singapore Dollar	2.2711	0.44032	2.2719	0.44016
Solomon Islands	SI Dollar	12.4682	0.080204	12.7244	0.078589
Somali Republic	Shilling	2161.21	0.0004627	2236.85	0.00044706
South Africa	Rand	13.0021	0.076911	12.4676	0.080208
Sri Lanka	Rupee	180.184	0.0055499	183.205	0.0054584
Sudan	Sudanese Pound	3.6544	0.27364	3.7308	0.26804
Surinam	Dollar	4.3020	0.23245	4.3741	0.22862
Swaziland	Lilangeni	12.9656	0.077127	12.3156	0.081198
Sweden	Krona	11.9491	0.083688	11.7215	0.085313
Switzerland	Franc	1.6968	0.58935	1.6961	0.58959
Syria	Pound	72.0249	0.013884	73.1795	0.013665
Taiwan	Dollar	51.6003	0.01938	51.7867	0.01931
Tanzania	Shilling	2071.20	0.00048281	2118.02	0.00047214
Thailand	Baht	53.6478	0.01864	53.7107	0.018618
Tonga Islands	Pa'anga	3.1526	0.3172	3.1071	0.32184
Trinidad & Tobago	Dollar	9.8537	0.10148	10.0652	0.099352
Tunisia	Dinar	2.1093	0.47409	2.1345	0.46849
Turkey	New Lira	2.4264	0.41213	2.4160	0.41391
Uganda	New Shilling	3177.46	0.00031472	3237.06	0.00030892
United Arab Emirates	Dirham	5.7445	0.17408	5.8497	0.17095
Uruguay	Peso Uruguay	35.2328	0.028383	34.3153	0.029142
USA	US Dollar	1.5633	0.63967	1.5962	0.62649
Venezuela	Bolivar Fuerte	3.3620	0.29744	1/4/09 to 10/1/10: 0.28987 11/1/10 to 31/3/10: 0.14969*	1/4/09 to 10/1/10: 3.4498 11/1/10 to 31/3/10: 6.6804*
Vietnam	Dong	28019.6	0.000035689	28974.5	0.000034513
Yemen	Rial	318.436	0.0031403	329.603	0.0030340
Zambia	Kwacha	7870.74	0.00012705	7741.14	0.00012918

* Rate shown for Venezuela from 11/1/10 is 'petro-dollar' rate, preferential rate is fixed at 2.6 to the US dollar

Table of spot rates on 31 December 2009 and 31 March 2010

		Table of Spot rates on 31 December 2009 and 31 March 2010			
		31 December 2009		**31 March 2010**	
Country	**Unit of Currency**	**Currency units per £1**	**Sterling value of currency unit £**	**Currency units per £1**	**Sterling value of currency unit £**
Australia	Australian Dollar	1.7956	0.55692	1.6527	0.60507
Canada	Canadian Dollar	1.6930	0.59067	1.5390	0.64977
Denmark	Danish Krone	8.3750	0.1194	8.3459	0.11982
European Union	Euro	1.1255	0.88849	1.1211	0.89198
Hong Kong	HK Dollar	12.5217	0.079861	11.7783	0.084902
Japan	Yen	150.335	0.0066518	141.739	0.0070552
Norway	Nor Krone	9.3287	0.1072	9.0038	0.11106
South Africa	Rand	11.8914	0.084094	11.1401	0.089766
Sweden	Krona	11.5302	0.086729	10.9171	0.091599
Switzerland	Franc	1.6693	0.59905	1.5967	0.62629
USA	US Dollar	1.6149	0.61923	1.5169	0.65924

2008–09 Foreign exchange rates

		Average rates for the year to 31 December 2008 and the year to 31 March 2009			
		Average for the year to 31 December 2008		**Average for the year to 31 March 2009**	
Country	**Unit of currency**	**Currency units per £1**	**Sterling value of currency unit £**	**Currency units per £1**	**Sterling value of currency unit £**
Algeria	Dinar	119.634	0.0083588	112.768	0.0088678
Argentina	Peso	5.8413	0.17119	5.559	0.17989
Australia	Australian Dollar	2.1869	0.45727	2.1814	0.45842
Bahrain	Dinar	0.6979	1.43287	0.6472	1.54512
Bangladesh	Taka	126.837	0.0078841	117.481	0.008512
Barbados	Barbados Dollar	3.7036	0.27001	3.4337	0.29123
Bolivia	Boliviano	13.4418	0.074395	12.2272	0.081785
Botswana	Pula	12.5687	0.079563	12.2141	0.081873
Brazil	Real	3.3579	0.29781	3.3307	0.30024
Brunei	Brunei Dollar	2.6016	0.38438	2.4531	0.40765
Bulgaria	Lev	2.4496	0.40823	2.3525	0.42508
Burma	Kyat	11.9263	0.083848	11.0485	0.09051
Burundi	Burundi Franc	2196.36	0.0004553	2060.04	0.00048542
Canada	Canadian Dollar	1.9615	0.50981	1.9112	0.52323
Cayman Islands	C.I Dollar	1.5166	0.65937	1.4031	0.71271
Chile	Chilean Peso	956.952	0.001045	946.012	0.0010571
China	Yuan	12.8301	0.077942	11.7475	0.085124
Colombia	Colombia Peso	3608.31	0.00027714	3535.02	0.00028288
Congo (Dem Rep)	Congolese Franc	1032.28	0.00096873	1023.63	0.00097692
Costa Rica	Colon	973.351	0.0010274	928.677	0.0010768
Cuba	Cuban Peso	1.826	0.54765	1.7008	0.58796
Czech Republic	Koruna	31.2163	0.032035	30.6209	0.032657
Denmark	Danish Krone	9.3823	0.10658	8.971	0.11147

2008–09 Average foreign exchange rates (cont'd)

		Average rates for the year to 31 December 2008 and the year to 31 March 2009			
		Average for the year to 31 December 2008		Average for the year to 31 March 2009	
Country	Unit of currency	Currency units per £1	Sterling value of currency unit £	Currency units per £1	Sterling value of currency unit £
Egypt	Egyptian £	10.0716	0.099289	9.3599	0.10684
El Salvador	Colon	16.1864	0.06178	14.9744	0.066781
Ethiopia	Ethiopian Birr	17.8542	0.056009	17.1711	0.058237
European Union	Euro	1.2586	0.79453	1.2042	0.83043
Fiji Islands	Fiji Dollar	2.9203	0.34243	2.8305	0.35329
French Cty/Africa	CFA Franc	821.42	0.0012174	788.89	0.0012676
French Pacific Islands	CFP Franc	149.33	0.0066966	143.417	0.0069727
Gambia	Dalasi	40.9522	0.024419	39.7935	0.025130
Ghana	Cedi	1.9891	0.50274	1.9975	0.50063
Grenada/Wind. Isles	E Carib Dollar	4.9999	0.200004	4.6356	0.21572
Guyana	Guyana Dollar	377.743	0.0026473	349.056	0.0028649
Honduras	Lempira	34.9474	0.028614	32.3282	0.030933
Hong Kong	HK Dollar	14.4291	0.069304	13.354	0.074884
Hungary	Forint	312.999	0.0031949	311.844	0.0032067
Iceland	Icelandic Krona	159.163	0.0062829	167.632	0.0059654
India	Indian Rupee	79.9647	0.012506	78.1871	0.01279
Indonesia	Rupiah	17758.16	0.000056312	17352.65	0.000057628
Iran	Rial	17472.49	0.000057233	16415.66	0.000060917
Iraq	New Iraq Dinar	2209.16	0.00045266	2024.15	0.00049403
Israel	Shekel	6.6178	0.15111	6.2823	0.15918
Jamaica	Jamaican Dollar	134.301	0.007446	130.009	0.0076918
Japan	Yen	192.26	0.0052013	173.793	0.005754
Jordan	Jordanian Dinar	1.3114	0.76254	1.2159	0.82244
Kenya	Kenyan Shilling	126.93	0.0078784	122.243	0.0081804
Korea (South)	Won	2016.25	0.00049597	2052.65	0.00048718
Kuwait	Kuwaiti Dinar	0.4978	2.00884	0.468	2.13675
Laos	New Kip	16140.15	0.000061957	14709.12	0.000067985
Latvia	Lats	0.8802	1.13611	0.848	1.17925
Lebanon	Lebanese Pound	2792.83	0.00035806	2584.94	0.00038686
Libya	Libyan Dinar	2.2503	0.44439	2.1135	0.47315
Lithuania	Litas	4.3238	0.23128	4.1526	0.24081
Malawi	Kwacha	260.21	0.003843	241.322	0.0041438
Malaysia	Ringgit	6.1456	0.16272	5.858	0.17071
Mauritius	Mauritius Rupee	52.2565	0.019136	50.51	0.019798
Mexico	Mexican Peso	20.4908	0.048802	20.3173	0.049219
Morocco	Dirham	14.2196	0.070325	13.5629	0.073731
Nepal	Nepalese Rupee	128.535	0.00778	125.743	0.0079527
N'nd Antilles	Antilles Guilder	3.3106	0.30206	3.0628	0.3265
New Zealand	NZ Dollar	2.6107	0.38304	2.657	0.37636
Nicaragua	Gold Cordoba	35.8091	0.027926	33.5155	0.029837
Nigeria	Naira	219.909	0.0045473	214.921	0.0046529
Norway	Nor Krone	10.3359	0.09675	10.1688	0.09834
Oman	Rial Omani	0.7129	1.40272	0.661	1.51286
Pakistan	Pakistan Rupee	129.686	0.0077109	127.419	0.0078481

2008–09 Average foreign exchange rates (cont'd)

Country	Unit of currency	Average rates for the year to 31 December 2008 and the year to 31 March 2009			
		Average for the year to 31 December 2008		Average for the year to 31 March 2009	
		Currency units per £1	Sterling value of currency unit £	Currency units per £1	Sterling value of currency unit £
Papua New Guinea	Kina	4.8787	0.20497	4.5214	0.22117
Paraguay	Guarani	8020.51	0.00012468	7557.59	0.00013232
Peru	New Sol	5.3906	0.18551	5.1117	0.19563
Phillipines	Peso	81.9749	0.012199	78.9259	0.01267
Poland	Zloty	4.3869	0.22795	4.5008	0.22218
Qatar	Riyal	6.7405	0.14836	6.2508	0.15998
Romania	New Leu	4.6269	0.21613	4.5851	0.2181
Russia	Rouble	45.8837	0.021794	46.5529	0.021481
Rwanda	Franc	1011.52	0.00098861	944.62	0.0010586
Saudi Arabia	Riyal	6.9462	0.14396	6.4408	0.15526
Seychelles	Rupee	17.1243	0.058397	19.1079	0.052334
Sierra Leone	Leone	5518.12	0.00018122	5152.67	0.00019407
Singapore	Singapore Dollar	2.613	0.3827	2.4609	0.40636
Slovakia	Koruna (to 31.12.08) (Euro from 1.1.09)	39.0363	0.025617	1.4.08 to 31.12.08: 37.7155 (Euro from 1.1.09)	1.4.08 to 31.12.08: 0.026514 (Euro from 1.1.09)
Solomon Islands	SI Dollar	14.1409	0.070717	13.2045	0.075732
Somali Republic	Shilling	2594.15	0.00038548	2388.10	0.00041874
South Africa	Rand	15.1357	0.066069	14.8671	0.067263
Sri Lanka	Rupee	200.476	0.0049881	188.497	0.0053051
Sudan	Sudanese Pound	3.8614	0.25897	3.6671	0.2727
Surinam	Dollar	5.0768	0.19697	4.6968	0.21291
Swaziland	Lilangeni	15.1142	0.066163	14.863	0.067281
Sweden	Krona	12.0887	0.082722	12.0213	0.083186
Switzerland	Franc	1.9979	0.50053	1.8833	0.53098
Syria	Pound	92.5003	0.010811	83.5987	0.011962
Taiwan	Dollar	58.2406	0.01717	54.854	0.01823
Tanzania	Shilling	2213.92	0.00045169	2111.78	0.00047353
Thailand	Baht	61.599	0.016234	58.3223	0.017146
Tonga Islands	Pa'anga	3.521	0.28401	3.3988	0.29422
Trinidad & Tobago	Dollar	11.5893	0.086286	10.7217	0.093269
Tunisia	Dinar	2.2674	0.44103	2.1824	0.45821
Turkey	New Lira	2.3965	0.41728	2.3961	0.41734
Uganda	New Shilling	3164.28	0.00031603	3045.77	0.00032832
United Arab Emirates	Dirham	6.8011	0.14704	6.3059	0.15858
Uruguay	Peso Uruguay	38.4107	0.026034	36.5457	0.027363
U S A	US Dollar	1.8511	0.54022	1.7138	0.5835
Venezuela	Bolivar Fuerte	3.9764	0.25148	3.6867	0.27125
Vietnam	Dong	30510.83	0.000032775	28859.78	0.00003465
Yemen	Rial	368.639	0.0027127	341.543	0.0029279
Zambia	Kwacha	6878.11	0.00014539	6952.69	0.00014383

Table of spot rates on 31 December 2008 and 31 March 2009

		Table of Spot rates on 31 December 2008 and 31 March 2009			
		31 December 2008		**31 March 2009**	
Country	**Unit of Currency**	**Currency units per £1**	**Sterling value of currency unit £**	**Currency units per £1**	**Sterling value of currency unit £**
Australia	Australian Dollar	2.0622	0.48492	2.0630	0.48473
Canada	Canadian Dollar	1.7749	0.56341	1.8034	0.55451
Denmark	Danish Krone	7.6987	0.12989	8.0409	0.12436
European Union	Euro	1.0344	0.96674	1.0796	0.92627
Hong Kong	HK Dollar	11.1429	0.089743	11.1085	0.090021
Japan	Yen	130.332	0.0076727	141.572	0.0070635
Norway	Nor Krone	10.0673	0.099331	9.6781	0.10333
South Africa	Rand	13.2920	0.075233	13.6312	0.073361
Sweden	Krona	11.3697	0.087953	11.8499	0.084389
Switzerland	Franc	1.5303	0.65347	1.6298	0.61357
U S A	US Dollar	1.4378	0.69551	1.4334	0.69764

2007–08 Foreign exchange rates

		Average rates for the year to 31 December 2007 and the year to 31 March 2008			
		Average for the year to 31 December 2007		**Average for the year to 31 March 2008**	
Country	**Unit of currency**	**Currency units per £1**	**Sterling value of currency unit £**	**Currency units per £1**	**Sterling value of currency unit £**
Algeria	Algerian Dinar	139.34	0.007177	137.08	0.007295
Argentina	Peso	6.2363	0.160351	6.283	0.15916
Australia	Australian Dollar	2.3907	0.418286	2.3153	0.431916
Bahrain	Bahrain Dinar	0.754	1.32626	0.7562	1.322401
Bangladesh	Taka	138.02	0.007245	138.23	0.007234
Barbados	Barbados Dollar	4.0023	0.249856	4.0151	0.24906
Bolivia	Boliviano	15.7073	0.063665	15.5431	0.064337
Botswana	Pula	12.2795	0.081437	12.4328	0.080432
Brazil	Real	3.8951	0.256733	3.7214	0.268716
Brunei	Brunei Dollar	3.0127	0.331928	2.9581	0.338055
Bulgaria	Lev	2.8506	0.350798	2.7593	0.362411
Burma	Kyat	12.8474	0.077837	12.8986	0.077528
Burundi	Burundi Franc	2180.06	0.0004587	2246.85	0.0004451
Canada	Canadian Dollar	2.1484	0.465473	2.0725	0.482501
Cayman Islands	C.I. Dollar	1.7029	0.587234	1.6912	0.591296
Chile	Chilean Peso	1043.21	0.0009586	1007.89	0.0009922
China	Yuan Renminbi	15.2109	0.065742	14.944	0.066916
Colombia	Colombia Peso	4150.21	0.00024095	4009.40	0.00024941
Congo (Dem Rep)	Congolese Franc	1111.48	0.0008997	1116.84	0.0008954

2007–08 Average foreign exchange rates (cont'd)

Average rates for the year to 31 December 2007 and the year to 31 March 2008

Country	Unit of currency	Average for the year to 31 December 2007		Average for the year to 31 March 2008	
		Currency units per £1	Sterling value of currency unit £	Currency units per £1	Sterling value of currency unit £
Costa Rica	Colon	1033.37	0.0009677	1025.41	0.0009752
Cuba	Cuban Peso	1.9787	0.505382	1.9719	0.507125
Cyprus	Cyprus Pound (up to 31/12/07) (Euro from 1/1/08)	0.8494	1.177302	1/4/07 to 31/12/07: 0.84398 (Euro from 1/1/08)	1/4/07 to 31/12/07: 1.184865 (Euro from 1/1/08)
Czech Republic	Koruna	40.4435	0.024726	38.2403	0.02615
Denmark	Danish Krone	10.8900	0.091828	10.5702	0.094606
Egypt	Egyptian £	11.2921	0.0885575	11.226	0.089079
El Salvador	Colon	17.5503	0.056979	17.6071	0.056795
Ethiopia	Ethiopian Birr	18.0963	0.055260	18.4057	0.054331
European Union	Euro	1.4604	0.684755	1.4178	0.70532
Fiji Islands	Fiji Dollar	3.2178	0.310771	3.1500	0.31746
French Cty/Africa	C.F.A. Franc	956.12	0.0010459	925.47	0.0010805
French Pacific Islands	C.F.P. Franc	173.82	0.005753	168.25	0.005944
Gambia	Dalasi	49.573	0.020172	46.5553	0.02148
Ghana	Ghanaian Cedi	1/1/07 to 30/6/07: 18264.02 1/7/07 to 31/12/07: 1.927	1/1/07 to 30/6/07: 0.00005475 1/7/07 to 31/12/07: 0.518950	1/4/07 to 30/6/07: 18434.15 1/7/07 to 31/3/08: 1.9257	1/4/07 to 30/6/07: 0.00005425 1/7/07 to 31/3/08: 0.519286
Grenada/Wind. Isles	East Caribbean Dollar	5.4032	0.185076	5.4204	0.184488
Guyana	Guyanese Dollar	406.10	0.0024624	409.02	0.002445
Honduras	Lempira	37.8929	0.02639	38.016	0.026305
Hong Kong	H.K. Dollar	15.6114	0.064056	15.659	0.063861
Hungary	Forint	366.12	0.002731	356.86	0.002802
Iceland	Icelandic Krona	127.99	0.007813	128.36	0.00779
India	Indian Rupee	82.6063	0.012106	80.7528	0.012383
Indonesia	I.Rupiah	18294.55	0.00005466	18425.14	0.00005427
Iran	Iranian Rial	18566.81	0.00005386	18630.05	0.00005368
Iraq	Iraq Dinar	2510.79	0.0003983	2479.81	0.00040325
Israel	Shekel	8.2105	0.121795	7.9471	0.125832
Jamaica	Jamaican Dollar	138.11	0.007241	140.35	0.007125
Japan	Japanese Yen	235.6273	0.004244	229.3116	0.0043609
Jordan	Jordanian Dinar	1.4178	0.705318	1.4222	0.703136
Kenya	Kenya Shilling	134.68	0.007425	134.00	0.007463
Korea (South)	Won	1861.77	0.0005371	1877.73	0.0005326
Kuwait	Kuwaiti Dinar	0.5687	1.758396	0.5618	1.779993
Laos	New Kip	19225.02	0.00005202	18955.83	0.00005275
Latvia	Lats	1.0206	0.979832	0.9855	1.014713
Lebanon	Lebanese Pound	3026.21	0.00033045	3035.80	0.0003294
Libya	Libyan Dinar	2.519	0.396983	2.4937	0.401011
Lithuania	Litas	5.0329	0.198694	4.8715	0.205275

Key Data

2007–08 Average foreign exchange rates (cont'd)

Country	Unit of currency	Average for the year to 31 December 2007		Average for the year to 31 March 2008	
		Currency units per £1	**Sterling value of currency unit £**	**Currency units per £1**	**Sterling value of currency unit £**
Malawi	Malawi Kwacha	280.16	0.0035693	281.54	0.003552
Malaysia	Ringgit	6.8706	0.145548	6.7553	0.148032
Malta	Maltese Lira (up to 31/12/07) (Euro from 1/1/08)	0.6271	1.594642	1/4/07 to 31/12/07: 0.62236 (Euro from 1/1/08)	1/4/07 to 31/12/07: 1.606799 (Euro from 1/1/08)
Mauritius	Mauritius Rupee	62.0963	0.016104	59.8987	0.016695
Mexico	Mexican Peso	21.8598	0.045746	21.8287	0.045811
Morocco	Dirham	16.3605	0.061123	15.9354	0.062753
Nepal	Nepalese Rupee	132.02	0.007575	129.13	0.007744
N'nd Antilles	Antilles Guilder	3.5895	0.27859	3.6011	0.277693
New Zealand	N.Z. Dollar	2.7195	0.367715	2.6436	0.378272
Nicaragua	Gold Cordoba	37.0597	0.026983	37.6291	0.026575
Nigeria	Nigerian Naira	251.46	0.003977	246.92	0.00405
Norway	N. Krone	11.7296	0.085254	11.3122	0.0884
Oman, Sultanate of	Rial Omani	0.7702	1.298364	0.7726	1.294331
Pakistan	Pakistan Rupee	121.51	0.00823	122.81	0.008143
Papua New Guinea	Kina	5.8123	0.172049	5.7172	0.174911
Paraguay	Guarani	10055.95	0.00009944	9823.32	0.0001018
Peru	New Sol	6.2554	0.159862	6.1231	0.163316
Phillipines	Phillipine Peso	92.1586	0.010851	88.695	0.011275
Poland	Zloty	5.4989	0.181855	5.2082	0.192005
Qatar	Qatar Riyal	7.2833	0.1373	7.3053	0.136887
Romania	Leu	4.8646	0.205567	4.8313	0.206984
Russia	Rouble	51.1028	0.019568	50.1627	0.019935
Rwanda	Rwanda Franc	1096.84	0.0009117	1098.52	0.0009103
Saudi Arabia	Saudi Riyal	7.4983	0.133364	7.5217	0.132949
Seychelles	Rupee	13.6354	0.073339	14.6353	0.068328
Sierra Leone	Leone	5972.91	0.0001674	5987.38	0.000167
Singapore	Singapore Dollar	3.0131	0.331884	2.9616	0.337655
Slovakia	Koruna	49.234	0.020311	47.1771	0.021197
Solomon Islands	S.I. Dollar	14.509	0.068923	14.6865	0.06809
Somali Republic	Shilling	2745.39	0.0003642	2770.69	0.0003609
South Africa	Rand	14.1085	0.070879	14.3067	0.069897
Sri Lanka	Rupee	221.39	0.004517	221.61	0.004512
Sudan	Sudanese Dinar (up to 30 June 2007) Sudanese Pound (from 1 July 2007)	1/1/07 to 30/6/07: 397.24 1/7/07 to 31/12/07: 4.1168	1/1/07 to 30/6/07: 0.0025174 1/7/07 to 31/12/07: 0.242907	1/4/07 to 30/6/07: 400.6417 1/7/07 to 31/3/08: 4.0913	1/4/07 to 30/6/07: 0.002496 1/7/07 to 31/3/08: 0.244418
Surinam	Surinam Guilder	5.5045	0.18167	5.5224	0.181081
Swaziland	Lilangeni	14.0461	0.071194	14.3204	0.069830
Sweden	Swedish Krona	13.5236	0.073945	13.1967	0.075776

2007–08 Average foreign exchange rates (cont'd)

		Average rates for the year to 31 December 2007 and the year to 31 March 2008			
		Average for the year to 31 December 2007		Average for the year to 31 March 2008	
Country	Unit of currency	Currency units per £1	Sterling value of currency unit £	Currency units per £1	Sterling value of currency unit £
Switzerland	Swiss Franc	2.4010	0.416498	2.3261	0.429896
Syria	Syrian Pound	103.71	0.009642	103.50	0.009662
Taiwan	T. Dollar	65.7326	0.015213	65.258	0.015324
Tanzania	Shilling	2481.21	0.000403	2437.04	0.0004103
Thailand	Thai Baht	68.5207	0.014594	67.7565	0.014759
Tonga Islands	Pa'Anga	3.908	0.255885	3.8389	0.260491
Trinidad & Tobago	Trinidad & Tobago Dollar	12.6152	0.079269	12.6561	0.079013
Tunisia	Dinar	2.5590	0.390778	2.5108	0.398279
Turkey	Turkish Lira	2.6067	0.383627	2.5166	0.397362
Uganda	New Shilling	3451.92	0.0002897	3429.98	0.00029155
United Arab Emirates	U.A.E Dirham	7.3481	0.13609	7.3712	0.135663
Uruguay	Uruguayan Peso	46.9076	0.021319	45.3662	0.022043
U.S.A	U.S. Dollar	2.0020	0.499493	2.0080	0.497998
Venezuela	V. Bolivar (2007) Bolivar Fuerte (2008)	5357.25	0.00018666	1/4/07 to 31/12/07: 4665.73 1/1/08 to 31/3/08: 4.2501	1/4/07 to 31/12/07: 0.00021433 1/1/08 to 31/3/08: 0.235287
Vietnam	Dong	32241.04	0.000031016	32340.43	0.00003092
Yemen	Rial	398.84	0.0025073	400.27	0.0024983
Zambia	Zambian Kwacha	7984.03	0.00012525	7769.02	0.00012872
Zimbabwe	Z. Dollar	01/01/07 to 5/9/07: 496.04 6/9/07 to 31/12/07: 61053.83	01/01/07 to 5/9/07: 0.00201596 6/9/07 to 31/12/07: 0.000016379	1/4/07 to 5/9/07: 500.60 6/9/07 to 31/3/08: 60335.72	1/4/07 to 5/9/07: 0.0019976 6/9/07 to 31/3/08: 0.000016574

Table of spot rates on 31 December 2007 and 31 March 2008

		31 December 2007		31 March 2008	
Country	Unit of Currency	Currency units per £1	Sterling value of currency unit £	Currency units per £1	Sterling value of currency unit £
Australia	Australian Dollar	2.2671	0.441092	2.1773	0.459284
Canada	Canadian Dollar	1.9646	0.509009	2.0393	0.490364
Denmark	Danish Krone	10.1522	0.098501	9.3536	0.106911
European Union	Euro	1.3615	0.734484	1.2543	0.797257
Hong Kong	H. K. Dollar	15.5215	0.064427	15.4685	0.064648
Japan	Japanese Yen	222.380	0.0044968	197.826	0.0050549
Norway	N. Krone	10.8087	0.092518	10.1000	0.099010
South Africa	Rand	13.6045	0.073505	16.1515	0.061914
Sweden	S.Krone	12.8656	0.077727	11.7858	0.084848
Switzerland	Swiss Franc	2.2536	0.443734	1.9658	0.508699
U.S.A	U.S. Dollar	1.9906	0.502361	1.9875	0.503145

Key Data

2006–07 Foreign exchange rates

| | | Average rates for the year to 31 December 2006 and the year to 31 March 2007 | | | |
| | | Average for the year to 31 December 2006 | | Average for the year to 31 March 2007 | |
Country	Unit of currency	Currency units per £1	Sterling value of currency unit £	Currency units per £1	Sterling value of currency unit £
Algeria	Algerian Dinar	134.0142	0.0074619	136.9221	0.00730342
Argentina	Peso	5.652	0.17692852	5.8223	0.17175343
Australia	Australian Dollar	2.4448	0.409031	2.4739	0.40422006
Bahrain	Bahrain Dinar	0.6952	1.43843498	0.7141	1.40036409
Bangladesh	Taka	127.3866	0.007850119	131.2303	0.007620191
Barbados	Barbados Dollar	3.6879	0.27115703	3.7884	0.26396368
Bolivia	Boliviano	14.7464	0.06781316	15.1462	0.06602316
Botswana	Pula	10.8192	0.092428276	11.4887	0.08704205
Brazil	Real	4.0028	0.24982512	4.0789	0.24516414
Brunei	Brunei Dollar	2.9251	0.341868654	2.9649	0.337279504
Burma	Kyat	11.8406	0.08445518	12.1615	0.08222670
Burundi	Burundi Franc	1846.6517	0.000541521	1932.3958	0.000517492
Canada	Canadian Dollar	2.0901	0.47844601	2.1567	0.4636713
Cayman Islands	C.I Dollar	1.5712	0.636456212	1.6242	0.615687723
Chile	Chilean Peso	977.173	0.00102336	1010.6452	0.00098947
China	Renminbi	14.7126	0.067968952	14.9935	0.066695568
Colombia	Colombia Peso	4348.138	0.00022998	4441.0926	0.00022517
Congo Dem (Rep) Zaire	Congolese Franc	859.2795	0.00116377	935.6975	0.00106872
Costa Rica	Colon	946.8613	0.001056121	981.3863	0.001018967
Cuba	Cuban Peso	1.8483	0.54103771	1.901	0.526038927
Cyprus	Cyprus Pound	0.8434	1.185677022	0.8508	1.175364363
Czech Republic	Koruna	41.4016	0.024153656	41.5989	0.024039097
Denmark	Danish Krone	10.9397	0.09141018	11.0014	0.0908975
Egypt	Egyptian £	10.5864	0.09446082	10.8563	0.09211241
El Salvador	Colon	16.1758	0.061820745	16.6369	0.060107352
Ethiopia	Ethiopian Birr	16.1638	0.06186664	16.7003	0.059879164
European Union	Euro	1.4666	0.68184917	1.475	0.6779661
Fiji Islands	Fiji Dollar	3.2042	0.312090381	3.2532	0.307389647
French Cty/Africa	C.F.A. Franc	960.8382	0.001040758	967.3428	0.00103376
French Pacific Islands	C.F.P. Franc	174.6763	0.005724875	175.8587	0.005686383
Gambia	Dalasi	51.8573	0.019283688	53.0478	0.018850923
Ghana	Ghanaian Cedi	16916.4967	0.0000591139	17447.0667	0.0000573162
Grenada/Wind. Isles	East Caribbean Dollar	4.9787	0.20085565	5.1144	0.19552636
Guyana	Guyanese Dollar	350.4058	0.00285383	365.1609	0.00273852
Honduras	Lempira	34.9226	0.028634752	35.9179	0.027841271
Hong Kong	H.K. Dollar	14.3132	0.06986558	14.724	0.0679163
Hungary	Forint	386.9914	0.002584037	388.1129	0.00257657
Iceland	Icelandic Krona	128.9847	0.00775286	133.7177	0.00747844
India	Indian Rupee	83.4523	0.01198289	85.6028	0.01168186

2006–07 Average foreign exchange rates (cont'd)

| | | Average rates for the year to 31 December 2006 and the year to 31 March 2007 | | | |
| | | Average for the year to 31 December 2006 | | Average for the year to 31 March 2007 | |
Country	Unit of currency	Currency units per £1	Sterling value of currency unit £	Currency units per £1	Sterling value of currency unit £
Indonesia	I.Rupiah	16875.1042	0.0000592589	17253.2658	0.00005796
Iran	Iranian Rial	16908.4704	0.000059142	17424.415	0.0000573907
Iraq	Iraq Dinar	2699.6693	0.00037042	2685.7928	0.00037233
Israel	Shekel	8.2066	0.12185314	8.2179	0.12168559
Jamaica	Jamaican Dollar	121.3518	0.00824050	125.8431	0.00794640
Japan	Japanese Yen	214.3005	0.0046663447	221.4527	0.004515637
Jordan	Jordanian Dinar	1.3066	0.76534517	1.3422	0.74504545
Kenya	Kenya Shilling	132.9039	0.0075423	135.298	0.00739109
Korea(South)	Won	1757.86	0.000568874	1794.2808	0.000557326
Kuwait	Kuwaiti Dinar	0.535	1.869158879	0.5483	1.82381908
Laos	New Kip	18530.2392	0.0000539658	18804.8133	0.0000531779
Lebanon	Lebanese Pound	2780.1683	0.00035969	2859.8993	0.00034966
Libya	Libyan Dinar	2.4064	0.41555851	2.4467	0.40871378
Malawi	Malawi Kwacha	251.0676	0.003983	262.3102	0.00381228
Malaysia	Ringgit	6.7564	0.148007815	6.832	0.14637002
Malta	Maltese Lira	0.63	1.58730159	0.6338	1.57778479
Mauritius	Rupee	57.9506	0.017256077	60.4041	0.01655517
Mexico	Mexican Peso	20.0984	0.0497552	20.8418	0.04798050
Morocco	Dirham	16.186	0.061781787	16.3655	0.061104152
Nepal	Nepalese Rupee	133.8618	0.007470391	137.3187	0.007282329
N'nd Antilles	Antilles Guilder	3.3084	0.302260912	3.4027	0.293884268
New Zealand	N.Z. Dollar	2.8425	0.35180299	2.8853	0.34658441
Nicaragua	Gold Cordoba	32.1564	0.031098008	33.5507	0.029805637
Nigeria	Nigerian Naira	236.971	0.00421993	242.9804	0.00411556
Norway	N. Krone	11.8095	0.08467759	11.9303	0.0838202
Oman, Sultanate of	Rial Omani	0.7099	1.408649	0.7293	1.371178
Pakistan	Pakistan Rupee	111.1701	0.00899522	114.5979	0.00872616
Papua New Guinea	Kina	5.5053	0.181643144	5.6454	0.177135367
Paraguay	Guarani	10373.1821	0.0000964024	10251.0069	0.0000975514
Peru	New Sol	6.0317	0.165791	6.1252	0.163260
Phillipines	Phillipine Peso	94.5009	0.01058191	95.5121	0.01046988
Poland	Zloty	5.7126	0.17505164	5.7668	0.173406395
Qatar	Qatar Riyal	6.7125	0.148976	6.8958	0.145016
Romania	Leu	5.1527	0.19407301	5.1239	0.19516384
Russia	Rouble (market)	50.0151	0.019993962	50.6508	0.019743025
Rwanda	Rwanda Franc	1010.6548	0.000989458	1042.4532	0.000959276
Saudi Arabia	Saudi Riyal	6.9151	0.144611	7.1037	0.140772
Seychelles	Rupee	10.2716	0.097355816	10.8403	0.09224837
Sierra Leone	Leone	5461.5218	0.0001830992	5631.4166	0.0001775752
Singapore	Singapore Dollar	2.9308	0.341204	2.966	0.337154
Solomon Islands	S.I. Dollar	13.597	0.073545635	13.9149	0.07186541
Somali Republic	Shilling	2615.015	0.000382407	2599.6275	0.00038467
South Africa	Rand	12.4976	0.08001536	13.341	0.0749569
Sri Lanka	Rupee	191.8051	0.00521363	200.1501	0.00499625

2006–07 Average foreign exchange rates (cont'd)

Average rates for the year to 31 December 2006 and the year to 31 March 2007

Country	Unit of currency	Average for the year to 31 December 2006		Average for the year to 31 March 2007	
		Currency units per £1	Sterling value of currency unit £	Currency units per £1	Sterling value of currency unit £
Sudan	Sudanese Dinar	399.0983	0.002505648	397.5664	0.002515303
Surinam	Surinam Guilder	5.0713	0.197188098	5.218	0.191644308
Swaziland	Lilangeni	12.6018	0.079353743	13.4435	0.074385391
Sweden	Swedish Krona	13.5672	0.07370718	13.593	0.0735673
Switzerland	Swiss Franc	2.3074	0.43338823	2.3425	0.42689434
Syria	Syrian Pound	96.5596	0.010356298	99.2471	0.010075861
Taiwan	New T. Dollar	59.9643	0.01667659	61.8966	0.01615598
Tanzania	Shilling	2311.7583	0.00043257	2411.6028	0.00041466
Thailand	Thai Baht	69.7902	0.014328659	69.3549	0.01441859
Tonga Islands	Pa'Anga	3.7453	0.267001308	3.8224	0.261615739
Trinidad & Tobago	Trinidad & Tobago Dollar	11.58	0.08635579	11.9098	0.083964
Tunisia	Dinar	2.4507	0.40804668	2.4998	0.400032
Turkey	Turkish Lira	2.6492	0.3774724	2.7546	0.363029
Uganda	New Shilling	3375.2477	0.000296275	3440.7299	0.00029064
United Arab Emirates	U.A.E Dirham	6.7727	0.147652	6.9571	0.143738
Uruguay	Uruguayan Peso	44.2834	0.022581825	45.5669	0.02194575
U.S.A	U.S. Dollar	1.8424	0.54277030	1.8932	0.5282062
Venezuela	V.Bolivar	5044.842	0.00019822	5747.9573	0.00017397
Vietnam	Dong	29567.2417	0.00003382	30455.15	0.00003284
Yemen	Rial	364.4703	0.002743708	376.1672	0.002658392
Zambia	Zambian Kwacha	6622.279	0.00015101	7244.9871	0.00013803
Zimbabwe	Z. Dollar	01/01/06–3/8/06 = 178951.06 04/08/06–31/12/06 = 476.63	01/01/06–03/08/06 = 0.00000558812 04/08/06–31/12/06 = 0.00209806	01/04/06–03/08/06 = 185137.83 04/08/06–31/03/07 = 481.06	01/04/06–03/08/06 = 0.0000540138 04/08/06–31/03/07 = 0.00207874

Table of spot rates on 31 December 2006 and 31 March 2007

Country	Unit of Currency	31 December 2006		31 March 2007	
		Currency units per £1	Sterling value of currency unit £	Currency units per £1	Sterling value of currency unit £
Australia	Australian Dollar	2.4779	0.40356754	2.4279	0.41187858
Canada	Canadian Dollar	2.2776	0.43905866	2.2627	0.44194988
Denmark	Danish Krone	11.0641	0.09038241	10.9789	0.09108381
European Union	Euro	1.4842	0.67376364	1.4735	0.67865626
Hong Kong	H K Dollar	15.2213	0.06569741	15.3265	0.06524647
Japan	Japanese Yen	233.204	0.00428809	231.586	0.00431805
Norway	N.Krone	12.1859	0.08206206	11.9723	0.08352614
South Africa	Rand	13.7994	0.07246692	14.2247	0.07030025
Sweden	S.Krone	13.3928	0.07466699	13.7611	0.07266861
Switzerland	Swiss Franc	2.3891	0.41856766	2.3945	0.41762372
U.S.A	U.S. Dollar	1.9572	0.51093399	1.9614	0.50983991

2005–06 Foreign exchange rates

		Average rates for the year to 31 December 2005 and the year to 31 March 2006			
		Average for the year to 31 December 2005		Average for the year to 31 March 2006	
Country	Unit of currency	Currency units per £1	Sterling value of currency unit £	Currency units per £1	Sterling value of currency unit £
Algeria	Algerian Dinar	132.3118	0.0075579	130.3635	0.007671
Argentina	Peso	5.3182	0.188033545	5.2768	0.189508793
Australia	Australian Dollar	2.3862	0.419076356	2.37825	0.420477
Bahrain	Bahrain Dinar	0.6859	1.457938	0.6729	1.486105
Bangladesh	Taka	116.7483	0.00856544	117.237	0.00853
Barbados	Barbados Dollar	3.639	0.274800769	3.57	0.28011204
Bolivia	Boliviano	14.666	0.068185	14.36	0.069638
Botswana	Pula	9.2512	0.10809409	9.51	0.10515
Brazil	Real	4.4133	0.226588	4.1126	0.24316
Brunei	Brunei Dollar	3.0182	0.33132331	2.9546	0.33846
Burma	Kyat	11.6811	0.085608	11.4616	0.08725
Burundi	Burundi Franc	1920.5317	0.0005207	1839.63	0.00054
Canada	Canadian Dollar	2.2063	0.45324752	2.1598	0.46300941
Cayman Islands	C.I Dollar	1.501	0.66622252	1.4774	0.67686
Chile	Chilean Peso	1018.873	0.000981	975.9229	0.001025
China	Renminbi	14.8666	0.0672488	14.4759	0.06908
Colombia	Colombia Peso	4227.3334	0.000236556	4107.4241	0.00024346
Congo Dem (Rep) Zaire	Congolese Franc	886.8474	0.00112759	864.3402	0.00115695
Costa Rica	Colon	869.6228	0.00114992	869.708	0.00115
Cuba	Cuban Peso	1.8162	0.55060015	1.7815	0.56132
Cyprus	Cyprus Pound	0.8438	1.18511496	0.8417	1.18807
Czech Republic	Koruna	43.66	0.02290426	43.1314	0.02318
Denmark	Danish Krone	10.8991	0.0917507	10.93255	0.09146997
Egypt	Egyptian £	10.538	0.094895	10.2955	0.09713
El Salvador	Colon	15.8952	0.06291207	15.5912	0.06414
Ethiopia	Ethiopian Birr	15.7915	0.06332521	15.5295	0.06439
European Union	Euro	1.4626	0.68371393	1.4664	0.681956
Fiji Islands	Fiji Dollar	3.0678	0.32596649	3.0556	0.32727
French Cty/Africa	C.F.A. Franc	959.9	0.00104178	961.102	0.00104
French Pacific Islands	C.F.P. Franc	174.5057	0.00573047	174.724	0.00572
Gambia	Dalasi	51.7924	0.01930785	50.3634	0.01986
Ghana	Ghanaian Cedi	16513.74	0.00006	16225.61	0.00006
Grenada/Wind. Isles	East Caribbean Dollar	4.9126	0.203558197	4.8195	0.2074904
Guyana	Guyanese Dollar	335.8187	0.0029778	334.5235	0.002989
Honduras	Lempira	34.1971	0.02924225	33.6188	0.02975
Hong Kong	H.K. Dollar	14.1526	0.07065839	13.9682	0.0715911
Hungary	Forint	363.5366	0.00275075	367.705	0.00272
Iceland	Icelandic Krona	114.2941	0.008749	113.7708	0.00879
India	Indian Rupee	80.099	0.012485	78.8637	0.01268

2005–2006 Foreign exchange rates (cont'd)

Average rates for the year to 31 December 2005 and the year to 31 March 2006

Country	Unit of currency	Average for the year to 31 December 2005		Average for the year to 31 March 2006	
		Currency units per £1	Sterling value of currency unit £	Currency units per £1	Sterling value of currency unit £
Indonesia	I.Rupiah	17636.33	0.0000567	17323.1629	0.0000577
Iran	Iranian Rial	16299.03	0.0000614	16111.9	0.000062
Iraq	Iraq Dinar	2667.384	0.000375	2620.743	0.000382
Israel	Shekel	8.1539	0.122641	8.1412	0.12283
Jamaica	Jamaican Dollar	112.8199	0.008864	112.3691	0.00889924
Japan	Japanese Yen	200.1041	0.0049974	201.2374	0.0049693
Jordan	Jordanian Dinar	1.2893	0.7756147	1.2648	0.79064
Kenya	Kenya Shilling	137.2843	0.007284	132.8881	0.007525
Korea (South)	Won	1852.275	0.00053988	1797.1	0.00056
Kuwait	Kuwaiti Dinar	0.5313	1.882176	0.5213	1.91828
Laos	New Kip	17674.3833	0.0000566	18440.6	0.0000542
Lebanon	Lebanese Pound	2744.3486	0.0003644	2687.5416	0.00037209
Libya	Libyan Dinar	2.3765	0.420787	2.3642	0.422976
Malawi	Malawi Kwacha	214.9901	0.004651	220.5461	0.004534
Malaysia	Ringgit	6.8872	0.145196887	6.7233	0.14873648
Malta	Maltese Lira	0.6285	1.59109	0.6293	1.58907
Mauritius	Rupee	53.4296	0.01602025	53.3423	0.01874685
Mexico	Mexican Peso	19.8317	0.050424	19.1852	0.05212
Morocco	Dirham	16.1185	0.06204051	16.0777	0.0622
Nepal	Nepalese Rupee	127.9483	0.00781566	125.954	0.00794
N'nd Antilles	Antilles Guilder	3.251	0.30759766	3.1888	0.3136
New Zealand	N.Z. Dollar	2.5815	0.387372	2.5841	0.38698193
Nicaragua	Gold Cordoba	29.7796	0.03358003	29.6126	0.03377
Nigeria	Nigerian Naira	241.7492	0.004137	235.493	0.00425
Norway	N. Krone	11.7178	0.08641325	11.6878	0.85559301
Oman, Sultanate of	Rial Omani	0.7006	1.427348	0.6873	1.4549687
Pakistan	Pakistan Rupee	108.417	0.009224	106.6047	0.0093804
Papua New Guinea	Kina	5.5303	0.18082202	5.4038	0.18505
Paraguay	Guarani	11239.12	0.0000889	10913.66	0.0000916
Peru	New Sol	5.9931	0.166859	5.9161	0.16903
Phillipines	Phillipine Peso	100.0778	0.009992226	96.8521	0.010325021
Poland	Zloty	5.5982	0.17862884	5.8289	0.17156
Qatar	Qatar Riyal	6.622	0.151012	6.4968	0.15392193
Romania	Leu	1/1/05-30/6/05 = 53404.4 1/7/05-31/12/05 = 5.2643	1/1/05-30/6/05 = 0.000018725 1/7/05-31/12/05 = 0.189959	1/1/05-30/6/05 = 53483.7 1/7/05-31/12/05 = 5.2306	1/1/05-30/6/05 = 0.000018697 1/7/05-31/12/05 = 0.191183
Russia	Rouble (market)	51.3674	0.0194676	50.4621	0.01982
Rwanda	Rwanda Franc	991.2927	0.00100878	967.81	0.00103
Saudi Arabia	Saudi Riyal	6.8237	0.146548	6.6944	0.14937859
Seychelles	Rupee	10.0265	0.0997357	9.8347	0.10168
Sierra Leone	Leone	5017.596	0.000199	5130.52	0.000195
Singapore	Singapore Dollar	3.0264	0.330425588	2.9663	0.337120318

2005–2006 Foreign exchange rates (cont'd)

		Average rates for the year to 31 December 2005 and the year to 31 March 2006			
		Average for the year to 31 December 2005		**Average for the year to 31 March 2006**	
Country	**Unit of currency**	**Currency units per £1**	**Sterling value of currency unit £**	**Currency units per £1**	**Sterling value of currency unit £**
Solomon Islands	S.I. Dollar	13.3353	0.07498894	13.1391	0.07611
Somali Republic	Shilling	4614.7308	0.0002167	3841.33	0.00026
South Africa	Rand	11.5723	0.08641325	11.4532	0.0873119
Sri Lanka	Rupee	182.1193	0.005491	180.6241	0.0053644
Sudan	Sudanese Dinar	442.4396	0.0022602	424.337	0.00236
Surinam	Surinam Guilder	4.9568	0.20174306	4.8734	0.2052
Swaziland	Lilangeni	11.5501	0.08657934	11.4034	0.08769
Sweden	Swedish Krona	13.5776	0.07365072	13.67855	0.073107
Switzerland	Swiss Franc	2.2681	0.440898	2.2756	0.43944
Syria	Syrian Pound	94.8321	0.01054495	93.0719	0.01074
Taiwan	New T. Dollar	58.4213	0.017117045	57.7011	0.01733
Tanzania	Shilling	2051.1569	0.00048753	2052.1933	0.0004873
Thailand	Thai Baht	73.1459	0.013671306	72.1171	0.0138663
Tonga Islands	Pa'Anga	3.253	0.30740855	3.2585	0.30689
Trinidad & Tobago	Trinidad & Tobago Dollar	11.3985	0.087730842	11.1882	0.08937988
Tunisia	Dinar	2.3573	0.424214	2.3656	0.422726
Turkey	Turkish Lira	2.4483	0.408447	2.4068	0.415489
Uganda	New Shilling	3234.669	0.000309	3221.231	0.00031
United Arab Emirates	U.A.E Dirham	6.6827	0.14964012	6.5562	0.152527379
Uruguay	Uruguayan Peso	44.461	0.0224916	43.1552	0.0231722
U.S.A	U.S. Dollar	1.8195	0.54960154	1.79738	0.556365
Venezuela	V.Bolivar	4916.2392	0.000203408	4751.6019	0.00021046
Vietnam	Dong	28797.3333	0.000035	28298.4	0.000035
Yemen	Rial	348.0178	0.00287342	345.207	0.0029
Zambia	Zambian Kwacha	8104.899	0.000123	7310.1153	0.0001368
Zimbabwe	Z. Dollar	1/1/05-21/10/05 = 22764.44 22/10/05-31/12/05 = 118470.7	1/1/05-21/10/05 = 0.0000439 22/10/05-31/12/05 = 0.00000844	1/1/05-21/10/05 = 27676.3 22/10/05-31/12/05 = 144586.5	1/1/05-21/10/05 = 0.000036 22/10/05-31/12/05 = 0.0000069

Table of spot rates on 31 December 2005 and 31 March 2006

		30 December 2005 (31 December is a Saturday)		**31 March 2006**	
Country	**Unit of currency**	**Currency units per £1**	**Sterling value of currency unit (£)**	**Currency units per £1**	**Sterling value of currency unit (£)**
Australia	Australian Dollar	2.3403	0.427296	2.4326	0.411083
Canada	Canadian Dollar	2.0054	0.498654	2.0235	0.494193
Denmark	Danish Krone	10.8558	0.092117	10.6962	0.093491
European Union	Euro	1.4554	0.687096	1.4333	0.697691
Hong Kong	H K Dollar	13.3109	0.075126	13.4598	0.074295
Japan	Japanese Yen	202.268	0.004944	204.660	0.004886
Norway	N.Krone	11.6245	0.086025	11.3835	0.087846

Country	Unit of currency	30 December 2005 (31 December is a Saturday)		31 March 2006	
		Currency units per £1	Sterling value of currency unit (£)	Currency units per £1	Sterling value of currency unit (£)
South Africa	Rand	10.8885	0.09184	10.6926	0.935226
Sweden	S.Krone	13.6629	0.073191	13.5185	0.073973
Switzerland	Swiss Franc	2.2681	0.440898	2.2668	0.44115
U.S.A	U.S. Dollar	1.7168	0.582479	1.7346	0.576502

2004–05 Foreign exchange rates

Country	Unit of currency	Average rates for the year to 31 December 2004 and the year to 31 March 2005			
		Average for the year to 31 December 2004		Average for the year to 31 March 2005	
		Currency units per £1	Sterling value of currency unit £	Currency units per £1	Sterling value of currency unit £
Algeria	Algerian Dinar	131.4975	0.007605	132.9205	0.007523
Argentina	Peso	5.402	0.18512	5.4508	0.18346
Australia	Australian Dollar	2.4912	0.401412974	2.4986	0.400224126
Bahrain	Bahrain Dinar	0.6917	1.445713	0.6968	1.435132
Bangladesh	Taka	108.9708	0.00917677	11.5317	0.008966
Barbados	Barbados Dollar	3.6574	0.273418	3.6848	0.271385
Bolivia	Boliviano	14.5681	0.068643	14.7661	0.067723
Botswana	Pula	8.5620	0.11679514	8.5027	0.117610
Brazil	Real	5.3511	0.18688	5.2779	0.18947
Brunei	Brunei Dollar	3.0908	0.32354083	3.0890	0.323729
Burma	Kyat	11.7790	0.08496850	11.8660	0.08427
Burundi	Burundi Franc	1941.2442	0.00051513	1963.573	0.000509
Canada	Canadian Dollar	2.3840	0.4194631	2.3573	0.4242141
Cayman Islands	C.I Dollar	1.5106	0.66198861	1.523	0.656599
Chile	Chilean Peso	1116.725	0.000895	1118.999	0.000894
China	Renminbi	15.1577	0.06597307	15.2827	0.065433
Colombia	Colombia Peso	4803.50	0.000208	4674.58	0.0002139
Congo Dem (Rep) Zaire	Congolese Franc	753.258	0.00132757	797.5428	0.00125385
Costa Rica	Colon	805.2731	0.00124181	830.7517	0.001204
Cuba	Cuban Peso	1.8314	0.54603036	1.8465	0.541565
Cyprus	Cyprus Pound	0.8572	1.16658889	0.8509	1.175226
Czech Republic	Koruna	47.0014	0.02127596	45.652	0.021905
Denmark	Danish Krone	10.9655	0.0911868	10.9121	0.0916414
Egypt	Egyptian £	11.3764	0.08791269	11.2929	0.08855
El Salvador	Colon	16.028	0.06239082	16.1604	0.06188
Ethiopia	Ethiopian Birr	15.7273	0.0635837	15.8847	0.062954
European Union	Euro	1.474	0.67842605	1.467	0.68166326
Fiji Islands	Fiji Dollar	3.1709	0.31536788	3.1678	0.315676
French Cty/Africa	C.F.A. Franc	966.9058	0.00103423	960.6808	0.001041
French Pacific Islands	C.F.P. Franc	175.0749	0.00571184	174.5547	0.005729
Gambia	Dalasi	53.9398	0.01853919	54.2474	0.018434

2004–2005 Foreign exchange rates (cont'd)

Country	Unit of currency	Average for the year to 31 December 2004		Average for the year to 31 March 2005	
		Currency units per £1	Sterling value of currency unit £	Currency units per £1	Sterling value of currency unit £
Ghana	Ghanaian Cedi	16488.517	0.00006064	16679.57	0.000059953
Grenada/Wind. Isles	East Caribbean Dollar	4.9525	0.2019182	4.99	0.2004008
Guyana	Guyanese Dollar	328.4189	0.0030449	330.8431	0.0030226
Honduras	Lempira	33.3949	0.02994469	34.0669	0.029354
Hong Kong	H.K. Dollar	14.268	0.70087	14.3762	0.069559
Hungary	Forint	369.4715	0.00270657	362.5755	0.002758
Iceland	Icelandic Krona	128.2386	0.007798	125.1205	0.0079923
India	Indian Rupee	82.9188	0.01206	82.8631	0.0120681
Indonesia	I.Rupiah	16422.433	0.0000608	16916.541	0.0000591
Iran	Iranian Rial	15816.065	0.0000632	16145.573	0.0000619
Iraq	Iraq Dinar	1/1/04-20/2/04 = 0.5734 21/2/04-31/12/04 = 2368.6802	1/1/04-20/2/04 = 1.74398325 21/2/04-31/12/04 = 0.00042217	2697.8116	0.0003707
Israel	Shekel	8.2138	0.1217463	8.2195	0.1216619
Jamaica	Jamaican Dollar	111.4187	0.0089752	112.6457	0.0088772
Japan	Japanese Yen	198.065	0.00505	198.171	0.00505
Jordan	Jordanian Dinar	1.3007	0.7688168	1.3102	0.7632423
Kenya	Kenya Shilling	145.2923	0.0068827	145.9332	0.0068525
Korea(South)	Won	2084.2033	0.0004798	2029.15	0.000493
Kuwait	Kuwaiti Dinar	0.5408	1.8491124	0.5435	1.8399264
Laos	New Kip	14397.408	0.000069456	14498.05	0.000068974
Lebanon	Lebanese Pound	2778.0553	0.00036	2798.3398	0.0003574
Libya	Libyan Dinar	2.3891	0.4185677	2.3908	0.41827
Malawi	Malawi Kwacha	198.5154	0.0050374	200.7741	0.0049807
Malaysia	Ringgit	6.9715	0.1434412	7.023	0.1423893
Malta	Maltese Lira	0.6306	1.5857913	0.6286	1.5908368
Mauritius	Rupee	50.5845	0.0197689	52.2987	0.0191209
Mexico	Mexican Peso	20.6952	0.0483204	20.9278	0.0477833
Morocco	Dirham	16.256	0.06151575	16.1825	0.061795
Nepal	Nepalese Rupee	132.5356	0.00754514	132.6487	0.007539
N'nd Antilles	Antilles Guilder	3.2781	0.30505476	3.3052	0.302554
New Zealand	N.Z. Dollar	2.7591	0.362437	2.7339	0.3657778
Nicaragua	Gold Cordoba	29.0374	0.03443835	29.5863	0.033799
Nigeria	Nigerian Naira	246.3451	0.0040593	246.7575	0.0040526
Norway	N. Krone	12.347	0.080991	12.1438	0.082347
Oman, Sultanate of	Rial Omani	0.7064	1.4156285	0.7117	1.4050864
Pakistan	Pakistan Rupee	107.2052	0.009327	108.9175	0.0091813
Papua New Guinea	Kina	5.7518	0.17385862	5.7245	0.174688
Paraguay	Guarani	10949.034	0.000953257	11145.829	0.0000897
Peru	New Sol	6.2532	0.1599181	6.2005	0.1612773
Phillipines	Phillipine Peso	102.9065	0.0097176	103.0777	0.0097014
Poland	Zloty	6.6646	0.15004651	6.0596	0.165027

2004–2005 Foreign exchange rates (cont'd)

Country	Unit of currency	Average for the year to 31 December 2004		Average for the year to 31 March 2005	
		Currency units per £1	Sterling value of currency unit £	Currency units per £1	Sterling value of currency unit £
Qatar	Qatar Riyal	6.6804	0.1496916	6.7288	0.1486149
Romania	Leu	59678.391	0.00001675	58049.01	0.000017226
Russia	Rouble (market)	52.6246	0.01900252	52.7342	0.018963
Rwanda	Rwanda Franc	1026.683	0.00097401	1031.425	0.00097
Saudi Arabia	Saudi Riyal	6.8814	0.1453193	6.9322	0.1442543
Seychelles	Rupee	10.1103	0.09890903	10.1938	0.098098
Sierra Leone	Leone	4501.4316	0.0002222	4552.6395	0.0002197
Singapore	Singapore Dollar	3.0974	0.3228514	3.0937	0.3232375
Solomon Islands	S.I. Dollar	13.6055	0.07349969	13.6218	0.073412
Somali Republic	Shilling	5035.7142	0.00019858	5293.099	0.000189
South Africa	Rand	11.81	0.084674	11.5364	0.086682
Sri Lanka	Rupee	185.8561	0.0053805	187.8602	0.0053231
Sudan	Sudanese Dinar	472.2258	0.00211763	471.232	0.002122
Surinam	Surinam Guilder	5.0088	0.19964862	5.0407	0.198385
Swaziland	Lilangeni	11.7582	0.08504703	11.5018	0.086943
Sweden	Swedish Krona	13.4526	0.07433507	13.3494	0.07491
Switzerland	Swiss Franc	2.2757	0.4394252	2.2596	0.4425562
Syria	Syrian Pound	92.1296	0.01085427	94.1199	0.010625
Taiwan	New T. Dollar	61.0875	0.01637	60.6512	0.0164877
Tanzania	Shilling	1995.077	0.0005012	2008.9023	0.0004978
Thailand	Thai Baht	73.7457	0.0135601	73.9875	0.0135158
Tonga Islands	Pa'Anga	3.6061	0.27730789	3.6002	0.277762
Trinidad & Tobago	Trinidad & Tobago Dollar	11.3504	0.0881026	11.488	0.0870474
Tunisia	Dinar	2.2834	0.4379434	2.3029	0.4342351
Turkey	Turkish Lira	2614460.3	0.00000038248	1/4/04-31/12/04 = 2672509.6 1/1/05-31/3/05 = 2.4998	1/4/04-31/12/04 = 0.00000037418 1/1/05-31/3/05 = 0.4000320
Uganda	New Shilling	3314.5158	0.0003017	3248.728	0.0003078
United Arab Emirates	U.A.E Dirham	6.7388	0.1483944	6.7884	0.1473101
Uruguay	Uruguayan Peso	52.5696	0.0190224	50.9267	0.0196361
U.S.A	U.S. Dollar	1.8318	0.5459111	1.8445	0.5421523
Venezuela	V.Bolivar	5128.1466	0.000195	4997.8741	0.0002001
Vietnam	Dong	28839.666	0.000035	29110.77	0.000034
Yemen	Rial	338.4705	0.00295447	342.6463	0.002918
Zambia	Zambian Kwacha	8742.492	0.0001144	8790.4958	0.0001138
Zimbabwe	Z. Dollar	1/1/04-23/1/04 = 1505.5 24/1/04-31/12/04 = 9319.984	1/1/04-23/1/04 = 0.00947867 24/1/04-31/12/04 = 0.00010729	10335.445	0.00009675

Table of spot rates on 31 December 2004 and 31 March 2005

		31 December 2004		31 March 2005	
Country	**Unit of currency**	**Currency units per £1**	**Sterling value of currency unit (£)**	**Currency units per £1**	**Sterling value of currency unit (£)**
Australia	Australian Dollar	2.4491	0.4001441	2.4428	0.409366
Canada	Canadian Dollar	2.3003	0.4347259	2.2861	0.437426
Denmark	Danish Krone	10.5068	0.0951764	10.8316	0.092322
European Union	Euro	1.4125	0.7079646	1.454	0.687757
Hong Kong	H K Dollar	14.9229	0.0670111	14.7377	0.067853
Japan	Japanese Yen	196.732	0.0050831	202.112	0.004947
Norway	N.Krone	11.6281	0.0859986	11.9316	0.083811
South Africa	Rand	10.8163	0.0924531	11.7604	0.085031
Sweden	S.Krone	12.7584	0.0783797	13.3089	0.075137
Switzerland	Swiss Franc	2.1832	0.4580432	2.2523	0.443990
U.S.A	U.S. Dollar	1.9199	0.5208605	1.8896	0.529212

INCOME TAX

1-180 Income tax rates

2010–11

	Taxable income band £	Tax rate %	Tax on band £
Basic rate	1–37,400	20	7,480.00
Higher rate	37,400–150,000	40	45,040
Additional rate	Over 150,000	50	

Rate on non-dividend savings income	10% up to £2,440 20% up to basic rate limit 40% up to higher rate limit 50% thereafter
Dividend ordinary rate	10% up to basic rate limit
Dividend higher rate	32.5% up to higher rate limit
Dividend additional rate	42.5% above higher rate limit
Trust rate	50%
Dividend trust rate	42.5%

2009–10

	Taxable income band £	Tax rate %	Tax on band £
Basic rate	0–37,400	20	7,480.00
Higher rate	Over 37,400	40	

Rate on non-dividend savings income	10% up to £2,440 20% up to basic rate limit 40% thereafter
Rate on dividend income	10% up to basic rate limit 32.5% thereafter
Trust rate	40%
Dividend trust rate	32.5%

2008–09

	Taxable income band £	Tax rate %	Tax on band £
Basic rate	0–34,800	20	6,960.00
Higher rate	Over 34,800	40	

Rate on non-dividend savings income	10% up to £2,320 20% up to basic rate limit 40% thereafter
Rate on dividend income	10% up to basic rate limit 32.5% thereafter
Trust rate	40%
Dividend trust rate	32.5%

2007–08

Taxable income band £	Tax rate[1] %	Tax on band £
0– 2,230	10	223
2,231–34,600	22	7,121.40
Over 34,600	40	

Note

[1] Savings income, other than dividends, is taxed at 10% up to the starting rate limit, at 20% above the starting rate limit and up to the basic rate limit, and at 40% above that. UK Dividend income is taxed at 10% up to the basic rate limit and at 32.5% thereafter.

2006–07

Taxable income band £	Tax rate[1] %	Tax on band £
0– 2,150	10	215
2,151–33,300	22	6,853
Over 33,300	40	

Note

[1] Savings income, other than dividends, is taxed at 10% up to the starting rate limit, at 20% above the starting rate limit and up to the basic rate limit, and at 40% above that. UK Dividend income is taxed at 10% up to the basic rate limit and at 32.5% thereafter.

2005–06

Taxable income band £	Tax rate[1] %	Tax on band £
0– 2,090	10	209
2,091–32,400	22	6,668
Over 32,400	40	

Note

[1] Savings income, other than dividends, is taxed at 10% up to the starting rate limit, at 20% above the starting rate limit and up to the basic rate limit, and at 40% above that. UK Dividend income is taxed at 10% up to the basic rate limit and at 32.5% thereafter.

2004–05

Taxable income band £	Tax rate[1] %	Tax on band £
0– 2,020	10	202
2,021–31,400	22	6,463
Over 31,400	40	

Note

[1] Savings income, other than dividends, is taxed at 10% up to the starting rate limit, at 20% above the starting rate limit and up to the basic rate limit, and at 40% above that. UK Dividend income is taxed at 10% up to the basic rate limit and at 32.5% thereafter.

2003–04

Taxable income band £	Tax rate[1] %	Tax on band £
0– 1,960	10	196
1,961–30,500	22	6,278
Over 30,500	40	

Note

[1] Savings income, other than dividends, is taxed at 10% up to the starting rate limit, at 20% above the starting rate limit and up to the basic rate limit, and at 40% above that. UK Dividend income is taxed at 10% up to the basic rate limit and at 32.5% thereafter.

1-200   Personal reliefs

Note: Individuals earning in excess of £100,000 have a reduced personal allowance from 2010–11 (FA 2009, s. 4)

Type of relief	2010–11 £	2009–10 £	2008–09 £	2007–08 £	2006–07 £	2005–06 £	2004–05 £
Personal allowance							
Age under 65	6,475	6,475	6,035	5,225	5,035	4,895	4,745
Age 65–74	9,490	9,490	9,030	7,550	7,280	7,090	6,830
Age 75 & over	9,640	9,640	9,180	7,690	7,420	7,220	6,950
Married couple's allowance[1]							
Born after 6 April 1935	–	–	–	–	–	–	–
Born before 6 April 1935; Age up to 74	–	6,865	6,535	6,285	6,065	5,905	5,725
Born before 6 April 1935; Age 75 & over	6,965	6,965	6,625	6,365	6,135	5,975	5,795
Minimum amount of allowance	2,670	2,670	2,540	2,440	2,350	2,280	2,210
Maximum income before abatement of reliefs for older taxpayers:	22,900	22,900	21,800	20,900	20,100	19,500	18,900
Abatement income ceiling Personal allowance:							
Age 65–74	28,930	28,930	27,790	25,550	24,590	23,890	23,070
Age 75 & over	29,230	29,230	28,090	25,830	24,870	24,150	23,220
Married couples allowance							
Born before 6 April 1935; Age up to 74	–	37,320	35,780	33,240	32,020	31,140	30,100
Born before 6 April 1935; Age 75 & over	37,820	37,820	36,260	33,680	32,440	31,540	30,390
Blind person's allowance	1,890	1,890	1,800	1,730	1,660	1,610	1,560
Life assurance relief (policies issued before 14 March 1984)	12.5% of premiums	12.5% of premiums	12.5% of premiums	12.5% of premiums	12.5% of premiums	12.5% of premiums	12.5% of premiums
'Rent-a-room' limit	4,250	4,250	4,250	4,250	4,250	4,250	4,250

Notes

[1] Relief is given at a rate of 10%.

Working tax credit – maximum rates 2005–06 to 2010–11

Element	2010–2011 £	2009–10 £	2008–09 £	2007–08 £	2006–07 £	2005–06 £
Basic element	1,920	1,890	1,800	1,730	1,665	1,620
Disability element (see note below)	2,570	2,530	2,405	2,310	2,225	2,165
30-hour element	790	775	735	705	680	660
Second adult element	1,890	1,860	1,770	1,700	1,640	1,595
Lone parent element	1,890	1,860	1,770	1,700	1,640	1,595

Element	2010–2011 £	2009–10 £	2008–09 £	2007–08 £	2006–07 £	2005–06 £
50-plus element;						
(a) working over 16 but less than 30 hours per week	1,320	1,300	1,235	1,185	1,140	1,110
(b) working over 30 hours per week (see note below)	1,965	1,935	1,840	1,770	1,705	1,660
Childcare element: percentage of eligible costs up to weekly maximum of:	80%				70%	70%
• for one child	£175				£175	£135
• for two or more	£300				£300	£200

Child tax credit – maximum rates 2005–06 to 2010–11

Element	Circumstance	2010–11 £	2009–10 £	2008–09 £	2007–08 £	2006–07 £	2005–06 £
Family	Normal case	545	545	545	545	545	545
	Where there is a child under the age of one	1,090	1,090	1,090	1,090	1,090	1,090
Individual	Each child or young person	2,300	2,235	2,085	1,845	1,765	1,690
	Each disabled child or young person	5,015	4,905	4,625	4,285	4,115	3,975
	Each severely disabled child or young person	6,110	5,980	5,645	5,265	5,060	4,895

Income thresholds and withdrawal rates 2005–06 to 2010–11

	2010–11	2009–10	2008–09	2007–08	2006–07	2005–06
First income threshold	£6,420	£6,420	£6,420	£5,220	£5,220	£5,220
First withdrawal rate	39%	39%	39%	37%	37%	37%
Second income threshold	£50,000	£50,000	£50,000	£50,000	£50,000	£50,000
Second withdrawal rate	6.67%	6.67%	6.67%	6.67%	6.67%	6.67%
First threshold for those entitled to Child Tax Credit only	£16,190	£16,040	£15,575	£14,495	£14,155	£13,910
Income disregard	£25,000	£25,000	£25,000	£25,000	£25,000	£2,500

Working Tax Credits – Daily rates 2005–06 to 2010–11

Credit element	2005–06 Daily rate £	2006–07 Daily rate £	2007–08 Daily rate £	2008–09 Daily rate £	2009–10 Daily rate £	2010–11 Daily rate £
Basic element of WTC	4.44	4.57	4.73	4.94	5.18	5.27
30-hour element of WTC	1.81	1.87	1.93	2.02	2.13	2.17
Second adult or lone parent element of WTC	4.37	4.50	4.65	4.85	5.10	5.18

Credit element	2005–06 Daily rate £	2006–07 Daily rate £	2007–08 Daily rate £	2008–09 Daily rate £	2009–10 Daily rate £	2010–11 Daily rate £
Disability element of WTC	5.93	6.10	6.32	6.59	6.94	7.05
Severe disability element of WTC	2.52	2.59	2.68	2.80	2.95	3.00
50-plus element of WTC, (16 hours +)	3.04	3.13	3.24	3.39	3.57	3.62
50-plus element of WTC, (30 hours +)	4.55	4.67	4.84	5.05	5.31	5.39

Working Tax Credits – Maximum daily rates for childcare 2005–06 to 2010–11

	2005–06 Daily rate £	2006–07 Daily rate £	2007–08 Daily rate £	2008–09 Daily rate £	2009–10 Daily rate £	2010–11 Daily rate £
One child	25.00	25.00	25.00	25.00	25.00	25.00
Two or more children	42.86	42.86	42.86	42.86	42.86	42.86

Child Tax Credits – Maximum daily rates 2005–06 to 2010–11

	2005–06 Daily rate £	2006–07 Daily rate £	2007–08 Daily rate £	2008–09 Daily rate £	2009–10 Daily rate £	2010–11 Daily rate £
Credit element						
Family element	1.50	1.50	1.49	1.50	1.50	1.50
– child under one year old (baby rate)	2.99	2.99	2.98	2.99	1.50	1.50
Child element	4.31	4.84	5.05	5.72	6.13	6.31
Disability element	6.27	6.44	6.67	6.96	7.32	7.44
Severe disability element	2.53	2.59	2.68	2.80	2.95	3.00

1-220   Payment dates 2009–10

(TMA 1970, s. 59A, 59B)

Tax is paid on 31 January next following the year of assessment as a single sum covering capital gains tax and income tax on all sources. Interim payments on account may be required. No interim payments are required for a year of assessment if the tax paid by assessment for the preceding year was less than £500 or 20% of the total tax liability for that year. This threshold will rise to £1,000 for payments on account due in January and July 2010. These will normally be half the amount of the net tax payable for the preceding year, but may be reduced to half the current year's liability if less. Net tax is previous year's tax after taking off tax deducted at source and tax on dividends. For 2009–10 the following due dates apply:

First interim payment	31 January 2010
Second interim payment	31 July 2010
Final balancing payment	31 January 2011

57

Note

If a return is not issued until after 31 October 2009 and the taxpayer has notified chargeability by 5 October 2009, the due date for the final payment becomes three months from the issue of the return (TMA 1970, s. 57B).

1-240   Time-limits for elections and claims

In the absence of any provision to the contrary, under self-assessment for the purposes of income tax, the normal rule is that claims are to be made within five years from 31 January next following the tax year to which they relate, previously six years from the end of the relevant chargeable period.

In certain cases the Board *may* permit an extension of the strict time-limit in relation to certain elections and claims.

Provision	Time-limit	Statutory reference
Averaging of profits of farmers or creative artists	12 months from 31 January next following end of the second tax year concerned	ITTOIA 2005, s. 222
Stock transferred to a connected party on cessation of trade to be valued at higher cost or sale price	2 years from end of accounting period in which trade ceased	ICTA 1988, s. 100(1C), ITTOIA 2005, s. 175
Post-cessation expenses relieved against income and chargeable gains	12 months from 31 January next following the tax year	ITA 2007, s. 96, ITTOIA 2005, s. 257(4)
Current and preceding year set-off of trading losses	12 months from 31 January next following the tax year loss arose	ITA 2007, s. 64, 71
Three-year carry-back of trading losses in opening years of trade	12 months from 31 January next following the tax year loss arose	ITA 2007, s. 72
Carry-forward of trading losses	5 years from 31 January next following tax year in which loss arose	ITA 2007, s. 83
Carry-back of terminal losses	5 years from 31 January next following tax year	ITA 2007, s. 89
Certain plant and machinery treated as 'short life' assets (income tax elections)	12 months from 31 January next following the tax year in which ends the chargeable period in which the qualifying expenditure was incurred	CAA 2001, s. 85
Transfer between connected parties of certain assets, eligible for capital allowances, at tax-written down value	2 years from date of sale	CAA 2001, s. 570(5)

1-260   Car, fuel and van benefits

Car benefit charges: normal rules

The benefit is calculated on a percentage of the list price of the car appropriate to the level of the car's CO_2 emissions, as follows:

- 15 per cent of the list price of cars emitting up to the lower threshold of emissions of carbon dioxide in grams per kilometre;
- increased by one per cent per 5g/km over the lower threshold, but

- capped at 35 per cent of the list price.

The lower threshold for each year from 2002–03 is as follows (ITEPA 2003, s. 139):

Tax year	Lower threshold (in g/km)
2010–11	130
2009–10	135
2008–09	135
2007–08	140
2006–07	140
2005–06	140
2004–05	145
2003–04	155
2002–03	165

If the exact CO_2 emissions figure does not end in 0 or 5, it should be rounded *down* to the nearest 5g/km before applying the above figures.

From 6 April 2008, lower rates apply to qualifying low emissions cars.

Discounts are given for cars using alternative fuels and technologies.

Diesel supplement

There is usually a three per cent penalty loading on diesel cars (subject to 35 per cent cap).

For years to 5 April 2006, no loading was applied to diesel cars that met the Euro IV emissions standard.

From 6 April 2006, the diesel loading applies to *all* diesel cars first registered from 1 January 2006 (as well as to older cars not meeting the standard).

Car benefit charges: table of taxable percentages

This table provides the 'appropriate percentage' figures for calculating the taxable benefit of a company car, based on CO_2 emissions figures for petrol cars (based on ITEPA 2003, s. 139, as amended).

CO_2 emissions (See note 1)	2010–11 %	2008–09 to 2009–10 %	2005–06 to 2007–08 %	2004–05 %	2003–04 %	2002–03 %
120	See note 2	See note 2				
130	15	15	15	15	15	15
135	16	15	15	15	15	15
140	17	16	15	15	15	15
145	18	17	16	15	15	15
150	19	18	17	16	15	15

CO_2 emissions (See note 1)	2010–11 %	2008–09 to 2009–10 %	2005–06 to 2007–08 %	2004–05 %	2003–04 %	2002–03 %
155	20	19	18	17	15	15
160	21	20	19	18	16	15
165	22	21	20	19	17	15
170	23	22	21	20	18	16
175	24	23	22	21	19	17
180	25	24	23	22	20	18
185	26	25	24	23	21	19
190	27	26	25	24	22	20
195	28	27	26	25	23	21
200	29	28	27	26	24	22
205	30	29	28	27	25	23
210	31	30	29	28	26	24
215	32	31	30	29	27	25
220	33	32	31	30	28	26
225	34	33	32	31	29	27
230	35	34	33	32	30	28
235	35	35	34	33	31	29
240	35	35	35	34	32	30
245	35	35	35	35	33	31
250	35	35	35	35	34	32
255	35	35	35	35	35	33
260	35	35	35	35	35	34
265	35	35	35	35	35	35

Notes

[1] The actual CO_2 emissions figure, if it is not a multiple of five, should be rounded down to the nearest multiple of five before applying this table.

[2] Since 6 April 2008, a new 10 per cent appropriate percentage has applied to company cars with CO_2 emissions of 120g/km or less (a 'qualifying low emissions car' or 'QUALEC').

Qualifying low emissions cars

From 6 April 2008, a lower tax charge is made if the vehicle is a 'qualifying low emissions car' ('QUALEC') for the tax year in which it is provided as a company car. In such a case, the appropriate percentage will be 10 per cent for petrol cars (but with a three per cent penalty loading, so a figure of 13 per cent, for most diesel cars).

A car is a QUALEC if its CO_2 emissions figure does not exceed the limit for the year, as specified at ITEPA 2003, s. 139(3A). For 2008–09, that limit is 120g/km.

Alternative fuel cars: current rules

Type of car	Discounted charge
Battery electric cars	15% of list price, less 6% discount – ie 9% of list price
Bi-fuel gas and petrol cars manufactured or converted before type approval	Appropriate percentage of list price, less 2% discount
Hybrid electric and petrol cars	Appropriate percentage of list price, less 3% discount
Cars capable of running on E85 fuel	Appropriate percentage of list price, less two per cent discount. (But NB discount applies only from 6 April 2008)
Note: the cost of conversion is ignored for bi-fuel gas and petrol cars converted after type approval, but no additional percentage discount is given.	

Alternative fuel cars: periods to 5 April 2006

Type of car	Discounted charge
Battery electric cars	15% of list price, less 6% discount – ie 9% of list price.
Hybrid electric cars	Appropriate percentage of list price, less 2% discount and a further 1% discount for each full 20 g/km that the CO_2 emissions figure is below the lower threshold.
Cars using liquid petroleum gas (LPG) or compressed natural gas (CNG) Cars running on road fuel gas alone	Appropriate percentage of list price, less 1% discount and a further 1% discount for each full 20 g/km that the CO_2 emissions figure is below the lower threshold.
Bi-fuel cars (both gas and petrol) *Cars first registered on or after 1 January 2000, and approved for running on both petrol and gas*	Appropriate percentage of list price applying to gas CO_2 emissions, less 1% discount and a further 1% discount for each full 20 g/km that the CO_2 emissions figure is below the lower threshold.

Type of car	Discounted charge
Cars first registered before 1 January 2000, and petrol cars that are retro-fitted	Appropriate percentage of list price applying to petrol CO_2 emissions, less 1% discount.

Fuel benefit charges: current rules

Since 6 April 2003, the additional taxable benefit of free fuel provided for a company car has been calculated using the same CO_2 figures as are used for calculating the company car charge.

The CO_2 percentage figure is applied to a fixed amount in accordance with the following table:

	£
2008–09	16,900
2007–08	14,400
2006–07	14,400
2005–06	14,400
2004–05	14,400
2003–04	14,400

The fuel benefit is reduced to nil if the employee is required to make good the full cost of all fuel provided for private use, and does so.

A proportionate reduction is made where the company car is only available for part of the year, where car fuel ceases to be provided part-way through the year, or where the benefit of the company car is shared.

The annual figure is expected to increase in line with RPI each year from April 2009.

Fuel types

Where there is a fuel benefit, employers must notify the Revenue of the type of fuel (or other power) by entering the appropriate 'key letter' on the form P11D. The key letters are as follows:

Key letter	Fuel or power type description
P	Petrol
D	Diesel not meeting Euro IV standard
L	Diesel meeting Euro IV standard
E	Electric only
H	Hybrid electric
B	Gas only, or bi-fuel with approved CO_2 emissions figure for gas when first registered (which must be from 1 January 2000)
G	Car manufactured to be capable of running on E85 fuel
C	Conversion, and all other bi-fuel cars with an approved CO_2 emissions figure for petrol only when first registered

In *Employer's Bulletin* 17, the Revenue wrote that:

'we have been asked to make it clear that the key letter shown in the P11D (Guide) refers to the car, not to the fuel in isolation.'

1-280   HMRC authorised mileage rates

Advisory fuel rates for company cars

HMRC have published rates that can be used for reimbursement of private mileage by company car drivers to their employers.

Rates applying from 1 June 2010

Engine size	Petrol	Diesel	LPG
1400cc or less	12p	11p	8p
1401cc to 2000cc	15p	11p	10p
Over 2000cc	21p	16p	14p

*Rates applying from 1 December 2009**

Engine size	Petrol	Diesel	LPG
1400cc or less	11p	11p	7p
1401cc to 2000cc	14p	11p	8p
Over 2000cc	20p	14p	12p

Petrol hybrid cars are treated as petrol cars for this purpose.

* The rates have effect for all journeys made from 1 December 2009.

Rates applying from 1 July (or 1 June) 2009

Engine size	Petrol	Diesel	LPG
1400cc or less	10p	10p	7p
1401cc to 2000cc	12p	10p	8p
Over 2000cc	18p	13p	12p

Petrol hybrid cars are treated as petrol cars for this purpose.

Rates applying from 1 January 2009 (or 2 December 2008)*

Engine size	Petrol	Diesel	LPG
1400cc or less	10p	11p	7p
1401cc to 2000cc	12p	11p	9p
Over 2000cc	17p	14p	12p

Petrol hybrid cars are treated as petrol cars for this purpose.

* The rates were announced on 2 December 2008, to have effect from 1 January 2009. However, HMRC then added the following comment:

'HMRC is content for the new rates to be implemented immediately where employers are able and wish to do so.'

Rates applying from 1 July 2008

Engine size	Petrol	Diesel	LPG
1400cc or less	12p	13p	7p
1401cc to 2000cc	15p	13p	9p
Over 2000cc	21p	17p	13p

Rates applying from 1 January 2008

Engine size	Petrol	Diesel	LPG
1400cc or less	11p	11p	7p
1401cc to 2000cc	13p	11p	8p
Over 2000cc	19p	14p	11p

Rates applying from 1 August 2007

Engine size	Petrol	Diesel	LPG
1400cc or less	10p	10p	6p
1401cc to 2000cc	13p	10p	8p
Over 2000cc	18p	13p	10p

Rates applying from 1 February 2007

Engine size	Petrol	Diesel	LPG
1400cc or less	9p	9p	6p
1401cc to 2000cc	11p	9p	7p
Over 2000cc	16p	12p	10p

Rates applying from 1 July 2006 to 31 January 2007

Engine size	Petrol	Diesel	LPG
1400cc or less	11p	10p	7p
1401cc to 2000cc	13p	10p	8p
Over 2000cc	18p	14p	11p

Rates applying from 1 July 2005 to 30 June 2006

Engine size	Petrol	Diesel	LPG
1400cc or less	10p	9p	7p
1401cc to 2000cc	12p	9p	8p
Over 2000cc	16p	13p	10p

Rates applying from 6 April 2004 to 30 June 2005

Engine size	Petrol	Diesel	LPG
1400cc or less	10p	9p	7p
1401cc to 2000cc	12p	9p	8p
Over 2000cc	14p	12p	10p

Rates applying to 5 April 2004

Engine size	Petrol	Diesel	LPG
1400cc or less	10p	9p	6p
1401cc to 2000cc	12p	9p	7p
Over 2000cc	14p	12p	9p

Mileage allowance payments

Statutory mileage rates 2002–03 onwards

From April 2002, statutory rates are set for mileage allowance payments (ITEPA 2003, s. 230). An employer may reimburse business mileage at more or less than the statutory rates; any excess is taxable and any shortfall is tax deductible.

Kind of vehicle	Rate per mile
Car or van	40p for the first 10,000 miles 25p after that
Motorcycle	24p
Cycle	20p

1-300   Taxable state benefits

The following benefits are liable to income tax (ITEPA 2003, s. 577, 580, 660).

Rates were most recently updated by the *Social Security Benefits Up-rating Regulations* 2008 (SI 2008/667).

Benefit	Weekly rate from						
	April 2010 £	April 2009 £	April 2008 £	April 2007 £	April 2006 £	April 2005 £	April 2004 £
Bereavement allowance	97.65	95.25	90.70	87.30	84.25	82.05	79.60
Carer's allowance	53.90	53.10	50.55	48.65	46.95	45.70	44.35
Dependent adults with retirement pension[1] with carer's allowance[1] with severe disablement allowance	57.05 31.70 31.90	57.05 31.70 31.90	54.35 30.20 30.40	52.30 29.05 29.25	50.50 28.05 28.05	49.15 27.30 27.50	47.65 26.50 26.65

Industrial death benefit:
Widow's pension
Permanent rate –
    higher
    lower
	
	97.65
	29.30
		
		95.25
		28.58
			
			90.70
			27.21
				
				87.30
				26.19
					
					84.25
					25.28
						
						82.05
						24.62
							
							79.60
							23.88

Key Data

Benefit	Weekly rate from						
	April 2010 £	April 2009 £	April 2008 £	April 2007 £	April 2006 £	April 2005 £	April 2004 £
Incapacity benefit (long term)							
Rate	91.40	89.80	84.50	81.35	78.50	76.45	74.15
Increase for age:							
higher rate	15.00	15.65	17.75	17.10	16.50	16.05	15.55
lower rate	5.80	6.55	8.90	8.55	8.25	8.05	7.80
Incapacity benefit (short term)							
Higher rate:							
under pensionable age[2]	81.60	80.15	75.40	72.55	70.05	68.20	66.15
over pensionable age[2]	91.40	89.80	84.50	81.35	78.50	76.45	74.15
Non-contributory retirement pension							
Standard rate	58.50	57.05	54.35	52.30	50.50	49.15	47.65
Age addition (at age 80)	0.25	0.25	0.25	0.25	0.25	0.25	0.25
Retirement pension							
Standard rate	97.65	95.25	90.70	87.30	84.25	82.05	79.60
Age addition (at age 80)	0.25	0.25	0.25	0.25	0.25	0.25	0.25
Widow's pension[3]							
Pension (standard rate)	97.65	95.25	90.70	87.30	84.25	82.05	79.60
Widowed parent's allowance	97.65	95.25	90.70	87.30	84.25	82.05	79.60

Notes

[1] No new claims for adult dependency increases payable with the state retirement pension or the carer's allowance may be made on or after 6 April 2010. Adult dependency increases already in payment immediately before 6 April 2010 are being phased out between 2010 and 2020.

[2] Pensionable age is 60 for women, 65 for men. From 6 April 2020, the state pension age for women will be 65, the same as for men. From 2010, women's state pension age is being gradually increased to bring it up to age 65 by 2020.

[3] Bereavement allowance replaced widow's pension from 9 April 2001 for all new claims by widows and widowers.

Website: www.dsdni.gov.uk/benefit_rates
www.rightsnet.org.uk/pdfs/Ben_Rates_2007_2008.pdf

1-320 Non-taxable state benefits

The following UK social security benefits are wholly exempt from tax (ITEPA 2003, s. 677(1), except where indicated otherwise. See also EIM 76100):

Benefit rates

Benefit	Weekly rate from						
	April 2010 £	April 2009 £	April 2008 £	April 2007 £	April 2006 £	April 2005 £	April 2004 £
Attendance allowance							
Higher rate (day and night)	71.40	70.35	67.00	64.50	62.25	60.60	58.80
Lower rate (day or night)	47.80	47.10	44.85	43.15	41.65	40.55	39.35
Child benefit[2]							
For the eldest qualifying child	20.30	20.00	18.80	18.10	17.45	17.00	16.55
For each other child	13.40	13.20	12.55	12.10	11.70	11.40	11.05
Constant attendance allowance							
Exceptional rate	116.80	115.00	109.60	105.40	101.80	99.20	96.20
Intermediate rate	87.60	86.25	82.20	79.05	76.35	74.40	72.15
Normal maximum rate	58.40	57.50	54.80	52.70	50.90	49.60	48.10
Part-time rate	29.20	28.75	27.40	26.35	25.45	24.80	24.05
Exceptionally severe disablement allowance	58.40	57.50	54.80	52.70	50.90	49.60	48.10
Disability living allowance (care component)							
Higher rate	71.40	70.35	67.00	64.50	62.25	60.60	58.80
Middle rate	47.80	47.10	44.85	43.15	41.65	40.55	39.35
Lower rate	18.95	18.65	17.75	17.10	16.50	16.05	15.55
Disability living allowance (mobility component)							
Higher rate	49.85	49.10	46.75	45.00	43.45	42.30	41.05
Lower rate	18.95	18.65	17.75	17.10	16.50	16.05	15.55
Incapacity benefit (short term)[3]							
Lower rate:							
under pensionable age[4]	68.95	67.75	63.75	61.35	59.20	57.65	55.90
over pensionable age[4]	87.75	86.20	81.10	78.05	75.35	73.35	71.15

Notes

[1] Child special allowance and child dependency increases with retirement pension, widow's benefit, short-term incapacity benefit at the higher rate and long-term incapacity benefit, invalid care allowance, severe disablement allowance, higher rate individual death benefit, unemployability supplement and short-term incapacity benefit if beneficiary over pension age.

[2] Child benefit increases for 2009 were paid from January rather than April 2009.

[3] Incapacity benefit (and contributory employment & support allowance) are taxable, under the *Income Tax (Earnings and Pensions) Act* 2003, except for short-term benefit payable at the lower rate. There is no tax charge, however, if the recipient started receiving invalidity benefit or sickness benefit before 6 April 1995 and has continued receiving incapacity benefit since then.

[4] Pensionable age is 60 for women, 65 for men. From 6 April 2020, the state pension age for women will be 65, the same as for men. From 2010, women's state pension age is gradually being increased to bring it up to age 65 by 2020.

1-340   Official rate of interest

(ITEPA 2003, s. 181)

The official rate of interest is used to calculate the cash equivalent of the benefit of an employment-related loan which is a taxable cheap loan. HMRC normally set a single rate in advance for the whole tax year and gave a commitment in January 2000, that (following announcement of the rate for any given tax year) the official rate may be reduced but will not be increased in the light of interest rate changes generally.

The official rate of interest was reduced with effect from 6 April 2010 and figures for recent periods have been as follows:

Date	Rate %	SI No.
From 6 April 2010	4.00	SI 2010/415
From 1 March 2009 to 5 April 2010	4.75	SI 2009/199
From 6 April 2007 to 28 February 2009	6.25	SI 2007/684
From 6 January 2002 to 5 April 2007	5.00	SI 2001/3860

The *average* official rates of interest are given below. These should be used if the loan was outstanding throughout the tax year and the normal averaging method of calculation is being used.

Year	Average official rate %
2009–10	4.75
2008–09	6.10
2007–08	6.25
2006–07	5.00
2005–06	5.00
2004–05	5.00
2003–04	5.00

1-360   Official rate of interest – foreign currency loans

The official rate of interest for certain employer-provided loans in Japanese yen or Swiss francs has been set as follows:

Loans in Swiss francs	
	Rate
Date	%
From 6 July 1994	5.5
From 6 June 1994 to 5 July 1994	5.7
Loans in Japanese yen	
	Rate
Date	%
From 6 June 1994	3.9

Note

There is no tax charge if all the employee's cheap or interest-free loans total no more than £5,000. Alternatively, where the employee's cheap or interest-free loans total more than £5,000, there is no tax charge in respect of 'non-qualifying' loans totalling no more than £5,000. A 'non-qualifying' loan is one in respect of which interest paid does not qualify for relief under ITA 2007, s. 24(1) (ignoring the exclusion of MIRAS loans) and is disallowed in computing the charge on trading profits.

The lower 'official rate' of interest for taxing loans in a foreign currency where interest rates in that country are significantly lower than interest rates in the UK only applies to a loan in another country's currency, to a person who normally lives in that country and has actually lived there in the year or previous five years.

Law: ITA 2007, s. 24(1)

1-380   Relocation allowance

Statutory relief

Tax relief for relocation expenses in relation to payments made or expenses provided in connection with an employee's change of residence where the employee's job or place of work is changed is generally subject to a statutory maximum from 6 April 1993. The maximum allowance is:

From	Maximum allowance £
6 April 1993	8,000

Law: ITEPA 2003, s. 288

1-400   Incidental overnight expenses

Benefits, reimbursements and expenses provided by an employer for employees' minor, personal expenditure whilst on business-related activities requiring overnight accommodation away from home are not taxable provided that the total amount reimbursed, etc. does not exceed the relevant maximum amount(s) per night, multiplied by the number of nights' absence. If the limit is exceeded the whole amount provided remains taxable.

From	Authorised maximum per night	
	In UK £	Outside the UK £
6 April 1995	5	10

Law: ITEPA 2003, s. 241

CORPORATION TAX

1-420   Corporation tax rates

Financial year	Full rate %	Small companies' rate %	Profit limit for small companies' rate (lower limit)	Profit limit for small companies' marginal relief (upper limit)	Marginal relief fraction for small companies	Starting rate %	Profit limit for starting rate (lower limit)	Profit limit for starting rate marginal relief (upper limit)	Marginal relief fraction for starting rate
2010	28	21	300,000	1,500,000	7/400	(5)	(5)	(5)	(5)
2009	28	21	300,000	1,500,000	7/400	(5)	(5)	(5)	(5)
2008	28	21	300,000	1,500,000	7/400	(5)	(5)	(5)	(5)
2007	30	20	300,000	1,500,000	1/40	(5)	(5)	(5)	(5)
2006	30	19	300,000	1,500,000	11/400	(5)	(5)	(5)	(5)
2005	30	19	300,000	1,500,000	11/400	0	10,000	50,000	19/400
2004	30	19	300,000	1,500,000	11/400	0	10,000	50,000	19/400

Notes

(1) The lower and upper limits for the small companies' rate and the small companies' marginal relief, as well as the similar lower and upper limits for the starting rate, are reduced proportionally:

- for accounting periods of less than 12 months, and
- in the case of associated companies, by dividing the limits by the total number of non-dormant associated companies.

(2) For companies with ring fence profits, the rates are as above except that:

- for financial years 2007, 2008, and 2009, the small companies' rate of tax is 19 per cent and the marginal relief fraction for small companies is 11/400; and
- for financial years 2008, 2009 and 2010, the main rate is 30 per cent.

For authorised unit trusts and open ended investment companies, the rate of corporation tax for a financial year is the rate at which income tax at the basic rate is charged for the year of assessment which begins on 6 April in that financial year (20 per cent for the financial year 2009). It was announced in the 2009 Pre-Budget Report that the Government is considering applying a reduced rate of corporation tax to income from patents from 2013.

(3) 'Close investment holding companies' do not receive the benefit of the small companies' rate or the starting rate and so are taxable entirely at the full rate regardless of the level of their profits.

(4) From 1 April 2006, the starting and non-corporate distribution rates are replaced with a new single banding for small companies set at the existing small companies' rate. The small companies' rate therefore applies to companies with taxable profits between £0 and £300,000.

(5) From 1 April 2004 to 31 March 2006, the benefit of the start5ng rate and marginal starting rate relief applied only to undistributed profits and profits distributed to other companies. Profits chargeable to corporation tax below the threshold for the small companies' rate that had been distributed to non-company shareholders were subject to a minimum rate (the 'non-corporate distribution rate': NCD rate which, for the financial years

2004 and 2005, was the equivalent to the small companies' rate). Profits distributed to other bodies subject to corporation tax were disregarded for the purpose of establishing whether the NCD rate applied.

Effective marginal rates

For marginal small companies' relief and marginal starting rate relief, there is an effective rate of tax in the margin, i.e. between the lower and upper limits given for each in the preceding table, which exceeds the full rate. These marginal rates are not prescribed by statute, but are derived from theappropriatee corporation tax rates and fractions. The applicable rates are as follows:

Financial year	Marginal small companies' rate %	Marginal starting rate %
2010	29.75	(1)
2009	29.75	(1)
2008	29.75	(1)
2007	32.5	(1)
2006	32.75	(1)
2005	32.75	23.75
2004	32.75	23.75

(1) From 1 April 2006, the starting rate is replaced with a new single banding for small companies set at the existing small companies' rate. The small companies' rate therefore applies to small companies with taxable profits between £0 and £300,000.

Marginal relief

$$\text{Deduction} = (\text{Upper Limit} - \text{Profits}) \times \frac{\text{Basic profits}}{\text{Profits}} \times \text{Marginal Relief Fraction}$$

'Profits' means profits as finally computed for corporation tax purposes *plus* franked investment income *excluding* franked investment income from companies in the same group. Distributions are treated as coming from within the group if they are received from a company which is a 51 per cent subsidiary or a consortium company, the recipient being a member of the consortium. For distributions received on or after 1 July 2009, the reference to franked investment income (and the exclusion for franked investment income received from group companies) includes distributions that are exempt from tax under the new broad exemption for distributions.

'Basic profits' means profits as finally computed for corporation tax purposes (also known as 'profits chargeable to corporation tax').

Similar provisions apply for calculating marginal relief for the starting rate effective from 1 April 2000.

1-440   Due dates

Liability	Due date
Mainstream tax (TMA 1970, s. 59D)	Nine months and one day after end of an accounting period[1]
Mainstream tax in instalments[2]:	The 14th day of the seventh, tenth, 13th and 16th months after start of a 12 month accounting period.
Income tax on interest, annual payments etc.	14 days after end of return period.[3]
Charge on loans to participators (CTA 2010, s. 455)	Nine months and one day after the end of the accounting period in which the loan was advanced.

Key Data

Notes

[1] FA 2009, s. 111 provides for companies to enter into voluntary payment plans with HMRC under which corporation tax liabilities can be paid in instalments spread equally before and after the due date. It should be noted that only corporation tax payable in accordance with TMA 1970, s. 59D (i.e. tax payable nine months and one day after the end of the accounting period) can be the subject of a managed payment plan. This excludes corporation tax payable by large companies in accordance with the quarterly instalment payment scheme. In addition, companies which have entered into a group payment arrangement can not enter into a managed payment plan. The payment plans will be launched in April 2011.

[2] TMA 1970, s. 59E and SI 1998/3175 provide for the payment of corporation tax by 'large' companies (defined in accordance with the small profits marginal relief upper limit) in instalments.

Companies which are 'large' because of the number of associated companies or because of substantial dividend income will not have to pay by instalments if their corporation tax liabilities are less than £10,000. Companies which become 'large' in an accounting period, having previously had profits below the upper limit, may be exempt from instalment arrangements in certain circumstances. Groups containing 'large' companies are able to pay corporation tax on a group-wide basis.

For accounting periods ending after 30 June 2005, corporation tax and the supplementary charge payable by oil companies on ring fence profits are payable in three equal instalments. Corporation tax due on other profits (i.e. non-ring fence) continues to be payable in quarterly instalments as above.

The payment dates for the three instalments once the transitional period (see below) has passed are as follows:

(1)   one-third payable six months and 13 days from the start of the accounting period (unless the date for instalment (3) is earlier);

(2)   one-third payable three months from the first instalment due date (unless (3) is earlier); and

(3)   the balance payable 14 days from the end of the accounting period (regardless of the length of the period).

Transitional arrangements apply for the first accounting period affected. These arrangements leave the first two quarterly instalments unchanged (at one-quarter each of the estimated liability for the period) but then require payment of the remainder of the estimated liability on ring fence profits for that accounting period to be paid on the new third instalment date.

(3) Return periods end on 31 March, 30 June, 30 September, 31 December and at the end of an accounting period.

The requirement for companies to deduct and account for income tax on certain payments is removed with effect for payments after 31 March 2001 of:

- interest, royalties, annuities and other annual payments made to companies within the charge to UK corporation tax on that income; and
- interest on quoted Eurobonds paid to non-residents.

1-460   Time-limits for elections and claims

In the absence of any provision to the contrary, the normal rule is that claims are to be made within six years from the end of the relevant chargeable period (FA 1998, Sch. 18, para. 46(1)) for accounting periods within self-assessment.

In certain cases the Board *may* permit an extension of the strict time-limit in relation to certain elections and claims.

Provision	Time limit	References
Stock transferred to a connected party on cessation of trade to be valued at higher cost or sale price	2 years from end of accounting period in which trade ceased	CTA 2009, s. 167(1)–(4)
Carry-forward of trading losses	Relief is given automatically	CTA 2010, s. 45
Set-off of trading losses against profits of the same, or an earlier, accounting period[1]	2 years from end of accounting period in which loss incurred	CTA 2010, s. 37(7)
Group relief	Claims to group relief must be made (or withdrawn) by the later of: (1) 12 months after the claimant company's filing date for the return for the accounting period covered by the claim; (2) 30 days after a closure notice is issued on the completion of an enquiry[2]; (3) 30 days after HMRC issue a notice of amendment to a return following the completion of an enquiry (issued where the company fails to amend the return itself); or (4) 30 days after the determination of any appeal against an HMRC amendment (as in (3) above).	FA 1998, Sch. 18, para. 74
Set-off of loss on disposal of shares in unquoted trading company against income of investment company	2 years from end of accounting period	CTA 2010, s. 70(4)
Surrender of company tax refund within group	Before refund made to surrendering company	CTA 2010, s. 963(3)

Provision	Time limit	References
Election to reallocate a chargeable gain or an allowable loss within a group [3]	2 years from end of accounting period during which the gain or loss accrues	TCGA 1992, s. 171A
Relief for a non-trading deficit on loan relationships (including any non-trading exchange losses)	2 years from end of period in which deficit arises, or, in the case of a claim to carry forward the deficit, 2 years from end of the accounting period following the deficit period, or within such further period as the Board may allow	CTA 2009, s. 460(1)

[1] The carry-back period is extended to three years for accounting periods ending in the period 23/11/08 to 24/11/2010 (FA 2009, s. 23, Sch. 6).

[2] 'Enquiry' in the above does not include a restricted enquiry into an amendment to a return (restricted because the time limit for making an enquiry into the return itself has expired), where the amendment consists of a group relief claim or withdrawal of claim. These time limits have priority over any other general time limits for amending returns and are subject to HMRC permitting an extension to the time limits.

[3] Following the enactment of the *Finance Act* 2009, it is now possible for chargeable gains and allowable losses to be transferred within a group. For gains and losses made before 21 July 2009, this result could only be achieved by electing for the notional transfer of an asset before its disposal to a third party (TCGA 1992, s. 171A prior to the changes made by FA 2009, s. 31, Sch. 12). The election had to be made jointly on or before the second anniversary of the end of the actual vendor group company's accounting period in which it made the disposal.

CAPITAL GAINS TAX

1-480 Rates, annual exemption, retirement relief, chattel exemption

Tax year	Annual exempt amount		Chattel exemption (max sale proceeds)[1]	Rate	
	Individuals, PRs[2], trusts for mentally disabled[3] £	Other trusts[3] £	£	Individuals %	Trustees and PRs %
2010–11	10,100	5,050	6,000	18[4]	18
2009–10	10,100	5,050	6,000	18[4]	18
2008–09	9,600	4,800	6,000	18[4]	18
2007–08	9,200	4,600	6,000	10/20/40[4]	40
2006–07	8,800	4,400	6,000	10/20/40[4]	40
2005–06	8,500	4,250	6,000	10/20/40[4]	40
2004–05	8,200	4,100	6,000	10/20/40[4]	40
2003–04	7,900	3,950	6,000	10/20/40[4]	34
2002–03	7,700	3,850	6,000	10/20/40[4]	34
2001–02	7,500	3,750	6,000	10/20/40[4]	34
2000–01	7,200	3,600	6,000	10/20/40[4]	34

Notes

[1] Where disposal proceeds exceed the exemption limit, marginal relief restricts any chargeable gain to $5/3$ of the excess. Where there is a loss and the proceeds are less than £6,000 the proceeds are deemed to be £6,000.

[2] For year of death and next two years in the case of personal representatives (PRs) of deceased persons.

[3] Multiple trusts created by the same settlor; each attracts relief equal to the annual amount divided by the number of such trusts (subject to a minimum of 10% of the full amount).

[4] For 2000–01 to 2007–08, capital gains are taxed as top slice of income at:

- starting rate to the extent to the starting rate limit;
- lower rate to the extent above the starting rate limit but to the basic rate limit; and
- higher rate to the extent above the basic rate limit.

1-500 Due dates

1996–97 and subsequent years

(1) Where a tax return for the tax year was issued to the taxpayer before 1 November of the following tax year, the due date of payment of capital gains tax for the tax year is 31 January following the end of the tax year in which the gain arises; and

(2) where a tax return for the tax year was issued to the taxpayer after 31 October of the following tax year, the due date of payment of capital gains tax for the tax year is three months after the date that the tax return was issued to the taxpayer.

1-520 Time-limits for elections and claims

In the absence of any provision to the contrary, under self-assessment the normal rule is that claims are to be made within five years from 31 January next following the tax year to which they relate, otherwise the limit is six years from the end of the relevant chargeable period (TMA 1970, s. 43(1)).

For details of time-limits relating to payment of tax, see 74.

In certain cases the Board *may* permit an extension of the strict time-limit in relation to certain elections and claims.

Provision	Time-limit	References
Post-cessation expenses relieved against gains	12 months from 31 January next following the tax year in which expenses paid	ITA 2007, s. 96
Trading losses relieved against gains	12 months from 31 January next following the tax year loss arose	ITA 2007, s. 64 and 71
Value of asset negligible	2 years from end of tax year (or accounting period if a company) in which deemed disposal/reacquisition takes place	TCGA 1992, s. 24(2)
Re-basing of all assets to 31 March 1982 values	Within 12 months from 31 January next following the tax year of disposal (or 2 years from end of accounting period of disposal if a company)	TCGA 1992, s. 35(6)
50% relief if deferred charge on gains before 31 March 1982	Within 12 months from 31 January next following the tax year of disposal (or 2 years from end of accounting period of disposal if a company)	TCGA 1992, s. 36 and Sch. 4, para. 9(1)
Variation within 2 years of death not to have CGT effect	6 months from date of variation (election not necessary for variations on or after 1 August 2002)	TCGA 1992, s. 62(7)
Specifying which "same day" share acquisitions (through employee share schemes) should be treated as disposed of first	Date of earliest disposal	TCGA 1992, s. 105A
Replacement of business assets (roll-over relief)	5 years from 31 January next following the tax year (or 6 years from the end of the accounting period if a company) Replacement asset to be purchased between 12 months before and 3 years after disposal of old asset	TCGA 1992, s. 152(1)
Disapplication of incorporation relief under TCGA 1992, s. 162	2 years from 31 January following the end of the year of assessment in which the business is transferred	TCGA 1992, s. 162A

Provision	Time-limit	References
Disposal of asset and re-investment in qualifying company (prior to 30 November 1993, applied only to disposal of qualifying shares or securities) (re-investment relief) (repealed for 1998–99 onwards)	5 years from 31 January next following the tax year	Former TCGA 1992, s. 164A(2)
Hold-over of gain on gift of business asset	5 years from 31 January next following the tax year	TCGA 1992, s. 165(1)
Determination of main residence	2 years from acquisition of second property (see ESC D21)	TCGA 1992, s. 222(5)
Irrecoverable loan to a trader	2 years from end of tax year (or accounting period if a company) otherwise effective from date claimed (see SP 8/90)	TCGA 1992, s. 253(3)
Retirement relief: ill-health grounds (pre 2003–04)	12 months from 31 January next following the year of assessment in which the disposal occurred	Former TCGA 1992, Sch. 6, para. 5(2)

1-540   Entrepreneurs' relief (from 6 April 2008 onwards)

Chargeable gains arising on disposals of qualifying business assets on or after 6 April 2008 are to be reduced by ⁴/₉ths before being charged to tax at the flat rate of 18%.

The qualifying gains eligible for this reduction are limited to a cap of £1m during the lifetime of the individual, or, in the case of a trustees' disposal, the lifetime of the qualifying beneficiary. That limit is increased to £2m in respect of disposals on or after 6 April 2010.

Transitional provisions allow relief to be claimed in certain circumstances where gains deferred from disposals made on or before 5 April 2008 subsequently become chargeable.

1-560   Exemptions and reliefs

Taper relief

(applies to individuals, trustees and personal representatives, NOT companies)

Introduced for gains realised on or after 6 April 1998 and before 6 April 2008. Indexation allowance to 5 April 1998 (see below) may also be available.

The chargeable gain is reduced according to how long the asset has been held or treated as held after 5 April 1998. Non-business assets acquired prior to 17 March 1998 qualify for an addition of one year to the period for which they are treated as held after 5 April 1998.

The taper is generally applied to the net chargeable gain for the year after deduction of any losses of the same tax year and of any losses carried forward from earlier years.

The amount of taper relief depends on:

(a)   the number of whole years in the qualifying holding period; and

(b)   the amounts of the chargeable gain treated as:

(i)   a gain on the disposal of a business asset; and

(ii) a gain on the disposal of a non-business asset.

The rules for determining the amounts of the chargeable gain that are treated as (i) a gain on the disposal of a business asset and (ii) a gain on the disposal of a non-business asset are set out in former TCGA 1992, Sch. A1, para. 3.

With respect to defining a business asset, the conditions for shares to qualify as business assets are set out in former TCGA 1992, Sch. A1, para. 4 and the conditions for other assets to qualify as business assets are set out in former para. 5.

The tables below show the percentage of chargeable gain that is subject to capital gains tax; i.e., after taper relief. Hence, if the percentage of gain chargeable is 100 per cent, then taper relief is 0 per cent; if the percentage of gain chargeable is 95 per cent, then taper relief is 5 per cent, and so on.

Business assets

Number of complete years after 5.4.98 for which asset held	Percentage of gains chargeable	
	All years from 2002–03 to 2007–08	2001–02
0	100	100
1	50	87.5
2	25	75
3	25	50
4 or more	25	25

Non-business assets

Number of complete years after 5.4.98 for which asset held	Percentage of gains chargeable (all years from 2001–02 to 2007–08)
0	100
1	100
2	100
3	95
4	90
5	85
6	80
7	75
8	70
9	65
10 or more	60

1-580 Treatment of shares and other securities (after 5 April 1998)

Pooling for capital gains tax (but not corporation tax) ceased for acquisitions on or after 6 April 1998.

Disposals after 5 April 1998 are identified with acquisitions in the following order:

(1) same day acquisitions (under existing rule);

(2) acquisitions within the following 30 days;

(3) previous acquisitions after 5 April 1998 on last-in first out (LIFO) basis;

(4) any shares in 'pool' as at 5 April 1998;

(5) any shares held at 5 April 1982; and

(6) any shares aquired before 6 April 1965.

If the above identification rules fail to exhaust the shares disposed of, they are identified with subsequent acquisitions.

Law: TCGA 1992, s. 106A

1-600 Enterprise Investment Scheme

(TCGA 1992, s. 150A and Sch. 5B)

Under the Enterprise Investment Scheme (EIS), income tax relief, CGT deferral relief and CGT disposal relief may be available and claimed. The income tax relief is based on the amount subscribed by a qualifying individual for eligible shares in a qualifying company. Income tax relief may be withdrawn under certain circumstances. With regards to the CGT reliefs:

(1) CGT Deferral Relief – Gains arising on the disposal of any asset can be deferred against subscriptions made by a qualifying individual for eligible shares in a qualifying company. For shares issued on or after 6 April 1998, shares no longer have to have EIS Income Tax Relief attributable to them in order to qualify for CGT Deferral Relief. The defered gains may crystallise on the disposal of the shares.

(2) CGT Disposal Relief – Gains arising on the disposal by a qualifying individual of eligible shares in a qualifying company are exempt from CGT provided the shares have been held for a minimum period or the EIS Income Tax Relief has not been withdrawn.

'Qualifying individual' is basically someone who is not connected with the qualifying company.

'Eligible shares' are basically ordinary unquoted shares in a company.

'Qualifying company' is basically an unquoted company existing wholly for the purposes of carrying on a 'qualifying trade', or whose business consists entirely in the holding of shares in, or the making of loans to, one or more 'qualifying subsidiaries'.

'Qualifying trade' is basically one that is conducted on a commercial basis with a view to realising profits other than specifically excluded activities.

'Qualifying subsidiary' is basically one carrying on a qualifying trade.

1-620   Roll-over relief

To qualify for roll-over or hold-over relief on the replacement of business assets, the items must be appropriate business assets and the reinvestment must take place within 12 months before, or three years after, the disposal of the old asset. For hold-over relief, the replacement asset is a depreciating asset (an asset with a predictable useful life of no more than 60 years).

Classes of assets qualifying for relief:

- land and buildings occupied and used exclusively for the purposes of a trade;
- fixed plant or machinery;
- ships, aircraft, hovercraft;
- satellites, space stations and spacecraft (including launch vehicles);
- goodwill;
- milk quotas, potato quotas and (from 29 March 1999) fish quotas;
- ewe and suckler cow premium quotas; and
- payment entitlements under the single payment scheme.

Law: TCGA 1992, s. 155

STAMP DUTIES

1-640   Rates, penalties and interest

Conveyance or transfer on sale of shares and securities (FA 1999, Sch. 13, para. 3)

Instrument	Rate of tax after 26 October 1986 %
Stock transfer	$1/_2$ [1][2]
Conversion of shares into depositary receipts	$1 1/_2$ [3]
Take overs and mergers	$1/_2$ [1][2]
Purchase by company of own shares	[1][2]
Letters of allotment	$1/_2$

Notes

[1] Because duty at $1/_2$% is equivalent to £5 per £1,000 of consideration and duty is rounded up to the next multiple of £5 (FA 1999, s. 112(1)(b)), duty is effectively £5 per £1,000 (or part of £1,000) of consideration.

[2] Loan capital is generally exempt from transfer on sale duty subject to specific exclusions (designed to prevent exemption applying to quasi-equity securities) (FA 1986, s. 79).

[3] FA 1986, s. 67(3).

Transfers of property (consideration paid)

Rates from 23 March 2006

Rate (%)	All land in the UK	
	Residential	Non-residential
Zero	£125,000	£150,000
1	Over £125,000–£250,000	Over £150,000–£250,000
3	Over £250,000–£500,000	Over £250,000–£500,000
4	Over £500,000	Over £500,000

Rates from 17 March 2005

Rate (%)	All land in the UK	
	Residential	Non-residential
Zero	£120,000	£150,000
1	Over £120,000–£250,000	Over £150,000–£250,000
3	Over £250,000–£500,000	Over £250,000–£500,000
4	Over £500,000	Over £500,000

Rate (%)	Land in disadvantaged areas	
	Residential	Non-residential
Zero	£150,000	All
1	Over £150,000–£250,000	
3	Over £250,000–£500,000	
4	Over £500,000	

Note:

Disadvantaged area relief for non-residential land transactions is not available for non-residential land transactions with an effective date on or after 17 March 2005.

However, the relief is preserved for:

- the completion of contracts entered into and substantially performed on or before 16 March 2005;
- the completion or substantial performance of other contracts entered into on or before 16 March 2005, provided that there is no variation or assignment of the contract or sub-sale of the property after 16 March 2005 and that the transaction is not in consequence of the exercise after 16 March 2005 of an option or right of pre-emption.

New leases (lease duty)

Duty on rent

Rate (%)	Net present value of rent	
	Residential	Non-residential
Zero	£0–£125,000	£0–£150,000
1	Over £125,000	Over £150,000

Note:

When calculating duty payable on the 'NPV' (net present value) of leases, reduce the 'NPV' calculation by the following before applying the 1% rate:

- Residential – £125,000 (£120,000 prior to 23 March 2006);
- Non-residential – £150,000.

Duty on premium is the same as for transfers of land (except special rules apply for premium where rent exceeds £600 annually).

The rate of stamp duty/stamp duty reserve tax on the transfer of shares and the securities is unchanged at 0.5% for 2006–07.

Rates from 1 December 2003 (implementation of stamp duty land tax)

Transfers of property (consideration paid)

Rate (%)	All land in the UK	
	Residential	Non-residential
Zero	£60,000	£150,000
1	Over £60,000–£250,000	Over £150,000–£250,000
3	Over £250,000–£500,000	Over £250,000–£500,000
4	Over £500,000	Over £500,000

Rate (%)	Land in disadvantaged areas	
	Residential	Non-residential
Zero	£150,000	All
1	Over £150,000–£250,000	
3	Over £250,000–£500,000	
4	Over £500,000	

Note

FA 2003, s. 125 confirms that property that is not land, shares or interests in partnerships is no longer subject to stamp duty from 1 December 2003.

Conveyance or transfer on sale of other property (e.g. freehold property)

Rates from 9 April 2003 to 30 November 2003

Rate (%)	All property	Disadvantaged areas	
		Residential	Non-residential
Zero	£0–£60,000	£0–£150,000	All
1	Over £60,000–£250,000	Over £150,000–£250,000	
3	Over £250,000–£500,000	Over £250,000–£500,000	
4	Over £500,000	Over £500,000	

Rates prior to 9 April 2003 (FA 1999, Sch. 13, para. 4)

	Thresholds			
Instruments executed	**Up to £60,000**	**Over £60,000 up to £250,000**	**Over £250,000 up to £500,000**	**Over £500,000**
On or after 28 March 2000[1]	Nil	1%	3%	4%
On or after 16 March 1999[2]	Nil	1%	2.5%	3.5%

Key Data

Notes

[1] Transfers executed on or after 28 March 2000 unless in pursuance of a contract made on or before 21 March 2000.

[2] Transfers executed on or after 16 March 1999 unless in pursuance of a contract made on or before 9 March 1999.

Stamp duty at the appropriate rate is charged on the *full* amount of the certified value, not just on any excess over a threshold.

Fixed duties (FA 1999, s. 112(2))

In relation to instruments executed on or after 1 October 1999, the amount of fixed stamp duty is £5.

Duty (pre-1/10/99)	**Amount**
Conveyance or transfer – miscellaneous	50p
Declaration of trust	50p
Duplicate or counterpart	50p
Exchange or partition	50p
Leases – small furnished letting	£1
miscellaneous	£2
Release or renunciation	50p
Surrender	50p

Note

FA 2003, s. 125 confirmed that property that is not land, shares or interests in partnerships is no longer subject to stamp duty from 1 December 2003.

Leases (and agreements for leases) (FA 1999, Sch. 13, para. 11–13)

Rates for instruments executed after 27 March 2000

Term (FA 1999, Sch. 13, para. 12(3))	**Rate %**
Under 7 years or indefinite:	
• rent £5,000 or less	Nil
• over £5,000	1

Term (FA 1999, Sch. 13, para. 12(3))	Rate %
Over 7 but not over 35 years	2
Over 35 but not over 100 years	12
Over 100 years	24

Notes

Leases for a definite term of less than one year: fixed duty of £5 (FA 1999, Sch. 13, para. 11 with effect from 1 October 1999).

Where a furnished property lease is granted for a premium, this will be subject to stamp duty with the nil rate only applying if the annual rent does not exceed £600 per annum.

An agreement for lease is liable to stamp duty as if it were an actual lease, but if a lease is subsequently granted which is in conformity with the agreement, or which relates to substantially the same property and term of years as the agreement, the duty on the lease is reduced by the duty already paid on the agreement.

Duty on new leases from 1 December 2003

Duty on rent

Rate (%)	Net present value of rent	
	Residential	Non-residential
Zero	£0–£60,000	£0–£150,000
1	Over £60,000	Over £150,000

Notes

These rates were introduced by FA 2003, s. 56 and Sch. 5.

Duty on *premium* is the same as for transfers of land (except special rules apply for premium where rent exceeds £600 annually).

Penalty for late presentation of documents for stamping

Documents executed after 30 September 1999 (SA 1891, s. 15B)

Type of document	Penalties applicable if document presented for stamping more than
Document executed in UK	30 days after execution
Document executed abroad relating to UK land and buildings	30 days after execution (wef Royal assent to FA 2002)
Other document executed abroad	30 days after document first received in UK[1]

Note

[1] Free standing penalty (see table further below) may apply if written information confirming date of receipt in UK is incorrect.

The maximum penalties are:

- £300 or the amount of duty, whichever is less; on documents submitted up to one year late; and
- £300 or the amount of duty, whichever is greater; on documents submitted more than one year late.

Mitigated penalties due on late stamping

The Stamp Office publishes tables (booklet SO10) of mitigated penalty levels that will be applied in straightforward cases.

Cases involving ad valorem duties

Months late	Up to £300	£300–£700	£705–£1,350	£1,355–£2,500	£2,505–£5,000	Over £5,000
Under 3	Nil	£20	£40	£60	£80	£100
Under 6	£20*	£40	£60	£80	£100	£150
Under 9	£40*	£60	£80	£100	£150	£200
Under 12	£60*	£80	£100	£150	£200	£300
Under 15	15% of the duty or £100 if greater					
Under 18	25% of the duty or £150 if greater					See
Under 21	35% of the duty or £200 if greater					below
Under 24	45% of the duty or £250 if greater					

Note

* Or the amount of the duty if that is less.

Cases over one year late involving duty over £5,000 and any case over two years late are considered individually.

Cases involving fixed duties

	Maximum penalty per document	Penalty after mitigation
Up to 12 months late	£5	Nil (100% mitigation)
Over 12 months late	£300	According to circumstances

In all cases above the penalties will not apply if the person responsible for stamping can show a 'reasonable excuse' for the failure to submit the document(s) within the time-limit. Interest is due on any unpaid penalty.

Free standing penalties (maximum amount)

- fraud in relation to stamp duty; (£3,000)
- failure to set out true facts, relating to stamp duty liability, in a document; (£3,000)
- failure to stamp document within 30 days of issue of a Notice of Decision on Adjudication; (£300)
- failure to allow inspection of documents; (£300)

- registering or enrolling a chargeable document that is not duly stamped; (£300)
- circulating a blank transfer; (£300)
- issuing an unstamped foreign security. (£300)

Duties abolished since March 1985

Duty	Effective date of abolition
Ad valorem	
• Capital duty	Transactions after 15 March 1988 – documents stamped after 21 March 1988
• Gifts inter vivos	Instruments executed after 18 March 1985, stamped after 25 March 1985
• Life assurance policy duty	Instruments executed after 31 December 1989
• Transfers on divorce etc.	Instruments executed after 25 March 1985
• Unit trust instrument duty	Instruments executed after 15 March 1988, stamped after 21 March 1988
• Variations and appropriations on death	Instruments executed after 25 March 1985
• Transfers of loan capital (subject to specific exclusions) generally (replaced previous provisions excepting certain categories of loan capital)	Instruments executed after 31 July 1986
• Duty on Northern Ireland bank notes etc.	1 January 1992
• Transfers of intellectual property	Instruments executed after 27 March 2000
• Transfers to Registered Social Landlords	Instruments executed after 28 July 2000
• Stamp duty reserve tax on transfers of units or shares in collective investment schemes held in individual pension accounts (IPAs)	Transactions from 1 April 2001
• Transfers of land and leases in designated disadvantaged areas (for consideration/ premium up to £150,000)	Instruments executed after 29 November 2001
• Transfers of goodwill	Instruments executed after 22 April 2002
• Transfers of debts	tba (late 2003)
Fixed duties	
• Agreement or contract made or entered into pursuant to the Highways Act. Appointment of a new trustee, and appointment in execution of a power of any property. Covenant. Deed of any kind whatsoever, not liable to other duties. Letter of power of attorney. Procuration. Revocation of any use or trust of any property by any writing, not being a will. Warrant of attorney. Letter of allotment and letter of renunciation. Scrip certificate, scrip.	Instruments executed after 25 March 1985
• Categories within the *Stamp Duty (Exempt Instruments) Regulations* 1987 (SI 1987/516):	Instruments executed after 30 April 1987

Duty	Effective date of abolition
A. Trust vesting instrument	
B. Transfer of bequeathed property to legatee	
C. Transfer of intestate property to person entitled	
D. Certain appropriations on death	
E. Transfer to beneficiary of entitlement to residue	
F. Certain transfers to beneficiaries entitled under settlements	
G. Certain transfers in consideration of marriage	
H. Transfers in connection with divorce	
I. Transfers by liquidator to shareholder	
J. Grant of easement for no consideration	
K. Grant of servitude for no consideration	
L. Conveyance as voluntary disposition for no consideration	
M. Variations on death	
N. Declaration of trust of life policy	Instruments executed after 30 September 1999

Note

FA 2003, s. 125 confirmed that property that is not land, shares or interests in partnerships is not subject to stamp duty from 1 December 2003.

Stamp duty reserve tax

Principal charge (FA 1986, s. 87)

Subject matter of charge	Rate of tax %
Agreements to transfer chargeable securities[1] for money or money's worth	0.5
Renounceable letters of allotment	0.5
Shares converted into depositary receipts	1.5
but transfer of shares or securities on which stamp duty payable	1
Shares put into clearance system	1.5
but transfer of shares or securities on which stamp duty payable	1

Note

[1] Chargeable securities = stocks, shares, loan capital, units under unit trust scheme (FA 1986, s. 99(3)).

Interest on stamp duty and stamp duty reserve tax (SDRT)

In respect of instruments executed on or after 1 October 1999, interest is chargeable on stamp duty that is not paid within 30 days of execution of a stampable document, wherever execution takes place (*Stamp Act* 1891, s. 15A). Interest is payable on repayments of overpaid duty, calculated from the later of 30 days from the date of execution of the instrument, or lodgement with the Stamp Office of the duty repayable (FA 1999, s. 110).

Interest is rounded down (if necessary) to the nearest multiple of £5. No interest is payable if that amount is under £25. The applicable interest rate is as prescribed under FA 1989, s. 178.

SDRT carries interest as follows:

- interest is charged on SDRT paid late (TMA 1970, s. 86 via SI 1986/1711, reg. 13);
- repayments of SDRT carry interest from the date that SDRT was paid (FA 1989, s. 178 via SI 1986/1711, reg. 11); and
- similarly, SDRT is repaid with interest if an instrument is duly stamped within six years of the date of the agreement (FA 1986, s. 92).

For interest periods from 1 October 1999 onwards, the rate of interest charged on underpaid or late paid stamp duty and SDRT exceeds that on repayments:

	Rate %	
Period of application	**Underpayments**	**Repayments**
From 6 September 2006	7.50	3.00
6 September 2005 to 5 September 2006	6.50	2.25
6 September 2004 to 5 September 2005	7.50	3.00
6 December 2003 to 5 September 2004	6.50	2.25
6 August 2003 to 5 December 2003	5.50	1.50
6 November 2001 to 5 August 2003	6.50	2.25
6 May 2001 to 5 November 2001	7.50	3.50
5 February 2000 to 5 May 2001	8.50	4.00
1 October 1999 to 5 February 2000	7.50	3.00

INHERITANCE TAX

1-660   Inheritance tax rates: general

There is a tapered reduction in the tax payable on transfers between seven and three years before death where the death occurs on or after 18 March 1986 (see below).

The following tables may be used for the purposes of 'grossing up' calculations (see 6620). The lower and upper limit of each rate-band may be ascertained by reference to the first column in each table and the rate of tax by reference to the second column.

1-680   Lifetime transfers: 2002 onwards

Lifetime transfers on or after 6 April 2010

Portion of value		Rate of tax %
Lower limit £	Upper limit £	
0	325,000	Nil
325,000	–	20

Grossing up table

Gross cumulative total £	Gross rate of tax %	Inheritance tax on band £	Cumulative inheritance tax payable £	Net cumulative total £	Tax on each £ over net cumulative total for grossing up
325,000	Nil	Nil	Nil	325,000	$^1/_4$
Over 325,000	20	–	–	–	–

Lifetime transfers on or after 6 April 2009

Portion of value		Rate of tax %
Lower limit £	Upper limit £	
0	325,000	Nil
325,000	–	20

Grossing up table

Gross cumulative total £	Gross rate of tax %	Inheritance tax on band £	Cumulative inheritance tax payable £	Net cumulative total £	Tax on each £ over net cumulative total for grossing up
325,000	Nil	Nil	Nil	325,000	$^1/_4$
Over 325,000	20	–	–	–	–

Lifetime transfers on or after 6 April 2008

Portion of value		Rate of tax %
Lower limit £	Upper limit £	
0	312,000	Nil
312,000	–	20

Grossing up table

Gross cumulative total £	Gross rate of tax %	Inheritance tax on band £	Cumulative inheritance tax payable £	Net cumulative total £	Tax on each £ over net cumulative total for grossing up
312,000	Nil	Nil	Nil	312,000	$^1/_4$
Over 312,000	20	–	–	–	–

Lifetime transfers on or after 6 April 2007

Portion of value		Rate of tax %
Lower limit £	Upper limit £	
0	300,000	Nil
300,000	–	20

Grossing up table

Gross cumulative total £	Gross rate of tax %	Inheritance tax on band £	Cumulative inheritance tax payable £	Net cumulative total £	Tax on each £ over net cumulative total for grossing up
300,000	Nil	Nil	Nil	300,000	$^1/_4$
Over 300,000	20	–	–	–	–

Lifetime transfers on or after 6 April 2006

Portion of value		Rate of tax
Lower limit £	Upper limit £	%
0	285,000	Nil
285,000	–	20

Grossing up table

Gross cumulative total £	Gross rate of tax %	Inheritance tax on band £	Cumulative inheritance tax payable £	Net cumulative total £	Tax on each £ over net cumulative total for grossing up
285,000	Nil	Nil	Nil	285,000	$^1/_4$
Over 285,000	20	–	–	–	–

Lifetime transfers on or after 6 April 2005

Portion of value		Rate of tax
Lower limit £	Upper limit £	%
0	275,000	Nil
275,000	–	20

Grossing up table

Gross cumulative total £	Gross rate of tax %	Inheritance tax on band £	Cumulative inheritance tax payable £	Net cumulative total £	Tax on each £ over net cumulative total for grossing up
275,000	Nil	Nil	Nil	275,000	$^1/_4$
Over 275,000	20	–	–	–	–

Lifetime transfers on or after 6 April 2004

Portion of value		Rate of tax
Lower limit £	Upper limit £	%
0	263,000	Nil
263,000	–	20

Grossing up table

Gross cumulative total £	Gross rate of tax %	Inheritance tax on band £	Cumulative inheritance tax payable £	Net cumulative total £	Tax on each £ over net cumulative total for grossing up
263,000	Nil	Nil	Nil	263,000	$^1/_4$
Over 263,000	20	–	–	–	–

Lifetime transfers on or after 6 April 2003

Portion of value		Rate of tax %
Lower limit £	Upper limit £	
0	255,000	Nil
255,000	–	20

Grossing up table

Gross cumulative total £	Gross rate of tax %	Inheritance tax on band £	Cumulative inheritance tax payable £	Net cumulative total £	Tax on each £ over net cumulative total for grossing up
255,000	Nil	Nil	Nil	255,000	$^1/_4$
Over 255,000	20	–	–	–	–

Lifetime transfers on or after 6 April 2002

Portion of value		Rate of tax %
Lower limit £	Upper limit £	
0	250,000	Nil
250,000	–	20

Grossing up table

Gross cumulative total £	Gross rate of tax %	Inheritance tax on band £	Cumulative inheritance tax payable £	Net cumulative total £	Tax on each £ over net cumulative total for grossing up
250,000	Nil	Nil	Nil	250,000	$^1/_4$
Over 250,000	20	–	–	–	–

1-700   Reliefs

Type of relief	Rate of relief for disposals			
	before 10/3/92 %	10/3/92– 31/8/95 %	1/9/95– 5/4/96 %	on or after 6/4/96 %
Agricultural property (IHTA 1984, s. 115ff.)[1]				
Vacant possession or right to obtain it within 12 months	50	100	100	100
Tenanted land with a vacant posession value	50	100	100	100
Entitled to 50% relief at 9 March 1981 and not since able to obtain vacant possession	50	100	100	100
Agricultural land let on or after 1 September 1995	N/A	N/A	100	100
Other circumstances	30	50	50	50
Business property (IHTA 1984, s. 103ff.) *Nature of property*				
Business or interest in business	50	100	100	100
Controlling shareholding in quoted company	50	50	50	50
Controlling shareholding in unquoted[2] company	50	100	100	100
Settled property used in life tenant's business	50/30[3]	100/50[3]	100/50[3]	100/50[3]
Shareholding in unquoted[2] company: more than 25% interest	50[4]	100	100	100
Minority shareholding in unquoted[2] company: 25% or less	30[5]	50	50	100
Land, buildings, machinery or plant used by transferor's company or partnership	30	50	50	50

Notes

[1] From 6 April 1995, short rotation coppice is regarded as agricultural property.

[2] With effect from 10 March 1992 'unquoted' means shares not quoted on a recognised stock exchange and therefore includes shares dealt in on the Unlisted Securities Market (USM) or Alternative Investment Market (AIM).

[3] The higher rate applies if the settled property is transferred along with business itself (*Fetherstonhaugh & Ors v IR Commrs* [1984] BTC 8,046).

[4] 30% if a minority interest transferred before 17 March 1987, or if transferor had not held at least 25% interest throughout preceding two years.

[5] The relief was 20% for transfers after 26 October 1977 but before 15 March 1983.

Taper relief

Years between gift and death		Percentage of full tax charge at death – rates actually due
More than	Not more than	%
3	4	80
4	5	60
5	6	40
6	7	20

Law: IHTA 1984, s. 7(4)

Quick succession relief

| Years between transfers | | Percentage applied to |
More than	Not more than	formula below
0	1	100
1	2	80
2	3	60
3	4	40
4	5	20

Formula

$$\text{Tax charge on earlier transfer} \times \frac{\text{Increase in transferee's estate}}{\text{Diminution in transferor's estate}}$$

Law: IHTA 1984, s. 141

Exemptions

Annual and small gift exemption

	On or after 6 April 1981 £	6 April 1980 to 5 April 1981 £	6 April 1976 to 5 April 1980 £
Annual	3,000	2,000	2,000
Small gift	250	250	100

Law: IHTA 1984, s. 19, 20

Gifts in consideration of marriage
(IHTA 1984, s. 22)

Donor	**Exemption limit** £
Parent of party to the marriage or civil partnership	5,000
Remote ancestor of party to the marriage or civil partnership	2,500
Party to the marriage or civil partnership	2,500
Any other person	1,000

Gift by UK-domiciled spouse or civil partner to non-UK domiciled spouse or civil partner
(IHTA 1984, s. 18)

Transfer on or after	**Exemption limit** £
9 March 1982	55,000

1-720   Due dates for delivery of accounts

Nature of transfer	Due Date
Chargeable lifetime transfer	Later of: – 12 months after end of month in which transfer occurred – 3 months after person became liable
Potentially exempt transfers which have become chargeable	12 months after end of month in which death of transferor occurred
Transfers on death	Later of: – 12 months after end of month in which death occurred – 3 months after personal representativers first act or have reason to believe an account is required
Gifts subject to reservation included in donor's estate at death	12 months after end of month in which death occurred
National heritage property	6 months after end of month in which chargeable event occurred

Values below which no account required

Excepted lifetime chargeable transfers on and after 6 April 2007	£
Where the property given away, or in which the interest subsists, is wholly attributable to cash or quoted stocks and securities, the cumulative total of all chargeable transfers made by the transfer in the seven years before the transfer must not exceed the nil rate band.	
Where the property given away, or in which the interest subsists, is wholly or partly attributable to property other than cash or quoted stocks and securities: (1) the value transferred by the chargeable transfer together with the cumulative total of all chargeable transfers made by the transferor in the seven years before the transfer must not exceed 80 per cent of the relevant IHT nil rate band; (2) the value transferred must not exceed the nil rate band that is available to the transferor at the time the disposal takes place.	
Excepted lifetime chargeable transfers on and after 1 April 1981 to 5 April 2007	
Transfer in question, together with all other chargeable transfers in same 12-month period ending on 5 April	10,000
Transfer in question, together with all previous chargeable transfers during preceding ten years	40,000

Excepted estates

Domiciled in the United Kingdom

Deaths on and after	But before	Total gross value[1] £	Total gross value of property outside UK £	Total value of settled property £	Aggregate value of 'specified transfers' £
6 April 2009	5 April 2010	325,000[1], [2]	100,000	150,000	150,000
6 April 2008	5 April 2009	312,000[1], [2]	100,000	150,000	150,000
6 April 2007	5 April 2008	300,000[1], [2]	100,000	150,000	150,000
6 April 2006	5 April 2007	285,000[1], [2]	100,000	150,000	150,000
6 April 2005	5 April 2006	275,000[1], [2]	100,000	150,000	150,000
6 April 2004	5 April 2005	263,000[1], [2]	100,000	150,000	150,000
6 April 2003	5 April 2004	240,000	75,000	100,000	100,000
6 April 2002	6 April 2003	220,000	75,000	100,000	100,000
6 April 2000	6 April 2002	210,000	50,000	–	75,000
6 April 1998	5 April 2000	180,000	30,000	–	50,000
6 April 1996	5 April 1998	180,000	30,000	–	50,000
6 April 1995	5 April 1996	145,000	15,000	–	–
1 April 1991	6 April 1995	125,000	15,000	–	–
1 April 1990	1 April 1991	115,000	15,000	–	–
1 April 1989	1 April 1990	100,000	15,000	–	–
1 April 1987	1 April 1989	70,000	10,000	–	–

Notes

[1] The aggregate of the gross value of that person's estate, the value transferred by any specified transfers made by that person, and the value transferred by any specified exempt transfers made by that person, must not exceed the IHT threshold. (Where the deceased dies after 5 April and before 6 August and application for probate or confirmation is made before 6 August in the same year as death, the inheritance tax threshold used is that for the preceding tax year.)

[2] An estate will qualify as an excepted estate where the gross value of the estate, plus the chargeable value of any transfers in the seven years to death, does not exceed £1,000,000 and the net chargeable estate after deduction of spouse or civil partner and/ or charity exemption **only** is less than the IHT threshold.

[3] For deaths on or after 6 April 2002, the limit applies to the aggregate of the gross value of the estate *plus* the value of 'specified transfers' which is extended and includes chargeable transfers, within seven years prior to death, of cash, quoted shares or securities, **or an interest in land and furnishings and chattels disposed of at the same time to the same person** (excluding property transferred subject to a reservation or property which becomes settled property).

For deaths on or after 6 April 1996 but before 6 April 2002, this limit applies to the total gross value of the estate *plus* the value of any transfers of cash or of quoted shares or securities made within seven years before death.

(4) If any of the sections IHTA 1984, s. 151A–151C dealing with alternatively secured pension funds apply by reason of an individual's death, that individual's estate does not qualify as an excepted estate (SI 2006/2141).

1-740   Due dates for payment of inheritance tax

Transfer	Due Date
Chargeable lifetime transfers between 6 April and 30 September	30 April in following year
Chargeable lifetime transfers between 1 October and 5 April	6 months after end of month in which transfer made
Potentially exempt transfers which become chargeable	6 months after end of month in which death occurred
Transfers on death; extra tax payable on chargeable lifetime transfers within seven years before death	6 months after end of month in which death occurred

Law: IHTA 1984, s. 226

VALUE ADDED TAX

1-760 VAT rates

Period of application	Standard rate %	Higher rate %
From 1/1/10	17.5	N/A
1/12/08–31/12/09	15	N/A
1/4/91–30/11/08	17.5	N/A
18/6/79–31/3/91	15	N/A
12/4/76–17/6/79	8	12.5
1/5/75–11/4/76	8	25*
18/11/74–30/4/75	8	25†
29/7/74–17/11/74	8	N/A
1/4/73–28/7/74	10	N/A

Notes

The increase from 1 January 2010 in the standard rate to 17.5 per cent from 15 per cent is as planned by the Chancellor of the Exchequer in his Pre-Budget Report of November 2008, but that plan may change.

* Re petrol, electrical appliances and luxury goods.

† Re petrol.

(1) Supplies of fuel and power for domestic, residential and charity non-business use and certain other supplies are charged at five per cent (VATA 1994, Sch. 7A).

(2) Imports of certain works of art, antiques and collectors' items are charged at an effective rate of five per cent from 27 July 1999 (VATA 1994, s. 21(4)–(6) as inserted by FA 1995, s. 22(1) and as amended by FA 1999, s. 12(1)(b)).

(3) The zero rate has applied from 1 April 1973 to date.

1-780 Registration limits

Taxable supplies

Period of application	1 year	Past turnover (£)[1] Unless turnover for next year will not exceed	Future turnover (£)[1] 30 days[2]
From 1/4/10	70,000	68,000	70,000
1/5/09–31/3/10	68,000	66,000	68,000
1/4/08–30/4/09	67,000	65,000	67,000

Period of application	1 year	Past turnover (£)[1] Unless turnover for next year will not exceed	Future turnover (£)[1] 30 days[2]
1/4/07–31/3/08	64,000	62,000	64,000
1/4/06–31/3/07	61,000	59,000	61,000
1/4/05–31/3/06	60,000	58,000	60,000
1/4/04–31/3/05	58,000	56,000	58,000
10/4/03–31/3/04	56,000	54,000	56,000
25/4/02–9/4/03	55,000	53,000	55,000
1/4/01–24/4/02	54,000	52,000	54,000
1/4/2000–31/3/01	52,000	50,000	52,000
1/4/99–31/3/2000	51,000	49,000	51,000
1/4/98–31/3/99	50,000	48,000	50,000
1/12/97–31/3/98	49,000	47,000	49,000
27/11/96–30/11/97	48,000	46,000	48,000

Notes

[1] Value of taxable supplies at the zero rate and all positive rates are included.

[2] A person is liable to register if there are reasonable grounds for believing that the value of his taxable supplies in the period of 30 days then beginning will exceed this limit.

Supplies from other member states – distance selling

Period of application	Cumulative relevant supplies from 1 January in year to any day in same year £
From 1/1/93	exceed 70,000

Notes

(VATA 1994, Sch. 2; Leaflet 700/1A).
If certain goods subject to excise duty are removed to the UK the person who removes the goods is liable to register in the UK because all such goods must be taxed in the country of destination. There is no de minimis limit.

Acquisitions from other member states

Period of application	Cumulative relevant acquisitions from 1 January in year to end of any month in same year £
From 1/4/10	70,000
1/5/09–31/3/10	68,000
1/4/08–30/4/09	67,000
1/4/07–31/3/08	64,000
1/4/06–31/3/07	61,000
1/4/05–31/3/06	60,000
1/4/04–31/3/05	58,000
10/4/03–31/3/04	56,000
25/4/02–9/4/03	55,000
1/4/01–24/4/02	54,000
1/4/2000–31/3/01	52,000
1/4/99–31/3/2000	51,000
1/4/98–31/3/99	50,000
1/1/98–31/3/98	49,000

Assets supplied in the UK by overseas persons

From 21 March 2000, any person without an establishment in the UK making or intending to make 'relevant' supplies must VAT register, regardless of the value of those supplies (VATA 1994, Sch. 3A). 'Relevant' supplies are taxable supplies of goods, including capital assets, in the UK where the supplier has recovered UK VAT under the eighth or thirteenth VAT directive. This applies where:

(1) the supplier (or his predecessor in business) was charged VAT on the purchase of the goods, or on anything incorporated in them, and has either claimed it back or intends to do so; or

(2) the VAT being claimed back was VAT paid on the import of goods into the UK.

1-800   De-registration limits

Taxable supplies

Period of application	Future turnover £
From 1/4/10	68,000
1/5/09–31/3/10	66,000
1/4/08–30/4/09	65,000
1/4/07–31/3/08	62,000
1/4/06–31/3/07	59,000
1/4/05–31/3/06	58,000
1/4/04–31/3/05	56,000
10/4/03–31/3/04	54,000
25/4/02–9/4/03	53,000
1/4/01–24/4/02	52,000
1/4/00–31/3/01	50,000
1/4/99–31/3/2000	49,000
1/4/98–31/3/99	48,000

Supplies from other member states

Period of application	Past relevant supplies in last year to 31 December £	Future relevant supplies in immediately following year £
From 1/1/93	70,000	70,000

Acquisitions from other member states

Period of application	Past relevant acquisitions in last year to 31 December £	Future relevant acquisitions in immediately following year £
From 1/4/10	70,000	70,000
1/5/09–31/3/10	68,000	68,000
1/4/08–30/04/09	67,000	67,000
1/4/07–31/3/08	64,000	64,000
1/4/06–31/3/07	61,000	61,000
1/4/05–31/3/06	60,000	60,000

Period of application	Past relevant acquisitions in last year to 31 December £	Future relevant acquisitions in immediately following year £
1/4/04–31/3/05	58,000	58,000
10/4/02–31/3/04	56,000	56,000
25/4/02–9/4/03	55,000	55,000
1/4/01–24/4/02	54,000	54,000
1/4/2000–31/3/01	52,000	52,000
1/4/99–31/3/2000	51,000	51,000
1/4/98–31/3/99	50,000	50,000
1/1/98–31/3/98	49,000	49,000

Special accounting limits

Cash accounting: admission to the scheme

Period of application	Annual turnover limit £
From 1/4/07	1,350,000
1/4/04–31/3/07	660,000
1/4/01–31/3/04	600,000
1/4/93–31/3/01	350,000
1/10/90–31/3/93	300,000
1/10/87–30/9/90	250,000

Notes

Annual turnover limit includes zero-rated supplies, but excludes any capital assets previously used in the business. Exempt supplies are also excluded.

A person must withdraw from the cash accounting scheme at the end of a prescribed accounting period if the value of his taxable supplies in the one year ending at the end of the prescribed accounting period has exceeded £1,600,000 (from 1 April 2007) (*Value Added Tax (Amendment) (No. 2) Regulations* 2007 (SI 2007/768)).

Outstanding VAT on supplies made and received while using the cash accounting scheme may be brought to account on a cash basis for a further six months after withdrawal from the scheme, but only where withdrawal was voluntary or because the turnover threshold was exceeded.

Annual accounting: admission to the scheme

Period of application	Annual turnover limit £
From 1/4/06	1,350,000
1/4/04–31/3/06	660,000
1/4/01–31/3/04	600,000
9/4/91–31/3/01	300,000

Notes

Annual turnover limit includes positive and zero-rated supplies but excludes any supplies of capital assets and any exempt supplies.

A person must withdraw from the annual accounting scheme at the end of a prescribed accounting period if the value of his taxable supplies in the one year ending at the end of the prescribed accounting period has exceeded £1,600,000 (£825,000 between April 2004 and 31 March 2006) (*Value Added Tax Regulations* 1995 (SI 1995/2518), Pt. VII).

Flat-rate scheme: admission to the scheme

Period of application	Annual taxable turnover limit[1] £	Annual total turnover limit [2] £
Returns ending after 10 April 2003	150,000	187,500
Returns ending after 25 April 2002	100,000	125,000

Notes

[1] Zero-rated and positive rated supplies excluding VAT. Exempt supplies are excluded.

[2] Total of VAT-exclusive taxable turnover and exempt and/or other non-taxable income.

[3] Net VAT liability is calculated by applying a flat-rate percentage to the VAT-inclusive turnover. The flat-rate percentage depends upon the trader sector (Notice 733).

1-820   VAT on private fuel

From 1 May 2010

For prescribed accounting periods beginning after 30 April 2010, the following table applies to assess output tax due on fuel used by cars for private journeys if it was provided at below cost from business resources (VATA 1994, s. 57(3)).

Fuel scale charges for 12-month period

CO$_2$ band, g/km	VAT fuel scale charge, 12 month period, £
120 or less	570.00
125	850.00
130	850.00
135	910.00
140	965.00
145	1,020.00
150	1,080.00
155	1,135.00
160	1,190.00
165	1,250.00
170	1,305.00
175	1,360.00
180	1,420.00
185	1,475.00
190	1,530.00
195	1,590.00
200	1,645.00
205	1,705.00
210	1,760.00
215	1,815.00
220	1,875.00
225	1,930.00
230 or more	1,985.00

Fuel scale charges for 3-month period

CO$_2$ band, g/km	VAT fuel scale charge, 3 month period, £
120 or less	141.00
125	212.00
130	212.00
135	227.00
140	241.00
145	255.00
150	269.00

CO$_2$ band, g/km	VAT fuel scale charge, 3 month period, £
155	283.00
160	297.00
165	312.00
170	326.00
175	340.00
180	354.00
185	368.00
190	383.00
195	397.00
200	411.00
205	425.00
210	439.00
215	454.00
220	468.00
225	482.00
230 or more	496.00

Fuel scale charges for 1-month period

CO$_2$ band, g/km	VAT fuel scale charge, 1 month period, £
120 or less	47.00
125	70.00
130	70.00
135	75.00
140	80.00
145	85.00
150	89.00
155	94.00
160	99.00
165	104.00
170	108.00
175	113.00
180	118.00
185	122.00
190	127.00
195	132.00
200	137.00
205	141.00
210	146.00

CO₂ band, g/km	VAT fuel scale charge, 1 month period, £
215	151.00
220	156.00
225	160.00
230 or more	165.00

1 January 2010 to 30 April 2010 (17.5 per cent rate)

The standard rate of VAT rose to 17.5 per cent from 15 per cent with effect from 1 January 2010, but there was no change to the amount of the fuel scale in VATA 1994, s. 57(3) which applies from 1 May 2009. However, the VAT on such charges must take account of the change in the standard rate.

Where the standard rate of 17.5 per cent applies, the following table applies to assess output tax due on fuel used by cars for private journeys if it was provided at below cost from business resources (VATA 199, s. 57(3)).

Fuel scale charges for 12-month period

CO₂ band, g/km	VAT fuel scale charge, 12 month period, £	VAT on 12 month charge, £	VAT exclusive 12 month charge, £
120 or less	505.00	75.21	429.79
125	755.00	112.45	642.55
130	755.00	112.45	642.55
135	755.00	112.45	642.55
140	805.00	119.89	685.11
145	855.00	127.34	727.66
150	905.00	134.79	770.21
155	960.00	142.98	817.02
160	1,010.00	150.43	859.57
165	1,060.00	157.87	902.13
170	1,110.00	165.32	944.68
175	1,160.00	172.77	987.23
180	1,210.00	180.21	1,029.79
185	1,260.00	187.66	1,072.34
190	1,310.00	195.11	1,114.89
195	1,360.00	202.55	1,157.45
200	1,410.00	210.00	1,200.00
205	1,465.00	218.19	1,246.81
210	1,515.00	225.64	1,289.36
215	1,565.00	233.09	1,331.91
220	1,615.00	240.53	1,347.47
225	1,665.00	247.98	1,417.02

CO$_2$ band, g/km	VAT fuel scale charge, 12 month period, £	VAT on 12 month charge, £	VAT exclusive 12 month charge, £
230	1,715.00	255.43	1,459.57
235 or more	1,765.00	262.87	1,502.13

Fuel scale charges for 3-month period

CO$_2$ band, g/km	VAT fuel scale charge, 3 month period, £	VAT on 3 month charge, £	VAT exclusive 3 month charge, £
120 or less	126.00	18.77	107.23
125	189.00	28.15	160.85
130	189.00	28.15	160.85
135	189.00	28.15	160.85
140	201.00	29.24	171.76
145	214.00	31.87	182.13
150	226.00	33.66	192.34
155	239.00	35.60	203.40
160	251.00	37.38	213.62
165	264.00	39.32	224.68
170	276.00	41.11	234.89
175	289.00	43.04	245.96
180	302.00	44.98	257.02
185	314.00	46.77	267.23
190	327.00	48.70	278.30
195	339.00	50.49	288.51
200	352.00	52.43	299.57
205	365.00	54.36	310.64
210	378.00	56.30	321.70
215	390.00	58.09	331.91
220	403.00	60.02	342.98
225	416.00	61.96	354.04
230	428.00	63.74	364.26
235 or more	441.00	65.68	357.32

Fuel scale charges for 1-month period

CO$_2$ band, g/km	VAT fuel scale charge, 1 month period, £	VAT on 1 month charge, £	VAT exclusive 1 month charge, £
120 or less	42.00	6.26	35.74
125	63.00	9.38	53.62
130	63.00	9.38	53.62

Key Data

CO$_2$ band, g/km	VAT fuel scale charge, 1 month period, £	VAT on 1 month charge, £	VAT exclusive 1 month charge, £
135	63.00	9.38	53.62
140	67.00	9.98	57.02
145	71.00	10.57	60.43
150	75.00	11.17	63.83
155	79.00	11.77	67.23
160	83.00	12.36	70.64
165	88.00	13.11	74.89
170	92.00	13.70	78.30
175	96.00	14.30	81.70
180	100.00	14.89	85.11
185	104.00	15.49	88.51
190	109.00	16.23	92.77
195	113.00	16.83	96.17
200	117.00	17.43	99.57
205	121.00	18.02	102.98
210	126.00	18.77	107.23
215	130.00	19.36	110.64
220	134.00	19.96	114.04
225	138.00	20.55	117.45
230	142.00	21.15	120.85
235 or more	147.00	21.89	125.11

From 1 May 2008, VAT fuel scale charges have changed. The former VAT fuel scale charges (see below), which were based on the engine size and fuel type of a car, have been replaced by a fuel scale charge based solely on the CO$_2$ rating of a car. Businesses must use the new scales from the start of their first accounting period beginning on or after 1 May 2008.

From 1 May 2009 to 31 December 2009 (15 per cent VAT rate)

For prescribed accounting periods *beginning* after 30 April 2009, where the standard rate of 15 per cent applies, the following table applies to assess output tax due on fuel used by cars for private journeys if it was provided at below cost from business resources (VATA 1994, s. 57(3)).

The standard rate of VAT is due to rise to 17.5 per cent from 15 per cent with effect from 1 January 2010, but there will probably be no change to the amount of the fuel scale charge in VATA 1994, s. 57(3) which applied from 1 May 2009. However, the VAT on such charges must take account of the change in the standard rate.

Fuel scale charges for 12-month period

CO_2 band, g/km	VAT fuel scale charge, 12 month period, £	VAT on 12 month charge, £	VAT exclusive 12 month charge, £
120 or less	505.00	65.87	439.13
125	755.00	98.48	656.52
130	755.00	98.48	656.52
135	755.00	98.48	656.52
140	805.00	105.00	700.00
145	855.00	111.52	743.48
150	905.00	118.04	786.96
155	960.00	125.22	834.78
160	1,010.00	131.74	878.26
165	1,060.00	138.26	921.74
170	1,110.00	144.78	965.22
175	1,160.00	151.30	1,008.70
180	1,210.00	157.83	1,052.17
185	1,260.00	164.35	1.095.65
190	1,310.00	170.87	1,139.13
195	1,360.00	177.39	1,182.61
200	1,410.00	183.91	1,226.09
205	1,465.00	194.09	1,270.91
210	1,515.00	197.61	1,317.39
215	1,565.00	204.13	1,360.87
220	1,615.00	210.65	1,404.35
225	1,665.00	217.17	1,447.83
230	1,715.00	223.70	1,491.30
235 or more	1,765.00	230.22	1,534.78

Fuel scale charges for 3-month period

CO_2 band, g/km	VAT fuel scale charge, 3 month period, £	VAT on 3 month charge, £	VAT exclusive 3 month charge, £
120 or less	126.00	16.43	109.57
125	189.00	24.65	164.35
130	189.00	24.65	164.35
135	189.00	24.65	164.35
140	201.00	26.22	174.78
145	214.00	27.91	186.09
150	226.00	29.48	196.52

Key Data

CO₂ band, g/km	VAT fuel scale charge, 3 month period, £	VAT on 3 month charge, £	VAT exclusive 3 month charge, £
155	239.00	31.17	207.83
160	251.00	32.74	218.26
165	264.00	34.43	229.57
170	276.00	36.00	240.00
175	289.00	37.70	251.30
180	302.00	39.39	262.61
185	314.00	40.96	273.04
190	327.00	42.65	284.35
195	339.00	44.22	294.78
200	352.00	45.91	306.09
205	365.00	47.61	317.39
210	378.00	49.30	328.70
215	390.00	50.87	339.13
220	403.00	52.57	350.43
225	416.00	54.26	361.74
230	428.00	55.83	372.17
235 or more	441.00	57.52	383.48

Fuel scale charges for 1-month period

CO₂ band, g/km	VAT fuel scale charge, 1 month period, £	VAT on 1 month charge, £	VAT exclusive 1 month charge, £
120 or less	42.00	5.48	36.52
125	63.00	8.22	54.78
130	63.00	8.22	54.78
135	63.00	8.22	54.78
140	67.00	8.74	58.26
145	71.00	9.26	61.74
150	75.00	9.78	65.22
155	79.00	10.30	68.70
160	83.00	10.83	72.17
165	88.00	11.48	76.52
170	92.00	12.00	80.00
175	96.00	12.52	83.48
180	100.00	13.04	86.96
185	104.00	13.57	90.43
190	109.00	14.22	94.78

CO$_2$ band, g/km	VAT fuel scale charge, 1 month period, £	VAT on 1 month charge, £	VAT exclusive 1 month charge, £
195	113.00	14.74	98.26
200	117.00	15.26	101.74
205	121.00	15.78	105.22
210	126.00	16.43	109.57
215	130.00	16.96	113.04
220	134.00	17.48	116.52
225	138.00	18.00	120.00
230	142.00	18.52	123.48
235 or more	147.00	19.17	127.83

From 1 December 2008–30 April 2009 (15 per cent VAT rate)

When the standard rate of VAT fell to 15 per cent from 17.5 per cent with effect from 1 December 2008, there was no change to the amount of the fuel scale charge in VATA 1994, s. 57(3) which applied from 1 May 2008. However, the VAT on such charges must take account of the change in the standard rate. The revised amounts are shown in the tables in Annex D to the HMRC guide *VAT – Change in the standard rate: a detailed guide for VAT-registered businesses* and are reproduced below.

Fuel scale charges for 12-month period

CO$_2$ band,	VAT fuel scale charge, 12 month period, £	VAT on 12 month charge, £	VAT exclusive 12 month charge, £
120 or less	555.00	72.39	482.61
125	830.00	108.26	721.74
130	830.00	108.26	721.74
135	830.00	108.26	721.74
140	885.00	115.43	769.57
145	940.00	122.61	817.39
150	995.00	129.78	865.22
155	1,050.00	136.96	913.04
160	1,105.00	144.13	960.87
165	1,160.00	151.30	1,008.70
170	1,215.00	158.48	1,056.52
175	1,270.00	165.65	1,104.35
180	1,325.00	172.83	1,152.17
185	1,380.00	180.00	1,200.00
190	1,435.00	187.17	1,247.83

Key Data

CO_2 band,	VAT fuel scale charge, 12 month period, £	VAT on 12 month charge, £	VAT exclusive 12 month charge, £
195	1,490.00	194.35	1,295.65
200	1,545.00	201.52	1,343.48
205	1,605.00	209.35	1,395.65
210	1,660.00	216.52	1,443.48
215	1,715.00	223.70	1,491.30
220	1,770.00	230.87	1,539.13
225	1,825.00	238.04	1,586.96
230	1,880.00	245.22	1,634.78
235 or more	1,935.00	252.39	1,682.61

Fuel scale charges for 3-month period

CO_2 band,	VAT fuel scale charge, 3 month period, £	VAT on 3 month charge, £	VAT exclusive 3 month charge, £
120 or less	138.00	18.00	120.00
125	207.00	27.00	180.00
130	207.00	27.00	180.00
135	207.00	27.00	180.00
140	221.00	28.83	192.17
145	234.00	30.52	203.48
150	248.00	32.35	215.65
155	262.00	34.17	227.83
160	276.00	36.00	240.00
165	290.00	37.83	252.17
170	303.00	39.52	263.48
175	317.00	41.35	275.65
180	331.00	43.17	287.83
185	345.00	45.00	300.00
190	359.00	46.83	312.17
195	373.00	48.65	324.35
200	386.00	50.35	335.65
205	400.00	52.17	347.83
210	414.00	54.00	360.00
215	428.00	55.83	372.17
220	442.00	57.65	384.35
225	455.00	59.35	395.65
230	469.00	61.17	407.83
235 or more	483.00	63.00	420.00

Fuel scale charges for 1-month period

CO₂ band,	VAT fuel scale charge, 1 month period, £	VAT on 1 month charge, £	VAT exclusive 1 month charge, £
120 or less	46.00	6.00	40.00
125	69.00	9.00	60.00
130	69.00	9.00	60.00
135	69.00	9.00	60.00
140	73.00	9.52	63.48
145	78.00	10.17	67.83
150	82.00	10.70	71.30
155	87.00	11.35	75.65
160	92.00	12.00	80.00
165	96.00	12.52	83.48
170	101.00	13.17	87.83
175	105.00	13.70	91.30
180	110.00	14.35	95.65
185	115.00	15.00	100.00
190	119.00	15.52	103.48
195	124.00	16.17	107.83
200	128.00	16.70	111.30
205	133.00	17.35	115.65
210	138.00	18.00	120.00
215	142.00	18.52	123.48
220	147.00	19.17	127.83
225	151.00	19.70	131.30
230	156.00	20.35	135.65
235 or more	161.00	21.00	140.00

Key Data

From 1 May 2008 – 30 November 2008 (17.5 per cent VAT rate)

For prescribed accounting periods *beginning* after 30 April 2008, where the standard rate of 17.5 per cent applied, the following table applies to assess output tax due on fuel used by cars for private journeys if it was provided at below cost from business resources (VATA 1994, s. 57(3)).

Fuel scale charges for 12-month period

CO₂ band, g/km	VAT fuel scale charge, 12 month period, £	VAT on 12 month charge, £	VAT exclusive 12 month charge, £
120 or less	555.00	82.66	472.34
125	830.00	123.62	706.38
130	830.00	123.62	706.38

CO$_2$ band, g/km	VAT fuel scale charge, 12 month period, £	VAT on 12 month charge, £	VAT exclusive 12 month charge, £
135	830.00	123.62	706.38
140	885.00	131.81	753.19
145	940.00	140.00	800.00
150	995.00	148.19	846.81
155	1,050.00	156.38	893.62
160	1,105.00	164.57	940.43
165	1,160.00	172.77	987.23
170	1,215.00	180.96	1,034.04
175	1,270.00	189.15	1,080.85
180	1,325.00	197.34	1,127.66
185	1,380.00	205.53	1,174.47
190	1,435.00	213.72	1,221.28
195	1,490.00	221.91	1,268.09
200	1,545.00	230.11	1,314.89
205	1,605.00	239.04	1,365.96
210	1,660.00	247.23	1,412.77
215	1,715.00	255.43	1,459.57
220	1,770.00	263.62	1,506.38
225	1,825.00	271.81	1,553.19
230	1,880.00	280.00	1,600.00
235 or more	1,935.00	288.19	1,646.81

Fuel scale charges for 3-month period

CO$_2$ band, g/km	VAT fuel scale charge, 3 month period, £	VAT on 3 month charge, £	VAT exclusive 3 month charge, £
120 or less	138.00	20.55	117.45
125	207.00	30.83	176.17
130	207.00	30.83	176.17
135	207.00	30.83	176.17
140	221.00	32.91	188.09
145	234.00	34.85	199.15
150	248.00	36.94	211.06
155	262.00	39.02	222.98
160	276.00	41.11	234.89
165	290.00	43.19	246.81
170	303.00	45.13	257.87

CO_2 band, g/km	VAT fuel scale charge, 3 month period, £	VAT on 3 month charge, £	VAT exclusive 3 month charge, £
175	317.00	47.21	269.79
180	331.00	49.30	281.70
185	345.00	51.38	293.62
190	359.00	53.47	305.53
195	373.00	55.55	317.45
200	386.00	57.49	328.51
205	400.00	59.57	340.43
210	414.00	61.66	352.34
215	428.00	63.74	364.26
220	442.00	65.83	376.17
225	455.00	67.77	387.23
230	469.00	69.85	399.15
235 or more	483.00	71.94	411.06

Fuel scale charges for 1-month period

CO_2 band, g/km	VAT fuel scale charge, 1 month period, £	VAT on 1 month charge, £	VAT exclusive 1 month charge, £
120 or less	46.00	6.85	39.15
125	69.00	10.28	58.72
130	69.00	10.28	58.72
135	69.00	10.28	58.72
140	73.00	10.87	62.13
145	78.00	11.62	66.38
150	82.00	12.21	69.79
155	87.00	12.96	74.04
160	92.00	13.70	78.30
165	96.00	14.30	81.70
170	101.00	15.04	85.96
175	105.00	15.64	89.36
180	110.00	16.38	93.62
185	115.00	17.13	97.87
190	119.00	17.72	101.28
195	124.00	18.47	105.53
200	128.00	19.06	108.94
205	133.00	19.81	113.19
210	138.00	20.55	117.45

Key Data

CO₂ band, g/km	VAT fuel scale charge, 1 month period, £	VAT on 1 month charge, £	VAT exclusive 1 month charge, £
215	142.00	21.15	120.85
220	147.00	21.89	125.11
225	151.00	22.49	128.51
230	156.00	23.23	132.77
235 or more	161.00	23.98	137.02

1-840 Value added tax – 'blocked' input tax

Any input tax charged on the following items is 'blocked', i.e. non-recoverable (see 8058):

- Motor cars, other than certain motor cars acquired by certain persons but after 31 July 1995 (1) any person can recover input tax on motor cars used exclusively for business and (2) only 50 per cent of VAT on car leasing charges is recoverable if lessee makes any private use of the car and if the lessor recovered the VAT on buying the car.
- Entertainment, except of employees.
- In the case of claims by builders, articles of a kind not ordinarily installed by builders as fixtures in new houses.
- Goods supplied under a second-hand scheme.
- Goods imported for private purposes.
- Non-business element of supplies to be used only partly for business purposes. This may contravene European law where the supplies are of goods: strictly the input tax is deductible, but output tax is due on non-business use. VAT on supplies not intended for business use does not rank as input tax, so cannot be recovered.
- Goods and services acquired by a tour operator for resupply as a designated travel service.
- Domestic accommodation for directors and their families to the extent of domestic purpose use.

In addition, 'exempt input tax' is not recoverable (see 8060). From 10 March 1999 the partial exemption simplification rule that allowed some businesses to claim back all their input tax, providing that their exempt input tax is only incurred in relation to certain exempt supplies, has been abolished.

NATIONAL INSURANCE CONTRIBUTIONS

1-860 NIC rates

Class 1 contributions

Class 1 primary (employee) contributions 2010–11	
Lower earnings limit (LEL)[1]	£97 weekly £421 monthly £5,044 yearly
Primary threshold	£110 weekly £476 monthly £5,715 yearly
Upper earnings limit (UEL)	£844 weekly £3,656 monthly £43,875 yearly
Upper accrual point (UAP)	£770 weekly £3,337 monthly £40,040 yearly
Rate on earnings up to primary threshold[1]	0%
Not contracted-out rate	11% on £110.01 to £844 weekly 1% on excess over £844
Contracted-out rate	9.4% on £110.01 to £770 weekly 11% on £770.01 to £844 weekly 1% on excess over £844
Reduced rate[2]	4.85% on £110.01 to £844 weekly 1% excess over £844 (no rebate even if contracted-out)

Notes

[1] Earnings from the LEL, up to and including the primary threshold (PT), count towards the employee's basic state pension, even though no contributions are paid on those earnings. Similarly, earnings between the LEL and the primary threshold count towards the employee's entitlement to certain benefits including the second state pension (S2P). Employees in contracted-out employment earn no S2P rights and receive a rebate of contributions of 1.6 per cent. This applies from the LEL to the UAP, so earnings from LEL to PT attract a 'negative' contribution of 1.6 per cent and the rate for earnings from PT to UAP becomes 9.4 per cent.

Monthly and annual LEL, UEL and UAP figures are calculated per SI 2001/1004, reg. 11.

[2] The reduced rate applies to married women or widows with a valid certificate of election.

Class 1 contributions

Class 1 primary (employee) contributions 2009–10	
Lower earnings limit (LEL)[1]	£95 weekly £412 monthly £4,940 yearly
Primary threshold	£110 weekly £476 monthly £5,715 yearly
Upper earnings limit (UEL)	£844 weekly £3,656 monthly £43,875 yearly
Upper accrual point (UAP)	£770 weekly £3,337 monthly £40,040 yearly
Rate on earnings up to primary threshold[1]	0%
Not contracted-out rate	11% on £110.01 to £844 weekly 1% on excess over £844
Contracted-out rate	9.4% on £110.01 to £770 weekly 11% on £770.01 to £844 weekly 1% on excess over £844
Reduced rate[2]	4.85% on £110.01 to £844 weekly 1% excess over £844 (no rebate even if contracted-out)

Notes

[1] Earnings from the LEL, up to and including the primary threshold (PT), count towards the employee's basic state pension, even though no contributions are paid on those earnings. Similarly, earnings between the LEL and the primary threshold count towards the employee's entitlement to certain benefits including the second state pension (S2P). Employees in contracted-out employment earn no S2P rights and receive a rebate of contributions of 1.6 per cent. This applies from the LEL to the UAP, so earnings from LEL to PT attract a 'negative' contribution of 1.6 per cent and the rate for earnings from PT to UAP becomes 9.4 per cent.

Monthly and annual LEL, UEL and UAP figures are calculated per SI 2001/1004, reg. 11.

[2] The reduced rate applies to married women or widows with a valid certificate of election.

Class 1 contributions

Class 1 primary (employee) contributions 2008–09	
Lower earnings limit (LEL)[1]	£90 weekly £390 monthly £4,680 yearly
Primary threshold	£105 weekly £453 monthly £5,435 yearly
Upper earnings limit (UEL)	£770 weekly £3,337 monthly £40,040 yearly
Rate on earnings up to primary threshold	0%
Not contracted-out rate	11% on £105.01 to £770 weekly 1% on excess over £770
Contracted-out rate	9.4% on £105.01 to £770 weekly 1% on excess over £770
Reduced rate[2]	4.85% on £105.01 to £770 weekly 1% excess over £770

Notes

[1]   Earnings from the lower earnings limit (LEL), up to and including the primary threshold will count towards the employee's basic 'flat rate' state pension, even though no contributions will have been paid on those earnings. Similarly, earnings between the LEL and the primary threshold count towards the employee's entitlement to certain benefits, including the second state pension. Monthly LEL and upper earnings limit (UEL) figures are calculated as per SI 2001/1004, reg. 1 (as amended by SI 2008/133). The equivalent annual figures are calculated as 52 × the weekly figure (NIM 12021).

[2]   The reduced rate applies to married women or widows with a valid certificate of election. Men over 65 and women over 60 pay no primary contributions, though employers still pay the secondary contribution at the usual rate. People under 16 and their employers pay no contributions.

Class 1 contributions

Class 1 primary (employee) contributions 2007–08[1]	
Lower earnings limit (LEL)[2]	£87 weekly £377 monthly £4,524 yearly
Primary threshold	£100 weekly £435 monthly £5,225 yearly
Rate up to primary threshold	0%
Rate between primary threshold and UEL (not contracted-out)	11%
Rate between primary threshold and UEL (contracted-out)	9.4%
Rate on earnings above UEL	1%
Reduced rate on earnings between primary threshold and UEL[3]	4.85%
Upper earnings limit (UEL)	£670 weekly £2,905 monthly £34,840 yearly

Notes

[1] Class 1 contributions are earnings related. Employees must pay primary Class 1 contributions on that part of their earnings which exceeds the primary threshold at the main rate of 11 per cent and on one per cent on earnings above the UEL.

[2] Earnings from the LEL, up to and including the primary threshold will count towards the employee's basic 'flat rate'' state pension, even though no contributions will have been paid on those earnings. Similarly, earnings between the lower earnings limit (LEL) and the primary threshold will count towards the employee's entitlement to certain benefits including the additional pension (SERPS), or, from April 2002, the second state pension.

[3] The reduced rate applies to married women or widows with a valid certificate of election. Men over 65 and women over 60 pay no primary contributions, though employers still pay the secondary contribution at the usual rate. People under 16 and their employers pay no contributions.

Class 1 contributions

Class 1 primary (employee) contributions 2006–07[1]	
Lower earnings limit (LEL)[2]	£84 weekly £364 monthly £4,368 yearly
Primary threshold	£97 weekly £420 monthly £5,035 yearly
Rate up to primary threshold	0%
Rate between primary threshold and UEL (not contracted-out)	11%
Rate between primary threshold and UEL (contracted-out)	9.4%
Rate on earnings above UEL	1%
Reduced rate on earnings between primary threshold and UEL[3]	4.85%
Upper earnings limit (UEL)	£645 weekly £2,795 monthly £33,540 yearly

Key Data

Notes

[1]   Class 1 contributions are earnings related. Employees must pay primary Class 1 contributions on that part of their earnings which exceeds the primary threshold at the main rate of 11 per cent and on one per cent on earnings above the UEL.

[2]   Earnings from the LEL, up to and including the primary threshold will count towards the employee's basic 'flat rate' state pension, even though no contributions will have been paid on those earnings. Similarly, earnings between the lower earnings limit (LEL) and the primary threshold will count towards the employee's entitlement to certain benefits including the additional pension (SERPS), or, from April 2002, the second state pension.

[3]   The reduced rate applies to married women or widows with a valid certificate of election. Men over 65 and women over 60 pay no primary contributions, though employers still pay the secondary contribution at the usual rate. People under 16 and their employers pay no contributions.

Class 1 contributions

Class 1 primary (employee) contributions 2005–06[1]	
Lower earnings limit (LEL)[2]	£82 weekly £355 monthly £4,264 yearly
Primary threshold	£94 weekly £407 monthly £4,888 yearly
Rate up to primary threshold	0%
Rate between primary threshold and UEL (not contracted-out)	11%
Rate between primary threshold and UEL (contracted-out)	9.4%
Rate on earnings above UEL	1%
Reduced rate on earnings between primary threshold and UEL[3]	4.85%
Upper earnings limit (UEL)	£630 weekly £2,730 monthly £32,760 yearly

Notes

[1] Class 1 contributions are earnings related. Employees must pay primary Class 1 contributions on that part of their earnings which exceeds the primary threshold at the main rate of 11 per cent and on one per cent on earnings above the UEL.

[2] Earnings from the LEL, up to and including the primary threshold will count towards the employee's basic 'flat rate' state pension, even though no contributions will have been paid on those earnings. Similarly, earnings between the lower earnings limit (LEL) and the primary threshold will count towards the employee's entitlement to certain benefits including the additional pension (SERPS), or, from April 2002, the second state pension.

[3] The reduced rate applies to married women or widows with a valid certificate of election. Men over 65 and women over 60 pay no primary contributions, though employers still pay the secondary contribution at the usual rate. People under 16 and their employers pay no contributions.

Class 1 contributions

Class 1 primary (employee) contributions 2004–05[1]	
Lower earnings limit (LEL)[2]	£79 weekly £343 monthly £4,108 yearly
Primary threshold	£91 weekly £395 monthly £4,732 yearly
Rate up to primary threshold	0%
Rate between primary threshold and UEL (not contracted-out)	11%
Rate between primary threshold and UEL (contracted-out)	9.4%
Rate on earnings above UEL	1%
Reduced rate on earnings between primary threshold and UEL[3]	4.85%
Upper earnings limit (UEL)	£610 weekly £2,643 monthly £31,720 yearly

Notes

[1] Class 1 contributions are earnings related. Employees must pay primary Class 1 contributions on that part of their earnings which exceeds the primary threshold at the main rate of 11 per cent and on one per cent on earnings above the UEL.

[2] Earnings from the LEL, up to and including the primary threshold will count towards the employee's basic 'flat rate' state pension, even though no contributions will have been paid on those earnings. Similarly, earnings between the lower earnings limit (LEL) and the primary threshold will count towards the employee's entitlement to certain benefits including the additional pension (SERPS), or, from April 2002, the second state pension.

[3] The reduced rate applies to married women or widows with a valid certificate of election. Men over 65 and women over 60 pay no primary contributions, though employers still pay the secondary contribution at the usual rate. People under 16 and their employers pay no contributions.

Key Data

Class 1 contributions

Class 1 primary (employee) contributions 2003–04[1]	
Lower earnings limit (LEL)[2]	£77 weekly £334 monthly £4,004 yearly
Primary threshold	£89 weekly £385 monthly 4,628 yearly
Rate up to primary threshold	0%
Rate between primary threshold and UEL (not contracted-out)	11%
Rate between primary threshold and UEL (contracted-out)	9.4%
Rate on earnings above UEL	1%
Reduced rate on earnings between primary threshold and UEL[3]	4.85%
Upper earnings limit (UEL)	£595 weekly £2,579 monthly £30,940 yearly

Notes

[1] Class 1 contributions are earnings related. Employees must pay primary Class 1 contributions on that part of their earnings which exceeds the primary threshold at the main rate of 11 per cent and on one per cent on earnings above the UEL.

[2] Earnings from the LEL, up to and including the primary threshold will count towards the employee's basic 'flat rate' state pension, even though no contributions will have been paid on those earnings. Similarly, earnings between the lower earnings limit (LEL) and the primary threshold will count towards the employee's entitlement to certain benefits including the additional pension (SERPS), or, from April 2002, the second state pension.

[3] The reduced rate applies to married women or widows with a valid certificate of election. Men over 65 and women over 60 pay no primary contributions, though employers still pay the secondary contribution at the usual rate. People under 16 and their employers pay no contributions.

Class 1 secondary (employer) contributions 2010–11	
Secondary earnings threshold	£110 weekly £476 monthly £5,715 yearly
Not contracted-out rate	12.8% on earnings above threshold

Class 1 secondary (employer) contributions 2010–11	
Contracted-out rate[1]	9.1% for salary-related (COSR) and 11.4% for money-purchase (COMP) schemes on earnings from secondary threshold to UAP (plus 3.7% and 1.4% rebates for earnings from LEL to secondary threshold), then 12.8% above UAP

Key Data

Notes

[1] As for employees, earnings between the LEL and the ST will count towards the employee's entitlement to S2P. Employers with contracted-out occupational pension schemes receive a rebate of contributions for scheme members of 3.7 per cent (COSR) or 1.4 per cent (COMP). This applies from the LEL to the UAP, so earnings from LEL to ST attract a 'negative' contribution and the rate for earnings from ST to UAP is reduced as shown

Class 1 secondary (employer) contributions 2009–10	
Secondary earnings threshold	£110 weekly £476 monthly £5,715 yearly
Not contracted-out rate	12.8% on earnings above threshold
Contracted-out rate[1]	9.1% for salary-related (COSR) and 11.4% for money-purchase (COMP) schemes on earnings from secondary threshold to UAP (plus 3.7% and 1.4% rebates for earnings from LEL to secondary threshold), then 12.8% above UAP

Notes

[1] As for employees, earnings between the LEL and the ST will count towards the employee's entitlement to S2P. Employers with contracted-out occupational pension schemes receive a rebate of contributions for scheme members of 3.7 per cent (COSR) or 1.4 per cent (COMP). This applies from the LEL to the UAP, so earnings from LEL to ST attract a 'negative' contribution and the rate for earnings from ST to UAP is reduced as shown

Class 1 secondary (employer) contributions 2008–09	
Secondary earnings threshold	£105 weekly £453 monthly £5,435 yearly
Not contracted-out rate	12.8% on earnings above threshold

Class 1 secondary (employer) contributions 2008–09	
Contracted-out rate	9.1% for salary-related (COSR) and 11.4% for money-purchase (COMP) schemes on earnings from secondary threshold to the UEL, then 12.8% on earnings above the UEL

Class 1 secondary (employer) contributions 2007–08[4]	
Earnings/secondary threshold	£100 weekly £435 monthly £5,225 yearly
Rates (not contracted-out)	12.8% above earnings threshold
Rates (contracted-out)[5]	9.1% for salary-related (COSR) and 11.4% for money-purchase (COMP) schemes (including 3.7% and 1.4% rebates for earnings from LEL to earnings threshold), then 12.8% above UEL.

Notes

[4] Class 1 contributions are earnings related. Employers must pay secondary Class 1 contributions on that part of an employee's earnings which exceeds the earnings threshold, without limit (i.e. without capping).

[5] With contracted-out salary related (COSR) schemes there is an employer's NIC rebate of 3.7% of earnings above the employer's earnings threshold, up to and including the upper earnings limit. With contracted-out money purchase (COMP) schemes there is an employer's NIC rebate of 1.4% of earnings above the employer's earnings threshold, up to and including the upper earnings limit, and a further age-related rebate is paid by the Inland Revenue National Insurance Contributions Office directly to the scheme (see table).

Class 1 secondary (employer) contributions 2006–07[4]	
Earnings/secondary threshold	£97 weekly £420 monthly £5,035 yearly
Rates (not contracted-out)	12.8% above earnings threshold
Rates (contracted-out)[5]	9.3% for salary-related (COSR) and 11.8% for money-purchase (COMP) schemes (including 3.5% and 1% rebates for earnings from LEL to earnings threshold), then 12.8% above UEL.

Notes

(4)   Class 1 contributions are earnings related. Employers must pay secondary Class 1 contributions on that part of an employee's earnings which exceeds the earnings threshold, without limit (i.e. without capping).

(5)   With contracted-out salary related (COSR) schemes there is an employer's NIC rebate of 3.5% of earnings above the employer's earnings threshold, up to and including the upper earnings limit. With contracted-out money purchase (COMP) schemes there is an employer's NIC rebate of 1.0% of earnings above the employer's earnings threshold, up to and including the upper earnings limit, and a further age-related rebate is paid by the Inland Revenue National Insurance Contributions Office directly to the scheme (see table).

Class 1 secondary (employer) contributions 2005–06(4)	
Earnings/secondary threshold	£94 weekly £407 monthly £4,888 yearly
Rates (not contracted-out)	12.8% above earnings threshold
Rates (contracted-out)(5)	9.3% for salary-related (COSR) and 11.8% for money-purchase (COMP) schemes (including 3.5% and 1% rebates for earnings from LEL to earnings threshold), then 12.8% above UEL.

Notes

(4)   Class 1 contributions are earnings related. Employers must pay secondary Class 1 contributions on that part of an employee's earnings which exceeds the earnings threshold, without limit (i.e. without capping).

(5)   With contracted-out salary related (COSR) schemes there is an employer's NIC rebate of 3.5% of earnings above the employer's earnings threshold, up to and including the upper earnings limit. With contracted-out money purchase (COMP) schemes there is an employer's NIC rebate of 1.0% of earnings above the employer's earnings threshold, up to and including the upper earnings limit, and a further age-related rebate is paid by the Inland Revenue National Insurance Contributions Office directly to the scheme (see table).

Class 1 secondary (employer) contributions 2004–05(4)	
Earnings/secondary threshold	£91 weekly £395 monthly £4,732 yearly
Rates (not contracted-out)	12.8% above earnings threshold

Rates (contracted-out)[5]	9.3% for salary-related (COSR) and 11.8% for money-purchase (COMP) schemes (including 3.5% and 1% rebates for earnings from LEL to earnings threshold), then 12.8% above UEL.

Notes

[4] Class 1 contributions are earnings related. Employers must pay secondary Class 1 contributions on that part of an employee's earnings which exceeds the earnings threshold, without limit (i.e. without capping).

[5] With contracted-out salary related (COSR) schemes there is an employer's NIC rebate of 3.5% of earnings above the employer's earnings threshold, up to and including the upper earnings limit. With contracted-out money purchase (COMP) schemes there is an employer's NIC rebate of 1.0% of earnings above the employer's earnings threshold, up to and including the upper earnings limit, and a further age-related rebate is paid by the Inland Revenue National Insurance Contributions Office directly to the scheme (see table).

Class 1 secondary (employer) contributions 2003–04[4]	
Earnings/secondary threshold	£89 weekly £385 monthly £4,615 yearly
Rates (not contracted-out)	12.8% above earnings threshold
Rates (contracted-out)[5]	9.3% for salary-related (COSR) and 11.8% for money-purchase (COMP) schemes (including 3.5% and 1% rebates for earnings from LEL to earnings threshold), then 12.8% above UEL.

Notes

[4] Class 1 contributions are earnings related. Employers must pay secondary Class 1 contributions on that part of an employee's earnings which exceeds the earnings threshold, without limit (i.e. without capping).

[5] With contracted-out salary related (COSR) schemes there is an employer's NIC rebate of 3.5% of earnings above the employer's earnings threshold, up to and including the upper earnings limit. With contracted-out money purchase (COMP) schemes there is an employer's NIC rebate of 1.0% of earnings above the employer's earnings threshold, up to and including the upper earnings limit, and a further age-related rebate is paid by the Inland Revenue National Insurance Contributions Office directly to the scheme (see table).

Flat-rate rebate Class 1 contracted-out rebates 2002–03 to 2009–10

	COSR (salary related) %	COMP (money purchase) %
Employees	1.6	1.6
Employers	3.7	1.4 + age-related percentage

Class 1A contributions

From 6 April 2000, employers (but not employees) pay NICs on an annual basis on benefits in kind provided to employees earning at the rate of £8,500 p.a. or more or to directors. The Class 1A rate for 2009–10 is 12.8 per cent. Contributions for the year 2008–09 are due on 19 July 2009.

From 5 April 1991 to 5 April 2000, employers (but not employees) paid NICs on an annual basis on cars or fuel provided for the private use of employees earning at the rate of £8,500 p.a. or more or for directors. The liability is calculated on the income tax car and fuel scale rates.

Rate of Class 1B contributions

From 6 April 1999 Class 1B contributions are payable by employers on the amount of emoluments in a PAYE settlement agreement (PSA) which are chargeable to Class 1 or Class 1A NICs, together with the total amount of income tax payable under the agreement. Class 1B contributions are charged at a rate equal to the secondary rate of NICs (12.8 per cent in 2009–10), with power for the Secretary of State to alter the rate by statutory instrument; but not so as to increase it to more than two per cent above the rate applicable at the end of the preceding year.

Class 2 contributions

Rates and SEE limit

Tax year	Weekly contribution rate			Small earnings exceptional limit £
	Rate £	Share fishermen £	Volunteer development workers £	
2010–11	2.40	3.05	4.75	5,075
2009–10	2.40	3.05	4.75	5,075
2008–09	2.30	2.95	4.50	4,825
2007–08	2.20	2.85	4.35	4,635
2006–07	2.10	2.75	4.20	4,465
2005–06	2.10	2.75	4.10	4,345
2004–05	2.05	2.70	3.95	4,215

Class 3 contributions

Class 3 contributions are paid voluntarily by persons not liable for contributions, or who have been excepted from Class 2 contributions, or whose contribution record is insufficient to qualify for benefits. They are paid at a flat rate.

Rate and earnings factor

Tax year	Weekly contribution rate £
2010–11	12.05
2009–10	12.05
2008–09	8.10
2007–08	7.80
2006–07	7.55
2005–06	7.35
2004–05	7.15
2003–04	6.95
2002–03	6.85
2001–02	6.75

Class 4 contributions

Self-employed people whose profits or gains are over a certain amount have to pay Class 4 contributions as well as Class 2 contributions.

Percentage rate and earnings limits

Tax year	Percentage rate %	Annual lower earnings limit £	Annual upper earnings limit £	Maximum contribution £
2010–11	8	5,715	43,875	(1)
2009–10	8	5,715	43,875	(1)
2008–09	8	5,435	40,040	(1)
2007–08	8	5,225	34,840	(1)
2006–07	8	5,035	33,540	(1)
2005–06	8	4,895	32,760	(1)
2004–05	8	4,745	31,720	(1)
2003–04	8	4,615	30,940	(1)

(1) Contributions are payable at the rate of one per cent on profits above the upper earnings level.

Law: SSCBA 1992, Sch. 1, para. 6(2) and (3)

INDIRECT TAXES

1-880   Insurance premium tax

Rate

Imposed on certain insurance premiums where the risk is located in the UK (FA 1994, Pt. III).

Period of application	Standard rate %	Higher rate %
From 1 July 1999	5	17.5
1 April 1997 to 30 June 1999	4	17.5
1 October 1994 to 31 March 1997	2.5	n/a

Note

[1] From 1 August 1998, the higher rate applies to all travel insurance.

Interest payable on certain assessments

Since 6 Februaury 1996, interest on insurance premium tax is charged at the same rate as under VATA 1994, s. 74.

1-900   Landfill tax

Landfill tax was introduced on 1 October 1996 and is collected from landfill site operators (FA 1996, Pt. III).

Exemption applies to mining and quarrying waste, dredging waste, pet cemeteries and waste from the reclamation of contaminated land.

From 1 October 1999, exemption applies to inert waste used in restoring licensed landfill sites, including the progressive backfilling of active mineral workings.

Type of waste	Rate (per tonne) £
Inactive waste	
From 1 April 2008	2.50
To 31 March 2008	2.00
Active waste:	
From 1 April 2010	48
From 1 April 2009	40
From 1 April 2008	32
1 April 2007 to March 2008	24
1 April 2006 to 31 March 2007	21
1 April 2005 to 31 March 2006	18
1 April 2004 to 31 March 2005	15

Key Data

Type of waste	Rate (per tonne) £
1 April 2003 to 31 March 2004	14
1 April 2002 to 31 March 2003	13
1 April 2001 to 31 March 2002	12
1 April 2000 to 31 March 2001	11
1 April 1999 to 31 March 2000	10
1 October 1996 to 31 March 1999	7

The lower rate of tax, which applies to land filled with inactive or inert wastes listed in the *Landfill Tax (Qualifying Material) Order* 1996 (SI 1996/1528), is £2.00 per tonne.

Interest payable on underdeclared landfill tax (FA 1996, Sch. 5, para. 26)

Since 1 April 1997, interest on landfill tax is charged at the same rate as under VATA 1994, s. 74.

Environmental trusts

Site operators making payments to environmental trusts set up for approved environmental purposes can claim a tax credit up to 90 per cent of their contribution – subject to a maximum of 20 per cent of their landfill tax bill in a 12-month period. From 1 August 1999, operators using the scheme have up to an additional month every quarter to claim tax credits. On 15 October 1996, Customs approved an independent body, ENTRUST, as the regulator of environmental trusts. It is responsible for enrolling environmental bodies, maintaining their operation and ensuring that all expenditure complies with the landfill tax requirements.

1-920   Aggregates levy

Rate

Period of application	Rate (per tonne) £
From 1 April 2008	1.95
1/4/02–31/3/08	1.60

There is no registration threshold for aggregates levy. Any person who commercially exploits aggregate in the UK after 31 March 2002 may be liable to register with Customs and account for aggregates levy (FA 2001, Sch. 4 and the *Aggregates Levy (Registration and Miscellaneous Provisions) Regulations* 2001 (SI 2001/4027), reg. 2).

Generally, 'aggregate' means any rock, gravel or sand together with any other substances which are for the time being incorporated in or naturally occurring with it.

'Commercially exploited' generally means in the course or furtherance of a business the earliest of (FA 2001, s. 16):

- removal from:
  - the originating site;
  - a connected site that is registered under the same name as the originating site; or
  - a site where it had been intended to apply an exempt process to it, but this process was not applied;

- agreement to supply to another person;
- use for construction purchases; and
- mixing with any material or substance other than water, except in permitted circumstances.

Interest payable on underdeclared aggregates levy (FA 2001, Sch. 5, para. 5ff.)

Since 1 April 2002, interest on aggregates levy is charged at the same rate as under VATA 1994, s. 74.

Income Tax

Self-employed users of mileage rates	141
Where does work start from?	141
Opening-year rules	142
Director but not an employee	142
IR35	143
Jury service	143
Directors' PAYE timings	144
Salary sacrifice training costs	145
Long service awards	145
Annual bash	146
Feeding your staff	146
Staff suggestions	147
Moving expenses	147
Overnight reimbursements	148
Overseas expenses	149
Ancillary accommodation expenses in exempt accommodation	149
Living accommodation	150
Air miles	151
Employee shares at undervalue	152
Convertible securities	152
Forced-value employee shares	153
Withdrawing share options	153
Qualifying EMI options to the maximum	154
Save as you earn	154
Enterprise management incentive	154
A caring employer	155
How much do you earn?	155
Recharged motoring costs	156
Cost allocation	156
Cost to employer	157
Part-time employee, full-time wife	157
Private computer use	157
Employee assets with costs	158
Employee assets transferred	158
Building the MD a home	159
Asset or accommodation?	159
Van benefits	160
Capital contribution towards use of a van	161
Is it a car? Is it a van? No, it's a horsebox!	162
Is there a benefit charge on a classic car?	162
Private use while on call	163

Income Tax

Normal commuting is private use	163
Company car prices	164
Private number plates	164
Pool cars	165
Leased cars	165
Company cars	166
Expensive cars	167
Company fuel	167
Company cars and petrol with repayments	168
Mileage allowances	168
Mileage allowances and self-employment	169
Double mileage rates	170
Overstated mileage claims	170
Beneficial loan interest	171
No such thing as free shares	171
Beneficial loans	172
Lending money to the family	173
Nursery care or family baby sitting?	174
Stockpiling childcare vouchers whilst on maternity leave	174
Childcare vouchers	175
Sacrifice for a phone	176
Termination payments after the termination	176
Group termination	176
Termination in kind	177
Goods taken for own use	177
Change of accounting dates	178
Partnership losses with profits	178
Partnership profit shares	179
Partnership interest	180
Partnership agreements	180
Partner rents to the partnership	181
Limited liability partnership losses	182
Patent royalties and gift aid	182
Payroll giving	183
Sports clubs	183
Farming: relief for fluctuating profits	184
Farmers averaging	184
Herd basis	185
Taxing a trust	185
Discretionary trust tax	186
Trust income	187
IIP trust income	188
Life interest income	189
Administration of estates	189
Income from an estate	190
Capital and income to the settlor	191

Settlor interested loans   191
School fees from trust income   191
Renting in two capacities   192
Furnished holiday lettings and capital allowances   193
Rent a room relief   193
How much of the premium is really rent?   194
Non-resident landlord   194
Chargeable events on death   194
Working overseas   195
Tax credits: method of calculating income   196
Tax credits   197
Married couple's allowance and wealthy pensioners   199
Foster care   200
Loan interest   201
Loan to my company   202
Employee control   202
Enterprise Investment Scheme relief   203
Less than maximum EIS relief   203
Trivial pensions   204
The effect of pensions   204
Annual allowance   205
Crystallisation events   206
Allowable continuing professional development?   206
Employer debit cards   207
Dealing with allowable expenses   207
Where do you work?   208
Taxi fares home   208
Meal vouchers   209
That's entertainment   209
A lecturer's suit   210
Excess pension contributions   210
Paying too much in pension contributions   211
Paying pension contributions whilst working abroad   211
Defending reputation   212
Lease premium   213
Pre-trade learning   213
Business equipment   214
Incorporation losses   214
Opening year losses   215
Temporary extension of loss carry-back rules   216
Terminal losses   217
Post-cessation expenses   218
Capital allowances introduction   218
When did you buy it?   219
When is an animal a plant?   220
Can I claim for my stolen van?   220

Income Tax

Effect of making a short-life asset election	221
The general pool	223
Writing down allowances	223
Flat conversion allowance	224
Renovating business premises	224
BPRA on retirement	224
PAYE settlement agreements	225
PAYE settlement agreement for all employees	225
Date of repayment for loss carry back	226
Pension PAYE effects	227
Notice of coding	227
Annual investment allowance	228
Sharing the annual investment allowance	228
Capital allowances on commercial investment properties	229
Capital allowances and property letting businesses	230
Capital allowances on prizes	230
Am I a non-dom?	231
Overseas employment and benefits in kind	231
Non-residents' living accommodation	232
Is death a reasonable excuse for non-payment?	233
Abolition of the starting rate	233
Does the business come under the CIS?	234
Using the remittance basis	235
Bad debts	236
How is the car scrappage scheme dealt with for tax?	237
SMP paid to foreign workers	237
Mixing up UK and foreign income	238
Compensation could be damaging	239

INCOME TAX

10-000 Self-employed users of mileage rates

> **Q.** As a sole trader I have been using the HMRC statutory mileage rates claiming 40p per mile for the first 10,000 business miles and 25p per mile thereafter. I am aware that I can only do this for as long as my turnover is below the VAT registration threshold. I have had a very successful year and will now have to register for VAT. How do I account for the transition to actual costs?

A. As the use of the statutory mileage rate is a measure to make claiming easier for the taxpayer the transition is also made easy. You are obliged to continue using the scheme until you change your car. At that point, and not until then, you measure your turnover and if you exceed the VAT threshold you will have to use the detailed 'expenditure' method of calculation. This may mean that you will continue to use the scheme for several years after you have exceeded the VAT registration threshold.

See *British Master Tax Guide* 61.

10-010 Where does work start from?

> **Q.** Our client is a self-employed taxi driver. Every morning he drives his cab to the taxi rank where he starts his day's trading. He has told us that other drivers who work from that rank claim the travel from home to the rank as an allowable expense. He writes up his books at home, and that is where he keeps all his records. Can we claim the home to rank travel as an allowable expense?

A. It is very unlikely that the cost will be allowable. The travel will be treated as home to work. The fact that he does some minor bookkeeping and administrative activities at home will not stop the rank being where his trading activities start.

There is a case where the facts are similar to the claim your client is trying to make. In the case of *Jackman v Powell*, Mr Powell was a self-employed milkman who tried to claim the cost of travel from his home to the milk depot. He claimed he ran his business from his home, as that was where he carried out the administration, but the nature of his trade was that he had to travel to his customers. In the High Court it was decided that his place of work was the roads where he made his deliveries and that travelling to the place he started his trading activities was not in the course of his business.

See *British Master Tax Guide* 1994.

10-020 Opening-year rules

Example

A business commences on 1 May 2010 and the first accounts are prepared to 31 March 2011.

Tax year	Accounts period	Period taxed
2010–11	1/5/10–31/3/11	1/5/10–31/3/11
2011–12	1/4/11–31/3/12	1/4/11–31/3/12
2012–13	1/4/12–31/3/13	1/4/12–31/3/13
2013–14	1/4/13–31/3/14	1/4/13–31/3/14

A business commences on 1 January 2010 and the first accounts are prepared to 31 December 2010.

Tax year	Accounts period	Period taxed
2009–10	1/1/10–31/12/10	1/1/10–5/4/10
2010–11	1/1/10–31/12/10	1/1/10–31/12/10
2011–12	1/1/11–31/12/11	1/1/11–31/12/11
2012–13	1/1/12–31/12/12	1/1/12–31/12/12
2013–14	1/1/13–31/12/13	1/1/13–31/12/13

Overlap profits are created from 1 January 2010 to 5 April 2010.

See *British Master Tax Guide* 183.

Law: ITTOIA 2005, s. 198–202

10-040 Director but not an employee

> **Q.** I have been offered the position of a non-executive director in a company with which I have business dealings. I am a self-employed consultant and would like the fees in respect of this position to be received as part of my business income. However, the company is advising me that PAYE will be applied to the fees. Do I have a choice in this matter?

A. Unfortunately not. Before 2003, there was doubt over whether PAYE applied in these cases as not all office holders were employees. The tax legislation was changed with effect from 6 April 2003 which made it clear that an office is treated in the same way as an employment. Therefore, PAYE must be applied to fees in respect of this office.

There is a concessionary treatment under Extra-statutory Concession A37 whereby, subject to various conditions being met, members of professional partnerships or companies can hold offices with the income being treated as part of the partnership/company business for tax purposes.

It is possible that in addition to the duties of the office, you are providing additional, separate services as a business consultant. In such a case the fees for these services should be invoiced from your business in the normal way. However, HMRC reserve the right to challenge the commerciality of the arrangements and so it is recommended that some formality is given to these. For example, the preparation of a company minute appointing you as non-executive director, stipulating your duties and the fee payable. Similarly, you should enter into a separate contract with the company as regards the consultancy services you are providing. Providing these arrangements are on arm's length terms, there is less risk of HMRC challenging them.

See *British Master Tax Guide* 250.

Law: ITEPA 2003, s. 5

10-060   IR35

Example

Rob provides computer consultancy services to Network Services Ltd via his personal services company, Rob Computing Ltd. The contract is between Network Services Ltd and Rob Computing Ltd and covers a 12-month period from 1 October 2010. Rob performs the work at the premises of Network Services Ltd, using their equipment and working the hours specified by them. Had the contract been between Rob and Network Services Ltd, Rob would have been an employee of Network Services Ltd.

The engagement is a relevant engagement as it meets all the necessary conditions. Rob performs the services personally for the client, Network Services Ltd. The services are provided under a contract between the client (Network Services Ltd) and the intermediary (Rob Computing Ltd) and the circumstances are such that had the contract been between Rob (the worker) and Network Services Ltd (the client), Rob would be viewed as an employee of Network Services Ltd.

See *British Master Tax Guide* 265.

10-080   Jury service

> **Q.**   What should we pay employees who are on jury service?

A.   There is no statutory entitlement for an employee to be paid by his employer during jury service. However, if the contract of employment has a clause covering such a situation, the employer must follow the terms of the contract.

Whilst on jury service, the employee is entitled to claim allowances from the court to cover travel and subsistence costs. In addition, a financial loss allowance may be claimed in respect of any loss of net earnings suffered as a result of attending the court.

The maximum financial loss allowance depends upon the number of hours served. These amounts are reviewed annually and at the time of writing are:

for up to 4 hours   £32.47 per day
for over 4 hours   £64.95 per day

If the juror serves more than ten days, the allowances effectively double from the eleventh day onwards, to £64.95 and £129.91 respectively.

The employer must fill in a Certificate of Loss of Earnings (supplied by the court), which includes information on whether or not the employee may return to work on the days or half-days that they are not required at court. The form asks the employer to report the net loss suffered by the employee. This net loss is the amount, which the court will then pay, subject to the limits above.

See *British Master Tax Guide* 1990.

10-100   Directors' PAYE timings

> **Q.**   The directors of a small company have not drawn any salary since the company was formed two years ago. A bonus was voted last March, but the directors chose not to draw the cash until this tax year. However as the amount is being paid within nine months of the end of the accounting period, it is shown in the previous year's accounts for corporation tax. In completing forms P46 for PAYE purposes, what should we put as the date the employment started?

A.   The date the employment started would have been the date they were appointed as directors, but that is not the important issue here. The question suggests that the bonus is about to be charged to PAYE but in the circumstances it appears that this should have been done last year.

In general, earnings are treated as received at the earliest of the following times:

- when payment is made of or on account of the earnings;
- when the person becomes entitled to payment of or on account of the earnings.

Unless there was any stipulation made at the time of voting, it would seem that the directors became entitled to be paid on the date of voting, they simply chose not to take the money.

However even if there was a stipulation restricting the availability of the bonus, for directors only, there are further rules which determine that earnings are treated as received at the earliest of the following times:

- when the amount is credited in the company accounts or records;
- if the amount of the earnings for a period is determined before the end of that period, the time when the period ends;
- if the amount of the earnings for a period is not determined until after the period has ended, the time when the amount is determined.

Using these rules it is clear that the bonus has been attributed to the previous year and consequently PAYE should already have been operated.

See *British Master Tax Guide* 274.

Law: ITEPA 2003, s. 62

10-120 Salary sacrifice training costs

> **Q.** I am proposing to undertake further education to gain a professional qualification relating to my work. As this is relevant to my employment I understand that my employer could meet the cost without any tax or National Insurance being due. Although my employer is not willing to stand the cost of the training, I understand that a salary sacrifice arrangement can be made to effectively pay the cost out of my existing salary and still obtain exemption from tax and NIC?

A. An exemption from a taxable benefit or National Insurance liability arises on the cost of employment-related training where this is either paid for directly by the employer or reimbursed to the employee. A salary sacrifice must be an actual contractual reduction to annual salary for a minimum period of one year, with no right to surrender the benefit in return for a reinstatement of salary. HMRC may question the validity of an arrangement where on completion of the training mid-year the salary is partially or fully restored to its pre-benefit level. It is important, therefore, that any such salary revision takes place on the normal pay review anniversary.

See *British Master Tax Guide* 279.

Law: ITEPA 2003, s. 119

10-140 Long service awards

Example

Joanna has worked for the same company for 25 years and it is decided to make a presentation to her.

The office manager recalls that five years previously, after 20 years of service, Joanna had already had an award. Drinks were offered at that earlier time to all staff in the office, a speech was made by the boss and Joanna was given some cosmetics worth £100.

Although 25 years at £50 per year would give an allowable value of £1,250, no tax-free award can be made at the 25-year stage as a previous award has already been made within the past 10 years.

See *British Master Tax Guide* 285.

Law: ITEPA 2003, s. 323

10-160   Annual bash

Example

An employer organises a summer dance for which the VAT-inclusive costs are as follows:

	£
Caterers	2,000
Drink	1,400
Public speaker	250
Accommodation for speaker	100
Total	3,750

Those attending the function are directors and employees (30 people), spouses, civil partners, boyfriends, girlfriends (25) and the speaker (1). As such, there are 56 people attending and the total cost is £67 per person (£3,750/56) which is well below the £150 per person limit.

See *British Master Tax Guide* 285.

Law: ITEPA 2003, s. 264

10-170   Feeding your staff

> **Q.** We sometimes ask a group of employees to stay on after work for a meeting. As this often means they will effectively be working late, we provide them with pizza. I have been told that this is going to create a benefit in kind on the employees. Is this correct?

A. Meals provided to employees will create a benefit in kind unless their provision is covered by ITEPA 2003, s. 317. The exemption provides that where free or subsidised meals are provided by the employer, on the employer's business premises, no income tax is charged in the following circumstances:

- the meals are provided on a reasonable scale: *and* **either**
- all employees may obtain free or subsidised meals on a reasonable scale, whether on the employer's premises or elsewhere, **or**

- the employer provides free or subsidised meal vouchers for staff for whom meals are not provided.

As the provision of pizzas to a group of employees is not covered by the exemption, a benefit in kind will arise based on the cost to the employer divided by the number of employees for whom pizza was provided.

Where the employer does not wish the employees to incur a tax charge they can enter into a PAYE settlement agreement (PSA) to meet the charge on the employees' behalf.

See *British Master Tax Guide* 412.

10-180   Staff suggestions

Example

Pete's employer sends large numbers of parcels abroad. Pete, who works in the post room, makes a suggestion that leads to a reduction in postage costs. His employer implements the suggestion and calculates that there will be a saving of around £3,000 per year. The employer can make an award of £1,500 tax-free and does so.

In actuality the reduction in postage costs is much larger than anticipated. The annual saving proves to be in the region of £12,000. As such, two years after the first award was made to Pete, he is paid a further £4,500.

The annual saving of £12,000 means that the financial benefit share is £6,000. However, the maximum tax-free award is capped at £5,000. As such, Pete can receive a further £3,500 tax-free but the last £1,000 is taxable.

See *British Master Tax Guide* 285.

Law: ITEPA 2003, s. 321

10-200   Moving expenses

Example

Ron starts a new job in Marlow and relocates from Coventry. His new employer meets the cost of the move as follows:

	£
Estate agent's fees	4,000
Legal fees	750
Stamp duty land tax	9,000
Removal fees	2,000
Total	15,750

As the eligible removal expenses and benefits are more than £8,000, the excess over £8,000 of £7,750 remains taxable and must be reported on the P11D.

See *British Master Tax Guide* 298.

Law: ITEPA 2003, Pt. 4, Ch. 7

10-220 Overnight reimbursements

Example

Tom is required to work away on business. He is away for five nights. He spends the first and last night in the UK, the remainder in France. His employer reimburses expenses as follows:

Night	Amount reimbursed £
1	6
2	9
3	12
4	8
5	4
Total	39

The permitted amount for the trip is £5 for each of the two nights spent in the UK and £10 for each of the three nights spent overseas. This gives a permitted amount for the trip of £40. The amount reimbursed for the trip was £39. The full amount is exempt. It does not matter that the limit was exceeded on two nights of the trip as the total for the trip fell within the permitted amount.

See *British Master Tax Guide* 302.

Law: ITEPA 2003, s. 240

10-230   Overseas expenses

> **Q.**   We regularly second employees overseas. Are there any agreed rates of allowances in respect of accommodation and subsistence?

A.   For travel within the UK, employers are able to apply for a specific dispensation based on a sample of actual expenditure incurred by employees. However, this is usually not possible for overseas travel because very few employers will have sufficient overseas employees to provide a meaningful sample.

HMRC agreed in January 2008 that employers may use the benchmark rates published by the Foreign and Commonwealth Office (FCO) when paying accommodation and subsistence expenses to employees whose duties require them to travel abroad, without the need for the employees to produce expenses receipts. However, the FCO subsequently advised HMRC that they had stopped producing worldwide subsistence rates tables because they no longer use these rates for their own staff. This means that the FCO rates can no longer be used by HMRC for the purposes of updating the benchmark rates published on its website. HMRC are in the process of reviewing the policy of providing benchmark rates for overseas subsistence rates and a further announcement will be made as soon as a decision is made. In the meantime, employers can continue to use the rates in the current version on its website until the end of the 2010–11 tax year (see the HMRC *Employment Income Manual* at EIM05250. Further details can be found on the HMRC website.

Accommodation and subsistence payments at or below the published rates will not be liable for income tax or National Insurance contributions for employees who travel abroad, and employers need not include them on forms P11D. However, if an employer decides to pay less than the published rates, its employees are not automatically entitled to tax relief for the shortfall. They can only obtain relief under the employee travel rules based on their actual, receipted expenses, less any amounts paid by the employer.

See *British Master Tax Guide* 1994.

Other guidance: http://www.hmrc.gov.uk/employers/emp-income-scale-rates.htm

10-240   Ancillary accommodation expenses in exempt accommodation

Example

Richard is a village policeman who lives in a police house in order to perform the duties of his employment better. The provision of the accommodation is exempt from tax. Richard incurs expenses on heat and light, cleaning and maintenance, as follows. His net earnings from the employment are £20,000 for the tax year in question.

	£
Heat and light	2,000
Cleaning	700
Maintenance	1,500
Total	4,200

The expenses are exempt from tax to the extent that they exceed 10% of Richard's earnings (£2,000).

In this case, Richard will be taxed on £2,000 of ancillary costs but not on the remaining £2,200.

See *British Master Tax Guide* 314, 398.

Law: ITEPA 2003, s. 99, 314–315

10-260   Living accommodation

Example 1

Basic charge
Michael occupies a flat owned by his employer. The flat cost £60,000 two years before the start of the tax year. The employer paid £5,000 on improvements. The gross rateable value is £800.

None of the special exemptions apply to Michael. He pays £50 per month as a nominal rent for the property but provides his own furniture and pays for all utilities himself.

	£
Rateable value	800
Deduct Michael's contributions	(600)
Taxable benefit	200

Example 2

Expensive property
Nigel is director of Nigel Enterprises Ltd. The company pays £410,000 for a property but Nigel personally contributes £10,000 towards the cost. The rateable value is £900. The official rate of interest on the first day of the tax year was 6.25%. Nigel pays the market rent of £1,000 per month and meets all his own bills.

	£
Rateable value	900
Additional benefit	
Cost, net of contribution	
400,000 − 75,000 × 6.25%	20,315
Calculated benefit	21,215
Less: rent paid	(12,000)
Taxable benefit	9,215

Example 3

Ancillary costs

Maria's employer bought a property three years ago for £150,000 and has spent £20,000 on improvements. The employer pays £500 to insure the property, £200 to insure the contents (all of which are owned by Maria) and half of the £1,600 fuel bills in the year. The rateable value is £1,200. The official rate of interest on the first day of the tax year was 6.25%. Maria is not within any of the exemptions. She pays £250 per month in rent.

	£
Rateable value	1,200
Additional benefit	
(150,000 + 20,000 − 75,000) × 6.25%	5,937
Less: contribution	(3,000)
	4,137
Property insurance	Nil
Contents insurance	200
Fuel	800
Total benefit	5,137

See *British Master Tax Guide* 314, 398.

Law: ITEPA 2003, s. 99–100, 314–315

10-280   Air miles

> **Q.**   Our sales staff are provided with a company credit card to meet the cost of fuel, etc. while travelling on business. They receive air miles from the credit card issuer relating to the use of these cards. Is this a taxable benefit of their employment?

A.   No, provided that the reward is received directly by the employee rather than via the employer, and the employee is the named card holder.

See *British Master Tax Guide* 318.

Law: ITEPA 2003, Pt. 3, Ch. 4

10-300   Employee shares at undervalue

Example

David acquires 100 shares for £1 each. At the date of acquisition, the market value of each fully paid-up share is £10. The market value of each partly-paid share is £4.

The difference between the value of the partly-paid shares and the amount paid for them is taxable under the general earnings rules. The balance of the underpayment is taxable as an interest-free loan.

In this case, therefore, David pays tax on £300 under the general rules and is also deemed to have received an interest-free loan from his employer of £600. The £5,000 de minimis exemption is still available if it is not used elsewhere.

See *British Master Tax Guide* 323.

Law: ITEPA 2003, s. 471–487

10-320   Convertible securities

Example

Helen acquires £500 of convertible loan stock from her employer with interest of 5%. The loan stock can be converted into 500 ordinary shares of £1 each after five years. At the time of acquisition, the shares have a market value of £2 per share and at the time of the conversion they have a market value of £4 per share. At the time of acquisition of the loan stock it is valued at £550 – £500 for the loan stock and £50 for the right to convert.

At acquisition, there is a tax charge based on the value of the loan stock, ignoring the right to convert, i.e. £500.

A further tax charge arises at the time of conversion. The loan stock, ignoring the right to convert, remains valued at £500. The market value of the shares is £2,000 (500 × £4 per share) less £500 (the value of the loan stock), i.e. £1,500. There is no deduction for the conversion rights of £50 as this was not charged to tax on acquisition.

See *British Master Tax Guide* 323.

10-340   Forced-value employee shares

Example

Karen is given 100 shares by virtue of her employment. As a result of things done by the company that were not for a 'genuine commercial purpose', the market value of the shares is £2 per share. Had these things not been done, the market value would be £3.50 per share.

A tax charge arises on acquisition of £150 (100 × (£3.50 − £2.00)).

A sum of £150 is treated as employment income for the year in which Karen acquires the shares.

See *British Master Tax Guide* 323, 329.

10-360   Withdrawing share options

Example

James, Henry and Rebecca are each awarded 100 free shares in the company which employs them. The shares are awarded on 1 December 2004, when the market value is £2.75 per share. James withdraws 50 shares from the plan on 1 January 2006 when the market value is £4.50 and Rebecca withdraws all of her shares on 1 November 2008 when the market value is £4.00. Henry leaves his shares in the plan until 1 May 2010, withdrawing them all on that date when the market value is £6.23.

As James withdraws 50 shares in the first three years, a tax charge arises based on the market value on 1 January 2006 of £4.50, the date on which the shares cease to be subject to the plan. He is thus taxed on £225 (50 × £4.50).

Rebecca withdraws her 100 shares between three and five years after the date of the award. The tax charge is based on the lower of £2.75 (the market value on 1 December 2004 when the shares are awarded) and £4.00 (the market value on 1 November 2008 when the shares cease to be subject to the plan).

Rebecca is thus taxed on £275 (£2.75 × 100).

As Henry does not withdraw his shares until five years have elapsed, no tax charge arises on withdrawal.

See *British Master Tax Guide* 329.

10-380   Qualifying EMI options to the maximum

Example

Natalie has unexercised options over shares in the company for which she works of £110,000. She is granted options over a further 150 shares. The new options have a value of £15,000. The first £10,000 of options in respect of the first 100 shares are qualifying options, taking her to the £120,000 limit. The options over the remaining 50 shares valued at £5,000 are not qualifying options, as they exceed the limit.

Where an employee has already been granted qualifying options with one company by reason of his or her employment with a total value of £120,000, any further option granted by reason of the employee's employment with that company, or if it is a member of the group of companies, with a group company, within the three-year restriction period cannot be a qualifying option. Likewise where an employee has been granted options with a total value of £120,000 with two or more companies of the same group, any further options granted by reason of the employee's employment with any member of the group within the three-year restriction period are not qualifying options. For the purposes of this restriction, it does not matter whether the qualifying options have been exercised or released.

See *British Master Tax Guide* 335.

10-400   Save as you earn

Example

Lilly participates in an approved SAYE share option scheme, entering into a five-year contract.

The scheme is an approved scheme and Lilly exercises the option when the contract finishes at year five. The conditions for exemption are met, so no tax charge arises on exercise.

However, from 18 June 2004, the exemption on exercise is only available if the avoidance of tax and National Insurance is not the main purpose or one of the main purposes of the arrangements under which the option was granted or exercised.

See *British Master Tax Guide* 330.

Law: ITEPA 2003, Sch. 3, 4

10-420   Enterprise management incentive

Example

Finn is granted a qualifying enterprise management incentive (EMI) option to buy 100 shares at £2 a share. At the time that the option is granted, the market value of the shares is

£3 per share. The options are exercised four years after grant at a time when the market value of the shares is £5 per share.

The charge on exercise is the difference between the market value at grant and the option price minus any amount paid on grant.

In this case the difference is £1 per share (£3 − £2) and so a charge of £100 will be made.

See *British Master Tax Guide* 335.

Law: ITEPA 2003, s. 527–531

10-440 A caring employer

> **Q.** I wish to pay for my employees' costs for periodic health checks. Is this taxable in the hands of my employees?

A. A statutory exemption for medical check-ups and health screening has existed since April 2007 giving statutory force to earlier practice, but imposing stricter conditions. The exemption applies to one health screening and one medical check-up per employee, per year. If the payments are in respect of members of the employee's household or family, and these members are not your employees, such payments would be taxable in the hands of your employee.

See *British Master Tax Guide* 382.

Law: ITEPA 2003, s. 70–72

10-460 How much do you earn?

Example

In year 2, an employee receives £7,000 as remuneration for his work in year 2. He also receives £2,000 as further remuneration for work he did in year 1. In year 3, he receives a further £1,000 for work done during year 2. For the purposes of the £8,500 test, his remuneration for year 2 is £8,000, even though he received £9,000 in the year. In this example, he would not be a P11D employee in year 2.

See *British Master Tax Guide* 382.

Law: ITEPA 2003, s. 70–72; *Income Tax (Exemption of Minor Benefits) (Amendment) Regulations* 2007 (SI 2007/2090)

155

10-480   Recharged motoring costs

> **Q.**   Barry has been reimbursing some of his employees for their daily costs incurred for parking and for congestion charges. Should these reimbursements have been put through the payroll and treated as earnings for PAYE and National Insurance as they are effectively meeting the employees' pecuniary liability?

A.   No liability to income tax arises in respect of the provision of workplace parking for an employee. This covers parking at or near the employee's place of work and is allowable for tax whether the cost is met directly by the employer or reimbursed to the employee.

The treatment of costs incurred as a result of congestion charging is dependent on the circumstances under which they were incurred. If they were incurred during the employee's ordinary commuting journey from home to work then this would indeed be meeting the employee's pecuniary liability and the reimbursement would be subject to PAYE and Class 1 NIC. However, reimbursement of congestion charges could be made tax- and NIC-free if they were incurred in the performance of business journeys.

See *British Master Tax Guide* 383.

Law: ITEPA 2003, s. 237

10-500   Cost allocation

Example

A company takes out a group private medical insurance policy to cover all of its 20 employees.

The cost of the policy is £8,260 p.a. The insurer does not provide a premium breakdown on an employee-by-employee basis. Employees make no contribution towards the cost.

To arrive at the cost per employee, the premium must be apportioned on a just and reasonable basis. A simple apportionment would be to divide the total premium by the number of employees covered. If this method were adopted, the cash equivalent of the benefit taxable on each P11D employee or director is £413 (£8,260 divided by 20 employees). It does not matter that some of the employees may be P9D employees.

See *British Master Tax Guide* 388.

Law: ITEPA 2003, s. 204

10-520   Cost to employer

Example

Julie is a hairdresser. One of her colleagues cuts her hair between clients. The colleague is paid a salary, irrespective of the number of clients she sees, and receives no extra money for cutting Julie's hair. The benefit is an in-house benefit and the marginal cost is zero. Thus the cost to the employer (and thus the taxable benefit) of providing the benefit is zero.

See *British Master Tax Guide* 388.

10-540   Part-time employee, full-time wife

Q.   Kate is the owner/director of her own business. She has a company car provided by the business and her husband also has a company car from the business. He helps out in the business for a couple of days per week but is paid below the earnings threshold. Am I right in assuming that there is no benefit to declare for the husband as he is a P9D employee (earning at the rate of less than £8,500 p.a.)?

A.   Under normal circumstances it would be true that there is no benefit to return in respect of a company car for a P9D employee. However, because of the husband and wife relationship it is unlikely that HMRC will take the view that the benefit is received purely in respect of the husband's employment. Is it likely that another part-time employee working two days per week in the business would be provided with a company car?

HMRC are likely to view the benefit as arising from the wife's employment and the benefit would therefore be taxable on his employment and returned on his P11D.

See *British Master Tax Guide* 394, 442.

10-560   Private computer use

Example

John has his own family company. The company buys computer equipment for £2,000 and it is used solely by John's teenage daughter for her schoolwork. Three years later, the daughter is going to university and John's company therefore buys a more modern laptop for her to use. The original computer is worth £100 and John pays that figure to buy it out of the company for use by a younger child.

Assuming that there are no incidental costs, the benefit on the use of the first computer will be calculated as £400 per year (£2,000 × 20%). This may, however, be exempt from tax by virtue of the home computer initiative rules if the computer was first provided for private use before 6 April 2006.

Income Tax

There will be no tax charge on the transfer of ownership of the computer if John pays the market value of £100.

See *British Master Tax Guide* 394, 396.

Law: ITEPA 2003, s. 206, 320

10-580 Employee assets with costs

Example

Bev is a director of her own family company. The company owns an antique bookcase which Bev keeps at her home. The market value of the bookcase is agreed as £1,000. In the year in question £300 was paid by the company to treat the bookcase for woodworm and to restore it generally.

The taxable benefit will be £500 (£1,000 @ 20% plus £300). Assuming no repairs are undertaken in the following year, the taxable benefit will revert to £200.

See *British Master Tax Guide* 396.

Law: ITEPA 2003, s. 203–207

10-600 Employee assets transferred

Example

A business buys a video camera, initially purely for work purposes, at a cost of £3,000 in January 2009. The project for which the camera was used is finished by the end of 2009 and so, from 1 January 2010, the camera is used for private purposes by employee A. The market value of the camera at 1 January 2010 is £2,000. Employee A uses the camera for private purposes for exactly one year and therefore pays tax on £400 (£2,000 × 20%). The market value at 1 January 2011 is £1,250 and at this date the employer gives the camera to employee B.

In accordance with these special rules, the taxable benefit on B is £1,600, calculated as £2,000 (the market value when the asset was first used as a benefit in kind) less £400 (the cost already taken into account as a benefit in kind). The market value of £1,250 at 1 January 2011 is ignored as this is less than the figure of £1,600.

If, however, the value at 1 January 2011 was £1,800 then this figure would be used and the figure of £1,600 would be ignored.

See *British Master Tax Guide* 396.

Law: ITEPA 2003, s. 203–207

10-620   Building the MD a home

> **Q.**   A property developing company, a close company, is completing a development and the managing director would like to take one of the houses for his own home. What will be the value of the benefit for his P11D?

A.   The general rule is that the value for tax purposes of a benefit or facility provided for an employee, or the employee's family is the expense incurred by the employing company, less the amount made good by the employee.

However, there is an important exception where the asset transferred can be sold for cash, and then the value of the benefit for tax purposes is the greater of the second-hand value of the asset in the employee's hands and the expense incurred by the employer.

In this situation, as the asset transferred is a house, the second-hand value of the property will be greater than the cost to the company. Thus the value that will go on the P11D will be the second-hand value.

See *British Master Tax Guide* 396.

Law: ITEPA 2003, s. 62, 204

10-640   Asset or accommodation?

> **Q.**   Tony is a director of a limited company. On 6 July 2009 the company bought a canal barge for £35,000. The director is able to use the barge at all times, and it is not available to any other employee. The company incurs costs of £3,000 on fuel, maintenance, insurance, etc. for the nine months from 6 July 2009 to 5 April 2010. The director used the barge for 40 days during the period for travel to a temporary place of work, and as overnight accommodation whilst working on the site. How is the benefit in kind calculated?

A.   When an asset is placed at the disposal of a director or employee, the amount of the cash equivalent of the benefit is the annual value plus additional expenses. The annual value is 20% of the market value of the barge when first provided to the director. So the basic benefit is calculated as follows:

	£
Annual value of barge (35,000 × 9/12 × 20%)	5,250
Additional expenses	3,000
Total amount of benefit	8,250

As the director's use of the barge for 40 days is wholly, exclusively and necessarily incurred in line with his duties he is entitled to a deduction for the amount of expenses incurred for business purposes that could have been deducted if they had been incurred by him personally. On the remaining 234 days the barge was at the disposal of the director to use as and when he wished and therefore the remainder will be chargeable to tax. The deduction is calculated as follows:

	£
Total amount of benefit	8,250
Less: deduction for business use (40/274 days)	(1,204)
Chargeable benefit	7,046

See *British Master Tax Guide* 396, 1992.

Law: ITEPA 2003, s. 205, 336

10-660   Van benefits

Example 1

John is sole shareholder of his own building company. He drives a van and uses it for both private and business purposes. John employs his 17-year-old son Steve in the business, paying him £5,000 per year for ten hours per week. Steve is also allowed to drive the vehicle and father and son make roughly equal use of the van overall, in each case with unrestricted private use. The overall taxable benefit is £3,000. In the ordinary way, this might be split £1,500 to each.

However, as Steve is in lower-paid employment, he would escape any tax liability on the van. In this case, his private use is ignored and John will pay tax on the full value of £3,000.

This anti-avoidance rule does not apply where the two employees are unconnected.

Example 2

Pete is employed as an electrician in Luton. His employer provides him with a van which he uses every day for work. Pete is allowed to use the van for private journeys within Bedfordshire, though he has to ask for permission if he wants to take the van outside the county. The van is replaced every three years. Pete paid tax on a benefit of £500 for each tax year up to 2005–06. However, from 2006–07 his taxable benefit increases to £3,000. Unless Pete pays for all his private fuel he also incurs a fuel scale charge of £500 from 2006–07, rising to £550 from 6 April 2010.

Example 3

Bob works as a plumber. He is provided with a van which is kept full of tools and plumbing accessories. Again, the van is replaced every three years. Bob is allowed to take the van home at the end of each day but is strictly forbidden to make any other private use. The insurance of the van reflects these conditions.

From 6 April 2005 Bob met the restricted private use condition as the only permitted private use was for ordinary commuting. From 2005–06 his taxable benefit has therefore been nil.

Example 4

Jack is director of a company that imports fruit and vegetables. He works almost entirely from the warehouse. Jack has a luxury car at home but on advice from his accountant he uses an (expensive) van for commuting to and from work, a round trip of 40 miles. The company pays for all expenses, including fuel. Nobody else drives the van. Jack tells his accountant that he almost never uses the van for purposes other than commuting to and from work.

Jack will pay tax on a benefit of £3,000. A fuel scale charge of £500 will also apply, rising to £550 from 6 April 2010. The fact that Jack may make occasional private use of the van for other purposes is not the main problem – other private use is not fatal as long as it is insignificant. However, it is clear on these facts that the van is not being made available mainly for the purposes of business travel. It therefore fails the second leg of the restricted private use condition. It also appears on these facts that there may be no formal restriction in place to prevent other private use.

See *British Master Tax Guide* 400.

Law: ITEPA 2003, s. 114, 154–155

10-670   Capital contribution towards use of a van

> **Q.**   My client is to be provided with a company van by his new employer which will be available for private use other than travel between home and work, and consequently, a van benefit charge will arise. My client is proposing to make a capital contribution to the cost of the vehicle. Can you please confirm whether this payment will result in a reduction to the annual benefit in kind charge, in the same way as it would for a company car?

A.   Unfortunately the van benefit provisions do not contain a similar provision to the company car benefit reduction on account of an employee's capital contribution to the vehicle's cost. They do, however, permit a reduction to the annual benefit charge for payments made in a year as a condition of the van being available for private use (ITEPA 2003, s. 158), in common with the company car provisions. Your client may therefore wish to explore this with the employer as an alternative to a one-off payment.

See *British Master Tax Guide* 400

Law: ITEPA 2003, s. 154–159.

10-680 Is it a car? Is it a van? No, it's a horsebox!

Q. Is a driven horse box a car or a van or is it classed as something else?

A. Vehicles under 3.5 tonnes are treated as vans. For vehicles over 3.5 tonnes the description is that of a commercial vehicle and this produces a benefit in kind of 20% of the market value of the asset where the user is an employee.

See *British Master Tax Guide* 400, 402.

Law: ITEPA 2003, s. 114, 239, 269

10-690 Is there a benefit charge on a classic car?

Q. My client company has spare cash which is currently earning interest at a low rate. The decision has been made to invest the money by buying a classic car. The vehicle is exempt from road tax and is uninsured; it is kept at the director's home. As it would be illegal to drive the car, is this exempt from a car benefit charge?

A. First, we must consider whether the car is made available to the director. There is no definition of 'available' in the relevant legislation and so the dictionary definition will be pertinent. The *Oxford English Dictionary* contains the definition:

'That may be availed of. Capable of being employed with advantage or turned to account; hence, capable of being made use of, at one's disposal, within one's reach.'

Even though it would be illegal to drive the car, it is still capable of being made use of and, as such, is available to the director.

This is confirmed by the commentary in HMRC's *Employment Income Manual* at EIM23175 which tells us:

'Neither does the car count as unavailable simply because there is no current:

- road tax
- MOT certificate, or
- Car insurance.'

In the circumstances given, a car benefit charge would arise, even if the car is never actually used.

See *British Master Tax Guide* 402.

Law: ITEPA 2003, s. 147

10-700   Private use while on call

> **Q.**   Pallett Ltd provides security services. Each of their security staff are provided with company vans. Private use of the vans is not generally permitted, however when a member of staff is on call at home, it seems logical for them to have their van with them if they leave their home. For example, if the individual needs to go to the local supermarket whilst on call, if they receive a call whilst in the supermarket they can get straight into the van and to work. However if they leave the van at home, using their personal vehicle to go to the supermarket they would have to go home to collect the van before leaving to attend the call. Does this constitute private use for the purpose of establishing whether a van benefit charge is due?

A.   The definition of private use has not changed under the new van benefit rules. The rules simply state that the charge is nil if the van is only available for business travel and commuting, and is not in fact used for any other purpose except to an insignificant extent, and is available mainly for use for the employee's business travel.

Business use is any travelling for which the expenses would be deductible if the employee incurred them. All use other than business travel is private use including when the employee is obliged to take the van home because the employee is on call.

There is special treatment for emergency vehicles where the person is employed in an emergency service but that is not the case here.

See *British Master Tax Guide* 400, 402.

Law: ITEPA 2003, s. 114–148

10-720   Normal commuting is private use

> **Q.**   The director of a small company commutes about 100 miles each day. It has been suggested that the company provide him with a van for this commute, and that there would be no benefit in kind chargeable. Following the change in the law allowing commuting not to be treated as private travel, is this correct?

A.   The problem you have is that there are two separate requirements to this test and both need to be satisfied in order to avoid the benefit in kind:

(1)   the commuter use requirement – this states that the van must not be available for private use other than ordinary commuting;

(2)   the business travel requirement – this states that the van must be available mainly for use for the employee's business travel.

And while it is true that commuting is not considered private travel, neither is it business travel.

See *British Master Tax Guide* 400.

Law: ITEPA 2003, s. 155, 171

10-740 Company car prices

> **Q.** The company managing director has arranged for the company to purchase his company car from abroad at a considerably lower price than the cost if acquired in the UK. Can we use this lower price to calculate the taxable car benefit?

A. Unfortunately not. The law states that the price to be used to calculate the cash equivalent of the benefit is 'the inclusive price appropriate for a car of that kind if sold in the UK, singly, in a retail sale in the open market on the day immediately before the date of the car's first registration'.

You will therefore need to find the price of the car in the UK at the time it was registered to calculate the benefit in kind.

See *British Master Tax Guide* 402.

Law: ITEPA 2003, s. 123

10-760 Private number plates

> **Q.** Our company has bought a personalised number plate. What allowances are claimable on such expenditure, and how will any benefit be taxable?

A. Assuming there is a demonstrable benefit to the trade in having such a number plate, the company will be able to claim the value of the number, in excess of the value of the metal, as an intangible asset, so claiming the amortisation in the accounts in accordance with generally accepted accounting practice (GAAP) or 4% p.a. if that is greater. The value of the metal or plastic is counted as part of the cost of the car and is available for capital allowances.

The provision of a personalised number plate does not, of itself, give rise to a taxable benefit on an employee, under the arrangements for taxing company cars, the number plate itself is a qualifying accessory.

See *British Master Tax Guide* 402.

10-780   Pool cars

> **Q.**   We have a car which is used during the day by various employees for business travel only. However there is no overnight parking facility at our business premises, so one of our employees takes the car home each night and parks it outside his house. He does not use the car privately, so are we right in assuming there will be no taxable benefit?

A.   No. To qualify for exemption under the pool car rules, the vehicle must not normally be kept overnight on or near the residence of any of the employees. In addition, home to work mileage is considered to be private so if the car is being taken home every night by the same employee then the private use is unlikely to be considered merely incidental. It would appear that a taxable benefit is arising for this individual.

See *British Master Tax Guide* 402.

10-790   Leased cars

> **Q.**   We provide a leased car to one of our employees. The car is available for private use but the employee reimburses us for the full cost of the lease. We assume that there is therefore no taxable benefit. Is this correct?

A.   No – the taxable benefit of the car is based on the list price of the vehicle, not the lease costs.

Section 144 of ITEPA 2003 states that, in order for an employee's payment to have any effect on the taxable benefit, it must be made 'as a condition of the car being available for private use'. HMRC's *Employment Income Manual* takes this even further and makes clear that payments for specific items or services such as insurance, road fund licence, etc. will not count. Therefore, simply reimbursing the employer for lease costs may not be accepted by HMRC as qualifying. Ideally, there should be a written condition that the employee is required to make a payment which is clearly identified as being in respect of the private use of the car and for no other purpose.

Having successfully negotiated that hurdle, the effect of the employee's payment is then to reduce the taxable benefit of the car pound for pound. It cannot be assumed that because the employer's cost has been fully covered that the taxable benefit will be zero – the two matters are unrelated.

See *British Master Tax Guide* 2368.

Income Tax

10-800   Company cars

Example 1

An employee pays tax at 40% and makes a capital contribution of £2,000 towards a company car supplied by her employer and costing £20,000. The car's 'appropriate percentage' is 35% on the basis of high CO_2 emissions and the car is kept for four years.

The contribution reduces the price of the car for tax purposes. As such, the individual will save £280 per year in tax (£2,000 × 35% × 40%). After four years, she will have saved a total of £1,120. If the car is then sold for say £8,000, then she can be reimbursed £800 tax-free (in line with her original 10% contribution). In total, she has therefore paid out £2,000 and received back £1,920.

However, her employer will also have saved National Insurance because of the capital contribution. If this is at a rate of 12.8% per year, the saving will be around £360 over the four years (£2,000 × 35% × 12.8% × 4).

Example 2

Eli starts working for her new employer on 3 March. She is immediately provided with a company car for £20,000 and the appropriate percentage for the year is 20%.

If the car had been available for the whole year, the taxable benefit would have been £4,000. In that year, however, the car is unavailable for 331 days. The £4,000 is therefore reduced by £3,627 (331/365 × £4,000).

The cash equivalent of the car is therefore £373.

Example 3

Paula runs an agency providing domestic staff. She works full-time in the business, which is operated through a limited company. Her husband is employed elsewhere and does not have a company car. Paula is a 40% higher-rate taxpayer.

The family need two cars – one large enough to travel around with the children and one mainly for the husband to drive to the station each morning. The larger vehicle is a company car.

They need to replace the second car and are thinking of spending £7,800 on a one-year-old vehicle with a list price of £10,000 and a CO_2 figure of 15%.

If the second car is bought through the company, the tax cost will be just £50 per month (£10,000 × 15% × 40%). The company can obtain full tax relief for all running costs and (by way of capital allowances) for the depreciation over the period of ownership. Even with the employer-National Insurance cost of nearly £200 for the year, this is likely to make good tax sense.

See *British Master Tax Guide* 402.

Law: ITEPA 2003, s. 114–148

10-810   Expensive cars

A car has a published price of £83,000 when first made available to Simon. The car is supplied with optional accessories with a list price of £3,000. Simon paid for the accessories (£3,000) plus a further £1,000 towards the cost of the car. The price of the car is established as follows:

	£
List price – car	83,000
List price – accessories	3,000
	86,000
Less: capital contribution	(4,000)
	82,000

Where the price of the car (or, in the case of a classic car – its market value) for a particular tax year exceeds £80,000 (including accessories) then the excess is ignored. Any deduction for a capital contribution is made before applying this restriction. As a result, a capital contribution to an expensive car may be wholly wasted as far as tax is concerned. So, in Simon's case, the £80,000 cap applies.

Note that the £80,000 cap referred to in this example is to be abolished from 2011–12 and subsequent tax years.

See *British Master Tax Guide* 2245.

Law: FA 2009, s. 53 and Sch. 28, para. 2

10-820   Company fuel

Example

Pauline drives a company car which has an appropriate percentage of 30%. Pauline is supplied with free fuel. She joined the company three months after the start of the tax year. In December, she was caught drink driving and received a six-week ban from 1 February to the middle of March.

Pauline's taxable benefit for free fuel will be £3,802 (£16,900 × 30 % × 9/12). She obtains a reduction for the first three months of the tax year, being a period before the car was first made available to her. She does not obtain a reduction for the period of the driving ban as the car is still available for her to use.

See *British Master Tax Guide* 403–405.

Law: ITEPA 2003, s. 149–153

10-840   Company cars and petrol with repayments

Example

Mary drives a 1,600cc petrol car with a list price of £12,000 and a CO_2 percentage of 25. All her fuel is provided by her employer. She drives 10,000 private miles in the year and is required to contribute 8p per private mile towards fuel. She is a higher-rate taxpayer.

Car benefit (12,000 × 25%)	£3,000
Fuel benefit (18,000 × 25%)	£4,500

The 8p per mile is inefficient from the tax point of view. It does not make good the full cost of the fuel (15p per mile on the basis of the advisory rates for a 1,600cc petrol car at 1 June 2010) so no tax reduction is obtained. It also fails to reduce the car benefit.

Mary's contribution will be £800 (10,000 private miles at 8p per mile). If the contribution had been made towards the use of the car then the taxable benefit would have been reduced by £800 saving tax of up to £320 (at the 40% higher rate), and some employer National Insurance on top.

See *British Master Tax Guide* 402–405.

Law: ITEPA 2003, s. 114–153

10-860   Mileage allowances

Example 1

Beryl travels on business several times each week. In the tax year ending on 5 April 2010 she covered 12,000 business miles. Her employer can reimburse her as follows without causing her to incur a tax charge:

	£
10,000 miles @ 40p per mile	4,000
2,000 miles @ 25p per mile	500
Total tax-free from employer	4,500

She has a fellow employee with her on business journeys totalling exactly 1,000 miles. She also drives one of the partners in the business for 200 business miles.

Beryl can be reimbursed an additional £50 tax-free (1,000 miles @ 5p per mile – not 1,200 miles, as the partner is not an employee).

Example 2

Jack drives 8,000 business miles and has a qualifying passenger for 5,000 of those miles. Jack's employer is entitled to pay up to £3,450 tax-free, (8,000 miles @ 40p per mile (£3,200) plus 5,000 miles at 5p per mile (£250)). Suppose, however, that his employer reimburses only £3,200.

If this is all expressed as being approved mileage allowance payments, with no passenger payments, then there is no tax liability but the employee cannot claim tax relief on the shortfall of £250. If, on the other hand, the employer states that he is paying £250 as a passenger payment and a reduced amount of £2,950 as the approved mileage payment, the employee can now claim tax relief on the shortfall of £250, saving up to £100 in tax.

See *British Master Tax Guide* 405.

10-870   Mileage allowances and self-employment

> **Q.**   My client has his own limited company and a quite separate self-employment. As he is trying to get the company on its feet he is only drawing a salary of £1,000 p.a. from the company; however, he does do a lot of travelling for the company. The company does not reimburse him. Can he claim the travelling at 40p per mile in his tax return and thus set the 'loss' on his employment against his self-employment income?

A.   An employee that is not reimbursed by his employer for business miles that he drives in his own car is able to claim a deduction from his employment income of a fixed sum in respect of those miles. This is also a possible deduction if the employer does actually make some contribution to the cost but below the approved mileage rate.

The approved rate for any tax year is 40p for the first 10,000 miles and 25p for any extra miles.

This is all very well but, as you say, your client does not receive sufficient income from this employment to obtain the relief for his business miles in full. The amount of the deduction is limited to the amount of the earnings from which it is to be deducted. It is not possible for the relief to create an allowable loss that could be relieved under any other section of the legislation. This loss cannot be set off against the self-employment profits.

Incidentally it would not help your client if he had another employment as it is not possible for any surplus expenses to be deducted from other employments (HMRC *Employment Income Manual* EIM31655).

See *British Master Tax Guide* 405.

10-880 Double mileage rates

Q. Claire has two employments and uses her own vehicle for business travel in each employment. She receives 40p per mile for the first 10,000 in each job. Will she have a tax liability as she has now received the higher mileage rate for 20,000 miles?

A. Where an employee gets mileage allowance payments from two or more employments that are not associated, the employee is entitled to payment at the higher rate for cars and vans for the first 10,000 miles travelled in each employment. Where an employee gets motor expenses payments from two or more associated employments, the reimbursed mileage must be aggregated for the purpose of deciding when 10,000 business miles is reached.

Employments are associated if the employer is the same or the employers are partnerships or bodies and an individual or another partnership or body has control over both of them or the employers are associated companies.

See *British Master Tax Guide* 405.

10-890 Overstated mileage claims

Q. At a recent compliance visit, it was discovered that a company car driver had been significantly overstating the business miles travelled and, as a result, had been paid mileage allowances in excess of HMRC limits. The Compliance Officer is arguing that because the employer did not adequately police the mileage claims, private fuel has effectively been provided for use in a company car and is levying the full fuel scale charge. Is he right?

A. Section 11.9 of the Booklet 490 states HMRC will not normally seek to recover the underpaid tax which has arisen as a result of inaccurate information supplied by an employee, where the employer can show that he or she has operated proper controls and has acted in good faith. In such circumstances, HMRC may pursue the employee instead.

However, this may be difficult for the employer to defend. In this case the employee had made significant overstatements of mileage that the employer really should have picked up and queried. The failure to do so could be viewed as condoning the offence and could even be interpreted as having deliberately turned a 'blind eye' in order to provide an additional award to the employee. This case demonstrates the importance of not only keeping expenses records, but also of checking them before allowing payment.

See *British Master Tax Guide* 405.

10-900   Beneficial loan interest

Q.   I have a loan of over £5,000 from my employer, on which interest is charged at the current HMRC official rate (4.75% for 2009–10). However, the interest is not payable until the end of the loan period. In the interim it is rolled up and carried forward. Does this give rise to a reportable benefit in kind?

A.   Initially, yes. A benefit on such a loan arises unless interest is paid on it for that year.

Clearly you will be paying interest for the year, but as yet it is not actually paid and therefore cannot be taken into account. If the interest is paid prior to the P11D return date, then it can be accounted for and the benefit will be negated but if it does not become payable until after that date, then the benefit should be reported on form P11D.

When the interest is subsequently paid, a retrospective claim for relief may be made. Such a claim should be admitted, though it is important to note that in order for interest to be allowed, it must be demonstrable that a legal obligation to pay the interest existed during the income tax year concerned. It is not sufficient to simply volunteer to pay interest in order to try and avoid a benefit.

See *British Master Tax Guide* 406.

Law: ITEPA 2003, s. 175, 191

10-920   No such thing as free shares

Example

Megan is given shares in the company for which she works. She makes no payment for the shares, which have a market value of £10,000. She is given the shares on 6 April. The official rate of interest for the tax year is 4.75%.

Megan is treated as having a notional loan of £10,000. The taxable sum is the amount of the loan multiplied by the official rate of interest for the year (£10,000 × 4.75% = £475). A sum of £475 is treated as specific employment income for the tax year in question.

See *British Master Tax Guide* 406.

Law: ITEPA 2003, s. 173–191

10-940   Beneficial loans

Example

Normal method

Graham's employer lends him £8,000 to enable him to pay off some private debts. The loan is made on 8 June. £2,000 is repaid on 1 December but the balance of the loan is still in force on the last day of the tax year. The official rate of interest is assumed to be 6.25% until 5 February and thereafter 5%.

The maximum outstanding when the loan was first made was £8,000.

The amount outstanding on 5 April at the end of the tax year was £6,000.

The average of these is £7,000.

The number of whole months the loan is outstanding is nine. (Months run from the sixth day to the fifth – the loan was not outstanding for the whole month 6 June to 5 July.)

Therefore:

£7,000 $\times$ 9/12 = £5,250

The average official rate is: 6.25 $\times$ (243/302) + 5 $\times$ (59/302) = 6%

If Graham has paid no interest on the loan, the taxable benefit is therefore £5,250 $\times$ 6% = £315. If interest has been paid for the year, it is deducted on a pound for pound basis. If Graham has paid interest of £315 or more for the year, the benefit is nil.

Alternative method

		£
8 June–1 December		
Amount outstanding	£8,000	
Interest rate	6.25%	
8,000 × 0.0625 × 177/365		242
2 December – 5 February		
Amount outstanding	£6,000	
Interest rate	6.25%	
6,000 × 0.0625 × 66/365		68
6 February – 5 April		
Amount outstanding	£6,000	
Interest rate	5%	
6,000 × 0.05 × 59/365		48
Cash equivalent		358

See *British Master Tax Guide* 406.

Law: ITEPA 2003, s. 173–191

10-960   Lending money to the family

> **Q.**   Aidan is a director and the sole shareholder of Company A. During the 2009–10 tax year Company A made an interest-free loan of £20,000 to a full-time employee (earning £30,000) who also happens to be Aidan's brother. The company also made a further interest-free loan of £25,000 to Aidan's mother, who is not involved in the business at all. What are the tax implications of these loans?

A.   Where a close company makes a loan to a participator or an associate of a participator, then a tax charge will apply. The company is required to notify HMRC within 12 months of the end of the accounting period in which the loan is made, and must pay tax equal to 25% of the amount of the loan by nine months and one day after the end of the accounting period. For these purposes 'associate' includes any relative of a participator.

In addition a director obtains a benefit when by reason of their employment he/she or any of his or her relatives are provided with an interest-free loan or low-cost loan. For these purposes 'relative' means husband or wife, or civil partner, parent or remoter forebear, child or remoter issue, or brother or sister and spouses of those persons.

As the brother is an employee earning more than £8,500 he will be taxable himself on the interest that would have been paid if he had been required to pay interest at the official rate

(4.75% for 2009–10). This will be shown on his own form P11D, and the company will be liable to Class 1A National Insurance in the usual way.

However, the loan to the director's mother should be shown on the director's form P11D; the benefit will be taxable on the director himself because his mother is not an employee. The company will be liable to pay Class 1A National Insurance on the benefit.

See *British Master Tax Guide* 406.

Law: CTA 2010, s. 455; ITEPA 2003, s. 175

10-980 Nursery care or family baby sitting?

> **Q.** One of our employee's children attends a nursery which is run on a commercial basis by her sister. We understand that a tax exemption of £55 per week is available but will not be available if children are looked after by relatives. Does this mean our employee will not qualify for this relief?

A. Your employee will still be able to benefit from the tax and National Insurance relief. Relief is available where the relative is a registered or approved childcarer and runs a childcare business looking after children she is not related to and looking after her sister's child is incidental to that business.

Relief would not be available if the childcare is provided by the relative in the child's own home.

See *British Master Tax Guide* 409.

10-990 Stockpiling childcare vouchers whilst on maternity leave

> **Q.** We operate a salary sacrifice scheme for the provision of childcare vouchers. Our voucher provider has informed us that HMRC have issued guidance regarding the situation when women in receipt of childcare vouchers are on maternity leave. They have told us that, although we must continue to provide the vouchers during maternity leave, if the vouchers are not used by the end of that leave, the woman must repay the value of the vouchers to the employer. Is this correct?
>
> We believe that many women continue to receive vouchers during maternity leave whilst looking after their child at home and 'stockpile' them for use once they return to work.

A: We have contacted HMRC and have been told by a member of their technical team that no such guidance has been issued.

The main problem around any such policy requiring the woman to repay the value of the unused vouchers would be one of discrimination. The salary sacrifice is a contractual arrangement and this is something that HMRC would be very reluctant to become involved with.

If you place limits on the use of the vouchers before the end of the woman's maternity leave but do not impose any such condition for people who are working, then you will be open to a woman bringing a case against you for causing her to suffer detriment for taking maternity leave.

HMRC's guidance states that to qualify for the exemption, the childcare vouchers provided in any qualifying week cannot exceed £55 per employee. Further, a 'qualifying week' for childcare vouchers is defined under ITEPA 2003, s. 270A(7) as 'a tax week in respect of which a qualifying childcare voucher is received'.

EIM22010 further covers a situation akin to the one you have described and states:

> 'This means that childcare vouchers can be stockpiled and used to pay for qualifying childcare when required – for example, during the school holidays.'

See *British Master Tax Guide* 409.

Law: ITEPA 2003, s. 318

11-000   Childcare vouchers

Example

An employee has a cash salary of £40,000 a year. The employee has a three-year-old daughter, who attends nursery whilst the employee is at work.

To take advantage of the exemption for childcare vouchers of £55 per week, the employer and employee arrange for the employee to take a pay-cut of £2,860 and instead to receive childcare vouchers to the value of £2,860. The employee swaps a cash salary of £40,000 for a cash salary of £37,140 and childcare vouchers with a face value of £2,860. The employee's total package remains at £40,000.

The vouchers are exempt from tax and National Insurance. The employee is a higher-rate taxpayer and as a result of the swap saves tax of £1,144 a year (£2,860 × 40%).

As the vouchers are exempt from NICs, the employer and employee both make savings.

See *British Master Tax Guide* 409.

Law: ITEPA 2003, s. 318

11-020   Sacrifice for a phone

Example

Beth pays 40% higher-rate tax. She agrees to a reduction in salary of £500 p.a. in return for which her employer allows her to use a mobile phone for which the employer pays, under contract, an amount of £40 per month. The provision of the phone is potentially tax-free. The cash cost to Beth of lost salary is just £295 (after tax at 40% and 1% NIC) and she saves mobile costs of £480, so she gains by £185. Her employer saves £20 (being the salary saved less the cost of the phone) plus National Insurance (at 12.8%) of £64 on the salary not taken.

See *British Master Tax Guide* 415.

Law: ITEPA 2003, s. 319

11-040   Termination payments after the termination

> **Q.**   We are making a senior executive redundant and offering an enhanced redundancy package in excess of £30,000. I am aware that the excess over £30,000 will be taxable, but the employee has asked for the payment to be made after the official leaving date as he says there will be less tax to pay. Why is this?

A.   There are special rules for payments after leaving. In this context, the term 'after leaving' essentially means after the P45 has already been issued. Employers should operate the tax code BR (non-cumulatively) on such payments. For higher-rate taxpayers this therefore means that there will be an initial tax saving of 20%. However, this apparent saving is in fact simply a deferment as tax will ultimately still be payable on the lump sum at the employees marginal rate (in this case 40%) via self-assessment.

See *British Master Tax Guide* 438, 440.

Law: ITEPA 2003, s. 309–310

11-060   Group termination

Example

Emma is the accountant for two group companies. One company is wholly owned by the other. She is made redundant from both jobs and receives compensation for loss of office of £25,000 from one company and £20,000 from the other company. Although neither payment exceeds £30,000, as the payments are made in respect of employment with associated employers, they must be aggregated before applying the £30,000 threshold. The total received is £45,000 and the excess over £30,000 (£15,000) is taxed as employment income.

See *British Master Tax Guide* 438–440.

Law: ITEPA 2003, s. 309–310

11-080 Termination in kind

Example

Jack is made redundant from his job as manager of a factory following the closure of the factory. He received an ex gratia lump sum of £20,000 as compensation for loss of office, plus the use of his company car for three years. The cash equivalent of the benefit of the car in the tax year of termination from the date of the termination is £2,000, £5,000 in the two following tax years and £3,000 in the final tax year to the third anniversary of the termination. The £30,000 is applied as follows:

- £22,000 in the year of termination covering in full the compensation for loss of office and the benefit of the car, leaving £8,000 to be carried forward;
- £5,000 against the car benefit in the tax year following termination leaving £3,000 to be carried forward;
- £3,000 to partially offset the benefit of the car in the next tax year.

This leaves £2,000 of the car benefit in year 2 and £3,000 car benefit in year three taxable as employment income.

See *British Master Tax Guide* 438–440.

Law: ITEPA 2003, s. 309–310

11-100 Goods taken for own use

Example

Arthur, a carpet trader, buys 50 small carpets for £100 each and enters the cost in his books as an expense. The selling price of the carpets is £200 each. At a later date Arthur takes five carpets home for his own use. These carpets cost him £500 but he could have sold them for £1,000. Even though Arthur has made no profit he must enter £1,000 into his books as the selling price and this will form part of his taxable income.

See *British Master Tax Guide* 636.

Law: ITTOIA 2005, s. 34

11-120   Change of accounting dates

Example 1

Rob draws up accounts to 31 May each year up to and including 31 May 2009. He then changes his accounting date to 30 April 2010 (and to 30 April each year thereafter). He meets all the necessary conditions for the change to be recognised.

His basis period for 2009–10 will be the year ended 31 May 2009.

His basis period for 2010–11 will be the year ended 30 April 2010.

The profits of the month of May 2009 are therefore counted twice and will generate overlap relief to be set against future profits.

Example 2

Steffi draws up accounts to 31 May each year up to and including 31 May 2009. She then changes her accounting date to 30 June 2010 (and to 30 June each year thereafter). She meets all the necessary conditions for the change to be recognised.

Her basis period for 2009–10 will be the year ended 31 May 2010.

Her basis period for 2010–11 will be the 13-month period from 1 June 2009 to 30 June 2010.

By definition, her previous accounting date of 31 May will mean that she will have overlap relief to set against these profits. She will be able to set one month's worth of overlap profits against the amount now taxed so that she is still taxed on 12 months' worth of profits.

See *British Master Tax Guide* 675.

Law: ITTOIA 2005, s. 216

11-140   Partnership losses with profits

Example

George, Jack, Eileen and Ian set up in partnership in June 2003. They prepare accounts to 30 September each year. Profits and losses are allocated in the ratio 5:2:2:1. For the year to 30 September 2010, they made a profit of £6,000. George and Eileen each received salaries of £8,000.

The partnership profits for 2010–11 assessment are initially allocated as follows:

	George £	Jack £	Eileen £	Ian £	Total £
Salaries	8,000	–	8,000	–	16,000
Balance allocated 5:2:2:1	(5,000)	(2,000)	(2,000)	(1,000)	(10,000)
Initial allocation	3,000	(2,000)	6,000	(1,000)	6,000

The above allocation produces a result that is not acceptable for tax purposes as there is no real loss to be allocated to any partner. The notional loss allocated to Jack and Ian is therefore reallocated between George and Eileen in proportion to the notional profit originally allocated to them, i.e. 3,000:6,000. The final position is as follows:

	George £	Jack £	Eileen £	Ian £	Total £
Salaries	8,000	–	8,000	–	16,000
Balance allocated 5:2:2:1	(5,000)	(2,000)	(2,000)	(1,000)	(10,000)
	3,000	(2,000)	6,000	(1,000)	6,000
Reallocation 3,000:6,000	(1,000)	2,000	(2,000)	1,000	–
Net allocated	2,000	–	4,000	–	6,000

See *British Master Tax Guide* 754.

11-160   Partnership profit shares

Example

Tom, Dick and Harry commenced trade in partnership on 12 May 2005. They prepare accounts to 31 December each year. Prior to 1 January 2009, profits and losses were shared equally. From 1 January 2009 they share profits and losses in the ratio 3:2:1. For the year to 31 December 2009, the partnership made a profit of £25,000. Tom received a salary of £4,000 and Harry received a salary of £3,000.

The partnership profits are allocated as follows for 2009–10:

	Tom £	Dick £	Harry £	Total £
Salaries	4,000	–	3,000	7,000
Balance of profits distributed 3:2:1	9,000	6,000	3,000	18,000
Total	13,000	6,000	6,000	25,000

See *British Master Tax Guide* 754.

Law: *Partnership Act* 1890, s. 24

11-180   Partnership interest

Example

Jane, Jean and Beth set up in partnership in October 2004. Jean contributed capital of £20,000 and Beth contributed capital of £30,000. Interest on capital is paid at 5% p.a. Jane receives a salary of £5,000 and Jean receives a salary of £10,000. For the year to 31 December 2009, the accounts show a profit of £50,000. Profits and losses are allocated in the ratio 2:3:5.

The allocation of profits for 2009–10 is as follows:

	Jane £	Jean £	Beth £	Total £
Salaries	5,000	10,000	–	15,000
Interest on capital	–	1,000	1,500	2,500
Balance allocated 2:3:5	6,500	9,750	16,250	32,500
Net allocated	11,500	20,750	17,750	50,000

See *British Master Tax Guide* 756.

11-200   Partnership agreements

Example

Ian and Peter have for several years traded in partnership. Their accounts for the year to 31 December 2009 show a profit of £16,000. Profits and losses are shared equally until 31 March 2009. From 1 April, profits and losses are shared in the ratio 7:9.

Profits for 2009–10 are allocated in accordance with the profit sharing arrangements in force during the year to 31 December 2009 as follows:

Three months to 31 March 2009

Profits for period:

3/12 × £16,000	£4,000
Allocated:	
Ian (1/2 × £4,000)	£2,000
Peter (1/2 × £4,000)	£2,000

Nine months to 31 December 2009

Profits for period:

9/12 × £16,000	£12,000
Allocated:	
Ian (7/16 × £12,000)	£5,250
Peter (9/16 × £12,000)	£6,750

Thus, profits for 2009–10 are allocated:

	Ian £	Peter £	Total £
1/1/09–31/3/09	2,000	2,000	4,000
1/4/09–31/12/09	5,250	6,750	12,000
Total	7,250	8,750	16,000

See *British Master Tax Guide* 756.

Law: ITTOIA 2005, s. 850

11-220   Partner rents to the partnership

> **Q.** The property from which a four-partner partnership trades is owned personally by one of the partners and a full rent is paid to him by the partnership. We are keen to claim the appropriate amount of tax relief available but presume that one-quarter of the rents paid must be disallowed, representing the share of rent paid by the property owner in his capacity as a partner. However, we are also concerned that HMRC may argue for a full disallowance of the rents paid on the basis of duality of purpose. What is the correct position?

A. The full rents paid by the partnership will be allowable as a deduction against taxable profits, subject to the amount paid not exceeding a market value rent. No partial or complete restriction is required due to the personal ownership of the property by a partner.

See *British Master Tax Guide* 759.

11-240   Limited liability partnership losses

Example

Matthew became a member of a trading limited liability partnership (LLP) on 6 April 2007 and introduced capital of £100,000. During the year to 5 April 2010 he makes a further capital contribution of £60,000. His share of the LLP's losses are as follows:

Year ended 5/4/08	£60,000
Year ended 5/4/09	£60,000
Year ended 5/4/10	£30,000

Matthew is entitled to relief against the losses as follows:

2007–08 (unrestricted)	£60,000
2008–09 (restricted to capital contribution)	£40,000
2009–10 (loss for year plus loss b/fwd)	£50,000

On 6 April 2010 there are unrelieved capital contributions carried forward of £10,000 (this equates to capital contributions of £160,000 less the relief given of £150,000).

See *British Master Tax Guide* 766–767.

Law: *Partnerships (Restrictions on Contributions to a Trade) Regulations* 2005 (SI 2005/2017)

11-260   Patent royalties and gift aid

Example

In 2009–10, Tom, a single man aged 30, has taxable earnings of £2,500, all from his trade. Tom makes net payments of patent royalties of £640 (equivalent to gross payments of £800). In the absence of other relevant factors his tax position will be as follows:

	£
Tom's earnings	2,500
Less: patent royalties payments (£640 × 100/80)	(800)
Statutory 'total income'	1,700
Less: personal allowances (restricted)	(900)
Taxable income (equal to the annual payment)	800
Tax due at the basic rate (£800 × 20%)	£160

If instead of paying patent royalties Tom made a net payment under the gift aid scheme of £640 (equivalent to £800 gross, with £160 of income tax deducted at source and, thus, subject to recovery) then the following calculation would be required:

	£
Statutory 'total income'	2,500
Less: personal allowances	(900)
Taxable income	1,600
Tax due at starting rate	
(£1,600 × 10%)	£160

The personal allowances have been restricted so that Tom's overall income tax liability of £160 (all charged at the starting rate) is equal to the basic rate tax deducted from the gift aid payment.

See *British Master Tax Guide* 902, 1406.

Law: ITA 2007, s. 429, 903

11-280   Payroll giving

Example

Sam's employer operates a payroll giving scheme. Sam chooses to donate £10 a month to a charity of his choice. Sam is a higher-rate taxpayer. The donation is made from gross pay and because he receives tax relief of 40%, it effectively costs him £6 per month.

The money is deducted from his pay by his employer and paid over to the payroll giving agency. The agency charges a 4% administration fee (40p per month). The charity therefore receives £9.60 per month.

See *British Master Tax Guide* 904.

Law: ITTOIA 2005, s. 72

11-300   Sports clubs

Avro Athletics has the following income and expenditure for the year to 31 December 2009 when it is registered as a Community Amateur Sports Club (CASC) for the entire period:

	£
Membership fees	10,000
Trading income exempt from tax (A)	8,000
	18,000

Expenditure on non-qualifying purposes (N)   4,000

Applying the formula:

8,000 − (8,000 × 4,000)/18,000 = £6,222

Total tax relief due to Avro Athletics for the year ended 31 December 2009 is £6,222.

See *British Master Tax Guide* 905.

Law: FA 2004, s. 56

11-310   Farming: relief for fluctuating profits

Example

Archer, a farmer, has assessable farming profits of £28,000 in 2008–09 and assessable profits of £13,800 in 2009–10. Since his profits in 2009–10 do not exceed 70% of his profits in 2008–09, if he makes a claim for profit averaging the result will be that his profits in each year are to be added together and his averaged profits for each year will become one-half of £28,000 plus one-half of £13,800, i.e. £20,900 in each year.

Law: ITTOIA 2005, s. 223

11-320   Farmers averaging

Example

In 2005–06, a farmer's profit is £10,000 and his tax and Class 4 NIC liability is £1,280.70. In 2006–07 his profit is £50,000 and his liability is £14,178.60. If a claim is made to average the two years, the profit figures for both years become £30,000.

The liability which would have arisen for 2005–06 on a profit of £30,000 would have been £7,280.70 and additional tax of £6,000 would have become due. Instead of revising the 2005–06 liability, this amount is added to the 2006–07 liability. The interim payments for 2006–07 remain unchanged at £640.35 each (one-half of £1,280.70) because the 2005–06 liability is not amended.

The 2006–07 liability is calculated on a profit of £30,000 and would be £7,231.50, to which would be added the £6,000 calculated above. The interim payments for 2007–08 would be £3,615.75 each being one-half of the 2006–07 liability ignoring the £6,000 adjustment.

See *British Master Tax Guide* 942.

Law: ITTOIA 2005, s. 221; TMA 1970, Sch. 1B

11-340   Herd basis

Example

Farmer Brown buys a herd of cows for £1,000. He elects for the herd basis to apply. There is therefore no tax relief in respect of the initial cost of £1,000, either as revenue or capital.

The next year, he sells two cows for £150 and buys two more for £130. He is therefore assessable on the difference of £20 as a trading receipt.

In the following year, he retires and sells his whole herd for £1,200. This receipt is not subject to tax.

See *British Master Tax Guide* 946.

Law: ITTOIA 2005, s. 116, 119

11-360   Taxing a trust

> **Q.**   Three years ago, when his daughter was 16, my client set up a discretionary trust with the intention of providing some income for his daughter during her years of higher education. The trustees had the power to accumulate income as an increase to the capital of the trust and indeed nothing was paid to beneficiaries while the daughter was a minor.
>
> Now that his daughter is over 18, if the accumulated income is now paid to her, will there be any tax consequences on her father? ITTOIA 2005, s. 631 would appear to catch this.

A.   I expect that the income was retained in the trust whilst the daughter was a minor to avoid the consequences of the rule in ITTOIA 2005, s. 629. This section states that where a parent has provided the initial funds and income arising from these funds is paid or made available to a minor child or step child of the settlor (who is nether married nor in a civil partnership) then the income is deemed to be that of the parent for tax purposes.

ITTOIA 2005, s. 631 extends s. 629 to bring in income that has previously been retained and accumulated in the trust that is paid to a 'child of the settlor who is unmarried or not in a civil partnership'. As you point out s. 631 omits the word 'minor'. The rationale behind this omission is unclear as ITTOIA 2005, s. 631 is a rewrite of ICTA 1988, s. 660B(2). The word 'minor' was present in ICTA 1988, s. 660B(2); the relevant words were 'unmarried minor child' of the settlor. There is no mention of this as an intentional change in the list of 'alterations to the law' for ITTOIA 2005.

However the purpose of s. 631 is only to clarify the amount of retained and accumulated income which can be treated as income for s. 629. This income would then be treated as the income of the settlor only if paid out to a minor child of the settlor, so that the omission of 'minor' in s. 631 does not actually cause a problem

As the accumulated income that you intend to distribute to the daughter now will not be treated as the income of the parent, because the daughter is no longer a minor, we need to ascertain the correct tax treatment for the payment.

From case law, a discretionary payment made out of accumulated income is usually regarded as a capital payment and not as the income of the beneficiary. The case was *Stevenson v Wishart*. These payments are only treated as the income of the beneficiary where, by the terms of the trust instrument, payments out of capital are required to be made, or may be made, in order to supplement regular income, which is obviously not the case with your trust.

Thus the payment to your client's daughter, once she has attained majority, will be treated as a capital payment out of the trust. There will be no accompanying tax credit available to be reclaimed and it will not be treated as the income of her father.

See *British Master Tax Guide* 987.

Law: *Stevenson v Wishart* [1987] BTC 283

11-380   Discretionary trust tax

Example

The Abacus discretionary trust has the following assessable income for the tax year 2007–08.

Allowable trust management expenses are as detailed below:

- Profit from property rental business: £2,000
- UK company dividends (net): £1,530
- Bank interest (net): £800
- Trust management expenses paid: £1,440

Taxable income for 2007–08

	Net income £	Grossed-up	Gross income £	Tax credit £
Rental income	2,000	n/a	2,000	n/a
Dividend	1,530 ×	100/90	1,700	170
Interest	800 ×	100/80	1,000	200
			4,700	370

The trust management expenses are treated as paid out of the dividend income in priority to other types of income. To the extent that the management expenses are paid out of a particular type of income (in this case dividend income) the income so used is taxed, not at the special trust rates, but at the appropriate basic, lower or dividend ordinary rate. The amount of income thus needed to pay the management expenses is the amount of gross income that would be needed, prior to the tax charged at the appropriate rate (in this case the dividend ordinary rate of 10%). The management expenses not subject to special trust rates are therefore the grossed-up expenses, as shown below:

	Non-savings (basic rate) £	Savings (lower rate) £	Dividend (dividend rate) £	Tax £
Taxable income	2,000	1,000	1,700	
Non-savings income (rental income)				
£1,000 at basic rate	(1,000)			
£1,000 × 22%				220.00
£1,000 at the rate applicable to trusts (RAT)	(1,000)			
£1,000 × 40%				400.00
Savings income (bank interest)				
£1,000 at the RAT		(1,000)		
£1,000 × 40%				400.00
Dividend income				
Income allocated to pay trust management expenses (grossed-up)				
£1,440 × 100/90			(1,600)	
Taxed at the dividend ordinary rate:				
£1,600 × 10%				160.00
Remaining dividend income taxed at the dividend trust rate:			(100)	
£100 × 32.5%				32.50
Total trust tax liability				1,212.50
Less:				
Tax deducted and tax credit (£170 + £200)				(370.00)
Tax payable				842.50

See *British Master Tax Guide* 989.

Law: FA 2005, s. 14

11-400   Trust income

Example

The Benificent Trust, a discretionary settlement, made a distribution of £3,250 to a beneficiary in 2009–10. The payment of £3,250 is treated as a net payment after tax at 40% has been deducted from the gross amount. The net payment is grossed-up in the hands of the beneficiary thus:

£3,250 × 100/(100 − 40) = £5,416.67

The beneficiary receives (for tax purposes) gross income of £5,416.67 with a tax credit of £2,166.67. These amounts will be included on the form 'R185 (Trust Income)'.

See *British Master Tax Guide* 991.

Law: ITA 2007, s. 498

11-420   IIP trust income

Example

Trust income (of an IIP trust, with a single beneficiary) for 2009–10 is as follows:

	Net £	Tax credit £	Gross £
Dividends	1,800	200	2,000
Bank interest	3,200	800	4,000
Rent	3,000	–	3,000
	8,000	1,000	9,000

The tax credit on the dividend income and the tax deducted at source from the savings income settle any trust liability in respect of those sources. Income tax of £600 will be due on rental income (£3,000 × 20%).

Trust administration expenses of £800 have been incurred.

	Rent £	Savings £	Dividends £
Total net income	3,000	3,200	1,800
Less: tax on rents	(600)		
Less: admin costs			(800)
	2,400	3,200	1,000

The maximum that the trust can distribute is £6,600 (£2,400 + £3,200 + £1,000). This is treated as the beneficiary's net income with the net amounts received with appropriate tax credits.

	Net	Tax credit	Gross
	£	**£**	**£**
Dividends	1,000	111	1,111
Bank interest	3,200	800	4,000
Rent	2,400	600	3,000
	6,600	1,511	8,111

See *British Master Tax Guide* 1001.

11-440   Life interest income

Example

John has a life interest in the residuary estate of Betty which is invested entirely in building society accounts. During the administration period, the executors pay John the following sums:

2007–08   £200
2008–09   £220
2009–10   £230

John is treated as having received £250, £275 and £287.50 respectively (being the amounts paid grossed up at the lower or basic rate relating to the year of payment). John is entitled to tax credits of £50, £55 and £57.50 respectively.

Where the estate has more than one beneficiary, payments of income bearing tax at different rates are apportioned between them on a just and reasonable basis according to their different interests. Otherwise, it is assumed that payments are made first out of income bearing tax at the basic rate, secondly out of income bearing tax at the lower rate and finally out of income bearing tax at the dividend ordinary rate.

See *British Master Tax Guide* 1006.

Law: ITTOIA 2005, s. 650, 653

11-460   Administration of estates

Example

Eleanor died in year 1 and the period of administration extended to year 4. The personal representatives are required to pass the income arising from the residue to Julia after paying a prior charge of £3,000 p.a. to Elissa.

Income arising from the residue before the prior charge is:

189

	£
Year 1	6,000
Year 2	2,000
Year 3	5,000
Year 4	4,000

Income assessable on Julia is calculated as follows:

	Total income £	Prior charge £	Reallocation £	Assessable income £
Year 1	6,000	(3,000)		3,000
Year 2	2,000	(3,000)	1,000	Nil
Year 3	5,000	(3,000)	(1,000)	1,000
Year 4	4,000	(3,000)		1,000

See *British Master Tax Guide* 1030–1031.

Law: ITTOIA 2005, s. 491

11-480   Income from an estate

> **Q.**   Betty has received a share of her deceased husband's estate. He had no children and died intestate. Betty received £200,000 plus half of the residue.
>
> The solicitor took three years to sort out the estate and Betty has been paid an extra 6% interest, which has been paid out of the capital of the estate. Is this taxable for Betty and if so should the income be spread over the three years?

A.   Legatees are entitled to interest at 6% (at present) from the end of the executors' year to the date of payment. The executors are given a year's grace to administer the estate without the need to pay interest to a beneficiary on any amounts that they are entitled to under the will. Although the interest is an allocation of estate capital, it is taxable income (interest) for the beneficiary. The interest is taxed in the year of assessment in which the income is received or placed at the disposal of the person entitled to it. In every case, therefore, it is income of the year in which it is paid and there are no provisions for spreading back the income to earlier years.

See *British Master Tax Guide* 1038.

Law: ITTOIA 2005, s. 649–682

11-500 Capital and income to the settlor

Example

Simon, the settlor, receives a capital payment of £100,000 in May 2007. The undistributed income of the settlement is as follows:

2007–08   £20,000
2008–09   £30,000
2009–10   £10,000

Assume that undistributed income for the 20 subsequent years is £1,000 p.a.

The sums of £20,000, £30,000 and £10,000 are treated as Simon's income in 2007–08, 2008–09 and 2009–10 respectively. £1,000 for each of the following eight years (i.e. 2010–11 to 2017–18) is also treated as Simon's income. Thus, in total, £68,000 of the capital sum will be treated as Simon's income.

See *British Master Tax Guide* 1071.

Law: ITTOIA 2005, s. 620, 634

11-520 Settlor interested loans

Example

Trustees of a settlement make a capital payment of £30,000 in May 2003 to Ann the wife of Stephen, the settlor, as a loan. Settlement income available for distribution is as follows:

2007–08   £9,000
2008–09   £8,000
2009–10   £7,000

The loan is repaid in 2008–09. Only £9,000 in 2007–08 and £8,000 in 2008–09 is treated as the settlor's income.

If in 2009–10 the trustees make a further loan of £20,000 to Stephen's wife, this sum would be treated as a capital payment of £3,000 (i.e. £20,000 − (£9,000 + £8,000)) and as the income of the settlor to that extent in 2009–10.

See *British Master Tax Guide* 1071.

11-540 School fees from trust income

Q. Ten years ago, on the birth of my son, I set up an accumulation and maintenance settlement in his favour. The income arising has been accumulated as I was advised that

191

income paid to my son when a minor would be treated as mine for income tax purposes. Is it possible to pay school fees out of trust capital and avoid such an income tax treatment?

In addition, as the trust is paying 50% income tax on the income, is it possible to pay accumulated income to my son when he reaches the age of 18 so that he can claim some of this tax back?

A. Income paid to or for an unmarried minor child of the settlor is treated as the settlor's income unless the gross income amounts to less than £100. The trust deed should allow payments to be made from capital. However, there may still be income tax charges on you.

If the payments are made to meet school fees, which are your liability as a parent, then these will be caught. The law treats capital payments to or for you as the settlor, as your income for the tax year of payment so far as there is income available at the end of the tax year.

Any excess of capital payments over income available is carried forward to subsequent years for similar matching, up to a maximum of ten years after the year of payment. These payments are treated as being made for you as they will be meeting your personal liability to pay the school fees. For this reason, a contract regarding school fees would have to be drawn up between the school and the trustees to avoid this applying.

See *British Master Tax Guide* 1075.

Law: ITTOIA 2005, s. 629, 631, 633

11-560   Renting in two capacities

Q. Joan has a property that she rented out in 2009–10 incurring a loss. She also has joint ownership with her sister of another property on which lettings exceed expenses. Can the loss on the first property be set against the profit on the second?

A. The loss can be offset as long as both properties are part of the same property income business. A taxpayer's property income business comprises all of the properties owned in the same legal capacity. In this particular situation, it is necessary to consider if the second property is owned by Joan in a different capacity, i.e. as a partner.

HMRC confirm that there is no difference between the partnership and sole trade ownerships and accordingly Joan owns both properties in the same capacity. The properties are part of the same property income business and therefore the losses would be set against the profit on the second property.

See *British Master Tax Guide* 1205, 1210.

Law: ITTOIA 2005, s. 270–272

11-570   Furnished holiday lettings and capital allowances

> **Q.**   Mr and Mrs Hove purchased a cottage in Wales in February 2009 with the intention of renting it out as a furnished holiday letting. The property was furnished during March and April, i.e. some of the additions were on or before 5 April 2009 and others were purchased after that date. The property was first let in May 2009. How and when will relief for the furnishings be given under the capital allowances provisions?

A.   The letting began in 2009–10. We need to apply the tests of availability, letting and pattern of occupation for the period of 12 months beginning with the first letting (HMRC *Property Income Manual* PIM4112). Assuming that the tests are met for that period then the property will be a furnished holiday letting for 2009–10 and capital allowances will be available in that year of assessment. A writing down allowance in respect of the pre-5 April expenditure will be brought into account as an expense on the first day of letting. Note that first-year allowances are not available in respect of those additions because they are assets for leasing. The additions after 5 April would be relieved by making a claim for annual investment allowance. If the cost of post-5 April 2009 additions exceeds £50,000 then the excess would go into the plant and machinery pool to be written down at 20% p.a. or, if the expenditure not covered by the annual investment claim pertains to integral features, the excess would go into a special rate pool to be written down at 10% p.a.

See *British Master Tax Guide* 1255.

Law: ITTOIA 2005, s. 323–326; CAA 2001, s. 46(2)

11-580   Rent a room relief

Example

Duncan has a total rent-a-room amount for 2009–10 of £5,200. He is not eligible for the basic relief and so will have to prepare an account for his property business, unless he elects for the alternative basis to apply. He has until 31 January 2012 to make the election for 2009–10. If he does make the election his taxable profit (to be assessed as a UK property business) for 2009–10 will be £950 (£5,200 – £4,250). The alternative basis will be applied for each subsequent year that his rent-a-room income exceeds the limit, until a formal withdrawal of the election is made.

See *British Master Tax Guide* 1254.

Law: ITTOIA 2005, s. 784–801

11-600   How much of the premium is really rent?

Example

Alpha Ltd pays £50,000 for the grant of a 20-year lease of a shop. The amount chargeable to income tax is:

	£
Premium	50,000
Less: capital element	
2% (20 − 1) × £50,000	(19,000)
Sch. A – taxed on the grantor	31,000

Relief for additional rent paid by the company is £1,550 p.a. (£31,000/20 years).

See *British Master Tax Guide* 1264.

Law: ITTOIA 2005, s. 277–279

11-620   Non-resident landlord

> **Q.**   John was a UK citizen and has now gone abroad to work indefinitely under a full-time contract. As his main residence is now empty he wishes to let it out. Assuming he is not resident anymore, does he have to pay UK tax on the rent?

A.   Yes. Generally, if you are non-resident and not ordinarily resident then you are liable to tax on rental income arising from letting out a UK property.

In this case, the Non Residents Landlord Scheme would apply. This basically requires the tenant, or the letting agent, to deduct basic rate tax on the rent less expenses and account for this quarterly to HMRC. The tenant does not have to deduct any tax if the gross rent is below £100 per week.

Being a UK citizen, John will currently still get his normal personal allowance to offset against the rental income.

See *British Master Tax Guide* 1368.

11-640   Chargeable events on death

> **Q.**   I am an executor of a deceased person's estate and I am dealing with their tax return to the date of death and the tax return of the estate. The deceased held an investment bond

with a UK insurance company and a chargeable event gain certificate was received some months ago showing a policy gain of £15,000 being the difference between the surrender value of £35,000 and the premium paid of £20,000.

Following my request for the surrender of the policy, the insurance company has now sent a cheque covering proceeds of £36,750 and a small interest payment of £200. No further certificate has been received. I know the gain should be shown on the tax return to the date of death and the interest is shown on the estate tax return. However, should the insurance company have sent me a revised chargeable event certificate? I am unsure what policy gain to declare.

A.   First, the insurance company is obliged to issue each policy holder with a certificate if a chargeable event gain arises. A certificate also needs to be supplied to HMRC but there are some de minimis limits here for the insurance company and so the HMRC certificates do not always have to be issued.

On the death of the policyholder the policy gain is calculated by reference to the surrender value of the policy but the policy gain for the personal representatives is calculated by reference to the policy sum actually payable. There is no double charge here as any gain arising to the deceased is deducted from the gain arising to the personal representatives.

Therefore what you may have is a policy gain of £15,000 arising to the deceased and a policy gain of £1,750 arising to the personal representatives. The insurance company should be able to clarify matters for you.

It is actually quite common for some insurance companies to issue one chargeable event certificate on the final payment of the policy proceeds. In practice, HMRC will usually accept the whole policy gain being shown on the tax return of the deceased. However, if the deceased was a higher-rate taxpayer it is often worthwhile checking the gain with the insurance company as the personal representatives have no higher-rate tax liability and so any part of the gain arising to them will reduce the tax liability.

See *British Master Tax Guide* 1465.

Law: ITTOIA 2005, s. 491; ICTA 1988, s. 552

11-660   Working overseas

Example

Alex had worked for his employer for eight years. His time spent abroad is such that exactly five years count as foreign service. He receives a compensation payment for loss of office of £70,000. The tax position will be as follows:

	£
Payment	70,000
Exemption (s. 403)	(30,000)
	40,000
Exemption (s. 414)	
5 years out of 8	(25,000)
Taxable	15,000

See *British Master Tax Guide* 440, 1583.

Law: ITEPA 2003, s. 403, 414

11-670   Tax credits: method of calculating income

Example

Below is an example of how the rules used to calculate income for tax credits described above operate. Tom and Samantha (who have three children) have the following sources of income for the 2010–11 tax year:

	£
Tom's salary	16,000
Profits from Samantha's business	18,000
Army disability pension (Samantha)	2,300
Net bank savings (joint)	760
ISA dividend (joint)	140
Rental income (joint)	3,500
Total	40,700

Tom pays a net amount of £2,305 into a stakeholder pension, and he and Samantha jointly make net Gift Aid donations of £702.

Their joint income for tax credits purposes is ascertained as follows:

Step 1	£
Investment income (bank savings)	
£760 × 100/80	950.00
Property income (rental)	3,500.00
Sub-total	4,450.00
Less: threshold	300.00
Total	4,150.00

Step 2   £
Employment (Tom)   16,000.00

Step 3
Total of steps one and two   20,150.00

Step 4
Add trading income (Samantha)   18,000.00

Add to step three   38,150.00

Deductions	£	
Grossed-up pension contribution (Tom)		
£2,305 × 100/80	2,881.25	
Grossed-up Gift Aid donations		
£702 × 100/80	877.50	
Less: total deductions		3,758.75
Total joint income for tax credits		34,391.25

Law: *Tax Credits (Definition and Calculation of Income) Regulations* 2002 (SI 2002/2006), reg. 3

11-680   Tax credits

Example

A couple has tax credits income of £54,000, two children and a baby due on 6 December 2010. Assuming the baby is born on that day, the exact calculations will be:

For first relevant period 6/4/10–5/12/10 (244 days)

	£	£	£
CTC – family element		1.50 × 244	366.00
Income (54,000 × 244/365)	36,098.63		
Threshold (50,000 × 244/365)	33,424.66		
	2,673.97 at 6.67%		(178.35)
			187.65

For second relevant period 6/12/10–5/4/11 (121 days)

	£		£	£
CTC – family element, baby rate			3.00 × 121	363.00
Income (54,000 × 121/365)	17,901.36			
Threshold (50,000 × 121/365)	16,575.35			
	1,326.01	at 6.67%		(88.44)
				274.56
Overall total for 2010–11 (187.65 + 274.56)				462.21

Working tax credit and the child elements of child tax credit are ignored in this example, because the income levels are too high for fast taper credits to be due.

However, if a family had an income of £73,000, four children, qualifying childcare costs of £280 per week, and worked at least 30 hours, although there would still be no fast taper credits payable, the existence of these credits would alter the level at which the family element of CTC was tapered away. The figures would come out as follows:

	£	£
WTC – basic	5.27	
WTC – second adult	5.18	
WTC – 30 hours	2.17	
CTC – child element × 4	25.24	
	37.86 × 365	13,818.90
WTC – childcare, £280 × 52 × 80%		11,648.00
		25,466.90
	£	
Income	73,000	
Threshold	6,420	
	66,580 at 39%	(25,966.20)
		Nil

The income level actually needed to reduce the entitlement to these credits to nil is £71,719.74 (71,719.74 − 6,420 = 65,299.74 at 39% = 25,466.90) so a threshold of £71,719.74 is used to determine the family element.

	£		£	£
CTC – family element			1.50 × 365	547.50
Income	73,000.00			
Threshold	71,719.74			
	1,280.26	at 6.67%		85.39
Total award for 2010–11				462.11

See *British Master Tax Guide* 1845–1848.

Law: *Tax Credits Act* 2002

11-700   Married couple's allowance and wealthy pensioners

Example

Horace and Edna have been married for 35 years. Horace celebrated his seventy-third birthday in July 2010 and Edna celebrated her seventy-seventh birthday in August 2010. Horace has income of £26,000 in 2010–11 and Edna has income of £15,400 in that year.

Horace is entitled to the age-related personal allowance of £9,490 for taxpayers aged 65–74 and the age-related married couple's allowance by virtue of Edna's age, of £6,965.

Horace's allowances are, however, restricted as follows:

Personal allowance

	£
Total income	26,000
Less: income limit	(22,900)
Excess	3,100

	£	£
Age-related personal allowance (65–74)		9,490
Less: restriction – lower of:		
(a) one-half excess (3,100 × 1/2); and	1,550	
(b) difference between age-related and standard personal allowance	3,015	
		(1,550)
Personal allowance		7,940

Married couple's allowance

	£	£
Age-related married couple's allowance (75 and over)		6,965
Less: restriction – lower of:		
(a) one-half excess (£3,100 × 1/2)	1,550	
Less: restriction of personal allowance	(1,550)	
	Nil	

and

	£	
(b) difference between age-related and minimum amount of married couple's allowance (£6,965 − £2,670)	4,295	
		(Nil)
		6,965

Thus, Horace is entitled to a restricted personal allowance of £7,940 and the full married couple's allowance of £6,965 for 2010–11.

As Edna's income does not exceed the income limit, she is entitled to the age-related personal allowance of £9,640 for taxpayers aged over 75.

See *British Master Tax Guide* 1853, 1874.

Law: ITA 2007, s. 42

11-720 Foster care

Example

Sue provides foster care from her home throughout the tax year. She fosters a seven-year-old boy for 30 weeks and a 14-year-old girl for 40 weeks during the year. Nobody else provides foster care from her home.

Her fixed amount is £10,000.

The amount per child for the boy is £6,000 (30 weeks at £200 per week) and for the girl is £10,000 (40 weeks at £250 per week).

Sue's limit is therefore calculated as £26,000.

If Sue draws accounts up to 5 April, and her total receipts are under £26,000, the foster income is exempt from tax.

See *British Master Tax Guide* 1879.

Law: FA 2003, s. 176, Sch. 36

11-740 Loan interest

Example

Christopher is a sole trader making profits of £47,000. In addition to this, he is a non-working shareholder in Exways Ltd, a trading company. In the year 2007–08 he received a dividend of £1,800 from that company. He also owns a property in the UK, which he lets at an annual rent, net of running expenses, of £5,000 in the year. He has three loans in connection with these interests being £50,000, which he used to buy the goodwill of his sole trader business, £40,000 to buy his shares in Exways Ltd and £100,000 to purchase the let UK property. The interest rate on these loans is at 6% p.a.

His income tax liability is as follows for 2007–08:

	£	£
Trading profits before interest	47,000	
Less: interest on £50,000 loan	(3,000)	44,000
UK property business – net rents before interest	5,000	
Less: interest on £100,000 loan	(6,000)	–
(Loss to carry forward £1,000)		
Dividend from Exways Ltd (gross)		2,000
		46,000
Less: interest on £40,000 loan to buy Exways Ltd		(2,400)
Net statutory income		43,600

The interest on the trade purposes and property purchase loans are deducted in arriving at the results of those particular sources and cannot be set against total income as such. The loan to purchase the shares in Exways Ltd is set off in the order which will produce the lowest income tax liability. This should, therefore, be by setting against the trading profits:

	£
Statutory income	43,600
Personal allowance	(5,225)
	38,375

Tax calculated at:

2,230 at 10%	223
32,370 at 22%	7,121
1,775 at 40%	710
2,000 at 32.5%	650
	8,704
Less: tax credit on dividends	(200)
Income tax payable	8,504

See *British Master Tax Guide* 1888, 2040, 2249.

Law: ITTOIA 2005, s. 272–275; ICTA 1988, s. 360

11-760　Loan to my company

Q.　I am currently repaying a bank loan which I took out some years ago to inject funds into my trading company. The company's trade ended last year but I have kept the company as I am planning to start a new business in due course. I have always claimed tax relief for the loan interest paid but my accountant advises me that no further tax relief is due on the loan interest. Is this correct?

A.　It is likely that your accountant is correct. Assuming that the company used your loan for the purposes of its business, tax relief is due providing that at the time the interest is paid the company is a qualifying company. To be a qualifying company it must carry on a qualifying business activity. The problem here is that the business seems to have ended last year, hence your accountant's comments.

See *British Master Tax Guide* 1888.

Law: ITTOIA 2005, s. 360

11-780　Employee control

Example

The 20 employees and three directors of XYZ Ltd acquire 60% of the issued ordinary share capital of XYZ Ltd. The three directors each acquire 15% of those shares and the balance is divided equally among the 20 full-time employees. This is not an employee-controlled company as 15% of the shares (5% for each director) are not regarded as being owned by a full-time employee.

See *British Master Tax Guide* 1892.

Other guidance: ITA 2007, s. 409(1)–(2), 410

11-800   Enterprise Investment Scheme relief

> **Q.**   Amanda invested £35,000 in Enterprise Investment Scheme (EIS) shares during 2009–10. She received income tax relief of £7,000 (£35,000 @ 20%). As the company was not performing very well Amanda sold her shares in January 2011 for £15,000. What are the income tax implications?

A.   Where EIS shares are sold before the expiration of the three-year period, and the disposal is at arm's length, the income tax relief withdrawn is equal to the disposal consideration received at the rate of tax on which the relief was originally given, i.e. £3,000 (£15,000 @ 20%). The income tax relief is withdrawn by the issue of an HMRC assessment for the year in which the relief was originally obtained, in this case 2009–10.

Had the disposal not been at arm's length, the full amount of the relief originally given would be withdrawn.

See *British Master Tax Guide* 1936, 1938.

Law: ITA 2007, s. 234, 240

11-820   Less than maximum EIS relief

Example

In November 2007 Sue invests £100,000 in 80,000 EIS shares. She obtains income tax relief for the investment equal to her income tax liability for the year of £10,000 (the maximum relief being £20,000). In June 2010 she sells all of the shares for £90,000.

Although Sue's investment was eligible for income tax relief of £20,000 (£100,000 at 20%) she obtained relief of only £10,000 because of her low tax figure. The amount of the relief withdrawn on sale is thus £9,000 (20% × £90,000 × £10,000/£20,000).

If instead she had sold the shares for £120,000 the full relief given of £10,000 would be withdrawn.

See *British Master Tax Guide* 1939.

Law: ITA 2007, s. 209

11-840   Trivial pensions

> **Q.**   I have reached the normal retirement date under one of my personal pension plans to which I ceased to actively contribute to a few years ago. The value of my fund is £8,000. The pension administrator has suggested I take the value of my fund up front as a lump, rather than a small pension over a number of years, under the commutation on the grounds of triviality rules. Can you confirm how I would be taxed on this, compared with taking a tax-free 25% lump sum and pension under the normal rules?

A.   Under the unified pension taxation rules a pension may be commuted on grounds of triviality where the value of the individual's pension fund is below 1% of the standard lifetime allowance. This currently equates to £18,000 (2010–11). Of the value taken, 25% may be taken tax-free. The balance is treated as taxable pension income in the year of receipt. In reaching your decision, consideration needs to be given to the tax payable on the taxable element of the lump sum in the year of receipt, i.e. whether this puts you into the higher rate of 40%, compared with the tax liability over the duration of the pension on the much smaller annual pension.

See *British Master Tax Guide* 432.

11-860   The effect of pensions

Example

Rebecca has taxable trading profits of £39,000 for 2007–08. In addition she has net bank interest of £1,800 and UK dividends of £1,350. She made a £10,000 investment qualifying for relief under the Enterprise Investment Scheme (EIS). Her income tax liability for 2007–08 is:

	£	£
Trading profits		39,000
Savings income		
Bank interest (gross)	2,250	
Dividends	1,500	3,750
		42,750
Less: personal allowance		(5,225)
Taxable income		37,525

	£
2,230 at 10%	223
31,035 at 22%	6,878
1,335 at 20%	267
1,425 at 40%	570
1,500 at 32.5%	488
	8,426

Less:	
EIS relief (£10,000 at 20%)	(2,000)
Income tax liability for year	6,426
Less: tax deducted at source	
Interest	(450)
Dividend tax credits	(150)
Payable by self-assessment	5,826

Suppose that Rebecca paid an allowable pension contribution of £1,884 net (£2,415 gross). Higher-rate relief is given by extending her basic rate limit, so the computation becomes:

	£
2,230 at 10%	223
31,545 at 22%	6,940
2,250 at 20%	450
1,500 at 10%	150
	7,763
Less: EIS relief	(2,000)
Less: deducted at source (as above)	(600)
Income tax liability for year	5,163

Thus, the reduction is £663, so that the total income tax relief on the pension contribution is £1,194 whereas 40% on the gross contribution is only £966.

See *British Master Tax Guide* 432.

11-880   Annual allowance

Example

Paul is a member of three pension schemes. The aggregate pension input amounts for 2009–10 for the three schemes are £268,000. The annual allowance for 2009–10 is £245,000. The excess of aggregate pension input amounts over the annual allowance is £23,000 (£268,000 less £245,000). Paul suffers the annual charge on the excess at 40% of £23,000 = £9,200.

See *British Master Tax Guide* 431.

Law: FA 2004, s. 227–234

11-900   Crystallisation events

Example

Mark crystallises a benefit with a value of £50,000. Previous crystallised benefits were valued at £2m. The standard lifetime allowance at the date of the benefit crystallisation is £2m. The lifetime allowance has been used up in full. Crystallisation of the benefit with a value of £50,000 triggers a lifetime allowance charge of £27,500 if the sum is taken as lump sum (£50,000 × 55%).

Lucy crystallises a benefit with a value of £800,000 at a time when the standard lifetime allowance was £2m. She previously crystallised a benefit of £500,000 when the standard lifetime allowance was £1.5m and a benefit of £200,000 when the standard lifetime allowance was £1.8m.

The adjusted previously used amount in relation to the first benefit crystallisation event is £666,667 being £500,000 × 2m/1.5m.

The adjusted previously used amount is relation to the second benefit crystallisation is £222,222 being £200,000 × 2m/1.8m.

The total of the previously used amounts is £888,889, leaving £1,111,111 of the £2m lifetime allowance to set against the crystallised benefit of £800,000. As this is covered by the remaining lifetime allowance, no lifetime allowance charge is payable in respect of that benefit crystallisation event.

See *British Master Tax Guide* 432.

11-920   Allowable continuing professional development?

Q.   Peter regularly goes on continuing professional development (CPD) courses in order to ensure that he meets the requirements of the professional qualification they hold. The qualification was deemed a pre-requisite for the position he holds. Can the costs of attending be allowed as part of their duties of employment?

A.   There is a general rule for the deduction of employee's expenses which allows for an amount if the employee if obliged to incur and pay it as a holder of the employment and the amount is incurred wholly and exclusively and necessarily in the performance of the duties of the employment.

However, following recent case law, HMRC have now revised their manuals to state that:

> 'the dividing line drawn by the Courts is between preparation for performing the duties of the employment, which may include attending educational courses, and actually performing those duties. CPD is not a duty of the employment and is therefore not necessary as required by law.'

See *British Master Tax Guide* 1992.

Law: ITEPA 2003, s. 336

11-930   Employer debit cards

> **Q.**   In HMRC's publication 480 *Expenses and benefits - A Tax Guide*, Chapter 3, the commentary tells me that expenses payments to an employee include expenses paid by the employee by means of a credit card in the employer's name. Does this also apply to a debit card provided by the employer?

A.   The provisions are contained in Pt. 3, Ch. 4 of ITEPA 2003 which, in s. 90(1) applies the legislation to credit tokens. Credit tokens are defined in s. 92 and include: credit cards, debit cards, a token, a document or other object given to a person by another person, on production of which, money, goods or services are provided by a third party and the token is used to pay that third party for what is supplied. Thus the use of a debit card should be taken into account when determining expenses payments in respect of an employee.

See *British Master Tax Guide* 318.

11-940   Dealing with allowable expenses

Example 1

Employee A earns £20,000 p.a. He incurs expenses of £100 which are agreed to be allowable for tax purposes. His employer does not reimburse the expenses. Employee A will pay tax on a net figure of £19,900.

Example 2

Employee B also earns £20,000 p.a. He too incurs expenses of £100 which are agreed to be allowable for tax purposes. His employer takes a different line and does reimburse the expenses. The reimbursement is treated as taxable income, so B's taxable income from the employment is £20,100 but he deducts the £100 expenses incurred and pays tax on a net figure of £20,000.

See *British Master Tax Guide* 1992.

Law: ITEPA 2003, s. 336

11-960   Where do you work?

Example 1

Andrew works full-time in Norwich. His employer asks him to manage an office in Great Yarmouth for a period of six months whilst the manager there is on maternity leave.

The Great Yarmouth office is a temporary workplace and Andrew can be reimbursed tax-free the full cost of travel from his home to Great Yarmouth. The task is of limited duration and it is not caught by the 24-month rule.

Example 2

Belinda works in Durham but her employer asks her to oversee a new project in Consett. It is anticipated that her role at Consett will last three years and this proves to be correct.

No relief is due for the cost of travel as Consett becomes her new permanent workplace, even if she eventually returns to work in Durham. Even if it can be described as a task of limited duration, the role is occupying more than 40% of Belinda's time over a period of more than two years.

Example 3

Carol is initially asked to accompany Belinda on identical terms. However, she is recalled to her original workplace after ten months.

Carol still obtains no relief because, although her duties at Consett did not exceed 24 months, the expectation was that they were going to do so.

Example 4

Edmund works in Guildford but is asked to spend one day a week in Reigate. This arrangement continues for many years.

Edmund can obtain tax relief on the cost of travel from home to Reigate because he is spending less than 40% of his working time in Reigate.

See *British Master Tax Guide* 1994.

Law: ITEPA 2003, s. 337–341

11-980   Taxi fares home

Example 1

Following a system failure, Julie is required to work late to meet a deadline. She finishes work at 11pm by which time her regular bus service has ceased to operate. Her employer provides a taxi for her journey home. This is the first time in the tax year that this has occurred. No liability to tax arises in respect of the provision of the taxi.

Example 2

Andrea and Claire operate a car-sharing arrangement, whereby Andrea drives them to work one week and Claire drives them to work the next week. During a week that Claire has driven, her daughter injures her arm at school and Claire has to leave early to take her to the hospital. The employer provides Andrea with a taxi home. This is a one-off occurrence. The exemption applies as the breakdown in the car-sharing arrangements was both due to exceptional circumstances and unforeseen.

See *British Master Tax Guide* 1994.

Law: ITEPA 2003, s. 248

12-000 Meal vouchers

Example

Karen receives meal vouchers each week to the value of £35. She works five days each week. The value for tax purposes is reduced by 15p for each working day (15p $\times$ 5 = 75p). The amount taxed is thus £34.25 (£35 − 75p).

See *British Master Tax Guide* 2000.

Law: ITEPA 2003, s. 89

12-020 That's entertainment

Example

Charlie successfully negotiates a contract with a new customer over dinner. Charlie pays the bill of £350. This is subsequently reimbursed by Charlie's employer. Charlie's employer is a trading concern. In computing the employer's profits for corporation tax purposes, business entertaining is disallowed. Condition A is met and the prohibition on the deduction of expenses is lifted, allowing Charlie to claim a deduction for the sum reimbursed, effectively offsetting any tax charge that would otherwise arise.

See *British Master Tax Guide* 2002.

Law: ITEPA 2003, s. 356–357

Income Tax

12-040   A lecturer's suit

> **Q.**   Christine is a self-employed fitness instructor who also travels the country giving lectures to other fitness professionals on sports science. She wishes to claim the costs of keeping a wardrobe of formal attire for the lectures plus the costs of make-up and contact lenses. I am told that actresses are now able to claim for their clothing and I am wondering if their situation is analogous to her.

A.   HMRC allow self-employed actors who supply their own clothing to be allowed a deduction for such expenditure if the clothes are meant to be worn in front of camera. This obviously begs the question for other people who provide public performances such as lecturers. HMRC guidance makes the distinction between a television interviewer purchasing a suit to wear on TV and the interviewee (an architect) purchasing a suit for the same interview. In the latter case, it is everyday clothing worn in pursuit of the architect's profession thus the case of *Mallalieu v Drummond* applies to disallow the expenditure. It is difficult, faced with such an example to say why Christine's purchases of formal clothing used exclusively for the purpose of lecturing the public or other professionals could not be allowed under the same principle. Whilst a case may be made for the make-up to be allowable on the same principle, it is unlikely that the cost of contact lenses will be deductible on the duality of purpose principle.

See *British Master Tax Guide* 2154.

Law: *Mallalieu v Drummond (HMIT)* [1983] BTC 380

12-060   Excess pension contributions

Example

Inzell pays pension contributions as follows:

Year ending:
31/3/09   £1,000,000
31/3/10   £3,500,000

210% of the contribution of £1,000,000 is £2,100,000. The contribution of £3,500,000 paid in the following year exceeds this amount, therefore the excess may need to be spread as follows:

	£
Contributions for year ending 31/3/10	3,500,000
Less: 110% of £1,000,000	(1,100,000)
'Excess' amount required to be spread	2,400,000

This is greater than £500,000 and so will be spread over the four years starting with the current period ending 31 March 2010. Thus, tax relief of £600,000 will be given in each of the years ending 31 March 2010, 2011, 2012 and 2013.

The total relief in the year ended 31 March 2010 would therefore be the £600,000 plus the non-excess amount of £1,100,000.

See *British Master Tax Guide* 2240.

12-080   Paying too much in pension contributions

Q. Gordon Ltd is making a large contribution into a registered pension scheme in the current tax year and realises that it may not be able to make full use of the tax relief if the whole amount is deducted from trading profits in the first year. Is there a limit on the amount of contribution it can make and is there any way it can put part of the contribution in the first year and perhaps carry forward some to the following year?

A. There is no limit on the amount an employer can contribute. If the contribution is deemed to be large, there is a spreading provision to enable part of the contribution to be treated as if it were paid in a later period of account. The initial contribution does not benefit from these provisions.

Spreading provisions apply when the pension contribution in the current period exceeds 210% of the amount paid in the previous period and the amount exceeding 110% of the amount paid in the previous period is at least £500,000.

If both of these apply then the maximum relief for the current period is 110% of the previous period's contribution plus a proportion of the excess.

The excess can be spread over two, three or four years dependent on the amount involved.

If the excess is between £500,000 and £1m, half the contribution is treated as paid in the current period and half in the next, and if the excess is between £1m and £2m, the spreading is based on a third in each chargeable period.

See *British Master Tax Guide* 2240.

12-090   Paying pension contributions whilst working abroad

Q. My client has left the UK intending to settle permanently in Australia, but will continue to work for a UK company. He has been a member of the company's in-house registered pension scheme for many years. He will continue to be paid from the UK, but will carry out all of his duties abroad. He has been UK resident, ordinarily resident and domiciled since birth.

We understand that, under certain circumstances, expatriates may continue to make net contributions to registered UK pension schemes for several years following emigration and still obtain UK tax relief. My client's only other UK arising income will be rental income relating to his former residence, and a small amount of bank interest. Can you please confirm accordingly?

A. To contribute to a UK registered pension and enjoy tax relief, an individual must come within the definition of a 'Relevant UK Individual' provided by FA 2004, s. 189(1). Subsection 189(1)(c) includes within that definition an individual that was UK resident both at some point in the five preceding tax years, and at the time he became a member of the pension scheme in question. On this basis, your client will be able to continue to contribute for five years, but note that his tax relief will be limited to the lower of £3,600 (gross) or his actual relevant earnings. As he carries out all of his duties abroad, the income from his UK employment will not count as relevant earnings for this purpose, and tax relief will be limited to £3,600 gross (£2,880 net) accordingly. However, despite this limit for tax relief, your client may actually contribute more than this, subject to the usual annual and lifetime limits for registered pension schemes.

See *British Master Tax Guide* 429.

Law: FA 2004, s. 189(1)

12-100 Defending reputation

Q. A firm of solicitors consisting of two partners received a professional negligence claim against one of the partners in connection with bad advice given to a client. The Law Society took action against the partner for professional misconduct and the partner was struck off. He ceased to be a partner with the business but the firm has continued with the introduction of a new partner. The partnership stood the legal costs incurred in defending the former partner. Are the costs allowable as a deduction against the partnership profits?

A. The legislation disallows any expenditure not incurred wholly and exclusively for the purposes of the trade, profession or vocation. This means that the rule is only satisfied if the taxpayer's sole purpose for incurring the expense is for the purposes of their trade, profession or vocation. If a non-trade purpose is identified the expense is not allowable.

The cost of defending title to trade or professional assets is generally allowable. However the costs of defending personal reputation are not allowable. A solicitor defending himself against an action, which if they lost, would preclude them from practising as a solicitor, has an automatic non-professional reason and the expenditure is disallowable.

See *British Master Tax Guide* 2242.

12-120   Lease premium

Example

Black is granted on 1 September a lease of offices by White Ltd for 21 years, at a premium of £70,000 and rental of £12,000 p.a. Black, who has calendar year periods of account, immediately occupies the offices for the purposes of his trade.

White Ltd pays tax on £42,000 calculated as follows:

	£
Premium	70,000
Less: 70,000 × 20/50	
(20 complete years)	(28,000)
	42,000

Black will get tax relief for £4,000 of actual rent paid in the first year, plus £668, calculated as £42,000 × 122 days/7,670 days.

See *British Master Tax Guide* 2245.

Law: ITTOIA 2005, s. 61

12-140   Pre-trade learning

> **Q.** Oliver has commenced trade as a self-employed swimming instructor. He has been a keen swimmer for many years, however in order to begin teaching he has had to obtain a teaching qualification. On the basis that he is unable to conduct his business without this qualification, can the expenditure on the cost of the training course and exams be deducted from his trading income as a pre-trading expense?

A. On the basis that this qualification has given the business proprietor new expertise and skills, it is said to provide an enduring benefit to the business and therefore the expenditure will be deemed to be of a capital nature.

The HMRC manual confirms that any expenditure that provides new expertise or knowledge should be disallowed, particularly where it brings into existence a recognised qualification.

Where the purpose of training is merely to update current expertise this can, for the self-employed, usually be regarded as revenue expenditure and is therefore deductible provided it is incurred wholly and exclusively for the purpose of the trade.

Income Tax

See *British Master Tax Guide* 2260.

Law: ITTOIA 2005, s. 33, 57

12-150   Business equipment

> **Q.**   I am setting up in practice for myself and want to know how much of the costs of
> my professional library I can claim against the profits of the business in the first year.

A.   In the Court of Appeal, in the case of *Munby v Furlong* it was decided that in the case
of a professional person the cost of periodicals were a revenue expense, claimable against
tax in the year in which the expenditure was incurred. It was also decided that textbooks,
which had an indefinite expected useful life, were plant, and capital allowances could be
claimed on them.

Therefore the costs of your textbooks and reference books can be claimed as plant, and a
writing-down allowance be claimed on the expenditure, the costs of professional magazines
can be claimed in full in the year in which you receive them.

As a general rule expenditure incurred before commencing practice will fall into one of
three categories:

(1)   expenditure allowable against profits in the first trading period, such as rental costs
incurred while setting up your practice;

(2)   expenditure subject to capital allowances, such as the cost of computers and furniture;

(3)   expenditure which will not be allowable, such as the cost of the course enabling you to
gain your professional qualification.

See *British Master Tax Guide* 2150.

Law: *Munby v Furlong (HMIT)* (1977) 50 TC 491

12-160   Incorporation losses

Example

On 1 May 2008 Hugh transfers his business to Y2 Ltd in return for shares. Hugh's business
has an outstanding loss of £20,000. Hugh owns the shares in Y2 Ltd at all material times. In
the year 2009–10 Hugh receives director's fees of £15,000 and a dividend of £1,500 gross.
If the relief is claimed, the loss will be set off against both types of income. The £3,500 loss
which remains outstanding is then carried forward and set off against income from the
company (salary before dividends) in 2010–11 and so on until the loss has been set off
completely.

See *British Master Tax Guide* 2292.

Law: ITA 2007, s. 86

12-180   Opening year losses

Example

Hugh started trading on 1 April 2006 and ceased trading on 30 April 2009. His tax-adjusted trading results (including capital allowances) show profits/(losses) as follows:

	£
Seven months to 31/7/06	(14,000)
Year to 31/7/07	(12,000)
Year to 31/7/08	36,000
Nine months to 30/4/09	20,000

The assessments (before loss relief) and available losses are computed as follows:

			Assessments £	Available losses £
2005–06	1/1/06 to 5/4/06			
	3/7 × (14,000)		Nil	(6,000)
2006–07	1/1/06 to 31/12/06			(14,000)
Less: overlap loss				6,000
5/12 × (12,000)	(5,000)		Nil	(5,000)
				(13,000)
2007–08	y/e 31/7/07		Nil	(12,000)
Less: overlap loss				5,000
				(7,000)
2008–09	y/e 31/7/08		36,000	
2009–10	9 months to 30/4/09		20,000	

If Hugh's general income was £10,445 in 2006–07, £44,645 in 2007–08 and £4,545 in 2008–09, he may decide to use the 2006–07 loss in the current year; the 2007–08 loss in the current year, and the 2008–09 loss in the previous year.

This avoids wasting personal allowances.

	2005–06 £	2006–07 £	2007–08 £
General income	10,445	44,645	4,545
Less: s. 64(2)	(6,000)		
Less: s. 64(2)		(13,000)	
Less: s. 64(2)		(7,000)	

See *British Master Tax Guide* 2297, 2302.

Law: ITA 2007, s. 64

12-190   Temporary extension of loss carry-back rules

> **Q.**   A sole trader has incurred trading losses in the two tax years 2008–09 and 2009–10. His business had been profit making prior to this. The details are as follows:
>
> - 2005–06 profit of £20,000;
> - 2006–07 profit of £80,000;
> - 2007–08 profit of £30,000;
> - 2008–09 loss of £90,000;
> - 2009–10 loss of £125,000.
>
> He wishes to take advantage of the extended carry-back loss provisions. To what extent will relief be given?

A.   Following the Pre-Budget Report 2008 and Budget 2009, trading losses incurred in 2008–09 and 2009–10 can be carried back for three years. Losses must be carried back to later years first, initially up to the maximum loss available for carry back against the total income of the previous 12 months and then up to a maximum of £50,000 covering the previous two years' trading profit only.

The above losses can be carried back as follows:

	2005–06	2006–07	2007–08	2008–09	2009–10
Profit/loss	£20,000	£80,000	£30,000	(£90,000)	(£125,000)
1-year carry back			(£30,000)	£30,000	
Extended carry back		(£50,000)		£50,000	
Extended carry back		(£30,000)			£30,000
Chargeable	£20,000	Nil	Nil		
Losses c/fwd				(£10,000)	(£95,000)

See *British Master Tax Guide* 2305.

Law: FA 2009, s. 23

12-200   Terminal losses

Example

Toby ceased trading on 30 June 2009. Toby's accounts for recent years have shown the following profits/(loss):

Year to 31 December	£
2006	12,000
2007	11,000
2008	8,000
Six months to 30/6/09	(5,000)

Toby has no other income but there is unused overlap relief of £4,000.

The assessments are calculated as follows:

	£	£
2006–07		12,000
2007–08		11,000
2008–09	8,000	
Less: terminal loss relief	(6,500)	1,500
2009–10	(5,000)	
	(4,000)	(9,000)

Calculation of terminal loss

	£
1/7/08–5/4/09	
6/12 × £8,000	4,000
3/6 × (£5,000)	(2,500)
	1,500 (treat as Nil)

	£
6/4/09–30/6/09	
3/6 × (£5,000)	(2,500)
Total loss	(2,500)
Add: overlap relief	(4,000)
Available terminal loss	(6,500)
Set against earlier profits	6,500
Unused loss	Nil

See *British Master Tax Guide* 2297, 2302.

Law: ITA 2007, s. 89

12-220 Post-cessation expenses

> **Q.** Gabby is a chartered surveyor and architect currently operating as a sole trader; she will be retiring at the end of May 2010. Following her retirement Gabby will need to continue paying her professional indemnity insurance premiums for five years in order to cover the work she has undertaken prior to the cessation of her business. Is there any tax relief for these expenses?

A. Relief is available for post-cessation expenses incurred within seven years of cessation provided that they are incurred wholly and exclusively in relation to the activities of a business that was previously carried on by an individual, either alone or in partnership. HMRC specifically list professional indemnity insurance as an acceptable example.

See *British Master Tax Guide* 2310.

Law: ITTOIA 2005, s. 250, 349–352

12-240 Capital allowances introduction

> *Note: The capital allowances regime was substantially reformed from 2008–09. The following example applies only for years up to and including 2007–08.*

Example

A trader has a value brought down from year one of £100,000. He incurs expenditure in 2007–08 of £25,000. He sells an asset in the year for £5,000 (which is less than the cost of the asset).

Assume that no first-year allowances are due. His computation for 2007–08 is as follows:

	£
Unrelieved qualifying expenditure b/fwd	100,000
Additional qualifying expenditure	25,000
Available qualifying expenditure	125,000
Total disposal receipts	(5,000)
	120,000
Writing-down allowance (25%)	(30,000)
Unrelieved qualifying expenditure c/fwd	90,000

If the business had an accounting period of just nine months the allowances would be calculated as follows:

	£
Unrelieved qualifying expenditure b/fwd	100,000
Additional qualifying expenditure	25,000
Available qualifying expenditure	125,000
Total disposal receipts	(5,000)
	120,000
Writing-down allowance (25% × 9/12)	(22,500)
Unrelieved qualifying expenditure c/fwd	97,500

If the business is carried on in the course of a 15-month period the allowances are calculated as follows:

	£
Unrelieved qualifying expenditure b/fwd	100,000
Additional qualifying expenditure	25,000
Available qualifying expenditure	125,000
Total disposal receipts	(5,000)
	120,000
Writing-down allowance (25% × 15/12)	(37,500)
Unrelieved qualifying expenditure c/fwd	82,500

See *British Master Tax Guide* 2332.

Law: CAA 2001, s. 6

12-260　When did you buy it?

> **Q.** Peter took delivery of new machinery that was used immediately in the manufacturing process of the trade. The machinery was delivered one month before the end of the accounting period and a contract to pay was agreed on the same day. The contract allowed a credit period of two months before the payment for the machinery became due. At what point in time is the expenditure recognised for capital allowance purposes?

A. The general rule is that expenditure is to be treated as incurred when there is an unconditional obligation to pay it. This applies even if all or some of the amount does not have to be paid until a later date. Legislation imposes a time-limit of four months after which the treatment differs. This subsection requires that, if the payment is due at a date

219

later than four months after the contract becoming unconditional, the effective date of expenditure is that date upon which the amount becomes payable.

See *British Master Tax Guide* 2334.

Law: ITTOIA 2005, s. 142

12-280   When is an animal a plant?

> **Q.**   Rachel has owned some horses for some time. She has now set up a riding school in which she is going to use the horses. What is the correct treatment of those horses and any of their foals that are reared for use in the business?

A.   Horses are plant when used in this way and they therefore qualify for writing-down allowances. As these horses were used by their owner for another purpose prior to being used in the riding school, the qualifying expenditure on which writing-down allowances are based is their market value on the date when first used in the business or the actual expenditure on them, if less.

As far as the foals being reared are concerned, trading deductions can be claimed for the expense of rearing the foals. At the point that they are introduced into the riding school, a trading receipt for that amount must be taxed and the same amount is the qualifying expenditure for writing-down purposes. The context of the treatment is the herd basis for farming which extends the treatment to trades other than farming.

See *British Master Tax Guide* 2360.

Law: CTA 2009, s. 50; ITTOIA 2005, s. 30; CAA 2001, s. 13

12-290   Can I claim for my stolen van?

> **Q.**   My client bought a van on hire purchase (HP), intending to use it in his trade. He was dissatisfied with it and returned it before he started to use it. Unfortunately the van was stolen and, following a court case, he is now liable to pay the HP company the full price. How can he get a deduction for the expenditure he will be incurring?

A.   Unfortunately your client will get no relief. Under CAA 2001, s. 67(3) items bought on HP will qualify for capital allowances when brought into use. Your client never brought the van into use, so he will not get capital allowances. However, the expenditure is still of a capital nature, so will not qualify for deduction as a revenue expense. Had he used it in the trade and it had subsequently been stolen, he would have been able to claim the capital allowances.

The *Capital Allowances Act* 2001, s. 67(3) states:

'At the time when the plant or machinery is brought into use for the purposes of the qualifying activity or corresponding overseas activity, the person is to be treated for the purposes of this Part as having incurred all capital expenditure in respect of the plant or machinery to be incurred by him under the contract after that time.'

See *British Master Tax Guide* 2324.

Law: CAA 2001, s. 67(3)

12-300   Effect of making a short-life asset election

Example

A business with qualifying expenditure of £160,000 brought forward buys a computer system costing £24,000 in year one. In year four it is scrapped. No other assets are bought or sold in the period in question. The annual investment allowance has been fully absorbed by another company in the group.

Without a short-life asset election, the position is as follows (applying the rates of writing-down allowances that have applied since April 2008, but ignoring transitional hybrid rates of allowance):

Main pool	£
Value b/fwd	160,000
Additions	24,000
	184,000
Less: Year 1 WDA	(36,800)
Value c/fwd	147,200
Less: Year 2 WDA	(29,440)
Value c/fwd	117,760
Less: Year 3 WDA	(23,552)
Value c/fwd	94,208
Less: Year 4 WDA	(18,842)
Value c/fwd	75,366

With no election, the total allowances given over the four-year period amount to £108,634.

If an election is made, the position is as follows:

Income Tax

	Main pool	*SLA pool*
	£	£
Value b/fwd	160,000	–
Additions	–	24,000
	160,000	24,000
Less: Year 1 WDA	(32,000)	(4,800)
Value c/fwd	128,000	19,200
Less: Year 2 WDA	(25,600)	(3,840)
Value c/fwd	102,400	15,360
Less: Year 3 WDA	(20,480)	(3,072)
Value c/fwd	81,920	12,288
Less: Year 4 WDA	(16,384)	
Proceeds		Nil
		(asset scrapped)
Balancing allowance		(12,288)
Value c/fwd	65,536	Nil

With the election, the total allowances given over the period amount to £118,464, an increase of £9,830.

To gain a fuller understanding of the position three points need to be considered.

(1) The effect of a short-life asset election is one of timing only. The increased allowances of £9,830 in the above example will eventually be offset by reduced allowances in future years. The carried forward value of £65,536 is therefore exactly £9,830 less than the figure of £75,366 where no election is made.

(2) The timing benefit of £9,830 all arises in the year of disposal (year four in the example). All that is happening is that a full balancing allowance is being given in that year instead of the standard 20 per cent writing-down allowance.

(3) By looking at the position at the start of the disposal period it can be seen (in this case too late – the time-limit for the irrevocable election has passed) whether or not the election will be beneficial. In the example, the brought forward value of the short-life asset is £12,288. As long as the asset is sold for less than 80 per cent of this figure then the election will prove beneficial. If it is sold for more, the election will be disadvantageous.

See *British Master Tax Guide* 2367.

Law: CAA 2001, s. 83–89

12-320   The general pool

Example

A business has expenditure brought down from the previous period of £20,000. An asset is sold for £6,000 and a replacement is bought for £10,000. For simplicity, it is assumed that the business is not entitled to any annual investment allowance (AIA) (probably because that allowance has been fully allocated to a connected business).

Available qualifying expenditure (AQE) will be £30,000, and the total of any disposal receipts (TDR) to be brought into account will be £6,000. Therefore, the allowance available is 20% of the net figure of £24,000, so £4,800. The balance of £19,200 is carried forward to the following period of account.

See *British Master Tax Guide* 59.

Law: CAA 2001, s. 53–66

12-330   Writing down allowances

Example

A trader has a value brought down from year 1 of £100,000. He incurs expenditure in year 2 of £25,000. He sells an asset in the year for £5,000 (which is less than the cost of the asset). Assume that no first-year allowances or annual investment allowances are due. His computation for year 2 is as follows:

	£
Unrelieved qualifying expenditure brought forward	100,000
Additional qualifying expenditure	25,000
Available qualifying expenditure	125,000
Total disposal receipts	(5,000)
	120,000
Writing-down allowance (20%)	24,000
Unrelieved qualifying expenditure carried forward	96,000

See *British Master Tax Guide* 59.

Law: CAA 2001, s. 53–66

12-340 Flat conversion allowance

Example

Zoe carries out work on renovating a flat during the year to 5 April 2010, and claims 100% tax relief on the costs in 2009–10. She obtains a tax refund as a result. Costs rise and Zoe cannot fund the remaining work. She therefore sells the property in November 2010, before the flats are ready for letting. The initial allowance is withdrawn and her 2009–10 tax liability is recalculated accordingly.

See *British Master Tax Guide* 2394.

Law: CAA 2001, s. 393I

12-360 Renovating business premises

> **Q.** An individual has recently bought a derelict building that he intends to renovate and use as business premises. Is there scope for claiming business premises renovations allowances?

A. Business premises renovation allowances apply to expenditure incurred in a period of at least five years running from 11 April 2007. Allowances of 100% can be claimed for the costs of renovating certain unused business property. A claim for allowances can be made by an individual or a company that incurs capital expenditure on bringing qualifying business premises back into business use. The allowances can be clawed back if there is a sale or other balancing event within seven years from the date on which the premises are first brought back into use. The subsequent purchaser of the property will have no entitlement to claim allowances.

See *British Master Tax Guide* 2390.

Law: FA 2005, s. 92 and Sch. 6

12-370 BPRA on retirement

> **Q.** My client is a trading partnership that met all of the relevant conditions to qualify for Business Premises Renovation Allowance (BPRA) for expenditure in 2007 and has received 100% writing-down allowances for the cost of the work. The partnership has five partners. One of the partners is considering retiring from the partnership. He would receive payment of his capital account at that point. The BPRA legislation makes clear that if there is a balancing event and that happens within seven years of the time that the property is first used after renovation, there would be a clawing back of the allowance. The definitions of balancing events in CAA 2001, s. 360O talk about sale of the property,

but what about the position if the retiring partner simply gives up his interest in the property for nil consideration?

A. The partner's retirement would not constitute the sale of the property according to the normal commercial meaning of a sale. However, CAA 2001, s. 573 vastly widens the definition of sale to include any disposal of the relevant interest in the property. Therefore, any arrangement under which the individual begins owning an interest in the property that entitles him to BPRA but ends up not owning a share in the property must result in a balancing event.

See *British Master Tax Guide* 2390.

Law: CAA 2001, s. 360O, 573

12-380   PAYE settlement agreements

Example

Ten higher-rate employees each receive benefits in kind valued at £200. The total value of benefits in kind is therefore £2,000 and, at 40%, the tax on this would amount to £800.

As the employer is going to meet this tax liability, it must be grossed up using the formula:

Tax liability $\times$ 100/(100 − 40)

The tax bill is therefore calculated as £800 $\times$ 100/60 = £1,333.33.

If the employer has other employees who are basic rate taxpayers then they must carry out a similar calculation for them and add the end result to the £1,333.33 so as to calculate the overall tax liability.

See *British Master Tax Guide* 2750.

Law: ITEPA 2003, s. 703–707

12-400   PAYE settlement agreement for all employees

Example

A company has agreed a PAYE settlement agreement (PSA) with HMRC. The employer provides a ball for the 200 employees to celebrate the company's ten-year anniversary. The cost of the ball is £100,000. Of the 200 employees, 150 pay tax at the basic rate and 50 pay tax at the higher rate.

The ball is outside the exemption for annual functions. However, it can be included within a PSA on the grounds of irregularity.

The employer's liability in respect of the PSA is found as follows:

Value of benefits provided to basic rate employees:

150/200 × £100,000   £75,000

Grossed-up value of benefits provided to basic rate employees:

£75,000 × 100/(100 − 20)   £93,750

Tax payable at basic rate:

£93,750 × 20%   £18,750

Value of benefits provided to higher-rate employees:

50/200 × £100,000   £25,000

Grossed-up value of benefits provided to higher-rate employees:

£25,000 × 100/(100 − 40)   £41,667

Tax payable at higher rate:

£41,667 × 40%   £16,667

Total tax payable by employer under PSA:

	£
Tax payable at basic rate	18,750
Tax payable at higher rate	16,667
Total tax payable under PSA	35,417

See *British Master Tax Guide* 285, 2750.

Law: ITEPA 2003, s. 264, 703–707

12-420   Date of repayment for loss carry back

> **Q.**   When a loss is carried back to an earlier year what is the effective date of payment for the credit generated?

A. If the resulting credit is to be set off against other liabilities then the effective date of payment is the later of the date the valid claim to relief was made and the relevant due date of the charge against which the relief is to be set.

If the credit is to be repaid then the effective date of payment is the fixed filing date of the later year's return.

Therefore a loss arising in 2009–10 and claimed on the 2010 return which was submitted on 1 June 2010 and carried back to May 2009 would have an effective date of payment for interest/surcharge purposes of 1 June 2010 but an effective date of payment for repayment supplement purposes of 31 January 2011.

See *British Master Tax Guide* 2764.

12-440   Pension PAYE effects

> **Q.** Andrea has given me her P60 but her taxable pay is less than her gross pay. The difference is equal to the amount of her employee pension contributions. Is this correct? The National Insurance table letter on the P60 is showing as A.

A. It appears that tax relief has been given at source for the employee's pension contributions. However, the corresponding table letter for National Insurance for an employee in an approved contracted-out pension scheme qualifying for tax relief at source under net pay arrangements would be either table D or F.

You will need to check that the table letter used is correct for the pension scheme contributions, which have been deducted. If the table letter shown is correct then the scheme does not have contracted-out status and tax relief at source should not have been applied. Her employers would be liable for the under-deduction of tax as they would have not operated PAYE correctly.

See *British Master Tax Guide* 2784.

12-460   Notice of coding

> **Q.** I have received a number of PAYE coding notices from HMRC in respect of my clients. It seems that HMRC have started to include estimates of non-PAYE income, such as bank and building society interest and rental income, in the PAYE codes. As the clients in question are self-assessment cases, I feel the inclusion of non-PAYE income in the coding notice is unnecessary. Can I ask HMRC to remove these items from the code?

A. Yes, an individual may ask HMRC to remove non-PAYE income from a code, and HMRC must then amend the code as requested.

See *British Master Tax Guide* 2784.

12-480 Annual investment allowance

Example

A business spends £90,000 on general plant and machinery and £25,000 on integral features. It will wish to treat the whole of the latter as annual investment allowance (AIA) qualifying expenditure so that the excess £15,000 (£90,000 plus £25,000, less £100,000) can attract allowances at the main writing down allowance (WDA) rate of 20% rather than at the lower rate of 10%.

See *British Master Tax Guide* 2324.

12-490 Sharing the annual investment allowance

Q. For several years Bob and Clive have run a trout farm as equal partners on some land on the outskirts of town. They prepare accounts for the trout farm annually to 31 May. Bob and Clive have also run another business with Derek (as equal partners) for several years repairing domestic appliances in a shed at the same site. The repair business draws its accounts up to 30 April each year.

In February 2009, the repair operation moved into a bigger unit a couple of miles away from the trout farm. The trout farm invested £30,000 in a refrigerated van for fish deliveries during the year ended 31 May 2009. During the year ended 30 April 2009, the repair business spent £25,000 on qualifying fixtures and new equipment for the expanded repair business at the new site.

Will the two partnerships be required to share a single annual investment allowance (AIA) between them for the tax year 2009–10?

A. The businesses will be required to share an AIA if they are controlled by the same person and they satisfy either or both of the shared premises conditions and the similar activities condition.

A partner is said to control a partnership for these purposes if he is entitled either to a majority of the capital of the partnership or a majority of the partnership's profits (CAA 2001, s. 51I(4) and 574(3). Clearly, no individual controls either partnership business under that definition. However, CAA 2001, s. 51I(5) goes on to say:

> 'Where partners who between them control one partnership also between them control another partnership, the qualifying activities carried on by the partnerships are to be treated as controlled by the same person.'

Together, Bob and Clive control the repair business and together they control the trout farm so the businesses are commonly controlled for these purposes.

The two partnerships will meet the similar activities condition if their NACE classification (classification of economic activities in the European Community) starts with the same letter of the alphabet. Classifications can be found on the EC website. The trout farm's activity is likely to fall into 'Freshwater aquaculture' (A3.2.2) and the repair business is likely to be classed as 'Repair of household appliances and home and garden equipment' (S95.2.2). So, the activities are not similar.

The shared premises test will be met if, 'at the end of the relevant chargeable period for one or both of the activities, the activities are carried on from the same premises'. (CAA 2001, s. 51J(3)). The relevant chargeable periods for the tax year 2009–10 are years ended 30 April 2009 and 31 May 2009. The repair business moved away in February so the businesses were not sharing premises at their year-ends. Therefore, the shared premises condition is not met in 2009–10.

The two partnerships are not required to split a single AIA between them because although the two activities are under common control, they do not meet either the shared premises or similar activities tests.

See *British Master Tax Guide* 2324.

Other guidance: http://ec.europa.eu/competition/mergers/cases/index/nace_all.html

12-500   Capital allowances on commercial investment properties

> **Q.**   My client's company has a large portfolio of commercial investment properties. He plans to carry out some extensive refurbishment work on several of the buildings in the near future, much of which would appear to qualify for capital plant and machinery allowances on fixtures and fittings. The expenditure is likely to be in excess of £100,000. Can you please confirm whether the 'annual investment allowance' (AIA) will be available on this expenditure, as I understand that new restrictions will apply to 'integral' plant and machinery?

A.   From 1 April 2008 (6 April 2008 for companies) the AIA is available to individuals, partnerships and companies, whether carrying on a rental business, trade, profession or vocation. Integral fixtures and fittings purchased from these dates are required to be held in a separate 'special rate' capital allowances pool and the written-down allowance will be restricted to 10% in this pool. However, the AIA will still be available in respect of such expenditure, in the same way as for moveable plant and machinery (HMRC Budget Notes 2008, BN 12). Your client will therefore be able to benefit from the AIA, but note, however, that the available relief is pro-rated both to the extent that an accounting period straddles

229

6 April 2008 (1 April 2008 for corporation tax) and to the extent that the accounting period is for more or less than 12 months. For an accounting period ending other than on 31 March, the relief on the remaining expenditure will attract written-down allowances at a 'hybrid' rate to reflect the reduction in the rate of relief from 25% to 10% as the following example illustrates:

Year-ended, say, 30 April 2008

£50,000 × 1/12 × 100% =	£4,167
£45,833 × 25% × (1/5/08 to 31/3/08) 11/12 = 22.91	
£45,833 × 10% × (1/4/08 to 30/4/08) 1/12 = 0.84 = 23.75% =	£10,885

See *British Master Tax Guide* 2324.

12-505 Capital allowances and property letting businesses

> **Q.** My client has income from three rental properties. He has recently purchased a personal computer to assist him in managing the business, for example, to produce rent statements, and spreadsheets recording expenditure. Are capital allowances available on the cost of the computer?

A. Yes, capital allowances are available on plant and machinery which is used in an income from property business. The types of plant and machinery that would qualify for allowances are vehicles, office equipment/furniture and tools used for maintenance of the property.

Allowances are not available for expenditure on furniture or household equipment provided for the tenants of a property (subject to special rules for furnished holiday lets), or on the cost of the building itself.

Capital allowances for a rental business are calculated in the same way as they are for a trade by virtue of CAA 2001, s. 15. Once calculated, they are deducted as an expense, and taken into account in arriving at the profit or loss from the letting business. Adjustments must be made for any private use of the assets, and the annual investment allowance will be available on qualifying assets.

See *British Master Tax Guide* 2324.

12-510 Capital allowances on prizes

> **Q.** My client is a self-employed plumber. He recently attended a meeting of his trade association and won a van which he immediately introduced into his business. What capital allowances are available to him?

A.   We must first establish what capital expenditure he will be treated as having incurred for capital allowance purposes. In fact, he has not incurred any expenditure on the van but CAA 2001, s. 14 treats him as having incurred expenditure equal to the market value of the van on the day it was first used in the plumbing business.

CAA 2001, s. 577 defines market value as 'the price the asset would fetch in the open market'. Therefore, even though the van has been taken immediately into use in the business, the capital expenditure is likely to be significantly lower than the list price. In terms of what capital allowances the van attracts, there is no problem claiming a writing down allowance of 20% but the asset would be denied annual investment allowance because of general exclusion 5 in CAA 2001, s. 38B.

See *British Master Tax Guide* 2324.

12-520   Am I a non-dom?

> **Q.**   When counting how many years a non-domiciled person has been resident do we count the year he arrived which was treated as a split year for residence purposes?

A.   For the purpose of determining the number of years it is necessary to count the number of years a person was resident, using the statutory definition of resident. As the split-year treatment is an extra statutory concession under ESC A11 you will have to ignore it for counting the years. Therefore the tax year of arrival will be treated as a year of residence.

See *British Master Tax Guide* 219.

12-540   Overseas employment and benefits in kind

> **Q.**   An individual who is resident, ordinarily resident and domiciled in the UK has taken up employment with an overseas employer. The employment is such that residence in the UK will continue. The remuneration package includes the provision of a company car which will be available for private use. Tax on this benefit will be paid on the provision of the car in the country where the duties of the employment are carried out. What is the tax position in respect of the car in the UK?

A.   Income that a person receives as the holder of an office or employment is charged to tax as 'employment income'. Employment income is defined in ITEPA 2003, s. 7 . It consists of 'general earnings' and 'specific employment income'.

General earnings is defined to include wages and salaries and also 'any gratuity or other profit or incidental benefit of any kind obtained by the employee if it is money or money's worth'. The definition of 'earnings' also includes 'anything else that constitutes an emolument'. This is a wide definition and ensures that all money payments that are similar to salaries, fees and wages are taxed as earnings. Examples are bonuses, commissions, tips, overtime pay and extra money earnings of any kind.

The main types of specific employment income include for example, payments and benefits on termination of employment, share related income, e.g. shares options and payments and benefits in respect of non-approved pension schemes.

The distinction between general earnings and specific employment income is an important one. There are special rules for taxing the general earnings of people who are not resident, or not ordinarily resident, or not domiciled in the UK for tax purposes. Those special rules do not apply to specific employment income.

Where an employee is at all times resident, ordinarily resident and domiciled in the UK the full amount of any general earnings which are received in a tax year is the amount of taxable earnings.

In this instance the company car benefit will be calculated as general earnings and included in the taxable earnings of the individual.

See *British Master Tax Guide* 10600.

12-560   Non-residents' living accommodation

> **Q.**   José is Spanish and his daughter has just been accepted at university in the UK. José intends to buy a house in the UK for use as accommodation for his daughter and for himself, as he intends to make frequent visits to England. These visits will combine seeing his daughter with the opportunity of furthering business contacts in England. José is concerned that the availability of accommodation in the UK may make him UK-resident for tax purposes.

A.   From the information that you give it should be arguable that José's visits to the UK are for 'temporary purposes'. The rules on the taxation of short-term visitors to the UK are in legislation, the *Income Tax Act* 2007, and in HMRC guidance, namely booklet HMRC6.

The *Income Tax Act* 2007, s. 831 and 832 apply to an individual who 'is in the United Kingdom for some temporary purpose only' and not with the intention of establishing his residence in the UK. Then he will be treated as non-resident in the UK in respect of relevant foreign income. An exception to these rules is, however, made if the person has in fact resided in the UK for six months or more in a tax year. Similar rules are made for CGT in TCGA 1992, s. 9(3).

The legislation makes it clear in s. 831 and 832 that the existence or otherwise of available accommodation must be ignored in determining whether an individual is in the UK for some temporary purpose and not with a view or intent of establishing his residence here.

HMRC practice is set out in booklet HMRC6. Again it is pointed out in HMRC6 (para. 1.5.22) that a taxpayer is always regarded as resident in a tax year if he is in the UK for 183 days or more in the year.

If José visits the UK regularly and after four tax years his visits during those years average 91 days or more a tax year then from para. 3.2, HMRC6, he will be treated by HMRC as resident from the start of the fifth year. It should be noted that from 2008 José will be counted as being in the UK on a particular day if he is in the UK at midnight on that day.

We can see from the above that the rules emphasise the purpose of the visits to the UK, i.e. are they for a settled or temporary purpose. If for a temporary purpose then José can rest assured that it is the number of days spent in the UK that is the relevant factor, and not the availability of accommodation here.

See *British Master Tax Guide* 11260.

12-580   Is death a reasonable excuse for non-payment?

Q.   My client died on 17 July so that no payment on account was made on the due date. It was more than a year before the personal representatives thought of making payments to HMRC for his income tax on his trading profits earned before he died. Is death a reasonable excuse from making payments on account?

A.   It is the duty of the personal representatives to administer the estate of the deceased and pay any liabilities that may be due. HMRC are not unreasonable and understand that the personal representatives cannot access the funds of the deceased before probate has been obtained. Extra-statutory Concession A17 provides a measure of relief.

The concession A17 states that where a taxpayer dies before a charge becomes due, then the due date is the later of either the normal due date or 30 days from grant of probate or letters of administration. Interest will run from this later due date until the date of payment.

Apparently, in the case of your client, probate was granted six months after the death so that the self-assessment tax due by the deceased should be settled without further delay.

See *British Master Tax Guide* 1030.

12-600   Abolition of the starting rate

Q.   How will the 10% starting rate for savings income apply to my 62-year-old client's building society interest of £2,200 paid net during the year? Her other income is £5,200 rent received from a lodger, salary from a part-time employment of £6,000 and dividends received of £4,000.

A. Your client's income needs to be classified as savings (the interest), dividends and other non-savings income (salary and rent). Her personal allowance applicable for 2010–11 is £6,475. The limit for the starting rate for savings income is £2,440 for 2010–11.

The revised legislation retains the order in which income is subject to income tax: non-savings income then savings then dividends.

The rent received is subject to rent-a-room relief, so the amount taxable is £950 (£5,200 – £4,250). Hence total non-savings income is £6,950. After the personal allowance has been applied to it, £475 remains taxable at 20%. The effect is also to 'use up' £475 of the starting rate band. Therefore, £1,965 of the interest income is taxed at 10%. The interest income of the year is £2,750 (£2,200 grossed up for 20% tax at source). The total tax on the interest is £353 (£1,965 @ 10% and £785 @ 20%). The tax due is recovered through self-assessment at the end of the year. The dividend income remains the highest slice of income and is taxed at 10% (the tax being covered by the notional tax credit because all of her income is below the top of the basic rate band.

See *British Master Tax Guide* 1366.

12-620   Does the business come under the CIS?

> **Q.** My client is a company which supplies and fits smoke and fire alarms and also full fire protection systems. They have engaged a building contractor to carry out improvements to their business premises and are unsure as to whether or not they need to apply Construction Industry Scheme (CIS) deductions to payments made to the builder. I believe that their current activities are outside of CIS and so would have to be a deemed contractor before they became obliged to operate CIS.

A. The requirement to operate CIS for the building work on your client's own business premises as a deemed contractor will only be a factor if they are not already a contractor under CIS for their operations in supplying and fitting fire protection systems.

If they engage subcontractors in the installation of the fire protection systems then they should already be operating CIS on payments to those subcontractors as the installation of fire protection systems is included within mainstream CIS operations. They would, therefore, already be classed as a contractor. As an existing CIS contractor they would have to operate CIS on any CIS activities for which they engage a subcontractor and the building work on their own business premises would be caught.

However, if your client uses it's own PAYE employees *only* in the installation of the fire protection systems then they would not be a contractor under CIS. To be required to operate CIS they would have to meet the deemed contractor criteria with an average expenditure of £1m p.a. on construction operations. However, even if they were a deemed contractor the construction work on their own business premises would be an operation exempted by the

Income Tax (Construction Industry Scheme) Regulations 2005 (SI 2005/2045), reg. 22(1), the payment would not be deemed as one to which CIS would be applied. Payment for construction operations relating to property used for the purposes of the business does not fall within CIS if the payment is made by someone who qualifies as a deemed contractor under FA 2004, s. 59(1)(l).

See *British Master Tax Guide* 2787.

12-640 Using the remittance basis

> **Q.** My client is not domiciled in the UK and has overseas capital gains and losses. In a previous year I set his overseas losses against the overseas gains but it was pointed out by HMRC that I had made a mistake and that the losses could not be used. In view of this it is important that I understand the new regime.
>
> My client will not be claiming the remittance basis every year but will make a decision each year. For 2009–10 he is likely to have foreign gains of £90,000, losses of £20,000, UK gains of £30,000 and UK losses of £40,000. He never remits the gain to the UK and will be claiming the remittance basis for 2009–10.

A. As you imply, up to and including 2007–08 there was no relief for any overseas capital losses made by foreign domiciliaries. Before 2008–09 the remittance basis for capital gains was automatic and not subject to a claim.

Finance Act 2008 introduced a form of loss relief for overseas losses from 6 April 2008. For a foreign domiciliary taxed on the remittance basis it will be possible to make an election. The election must be made for the first year in which the remittance basis is claimed. If an election is not made, then overseas losses of that tax year and all future years will not be allowable losses. They will be disallowed even if the taxpayer in a later year opts to be taxed on an arising basis rather than remittance basis unless he accepts that he is domiciled in the UK for all purposes.

You must think carefully before an election is made because it can cause surprising results. The order of set-off can cause problems. If the remittance basis is claimed for the tax year in which overseas capital gains are made, the total allowable losses (overseas and UK) are deducted first from foreign gains arising and remitted in the year, then against unremitted foreign gains and lastly against UK gains.

For your client, who does not remit overseas gains for 2009–10:

With election to use foreign losses

Total losses foreign £20,000 + UK £40,000 = £60,000

Set off against foreign gains of £90,000

Leave foreign gains of £30,000 – not taxed as not remitted

UK gains £30,000 subject to tax

With no election to use foreign losses

Total losses foreign £20,000 + UK £40,000 = £60,000

Foreign gains of £90,000 not subject to tax

UK gains £30,000 less UK losses £40,000 leave no gain taxable and £10,000 loss to carry forward

It can be seen that in this case an election to take advantage of foreign losses will lead to a higher tax charge.

See *British Master Tax Guide* 11150.

12-660 Bad debts

> **Q.** We trade as a partnership, have a large number of clients, not one of whom owes a large amount. It would be extremely onerous to examine each creditor to determine a specific bad debt. Are we nonetheless able to claim the provision as allowable for tax?

A. The place to start in the consideration of allowability in this instance is ITTOIA 2005, s. 35:

'Bad and doubtful debts

(1) In calculating the profits of a trade, no deduction is allowed for a debt owed to the person carrying on the trade, except so far as–

    (a) the debt is bad;

    (b) the debt is estimated to be bad; or

    (c) the debt is released wholly and exclusively for the purposes of the trade as part of a statutory insolvency arrangement.

(2) If the debtor is bankrupt or insolvent, the whole of the debt is estimated to be bad for the purposes of subsection (1)(b), except so far as any amount may reasonably be expected to be received on the debt.'

This section clearly indicates that general bad debt provisions will not be allowed. Subsection (1)(b) makes it clear that only the estimate for a specific debt which is considered bad will be allowed. However, HMRC have agreed a relaxation in the strict interpretation of the legislation in specific circumstances.

General bad debt provisions, i.e. not relating to specific debts, are not deductible. However where there are a large number of comparatively small debts, making the 'valuation' of individual debts impracticable, HMRC will normally agree to an allowance in accordance with a formula based on the bad debt experience of the business.

Under the circumstances you have indicated, a general provision, based on an accurate estimate of historical bad debt percentages, would be allowable.

See *British Master Tax Guide* 2150.

12-680   How is the car scrappage scheme dealt with for tax?

Q.   During the year under review, my client purchased a new car for his business under the scrappage scheme. Does the £2,000 discount count as disposal proceeds for the old car?

A.   Whether your client is a limited company or an unincorporated business, capital allowances can be claimed on cars purchased for business use. When a business purchases a car under the scrappage scheme, capital allowances are available on the amount actually paid for the car, i.e. the list price less the £2,000 deduction.

The car that has been scrapped is treated as having been disposed of for no proceeds. The £2,000 discount is not treated as consideration for the scrapped vehicle and as such does not constitute taxable disposal proceeds for capital allowances purposes.

Of course, if your client is an unincorporated business, any capital allowances claimed must be reduced by the appropriate percentage representing the private use of the car.

See *British Master Tax Guide* 2324.

12-700   SMP paid to foreign workers

Q.   We have employed a woman from Albania who has a work visa which states 'no access to public funds'. She is now pregnant and has presented us with form MatB1 showing an expected date of confinement of 21/12/09. Are we right to refuse to pay Statutory Maternity Pay (SMP) as she has no right to public funds. Her visa also shows an expiry date of 31 August 2009.

A.   SMP is not a benefit paid from public funds but rather a statutory right which is 'earned' from employment and earnings which are subject to Class 1 National Insurance and paid during the set period ending with the payment in or before the fifteenth week before the expected week of confinement (EWC). Twenty-six weeks' continuous employment is required by the end of the fifteenth week before the EWC.

For an expected date of confinement of 21/12/09 the fifteenth week before would be 6–12 September 2009. In this instance there would be no requirement to calculate the average earnings or length of qualifying service as by the time of the fifteenth week the employee would no longer be a legal employee as her work permit will have expired.

However, if her work permit is renewed with an effective renewal before the end of the fifteenth week before the EWC then she would be eligible for SMP on the same criteria as any other employee.

See *British Master Tax Guide* 294.

12-720   Mixing up UK and foreign income

> **Q.** My client is a UK-resident individual. During 2008–09, he received the following income: a minimal salary of £5,435 from his own UK company, a dividend of £40,000 from that company, interest of £3,000 from a bank in India which had been taxed at the treaty rate of 15% and a dividend of £750 from a Spanish company after tax at the treaty rate of 15% had been withheld. What double taxation relief is available to him by crediting the overseas tax against his UK liability?

A. The limit of credit of overseas tax is the lower of the foreign tax and the UK tax charged on that income. Because he has more than one source of income for the year, we need a method for establishing the UK tax on the overseas income. HMRC's *International Manual* at INTM165040 provides commentary on the calculations. First, calculate the income tax liability on his total income. With a personal allowance of £5,435 this comes to £7,848.

Note that the Spanish dividend income is £1,111 because the taxpayer (who is a minority shareholder) was entitled to a 10% notional credit. Arguably the foreign interest is liable to UK tax at 10% or 20% and the foreign dividends at a rate of 10%. That would imply a restriction of the foreign taxes at the higher rate of 15%. However, INTM165040 states that the taxpayer's foreign income:

> 'is to be treated as forming the top slice of his total income so that the maximum amount of UK tax can be attributed to it.'

Therefore, for the purpose of establishing the crediting limit, we treat the foreign income as if it were taxed at the taxpayer's highest rate of 32.5% and therefore the foreign taxes can be fully credited against his UK tax liability.

See *British Master Tax Guide* 1780.

12-740 Compensation could be damaging

> **Q.** My client recently won a long-standing claim for damages, which involved their minor child several years ago. They were finally awarded over £4m as compensation which they are told will be paid to them not as a lump sum but as a set regular figure decided by the courts. They have been told by their solicitors that this amount will be taxed on them as parents at their marginal rate.
>
> My clients understandably, are particularly anxious as they will now have to find funds to settle their tax bill. Are they able to delay payment or are there any reliefs available to them?

A. Claims for personal injury can be paid in a number of ways. They can be settled via a lump sum to the individual party, or, as is more often the case, a periodical payment is made to the individual for the rest of his or her life; this is referred to as a structured settlement and usually involves a minor.

From 1 April 2005, courts have the power to impose an order providing for periodical payments to the injured person without the consent of the parties. Previously, an order providing for periodical payments could only be made if both parties agreed.

Within ITTOIA 2005, s. 731, the payment can be made by the person liable for the damages, by an insurance company who acts on behalf of the person liable, by way of an annuity, or by the Motor Insurers Bureau (MIB) where the driver is uninsured or untraceable, as long as it meets the conditions within s. 731(2)(a)–(e).

ITTOIA 2005, s. 733 clearly states that certain people entitled to receive the sums awarded are not liable to tax. These include:

- the injured person;
- a person who receives a periodical payment on behalf of the injured person, such as a parent or guardian;
- a person given power of attorney where the injured person is incapacitated;
- a trustee who receives a periodical payment on trust for the benefit of the injured person, provided the injured person is the only beneficiary in life.

Therefore, there will be no tax liability on your client by virtue of ITTOIA 2005, s. 733.

See *British Master Tax Guide* 1376.

Corporation Tax

Relief for income tax suffered	243
Comprehensive example of adjustments to calculate taxable trading profits	244
Bad debt provisions	249
Typical corporation tax computation	249
Period of account exceeding 12 months	250
Accounting period for a newly formed company	252
Accounting periods for a company in liquidation	252
Relief for 'loan relationship' non-trading deficit	253
Related loans	253
Group loans and gains	254
Bad debts in a group	254
Revenue or capital computer	255
Intangible amortisation	256
Accounting period straddling 31 March	256
Small companies' rate	256
Marginal relief	257
Foreign tax suffered	257
Should I withhold withholding tax?	258
Post cessation carry forward of losses	259
Terminal losses	259
Carry back of trading losses	260
Government loans	261
Buying losses	262
Pre-rental expenditure	262
Pre-trading expenditure	263
Losses on a company restructuring	263
Converting loans into shares	265
Who's in control?	265
Change in trade	266
Purchase of own shares	266
Hive down of trade with transferor company left insolvent	267
Identifying the group return period	268
Can it be a group company?	269
Sale of trading stock on intra-group transfer of trade	269
Pre-entry losses	270
Notional group transfer	271
Degrouping charge	271
Degrouping goodwill	272
Consortium relief	273
Wasting losses and double tax	274
Group relieved capital allowances	274

Corporation Tax

Calculation of profits available for group relief   275
Computation of group relief from newly acquired subsidiary   276
Comprehensive example of group relief   277
A group and a consortium   278
Substantial shareholdings   279
Substantial shareholdings and the nil gain nil loss rules   280
Substantial share for share exchange   280
Does my company live where I live?   281
How is my overseas company taxed?   281
Pre-sale sales   282
How close are they?   282
Are limited liability partnerships associated?   283
Group or association   283
Minimum controlling combinations   284
Participator loans participate in penalty calculation   285
Effect of a director's loan on penalty and interest   286
Buy-back of shares   286
Selling the company assets and my liabilities   287
Life company taxation   288
R&D claims   289
R&D group   290
Pension contributions and R&D   290
Enhanced SME relief for R&D subcontracted to fellow group company   291
Tell HMRC when you start   291
Paying by instalments   292
Changing the quarters   292
Interest on unpaid tax   293
Interest on tax repaid   294
Computation of penalties and interest   294
Late filing penalty   295
Stock or fixed assets   295
Construction industry company   296
UITF 40 adjustment   296
Company loans to family members   297
Rationalising associated company's structure   297
Who's associated with who?   298
Purchasing energy-saving equipment   298
Capital allowances under the new regime   300
How does the family company claim AIAs?   300
How does the family company share capital allowances on long-life plant?   301
How is a VAT repayment dealt with for corporation tax purposes?   302
Claim for double tax relief   302
Tax on foreign company dividends   303
Bad debts on cessation of business   303
Capital allowances on leased vehicles   304

CORPORATION TAX

20-000　Relief for income tax suffered

Example

Geranium Ltd prepares accounts to 31 March each year. Its corporation tax computation for the year ended 31 March 2010 is as follows:

	£	£
Tax-adjusted trading profits		1,887,500
Non-trade loan relationship profits		
Loan interest receivable	37,500	
Bank interest payable	(7,000)	30,500
		1,918,000
Less: qualifying charitable donation		(8,000)
PCTCT		1,910,000

	£
Corporation tax liability	
£1,910,000 × 28%	534,800
Less: excess of income tax suffered	
over tax deducted from own charges	(4,200)
Amount payable	530,600

Trading profits include patent royalties of £4,000 paid overseas to Super Nova Ltd (a Guernsey resident company).

Income tax suffered/(paid)

	£
Loan interest 10% Cranesbill plc loan note £500,000	
issued to company on 30/6/09	
Interest received on 31/12/09	
(£500,000 × 10% × 6/12 = £25,000 × 20%)	5,000
Less: income tax paid on patent royalty (£4,000 × 20%)	(800)
Net income tax suffered by deduction	4,200

See *British Master Tax Guide* 3020.

Law: ITTOIA 2005, s. 602

20-020 Comprehensive example of adjustments to calculate taxable trading profits

Example

Acorus Ltd is a UK resident company which has traded as a manufacturer of gardening tools for many years. It has no associated companies. The company is a medium-sized company.

The company's summarised profit and loss account for the year ended 30 September 2009 showed the following:

	£	£
Sales		3,942,000
Less: cost of sales		(1,995,460)
Gross trading profit		1,946,540
Other income (note (a))		127,960
		2,074,500
Less:		
Rent and establishment costs	215,825	
Salaries and staff costs	535,900	
Directors' remuneration	135,400	
Pension contributions (note (b))	62,400	
Bad debts (note (c))	60,600	
Legal and professional costs (note (d))	12,000	
Audit and accountancy	60,000	
UK patent royalties	8,000	
Repairs and renewals (note (e))	27,400	
Depreciation (note (f))	428,000	
Sundries (note (g))	58,980	
Interest (note (h))	46,875	(1,651,380)
Profit before exceptional items		423,120
Less: exceptional items (note (i))		(471,000)
Loss before taxation		(47,880)

The following additional notes have been provided:

(a) Other income

	£
Franked investment income	30,500
Proceeds from sale of know-how	76,460
Bank interest receivable	21,000
	127,960

(b)   Pension contributions of £45,000 were paid during the year to 30 September 2009.

(c)   The bad debts account is analysed as follows:

	Dr £	Cr £
Balance at 1/10/08		
General provision	30,000	
Specific provision	23,000	
Profit and loss account	60,600	
Loss arising from staff pilferage		18,000
Balance at 30/9/09		
General provision		20,000
Specific provision		75,600
	113,600	113,600

(d)   Legal and professional costs are analysed as follows:

	£
Company secretarial costs	6,000
Debt collection	1,750
Patent infringement claim work	1,200
Claim for unfair dismissal	700
Assignment of short lease	2,350
	12,000

(e)   Repairs and renewals:

	£
Lorry park security fencing	2,050
Machinery protection guards	1,870
Factory storage shelving	13,230
General repairs provision	10,000
General factory maintenance (all allowable)	250
	27,400

Corporation Tax

245

(f) Depreciation is made up as follows:

	£
Owned assets	
Land and buildings	20,000
Plant and machinery	288,000
Finance lease assets	
Lorry fleet	120,000
	428,000

The company acquires all of its delivery lorries under finance leases. The lorries are depreciated at the rate of 25% with a full charge being made in the year of purchase and none in the year of disposal.

(g) Sundries are analysed as follows:

	£
Computer maintenance	16,600
Security costs	7,400
Damages paid to purchaser for supply of defective goods	4,000
Gift aid donation paid to BBC 'Children in Need' appeal	5,000
VAT serious misdeclaration penalty	3,600
Canteen expenses	21,700
Sundries (all allowable)	680
	58,980

(h) Interest is analysed as follows:

	£
Finance charge on finance leases	45,000
Loan stock interest accrued at 30/9/09	1,875
	46,875

(i)   Exceptional items:

	£	£
Loan stock issue expenses		
Accountants' fees	50,000	
Solicitors' fees	25,000	
Bank guarantee charges	15,000	90,000
Rationalisation costs		
Cost of transferring equipment	25,000	
Redundancy costs		
Paid in period	96,000	
Provision for future redundancies at 30/9/09	180,000	
Provision for other closure costs at 30/9/09	80,000	381,000
		471,000

The company issued £100,000 10% loan stock on 20 July 2009. (The amount borrowed is to be used for capital investment in a new factory.)

The company has a constructive obligation to carry out the rationalisation programme, at 30 September 2009, having taken steps to move plant and notify its suppliers and customers. The rationalisation primarily relates to the closure of its Prunella Road factory. The provision for future redundancies at 30 September 2009 has been calculated by reference to the amounts due to the relevant employees who are to be made redundant on 31 October 2009. The provisions for redundancy and closure costs are validly made under FRS 12.

(j)   The company can claim £42,703 in capital allowances.

(k)   The company can claim £12,482 in industrial buildings allowances.

Acorus Ltd's adjusted taxable trading profit and profit chargeable to corporation tax for the year ended 30 September 2009 is as follows:

Corporation Tax

	£	£
Loss before taxation		(47,880)
Add:		
Pension contributions charged	62,400	
Legal and professional costs – assignment of short lease	2,350	
Repairs and renewals (W2)	27,150	
Depreciation on 'owned' assets (£20,000 + £288,000)	308,000	
Sundries – VAT serious misdeclaration penalty	3,600	403,500
Less:		
Franked investment income	(30,500)	
Bank interest received	(21,000)	
Pension contributions paid	(45,000)	
Reduction in general provision for bad debts (£30,000 − £20,000) (W1)	(10,000)	
Capital allowances – plant	(42,703)	
Industrial buildings allowances	(12,482)	(161,685)
Tax-adjusted trading profit		193,935
Non-trading loan relationship income		21,000
Profits chargeable to corporation tax		214,935

Workings and notes

W1   The loss arising from staff pilferage would be accepted as allowable as this would be an ordinary risk of the trade.

W2   Repairs and renewals

		Disallowable
	£	£
General repairs provision	10,000	10,000
Lorry park security fencing	2,050	2,050
Machinery protection guards	1,870	1,870
Factory storage shelving	13,230	13,230
General factory maintenance	250	
	27,400	27,150

W3   The company is obliged (constructively) to the closure of the factory and the redundancy programme. The redundancy cost provision (calculated accurately by reference to the relevant individual employees) and the provisions for other closure costs are made in accordance with FRS 12, and hence allowed for tax purposes.

See *British Master Tax Guide* 3026–3029, 3036–3038.

Law: CTA 2009, s. 2–9; FA 1998, Sch. 18

20-040   Bad debt provisions

Example

A summary of Jasmine Ltd's bad debts account for the year ended 31 December 2009 is given below.

	£	£
Trade debts written off in the year (net of recoveries of £2,960)		19,950
Staff loan written off		600
		20,550
Provisions carried forward at 31/12/09:		
General	36,000	
Specific	22,360	58,360
Less: provisions brought forward at 1/1/06:		
General	(20,000)	
Specific	(27,450)	(47,450)
Charged to profit and loss account		31,460

The following amounts would be added back for tax purposes:

	£
Increase in general provision (36,000 − 20,000)	16,000
Staff loan written off	600
Disallowed	16,600

See *British Master Tax Guide* 3027.

20-060   Typical corporation tax computation

Example

Cornflower Ltd had the following income and capital gains for the year ended 31 December 2009, as adjusted for tax purposes.

	£
Trading profit (after deducting capital allowances)	275,000
Net income from rental of unfurnished property	18,000
Bank deposit interest	7,500
Dividends from overseas company (including foreign taxes of 25%)	8,000
Chargeable gains	50,000

The company also paid gross interest (i.e. including the income tax deducted at source) amounting to £36,000 on a £450,000 loan note issued to Mrs Search as part consideration for the acquisition of her company in December 2000.

Based on the above information, the corporation tax computation would be set out as follows:

Cornflower Ltd

Corporation tax computation based on the accounts for the year ended 31 December 2009.

	£
Adjusted trading profit	275,000
Net business rental income	18,000
Dividends from overseas companies	8,000
Chargeable gains	50,000
	351,000
Less: non-trading deficit (see below)	(28,500)
Profits chargeable to corporation tax (PCTCT)	322,500

	£
The non-trading deficit comprises:	
Loan note interest incurred	36,000
Bank deposit interest	(7,500)
	28,500

See *British Master Tax Guide* 3027–3028.

Law: CTA 2009, s. 2–9

20-080   Period of account exceeding 12 months

Example

Amaryllis Ltd has traded for some years and accounts have previously been prepared annually to 31 March. As a result of being taken over, the company has prepared accounts for the 18-month period to 30 September 2009.

The following information has been extracted:

- Trading profits for the period, as adjusted for taxation purposes, but before capital allowances, were £137,250.
- The company is entitled to capital allowances on plant and machinery of £5,220 for the 12 months to 31 March 2009 and £2,750 for the six months to 30 September 2009.
- The accounts for the period showed the following investment income:

	£
Bank deposit interest	1,530
Dividends from UK companies	4,000

- Interest of £18,000 was charged on a 12% £100,000 loan note issued for a £100,000 loan which was advanced to the company on 1 January 2005.
- The company covenanted to make an annual payment of £1,000 to Oxfam on 31 December each year. The first £1,000 was paid on 6 January 2009.

As the period of account exceeds 12 months, the company would have to prepare corporation tax computations for the following two accounting periods:

(1) 1 April 2008 to 31 March 2009 (12 months);

(2) 1 April 2009 to 30 September 2009 (6 months, ending on the date to which accounts are prepared).

Amaryllis Ltd

Corporation tax computation based on the accounts for the 18 months to 30 September 2009.

	1/4/08 to 31/3/09	1/4/09 to 30/9/09
	£	£
Adjusted trading profit	91,500	45,750
Capital allowances on plant	(5,220)	(2,750)
Trading profit	86,280	43,000
Less: current non-trading deficit	(10,980)	(5,490)
Profits before charges	75,300	37,510
Less: charges on income (gross):		
Gift Aid deduction	(1,000)	–
Profits chargeable to corporation tax	74,300	37,510

Current year non-trading deficit is made up as follows:

	£
Bank deposit interest income	1,530
12% loan note interest payable	(18,000)
	(16,470)

See *British Master Tax Guide* 3026–3028.

Law: CTA 2009, s. 2–9

20-100 Accounting period for a newly formed company

Example

Begonia Ltd was incorporated on 7 February 2010. It issued 50,000 ordinary shares on 25 April 2010 and most of the subscription moneys were placed in a bank deposit account on 29 April 2010. The company commenced trading on 1 July 2010 and registered to draw up its accounts to 31 December each year. Begonia Ltd's accounting periods would be as follows:

29 April 2010 to 30 June 2010

This period begins when Begonia Ltd acquires a source of income (the bank deposit account) and, in practice, would end on the day before trading commences.

1 July 2010 to 31 December 2010

This period starts on the day after the expiry of the previous period and ends on the date to which accounts are first drawn up.

Thereafter, Begonia Ltd will have a period ending on 31 December each year.

See *British Master Tax Guide* 3028.

Law: CTA 2009, s. 8–10

20-120 Accounting periods for a company in liquidation

Example

Magpie Ltd has traded for many years, making up accounts to 30 September each year. The shareholders of the company decided to put the company into liquidation and the relevant special resolution was passed on 10 June 2010. The liquidation of the company was completed on 15 January 2012.

Magpie Ltd would have the following accounting periods:

1 October 2008 to 30 September 2009

This would be a normal 12-month accounting period ending on the company's accounts date.

1 October 2009 to 9 June 2010

This accounting period will end immediately before the company is wound up.

10 June 2010 to 9 June 2011

This accounting period begins when the liquidation commences and runs for 12 months.

10 June 2011 to 15 January 2012

The completion of the liquidation terminates the accounting period.

See *British Master Tax Guide* 3028.

Law: CTA 2009, s. 8–10

20-140 Relief for 'loan relationship' non-trading deficit

Example

Autumnalis Ltd's summarised corporation tax results for the year ended 31 March 2009 are as follows:

	£'000	£'000
Adjusted trading profits		584
Rental income		42
Capital gain		15
Non-trading deficit, comprising:		
Interest payable (loan to finance investment property)	(64)	
Bad debt re loan to employee written-off	(7)	
Bank interest receivable	12	(59)
PCTCT (having offset the non-trading deficit in year)		582

The loss could also have been carried forward against a future non-trading surplus.

See *British Master Tax Guide* 3036–3038.

Law: CTA 2009, Pt. 5

20-160 Related loans

Example

The Jones partnership lends £100,000 to Pride Ltd. The composition of the partnership consists of Mr Jones, Pride Ltd and Proud Ltd. The loan carries interest at 10% p.a.

For the purposes of their respective tax calculations, Pride Ltd and Proud Ltd are each treated as being the creditor in a £100,000 loan relationship. Each company will have gross credits of £10,000, the interest accruing on the loan.

Where the money debt is not a transaction for the lending of money, the company partner can be treated as being party to a deemed loan relationship which brings in interest and exchange gains and losses on debts that are not loan relationships.

See *British Master Tax Guide* 3036–3037.

Law: CTA 2009, Pt. 5

20-180   Group loans and gains

Example

A Ltd has a loan relationship asset which is accounted for at cost £1m. In the year ended 31 March 2010, it transfers the asset to B Ltd, a 100% subsidiary of A Ltd, for its then fair value of £1.4m. B Ltd is a special purpose vehicle, which has no assets apart from the loan relationship. It issues shares of £1.4m in consideration of the transfer.

In the year ended 31 March 2011, the fair value of the loan relationship held by B is £1.6m. At this point, A Ltd sells the shares in B Ltd to an unconnected party for £1.6m. It realises a capital gain of £200,000 on the share disposal but A Ltd is not taxed at all on the growth in value of the asset, from £1m to £1.4m, prior to the intra-group transfer to B Ltd.

See *British Master Tax Guide* 3037.

Law: CTA 2009, Pt. 5

20-200   Bad debts in a group

> **Q.**   I know that loans written off are taxable or allowable in the respective companies under the loan relationship rules. But I've heard that this doesn't apply when the companies are connected – is this true?

A.   Yes. Generally bad debt relief is not available to the lender in respect of a loan made to a connected party. Conversely, the loan written off is not taxable on the borrower either.

However, there are circumstances in which bad debt relief is allowed between connected parties. A deduction is permitted where the connected parties are both companies and the connection arises only because the creditor company accepts equity in the debtor company in return for waiver of the loan.

Furthermore, for accounting periods beginning on or after 1 October 2002 bad debt relief is also allowable where the creditor company is in insolvent liquidation. The legislation provides however that should the company cease to be in liquidation without being wound up, the normal connection rules will apply.

See *British Master Tax Guide* 3037.

20-220 Revenue or capital computer

Q. A company incurs expenditure on computer software. What is the tax treatment?

A. Consideration should be made as to whether the licence for the purchase of software is a capital asset of the trade. The function of the licensed software should be looked at in the context of the licensee's trade. Usually the software will be expected to act as a tool of the trade over a period of several years and on occasion the benefit of the software may only be temporary so that the expenditure can be treated as revenue expenditure.

In general, where the software is expected to have a useful economic life of less than two years HMRC will accept that the expenditure is revenue. In these circumstances the timing of the deduction will depend on the correct accounting treatment as it does for regular payments.

Computer equipment is often purchased as a package including the hardware and the software. In these cases the expenditure should be apportioned between the two elements. Capital allowances under the plant and machinery rules will be due on the expenditure attributable to the hardware. In practice it is not necessary to apportion the expenditure between hardware and software if it is acquired on capital account. In those cases the expenditure in full goes into the plant and machinery pool for capital allowances purposes.

Most software is acquired under licence however there are some instances where larger organisations develop their own software. The same principles apply in both cases.

Where a limited company acquires software the expenditure can be classed as an intangible asset. This rule overrides the capital allowances treatment. Software which is not acquired with hardware falls within the intangible asset regime and amortisation applies accordingly.

Companies can make an election in respect of capital expenditure on computer software making capital allowances available.

See *British Master Tax Guide* 3042.

Law: CTA 2009, Pt. 8

20-240　Intangible amortisation

Example

In purchasing the trade and net assets of a business, Lobbs Ltd acquires goodwill for £200,000. For accounting purposes the goodwill is written off over ten years on a straight-line basis. For tax purposes the cost is reduced by £50,000 as a result of roll-over relief. The amortisation charge in both year 1 and year 2 is £20,000. The tax debit in year 1 is £20,000 × £150,000/£200,000 = £15,000. The tax debit in year 2 is £20,000 × £135,000/£180,000 = £15,000 and so on.

See *British Master Tax Guide* 3045.

Law: CTA 2009, Pt. 8

20-260　Accounting period straddling 31 March

Example

Allyssum Ltd draws up accounts to 31 December each year. During the year ended 31 December 2009 its profits (as adjusted for tax purposes) were £2,190,000.

The corporation tax liability would be computed as follows:

	FY 2008 **(90 days)** **(90/365)**	**FY 2009** **(275 days)** **(275/365)**
	£	£
Lower limit	73,973	226,027
Upper limit	369,863	1,130,137
PCTCT	540,000	1,650,000
Corporation tax liability		
FY 2008 – £540,000 at 30%	162,000	
FY 2009 – £1,650,000 at 28%	462,000	
Total CT liability	624,000	

See *British Master Tax Guide* 3090.

20-280　Small companies' rate

Example

Malope Ltd, a trading company, had profits chargeable to corporation tax of £204,400 during the year ended 31 December 2008. (The company did not receive any franked investment income). Malope Ltd's 2008 tax liability is £42,420, calculated as follows:

	£
FY 2007 (£204,400 × 90/365) = £50,400 × 20%	10,080
FY 2008 (£204,400 × 275/365) = £154,000 × 21%	32,340
	42,420

See *British Master Tax Guide* 3092.

20-300   Marginal relief

Example

Foxglove Ltd had taxable profits of £500,000 during the year ended 31 March 2009.

	£
Corporation tax liability £500,000 × 28%	140,000
Less: marginal relief 7/400 × (£1,500,000 − £500,000)	(17,500)
	122,500

See *British Master Tax Guide* 3094.

Law: CTA 2010, s. 19

20-320   Foreign tax suffered

Example

Wurlie plc had the following results for its year ended 31 March 2009:

	£
Trading profit – UK	1,482,000
Property income	350,000
Dividend income	278,000

In addition, the company paid charges of £400,000 (gross) during the year.

The dividend from overseas had suffered foreign tax of £27,800, which is eligible for double tax relief.

	UK income	Overseas income	Total
	£	£	£
Trading income	1,482,000		1,482,000
Property income	350,000		350,000
Dividend income		278,000	278,000
	1,832,000	278,000	2,110,000
Less: charges	(400,000)		(400,000)
	1,432,000	278,000	1,710,000

			£
UK CT @ 28%	400,960	77,840	478,800
Less: relief for overseas tax, lower of:			
UK tax on foreign income:			
28% × 278,000 = 77,840			
Foreign tax suffered (27,800)			(27,800)
Mainstream corporation tax			451,000

See *British Master Tax Guide* 3097.

Law: TIOPA 2010, s. 42

20-340 Should I withhold withholding tax?

> **Q.** Reid Ltd is a UK company which will be paying royalties to its Canadian parent company. Does the company have to operate withholding tax on the royalty payments?

A. The rules on deduction of withholding taxes on royalty payments made by UK companies to non-UK resident companies were amended for payments being made on or after 1 October 2002. Prior to this date, income tax had to be withheld from the payments at the basic rate of tax unless the recipient company had applied to the Centre for Non-Residents for a reduced treaty withholding rate to be applied. For payments after that date, however, paying companies may instead opt to deduct income tax from the royalty payments at the appropriate treaty rate (occasionally 0%) provided the company making the payment believes that the recipient is entitled to claim relief under the terms of a double taxation agreement. As a result, formal clearance from HMRC that the treaty rate applies is no longer required. Details of any payments made by the UK company have to be reported on the UK company's CTSA return.

If there is any doubt as to whether the overseas company would be entitled to relief, Reid Ltd should continue to withhold income tax at the basic rate. This is because if treaty relief turns out not to be due, the UK company will be liable for payment of the withholding tax together with interest. In addition, penalties could be levied against the UK company where withholding tax has not been deducted but the UK company could not have reasonably believed that treaty relief would be due. As a result, many UK companies may prefer to continue operating withholding tax until the overseas company makes a formal application for the treaty withholding rate to apply.

Special forms for such applications are available for a number of countries from the Centre for Non-Residents pages of the HMRC website.

See *British Master Tax Guide* 3097.

Law: TIOPA 2010, s. 42

20-360   Post cessation carry forward of losses

> **Q.**   Murray Ltd ceased to trade on 31 December 2010 having accrued trading losses. In the following year, the company received bank interest. Can the trading losses brought forward be set against the interest income?

A.   The normal treatment of a company's trading losses is for them to be carried forward and relieved against the earliest available trading income of that trade in later accounting periods.

Legislation also provides for certain kinds of interest to be relieved by trading losses brought forward where they cannot be wholly relieved against trading income. In this situation, it is clear that trading losses brought forward will never be fully relieved against trading income because the trade has ceased. Therefore, relief can be granted for the losses against the interest received.

See *British Master Tax Guide* 3106.

Law: CTA 2010, s. 45

20-400   Terminal losses

Example

Mango Ltd had the following results for the accounting periods up to cessation of trade on 30 September 2010.

	Y/e 31/3/07	Y/e 31/3/08	Y/e 31/3/09	Y/e 31/3/10	9 months to 30/9/10
	£	£	£	£	£
Trading profit/loss	70,000	50,000	15,000	(100,000)	(80,000)
Property income	15,000	15,000	15,000	15,000	–
Gains	10,000		5,000		30,000
Trade charge	2,500	2,500	2,500	2,500	1,875

Assuming that losses are relieved in the most tax-efficient way the solution to the above will look like this:

	Y/e 31/3/07	Y/e 31/3/08	Y/e 31/3/09	Y/e 31/3/10	9 months to 30/9/10
	£	£	£	£	£
Trading profit/loss	70,000	50,000	15,000	–	–
Property income	15,000	15,000	15,000	15,000	–
Gains	10,000		5,000		30,000
	95,000	65,000	35,000	15,000	30,000
s. 37(3)(a)					
31/3/10				(15,000)	
30/9/10					(30,000)
	95,000	65,000	35,000	–	–
Charge	(2,500)	(2,500)	(2,500)		
	92,500	62,500	32,500	–	–
s. 37(3)(a)		(51,250)	(32,500)		
	92,500	11,250	–	–	–
s. 37(3)(a)	(40,625)	(11,250)			
PCTCT	51,875	Nil	Nil	Nil	Nil

See *British Master Tax Guide* 3109.

Law: CTA 2010, s. 37

20-420 Carry back of trading losses

Example 1

For its accounting period ended 31 December 2009, B Ltd had total profits of £100,000 and a trading loss of £300,000. For its 18-month accounting period ended on 31 December 2008, its total profits were £120,000. As 12 months of the 18-month accounting period ended 31 December 2008 fell with the required period, the amount of the loss which can be carried back to the accounting period ended 31 December 2008 is £80,000 (12/18 × £120,000). Therefore, £100,000 of the loss can be claimed against total profits for the period ended 31 December 2009 and £80,000 against total profits for the period ended 31 December 2008. The remaining loss of £120,000 is carried forward.

Example 2

The facts with regard to the period ended 31 December 2009 above are the same. However, the previous accounting period is the 6 months ended on 31 December 2008 for which total profits were £40,000. Total profits for the 12-month accounting period ended on 30 June 2008 were £80,000. As above, sideways relief of £100,000 can be claimed in respect of the accounting period ended on 31 December 2009. A loss of £40,000 can be claimed against total profits of the period ended 31 December 2008 (as it falls wholly within the required period) and a loss of £40,000 can be claimed in respect of the accounting period ended 30 June 2008 (as this period falls partly within the required period, relief is restricted to 6/12 × £80,000 = £40,000).

See *British Master Tax Guide* 3106–3109.

Law: CTA 2010, s. 37(3)(b)

20-440   Government loans

Example

The Government lent A Ltd £60,000 and A Ltd makes up its accounts to 31 December each year. In the year ended 31 December 2009, A Ltd sustained a loss of £30,000. The company also has a capital loss of £10,000, £1,000 trade charges and capital allowances of £5,000. The Government wrote off £40,000 of the loan in March 2010.

	£
Y/e 31/12/09:	
Trading losses	30,000
Capital allowances	5,000
Trade charges	1,000
Losses c/fwd (CTA 2010, s. 45)	36,000
Capital losses c/fwd	10,000

The £40,000 written off by the Government is set against A Ltd's tax losses at the end of the accounting period ending on 31 December 2009 and the revised losses will be as follows:

	£
Trading losses	36,000
Less: government debt written off	(36,000)
	Nil
Capital losses	10,000
Less: balance of government debt	(4,000)
Revised capital losses available	6,000

See *British Master Tax Guide* 3116.

Law: CTA 2010, s. 92

20-460 Buying losses

Example

Precious Ltd transferred its trade to Pinner Ltd. At the time of the transfer Precious Ltd's assets and liabilities are as follows:

	Assets retained	Assets transferred	Total
	£	£	£
Assets	500,000	400,000	900,000
Liabilities	1,100,000	350,000	1,450,000

Pinner Ltd makes a payment of £150,000 to Precious Ltd in respect of the transfer. Precious Ltd has accumulated losses of £850,000, which Pinner Ltd wishes to inherit.

Relevant assets (£500,000 + £150,000)	£650,000
Relevant liabilities	£1,100,000
Losses available to Precious Ltd are restricted to	
£850,000 − (£1,100,000 − £650,000)	£400,000

See *British Master Tax Guide* 3125.

Law: CTA 2010, s. 945(1), (4), (5), Sch. 2, para. 99

20-480 Pre-rental expenditure

Example

Brown Ltd carries on a business of letting bed-sitting rooms in a large house to students. Within seven years before commencing letting Brown Ltd incurred expenditure in respect of rent for the house while it was being prepared for the lettings and alterations and improvements to the rooms to fit them out for the purposes of letting.

The rent is relievable but not the improvements since that is capital, not revenue, expenditure. Allowable pre-trading expenditure is treated as incurred on the day on which the rental business is first carried on, and is deducted in the accounts as a business expense.

See *British Master Tax Guide* 3138.

Law: CTA 2009, s. 61

20-490 Pre-trading expenditure

> **Q.** I recently set up a company from which I am planning to run a small hotel. At present the company has taken out a bank loan to acquire a property which will be refurbished over a period of perhaps 18 to 24 months. I understand the rebuilding costs are part of the capital gains cost of the property but can the company carry forward the loan interest payments to offset against future hotel profits?

A. Relief can be claimed for pre-trading expenses incurred in the seven years prior to the commencement of the company's trade under CTA 2009, s. 61. However, loan interest is covered under the loan relationship regime in Pt. 5 of CTA 2009. In the period when no trade is being carried on, the interest payments will be classed as a 'non trade loan relationship deficit'. Such non-trade deficits can only be carried forward against non-trading profits and so may be of little use to your company. An election is available under CTA 2009, s. 330 whereby within two years of the end of the accounting period in which the non-trading deficits are incurred, they can be treated as though they were pre-trading expenses making them allowable against future trading income.

Unfortunately, HMRC appear to have decided that as s. 330 relates to accounting periods, there may be occasions when an election is not possible, i.e. where there is no accounting period for tax purposes. This is explained in HMRC's *Corporate Finance Manual* at CFM5321. A company has to be within the charge to corporation tax in order to have an accounting period for tax purposes. Therefore, ensuring a taxable source of income arises such as a small amount of funds on bank deposit account should ensure the election remains available.

See *British Master Tax Guide* 3138.

Law:

CTA 2009, s. 61, 330

20-500 Losses on a company restructuring

Example

Blair Ltd and Brown Ltd are both wholly owned subsidiaries of Gordon Ltd. Brown Ltd transferred the whole of its trade to Blair Ltd on 1 January 2010, together with the stock and plant in return for £200,000. The consideration took the form of cash and the liabilities of Brown Ltd were retained in that company. Brown Ltd had trading losses of £750,000 available to be carried forward under CTA 2010, s. 45 immediately before the transfer. Blair Ltd will also take over a trade creditor of £70,000 relating to stock.

The balance sheet of Brown Ltd immediately before the transfer was:

	£
Tangible fixed assets	250,000
Stock	170,000
Debtors (trade-related)	170,000
Cash	10,000
Plant	30,000
	630,000

	£
Creditors	1,000,000
Bank loan	370,000
Share capital	40,000
Inter-company loan	20,000
Profit and loss account	(800,000)
	630,000

Brown Ltd's relevant assets (assets retained):

	£
Tangible fixed assets	250,000
Trade debtors	170,000
Cash	10,000
Consideration received from Blair Ltd	200,000
	630,000

Brown Ltd's relevant liabilities (liabilities retained):

	£
Bank loan	370,000
Inter-company loan	20,000
Trade creditors (£1,000,000 − £70,000)	930,000
	(1,320,000)

	£
Excess relevant liabilities over relevant assets	(690,000)
CTA 2010, s. 45 relief available to Brown Ltd	750,000
Less: excess relevant liabilities over relevant assets	(690,000)
Amount available to Blair Ltd	60,000

The losses available to be carried forward (trading losses transferable) in Blair Ltd would be £60,000.

See *British Master Tax Guide* 3140.

Law: CTA 2010, s. 45

20-510   Converting loans into shares

> **Q.**   Mrs Smith is director and shareholder of Smith Ltd. In recent years the company has struggled to trade profitably. As a consequence the balance sheet at 31 August 2009 shows a deficit of £50,000 after taking into account a loan made to the company by Mrs Smith of £25,000. It has been suggested that Mrs Smith converts her loan capital into shares so that the net deficit of the company is reduced to £25,000. What are the consequences of the suggested transaction on any later loss claims that could be made?

A.   It is occasionally suggested that shareholders in trading companies, which are going through a difficult time and where it might be anticipated that the company may go into insolvent liquidation at some point in the future, would be advised to convert loan capital in the company into share capital. This is so that they might take advantage, at a future date, of a claim for income tax relief under ITA 2007, s. 132, i.e. share loss relief claim against general income. However relief is unlikely to be available because the subscription for the shares is deemed to take place at market value in line with TCGA 1992, s. 17. If the company is insolvent at the time of the conversion to shares then the acquisition value for the shares may well be nil.

Equally a claim for capital loss relief under TCGA 1992, s. 253 may well be denied. A shareholder who converts a loan into share capital in circumstances where the company is or becomes insolvent cannot then make a claim for relief under TCGA 1992, s. 253 because at the date of liquidation the loan no longer exists.

See *British Master Tax Guide* 6183.

20-520   Who's in control?

Example

A Ltd is the parent company of B Ltd and C Ltd. B Ltd controls 75% of the shares in D Ltd and A Ltd controls the remaining 25%.

D Ltd has substantial trading losses brought forward. X Ltd acquired entire share capital of B Ltd and A Ltd's 25% shareholding in D Ltd.

There is no direct change in ownership of D Ltd but there is a change in ownership of D Ltd for the purposes of CTA 2010, s. 719. This is because the law treats X Ltd as if it acquired B Ltd's 75% shareholding in D Ltd directly.

See *British Master Tax Guide* 3143–3145.

Law: CTA 2010, s. 719

20-540   Change in trade

Example

Streamline Ltd, a 75% subsidiary of Fast Track Ltd, operated a dealership in saloon cars. Its accounting period is the calendar year. On 31 December 2009, Fast Track granted an option for the sale of its 75% holding in Streamline Ltd to Lime & Clay Ltd, agricultural contractors. On 1 April 2009, Streamline leased its entire fleet of saloon cars to Fast Track Ltd. On 1 March 2011, the sale to Lime & Clay was completed by Lime & Clay exercising the option of 31 December 2008. Shortly thereafter, Streamline switched to dealing in tractors.

Streamline's substantial corporation tax liability for its accounting period ended 31 December 2009 was finally settled by agreement on 1 September 2010. Following the sale to Lime & Clay, Streamline's tax bill was still unsettled.

HMRC may look to Fast Track Ltd, or any other company under Fast Track's control, for settlement of Streamline's outstanding tax liability. There was clearly a change of ownership on 1 March 2011 and the switch from dealing in saloon cars to tractors constituted a major change in the nature or conduct of the trade carried on by the company. The leasing of the fleet of saloon cars to Fast Track constituted a transfer of assets and both events occurred within three years before the change of ownership.

See *British Master Tax Guide* 3143.

Law: CTA 2010, s. 719

20-560   Purchase of own shares

Example 1

Melody subscribed for £100,000 shares in her personal company, Precious Ltd at par in January 2004. In February 2007, she sells the shares back to the company at £5, since she intends to retire and the family wishes to retain control of the company. The amount subject to CGT would be calculated as:

	£
Proceeds	500,000
Less: cost	(100,000)
Untapered gain	400,000
Less: taper relief	(300,000)
Chargeable	100,000

Example 2

The issued share capital of Brown Ltd comprises 1,000 ordinary shares of £1 each. Mr Brown owns 400 of these shares with the remaining 600 being held by unconnected parties.

If Brown Ltd acquires 100 of Mr Brown's shares, Mr Brown will have retained 300 shares and the company's issue share capital will be 900.

Mr Brown's interest will have fallen from 40% to $33^1/_3$%, which is less than a one-quarter reduction. In order to attain the necessary reduction, Mr Brown must dispose of at least 143 shares to Brown Ltd. This is determined by using the formula below.

$$R = (A \times B) / (4B - 3A)$$

where:

R   is the minimum number of shares needed to achieve a substantial reduction;
A   is the nominal value (before the sale) of the vendor's shares;
B   is the nominal value (before the sale) of the company's issued share capital.

Thus:

$(400 \times 1,000) / (4,000 - 1,200) = 400,000 / 2,800 = 143$ shares

See *British Master Tax Guide* 3220–3245.

Law: CTA 2010, Pt. 23, Ch. 3

20-580   Hive down of trade with transferor company left insolvent

Example

On 10 September 2010, Clematis Ltd went into receivership. On 1 October 2010, the receiver decided to hive down the trade and assets of Clematis Ltd to a wholly owned subsidiary, Clematis (2010) Ltd. All the assets and trade creditors were transferred to

Clematis (2010) Ltd, except the unsecured bank overdraft. The consideration for the trade and assets transferred was £475,000.

The company had unrelieved trading losses of £450,000 at 30 September 2010.

The summarised balance sheet of Clematis Ltd immediately after the transfer was as follows:

	£
Consideration due from Clematis (2010) Ltd	475,000
Bank overdraft	(760,000)
	(285,000)
Share capital	1,000
Profit and loss account	(286,000)
	(285,000)

The unrelieved losses which are available for transfer to Clematis (2010) Ltd will be restricted as Clematis Ltd is left insolvent after the transfer. Only £165,000 of the losses can be transferred, calculated as follows:

	£	£
Unrelieved losses		450,000
Less: Excess relevant liability:		
Relevant liability	760,000	
Relevant asset	(475,000)	(285,000)
Losses available to Clematis (2010) Ltd		165,000

See *British Master Tax Guide* 3320.

20-600   Identifying the group return period

Example

In January 2004, the Helleborus Group Ltd receives return notices for four of its subsidiary companies, Atrorubens Ltd, Corsicus Ltd, Orientalis Ltd and Niger Ltd. All notices have specified a return period of 1 January 2009 to 31 December 2009, which is the group's accounting reference date.

Atrorubens Ltd has traded for many years and has drawn up accounts for the year to 31 December 2009. Atrorubens Ltd will complete its return for the period from 1 January 2009 to 31 December 2009.

Corsicus Ltd was acquired by the group on 1 June 2009. Statutory accounts were prepared for the year ended 30 April 2009 and for the period to 31 December 2009.

Corsicus Ltd will complete two returns – the first for the 12-month accounting period to 30 April 2009 and the second for the 8-month accounting period to 31 December 2009.

Orientalis Ltd was incorporated by the Helleborus Group Ltd on 1 September 2009 and the company started trading on 10 October 2009. Its first accounts will be drawn up to 31 December 2010.

Orientalis Ltd will complete a return for the period 1 September 2009 to 9 October 2009 only.

Niger Ltd was incorporated by the Helleborus Group Ltd on 1 April 2009. The company commenced trading on 10 May 2009 and drew up accounts to 31 December 2009.

Niger Ltd will complete a return for the period 10 May 2009 to 31 December 2009.

See *British Master Tax Guide* 3028, 3650.

20-620   Can it be a group company?

> **Q.** A members' unincorporated association owns 100% of the share capital of a company. Given that any unincorporated association falls within the definition of company, do these two entities constitute a group for the purposes of group relief and transfers at no gain/no loss?

A.   This arrangement does not facilitate either group relief or transferring assets at nil gain/ nil loss. A company for group relief and capital relief is defined as any body corporate which this is not.

HMRC's *Capital Gains Manual* also confirms that an unincorporated association cannot be part of a group for capital gains purposes.

See *British Master Tax Guide* 3004, 3653.

Law: CTA 2010, s. 1154; CTA 2009, s. 2

20-640   Sale of trading stock on intra-group transfer of trade

Example

On 31 December 2009, Electra Ltd transferred its trade and assets to its parent company, Silene plc, as part of a group divisionalisation.

Corporation Tax

For these purposes, Electra Ltd transferred its trading stock at net book value, being £280,000. The arm's-length price of the stock is £350,000.

Electra Ltd's tax-adjusted trading profit for the period to 31 December 2009 would be increased by £70,000 (£350,000 less £280,000) to reflect the transfer of the stock at its actual market value for tax purposes (being a transfer between connected persons).

However, provided Electra Ltd and Silene plc make a joint election the stock can be treated as sold at its net book value of £280,000 (thus avoiding the £70,000 increase in Electra Ltd's taxable trading profit and Silene plc's acquisition value).

See *British Master Tax Guide* 3653, 3665.

Law: CTA 2009, s. 190

20-660   Pre-entry losses

> **Q.**   A group of companies wishes to purchase the shares of A Ltd. A Ltd holds 100% of the shares in B Ltd. A Ltd is not a trading company. The acquiring group proposes to dispose of the shares in B Ltd. The shares will produce a capital loss. Can the group use the losses against group gains?

A.   Anti-avoidance provisions were introduced in *Finance Act* 2006 to prevent groups of companies avoiding tax on capital gains by acquiring a company with capital losses. In general, a company's capital losses should only be available against its own capital gains or those of companies that were under the same economic ownership when the loss arose and when the loss is utilised.

The legislation is applied whenever there is a change of ownership of a company and the change of ownership occurs directly, or indirectly in consequence of, or otherwise in connection with, any arrangements the main purpose, or one of the main purposes, of which is to secure a tax advantage and the advantage involves the deduction of a loss.

All of the circumstances in which the arrangements were entered into need to be taken into consideration to determine whether obtaining a tax advantage is the main purpose. The existence of a tax advantage, such as obtaining a deduction for tax purposes, is not enough in itself to show that the arrangements have a main purpose of obtaining a tax advantage. It would be necessary to consider whether the transaction would take place at all if the company has not been in possession of the capital losses.

The effect of the legislation in relation to loss buying is that a loss which arises to a company on a disposal of a pre-change asset may not be set against any gains, except in certain very limited circumstances. A pre-change asset is defined as an asset owned by the relevant company before the change of ownership.

In this instance the loss accrues on a pre-change asset. The loss therefore cannot be deducted from any gains made by the group following the change of ownership.

See *British Master Tax Guide* 3682, 3684.

Law: TCGA 1992, s. 170–171

20-680   Notional group transfer

Example

Brown Ltd sold an asset outside the group for £70,000 and realised a chargeable gain of £30,000. Brown Ltd and Red Ltd may enter into an election whereby 100% of the asset is deemed to have been transferred to Red Ltd. The effect is that 100% of the gain will be treated as accruing to Red Ltd.

See *British Master Tax Guide* 3685.

20-700   Degrouping charge

Example

In January 2008, Mabel Ltd acquired a warehouse from a fellow subsidiary, Spotlight Ltd, when it was worth £200,000. Spotlight Ltd had purchased the warehouse in March 2004 for £100,000. Mabel Ltd was sold by the group in November 2009.

The deemed gain arising in Mabel Ltd's tax computation for the year ended 31 December 2009 is computed as follows:

	£
Market value (at January 2008)	200,000
Less: Original cost	(100,000)
Indexation March 2004 to January 2008 (£100,000 × say 10%)	(10,000)
Chargeable gain	90,000

The gain is deemed to arise on 1 January 2009.

See *British Master Tax Guide* 3686, 3692.

Law: TCGA 1992, s. 179

Corporation Tax

20-720   Degrouping goodwill

Q. Company X acquired goodwill for £100,000 on 1 January 2008. A year later on 1 January 2009 the goodwill was transferred to a group company, Company Y. The book value at the time of transfer was £90,000; however, the market value was £150,000. Company Y left the group on 1 January 2010. The accounts of the group are drawn up to 31 December each year and the goodwill has been written off on a straight line basis over ten years. What is the degrouping charge when Company Y leaves the group?

A. The *Corporation Tax Act* 2009, Pt. 8 deals with the degrouping provisions applying to a group company where an intangible asset has been transferred on a tax neutral basis. A degrouping charge will apply where the company leaving the group still owns the intangible asset at the time of leaving.

Although the calculation of any gain or loss on disposal is calculated by reference to the market value of the asset at the time immediately following the disposal by a group member to the transferee company, the taxable credit or deductible debit resulting is brought into the computation in the period in which the company leaves the group.

The degrouping charge will apply if the company leaves the group within six years from the date of the transfer. There are no degrouping charges if the company is leaving the group as a result of a demerger that is carried out for bona fide commercial reasons.

In this instance Company X will have a tax debit of £10,000 in year ended 31 December 2008.

Company Y will continue to write down the goodwill on the same basis and will obtain a tax debit of £10,000 in year ended 31 December 2009.

Company Y is deemed to have realised and reacquired goodwill on 1 January 2009. This results in a tax credit representing the excess market value over the tax written-down value, i.e. £150,000 − £90,000 = £60,000.

Company Y's acquisition cost is now £150,000 and the annual tax debit is based on this figure. Over the life of the asset the degrouping tax credit is balanced by extra deductions for sums written off the asset.

See *British Master Tax Guide* 3687.

Law: TCGA 1992, s. 178–179

20-740   Consortium relief

Example

Viola Ltd is owned by a consortium, as illustrated below:

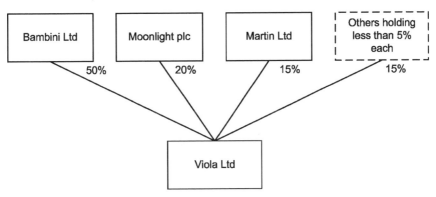

Viola Ltd incurred a loss of £360,000 during the year ended 31 March 2010. All consortium members prepared accounts to 31 December each year.

The tax results and the consortium relief claims for the consortium members for the year ended 31 March 2010 are summarised below:

	Bambini Ltd £	Moonlight plc £
Taxable profits	250,000	98,000
Consortium relief for		
Viola Ltd's loss of £360,000 (50%:20%)	(180,000)	(72,000)
PCTCT	70,000	26,000

While the shares held by Martin SpA (a non-UK resident company) are included in determining that a 'consortium' relationship exists, Martin SpA cannot be a party to the consortium relief claim.

If Bambini Ltd had a non-trading loan relationship deficit of £80,000 during the year ended 31 March 2005 and Viola Ltd had taxable profits of £100,000, Bambini Ltd could surrender up to £50,000 (50% of Viola Ltd's taxable profits of £100,000) to Viola Ltd.

See *British Master Tax Guide* 3809–3821.

Law: CTA 2010, Pt. 5, Ch. 4

Corporation Tax

20-760   Wasting losses and double tax

Example

Apple Ltd has £150,000 (gross and withholding tax of £37,500) of foreign source income and a trading loss of £140,000, Orange Ltd is a fellow group member, has a trading profit of £150,000. The loss can be group relieved or set off in the same company:

	CTA 2010, s. 37		CTA 2010, s. 99	
	Apple Ltd	**Orange Ltd**	**Apple Ltd**	**Orange Ltd**
	£	£	£	£
Trading profit	Nil	150,000	Nil	150,000
Other income	150,000	Nil	150,000	Nil
	150,000	150,000	150,000	150,000
Less: CTA 2010, s. 37	(140,000)			
Less: CTA 2010, s. 99				(140,000)
PCTCT	10,000	150,000	150,000	10,000
	£	£	£	£
Corporation tax	3,000	45,000	45,000	3,000
Less: double tax relief (DTR)	(3,000)		(37,500)	
	Nil	45,000	7,500	3,000
Total		45,000		10,500
DTR wasted		34,500		

By surrendering the losses of £140,000 to Orange Ltd, there is a tax saving of £24,000 for the group as a whole and it eliminates the wastage of DTR.

See *British Master Tax Guide* 3106, 3812.

Law: CTA 2010, s. 37, 99

20-780   Group relieved capital allowances

Example

Apple Ltd is a wholly owned subsidiary of Peach Ltd. Both companies make up their accounts to 31 March each year. The accounts and computations of both the companies for the accounting period ended 31 March 2010 are as follows:

	£
Peach Ltd	
Trading profits	5,000
Income from special leasing	2,000
Capital allowances in respect of special leasing	3,000
Apple Ltd	
Trading profits	3,000

Peach Ltd consented for Apple Ltd to claim relief in respect of its excess capital allowances of £1,000 (£3,000 less £2,000). Note that Peach Ltd can surrender all its excess capital allowances, notwithstanding it has other profits for the accounting period.

The tax computation for the year ended 31 March 2010 will look like this:

	£
Peach Ltd	
Trading profit	5,000
Other income	Nil
PCTCT	5,000

	£
Apple Ltd	
Trading profit	3,000
Less: group relief	(1,000)
PCTCT	2,000

See *British Master Tax Guide* 3815.

Law: CTA 2010, Pt. 5, Ch. 2

20-800   Calculation of profits available for group relief

Example

Pipit Ltd, which is a member of the Narcissi Group, had the following tax results for the year ended 31 December 2009:

	£
Trading loss	(75,700)
Non-trading income	5,200
Chargeable gain	150,000
Profits (subject to group relief)	155,200

The final group tax plan for 2009 indicates that there are sufficient losses available for surrender to Pipit Ltd. The company is likely to make substantial profits in 2010.

Pipit Ltd can only claim group relief of £79,500, even if the company carries its trading loss forward under CTA 2010, s. 45:

	£
Loan relationship income	5,200
Chargeable gain	150,000
	155,200
Less: assumed current year loss offset	(75,700)
PCTCT	79,500

See *British Master Tax Guide* 3815.

Law: CTA 2010, Pt. 5, Ch. 2

20-820   Computation of group relief from newly acquired subsidiary

Example

Mahonia Ltd acquired the entire share capital of Bealei Ltd on 1 April 2009.

Mahonia Ltd made a trading profit of £960,000 during its year ended 31 December 2009.

Bealei Ltd incurred a trading loss of £720,000 in respect of the year ended 31 October 2009.

The amount of group relief which could be claimed by Mahonia Ltd is computed based on the corresponding accounting period which is 1 April 2009 to 31 October 2009 (seven months).

Mahonia Ltd could only claim £420,000 group relief for this period, which is the lower of:

- $7/12$ of Mahonia Ltd's profit – $7/12 \times$ £960,000 = £560,000, and
- $7/12$ of Bealei Ltd's loss – $7/12 \times$ £720,000 = £420,000.

See *British Master Tax Guide* 3815.

Law: CTA 2010, Pt. 5, Ch. 2

20-840   Comprehensive example of group relief

Example

Aster (Holdings) plc has four wholly owned subsidiaries: Lilliput Ltd, Meteor Ltd, Milady Ltd and Pompone Ltd. Milady Ltd was acquired on 1 November 2009.

All companies prepared accounts for the year ended 31 March 2010. A summary of the tax computations, incorporating the group relief claims, is shown below:

	Aster plc £	Lilliput Ltd £	Meteor Ltd £	Milady Ltd £	Pompone Ltd £
Trading profit/(loss)	1,777,100	460,900	217,300	(78,000)	143,300
Trading profit/(loss) b/fwd		(672,000)			
Trading profit/(loss) c/fwd		(211,100)			
Non-trading income (receivable from Meteor Ltd)	425,000	1,400			1,200
Rental income			12,400		(20,700)
Chargeable gain	33,400				4,600
Non-trading loan (interest paid to Aster (Holdings) plc)			(425,000)		
Gift aid donation	(5,000)				
	2,230,500	1,400	(195,300)	(78,000)	128,400
Less: group relief					
Non-trading loan deficit	(126,900)		195,300		(68,400)
Milady Ltd's trading losses	(32,500)			32,500	
PCTCT	2,071,100	1,400	Nil		60,000
Loss c/fwd		(211,100)		(45,500)	
CT payable					
at 28%	579,908				
at 21%		294			12,000

Lilliput Ltd cannot surrender its brought forward losses.

Meteor Ltd can make a claim to surrender £195,300 of its loan relationship deficit by way of group relief. It does not have to apply its loan relationship deficit in reducing its other profits first but may do so. £68,400 is allocated first to Pompone Ltd to bring its profits down to the lower limit for small profits rate purposes – £60,000 (i.e. £300,000 ÷ 5). The balance is surrendered to Aster (Holdings) plc.

As Milady Ltd joined the group on 1 November 2009, it can only surrender $5/_{12}$ of its loss of £78,000. The remaining £45,500 has been carried forward.

Pompone Ltd's rental business loss of £20,700 cannot be group-relieved as it does not exceed the company's total profits.

See *British Master Tax Guide* 3815.

Law: CTA 2010, Pt. 5, Ch. 2

20-860   A group and a consortium

Example

Consider the following group/consortium structure:

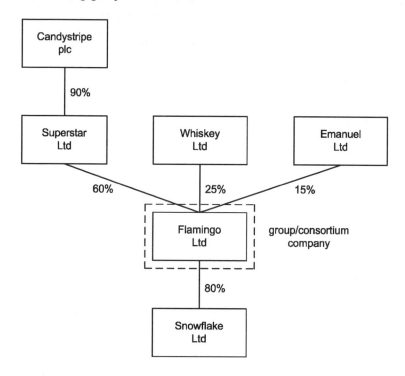

During the year ended 31 December 2009 the relevant tax results were:

		£
Superstar Ltd	Total profits	250,000
Flamingo Ltd	Trading loss	(360,000)
Snowflake Ltd	Total profits	90,000

Flamingo Ltd is a group/consortium company.

Superstar Ltd's claim for consortium relief against its profits would be 60% of Flamingo Ltd's loss after taking into account the potential group relief claim by Snowflake Ltd (whether or not the claim is actually made), i.e. £162,000 (60% × (£360,000 – £90,000)).

As £162,000 is lower than Superstar Ltd's available profits of £250,000, the amount surrendered is £162,000.

Superstar Ltd's final taxable profits would then be:

	£
Profits	250,000
Less: consortium relief	(162,000)
Taxable profits	88,000

If the tax results for the relevant companies for the year ended 31 December 2009 were as follows:

		£
Candystripe plc	Total profits	328,000
Superstar Ltd	Total profits	80,000
Flamingo Ltd	Trading loss	(220,000)
Snowflake Ltd	Trading loss	(10,000)

Then the maximum loss which Flamingo Ltd can surrender to Superstar Ltd is £132,000 (60% × £220,000). This would then be reduced to £80,000, being Superstar Ltd's total profits available to relieve the surrendered loss.

However, the surrender of the full £132,000 can be split between Candystripe plc and Superstar Ltd, in whatever proportion they may decide.

See *British Master Tax Guide* 3815.

Law: CTA 2010, Pt. 5, Ch. 2

20-880   Substantial shareholdings

Example

A Ltd acquired a 15% shareholding in B Ltd on 1 July 2006. On 31 January 2010, A Ltd disposed of 6% of the shares in B Ltd. On 31 October 2010, A Ltd disposed of the remaining 9% of the shares in B Ltd.

On 31 October 2010, A Ltd only owned 9% of the shares in B Ltd. However, in the two-year period prior to this date (1 November 2008 to 31 October 2010), A Ltd held at least 10% of the shares of B Ltd for a period of 15 months (1 November 2008 to 31 January 2010). Subject to the other requirements being met, therefore, any gain on the sale of B Ltd would not be taxable under the substantial shareholding rules.

See *British Master Tax Guide* 4035–4037.

Corporation Tax

20-900   Substantial shareholdings and the nil gain nil loss rules

Example

A Ltd owns a 100% shareholding in B Ltd. On 1 May 2009, A Ltd acquires a 100% shareholding in C Ltd for £3m. On 30 June 2010, A Ltd transfers its shares in C Ltd to B Ltd. On 31 August 2010, B Ltd sells C Ltd for £5m.

Although B Ltd has only owned the shares in C Ltd for two months, it acquired them by way of a no gain/no loss transfer from A Ltd. It is therefore possible for B Ltd to include the period of ownership by A Ltd (14 months) in determining whether the minimum ownership period applies. As the total period of ownership is 16 months, then B Ltd will be deemed to have held the shares in C Ltd for at least 12 months, beginning not more than two years before the day on which the disposal took place. Subject to the other requirements being met, therefore, the gain on the sale of C Ltd would not be taxable.

See *British Master Tax Guide* 4035–4037.

20-920   Substantial share for share exchange

> **Q.**   Paper Ltd held 35% of the share capital in Scissors Ltd until February 2010, when Stone Ltd purchased Scissors Ltd. Paper Ltd did not receive cash for its shares; instead it received shares in Stone Ltd as consideration for the shares in Scissors Ltd. How do the substantial shareholdings rules interact with the share for share provisions?

A.   As Paper Ltd has received shares in return for the shares it held in Scissors Ltd, the share for share rules say that there is no disposal. Instead the new shares in Stone Ltd are deemed to stand in the shoes of the original Scissors Ltd shares.

However, in order to decide whether the share for share rules take precedence over the substantial shareholdings rules one needs to ask if a disposal has taken place in the absence of the share for share rules. If the answer is yes, then the substantial shareholdings rules take precedence.

In these circumstances if Paper Ltd had sold its shares in Scissors Ltd for cash a disposal would have arisen, so the substantial shareholdings rules will override.

Assuming the conditions for the substantial shareholdings exemption are all met, the disposal of shares in Scissors Ltd by Paper Ltd is treated as giving rise to an exempt gain. Paper Ltd is treated as having acquired the shares in Stone Ltd at their market value.

See *British Master Tax Guide* 4035, 4037, 5903.

Law: TCGA 1992, s. 192

20-940   Does my company live where I live?

> **Q.**   I presently run a personal consultancy company and am considering emigrating in the next few years. The nature of the services I provide through the company means that most of the company's business is dealt with from my home via e-mail, with little or no personal contact with my clients. Therefore I intend to continue running the company after I emigrate to serve the existing clients, all of whom are based in the UK. As this is a UK registered company, does this mean that the company continues to pay UK corporation tax even if I personally am not resident in the UK?

A.   The answer depends on which country you are emigrating to as the tax rules of that country and the terms of the double taxation treaty between the UK and that country will determine the company's tax position.

Companies are deemed to be resident in the UK if they are either registered in the UK or are centrally managed and controlled in the UK. Therefore the first condition will still be met even after you emigrate. However, the country you move to may have a rule which determines that, as the company is carrying on a business in that country, it is resident there. Your company will then be a dual resident company and subject to tax in both countries. The terms of the double taxation agreement will then have to be reviewed to see whether the agreement contains an article which overrides domestic legislation. Most double taxation agreements (but not all) have a tie-breaker which will determine in which country the company is resident, usually by reference to the place of effective management. If there is no such tie-breaker, then the company will be dual resident and the double taxation agreement will determine which country taxes the income first, and the amount of credit for such tax that will be allowed by the other country against the tax it charges. If there is no double taxation agreement with the country you move to, then the company will continue to be treated as UK resident.

If your company is to be treated as non-resident under the above rules, then it is deemed to have ceased for UK tax purposes and to have sold its chargeable assets and its intangible assets at market value. A final company tax return up to the date of emigration will, therefore, be required. The company is obliged to give notice to HMRC that the company intends to emigrate, what its liabilities are, how it will pay these liabilities, and ask for agreement to the proposals.

See *British Master Tax Guide* 4072.

Law: SP 1/90

20-950   How is my overseas company taxed?

> **Q.**   My client, a non-resident company, owns an investment property in the UK, a portfolio of small shareholdings in quoted UK companies and deposits invested in a UK

bank account. During the year ended 5 April 2009, the company granted a 12-year lease for a premium of £50,000; it also received rent of £7,000, interest of £2,500 and dividends of £23,560. What is the company's liability to UK tax?

A. The company is not liable to corporation tax because it is not resident here and it is not trading here through a permanent establishment. Its sources of income are subject to income tax at the basic rate (ITA 2007, s. 11) and must be reported on SA700 (Tax Return For A Non-Resident Company Liable To Income Tax). Because the premium is in respect of the granting of a short lease, some of it (£39,000) is treated as rental income in the year. Therefore, the company has £46,000 of rental income during the year. The interest and dividend income is disregarded for determining the company's liability to UK income tax but if any tax has been deducted at source on the interest, the company remains liable for that amount. Therefore, the company's income tax liability for the year is £10,120 assuming no tax was deducted at source for the interest.

See *British Master Tax Guide* 3014.

Law: ITA 2007, s. 815, 825

20-960 Pre-sale sales

Example

Company X wishes to dispose of its shares in its wholly owned UK subsidiary, Company Y. In turn, Company Y owns shares in Company Z (a 75% subsidiary). Company Z revalues an asset in its books and, by virtue of the fact that it is registered and incorporated in Zedland, it then distributes the accounting surplus to Company Y, which distributes it to Company X, thereby reducing the value of Company Y.

The chargeable gain accruing to Company X on the disposal of its shares in Company Y is thereby reduced in a similar manner to that in relation to intra-group transfers and exchange of securities.

See *British Master Tax Guide* 4164.

20-980 How close are they?

Example

Mr and Mrs X each own 25% of A Ltd and the same percentage in B Ltd. Mr Y, who owns 40% of A Ltd and 50% of B Ltd (the other 10% of A Ltd being owned by another individual).

Mr and Mrs X will each be deemed to have a 50% interest in both A Ltd and B Ltd because they are each attributed the other's rights and powers. Since Mr Y also has at least a 40%

interest in each company, each individual is a major participant in both companies, therefore they are all indirect participants in both A Ltd and B Ltd, so A Ltd and B Ltd have the special relationship required in order for the basic rules to apply.

See *British Master Tax Guide* 4253.

Law: CTA 2009, Sch. 1, para. 272(2); CTA 2010, s. 439

21-000   Are limited liability partnerships associated?

Q.   I know four individuals who own two companies. They want to create another entity to be a service company. If they set up a limited liability partnership (LLP) will that count as an associated company and increase their corporation tax liability? They do have other businesses individually so they are anxious to limit their exposure via an LLP rather than a normal partnership.

A.   An LLP is not a company and it will not count as an associated company. This applies to all LLPs that carry on a trade, profession or other business with a view to profit.

However you mention that the partners have other businesses. If these businesses are also limited companies you must be very careful as the creation of an LLP, or indeed an ordinary partnership, will mean that the individual partners will be associates of each other for tax purposes. The number of associated companies will increase to include their own personal companies and indeed their own personal companies will have associated companies.

As you can see this is a nightmare scenario and so you may be better just to create one more company with the four individuals as shareholders.

See *British Master Tax Guide* 4268, 4271.

Law: CTA 2010, s. 449

21-020   Group or association

Q.   A company owns an intangible asset which has been written down in accordance with the provisions of CTA 2009, Pt. 8 (former FA 2002, Sch. 29). It cost £1,000 and is now valued at £1,500. The company wants to sell it to another company. Both companies are owned equally by the same three directors. What proceeds should be attributed to the transfer?

A.   If the disposal is to a related party, proceeds are deemed to be the market value and if to another member of the same group of companies, the transfer is deemed to take place at the tax written-down value (TWDV) of the asset. If neither of these applies, the actual consideration is used.

These companies are not in a group because a group consists of a company and its 75% subsidiaries so the disposal is not tax-neutral (i.e. not at TWDV).

The companies are related if under the control of the same individual. For each of these companies, the holding of any of the shareholders on its own is not enough to control it. However, it is necessary to consider whether there are any connected persons whose shareholdings should be aggregated to determine control. A person is connected with an individual if that person is the individual's spouse or civil partner, or is a relative, or the spouse or civil partner or a relative, of the individual or of the individual's spouse or civil partner.

For the purposes of this sub-paragraph relative means brother, sister, ancestor or lineal descendant.

In this instance, the directors are not connected so the two companies are not related and the credit to bring in for the disposal is actual proceeds.

See *British Master Tax Guide* 4271.

Law: CTA 2010, s. 449

21-040   Minimum controlling combinations

Q. I act for three companies which are owned as follows:

Company A   100% by Shareholder X

Company B   40%/40% by Shareholders X & Y with three other shareholders

Company C   50%/50% by Shareholders X & Y

None of the shareholders are connected with each other. Company C is a new venture and shareholder X has made a substantial loan to the company which almost entirely covers the company's assets. I am unsure which companies are associated for corporation tax purposes. I am aware that HMRC have a rule that looks for the minimum control group, which seemingly would mean that shareholder X alone controls Company C. Is this correct?

A. There is a general rule whereby a participator (shareholder or loan creditor) controls a company if he controls the affairs of a company and then four specific tests where control depends on having the greater share of:

- the issued share capital;
- the voting power;
- the income;
- the assets on a winding up.

The tests are mutually exclusive and so each must be considered in turn. Assuming each of the company shares are of the same class, no-one has a casting vote and there are no shareholder loans in Company B, then the associated companies are as follows:

Company A is associated with Company C as shareholder X is entitled to the greater part of the assets on a winding up.

Company B is associated with Company C as the Shareholders X and Y have the greater issued shares/voting power.

Shareholder X alone does control Company C under the assets test. However, the issued share/voting power tests produce a minimum controlling group of shareholders X and Y.

If the shareholders are also directors, it is likely that directors' loan accounts exist and so the daily balances will need to be checked. For example, if shareholder X's loan account in Company B was higher on any one day than that of shareholder Y then he may control Company B under the assets test, depending on the amounts of the loan and the company's assets, and so all three companies could be associated. Companies are associated if a participator has control of them at any time in the accounting period or in the previous 12 months.

See *British Master Tax Guide* 4271.

Law: CTA 2010, s. 449

21-060   Participator loans participate in penalty calculation

> **Q.**   Is the tax-geared penalty imposed on a company for filing its return late calculated in respect of corporation tax charged on loans to participators under CTA 2010, s. 455?

A.   The provision for these penalties states that no account will be taken of relief claimed in respect of s. 455 tax if the loans have been repaid or released. The implication is therefore that s. 455 tax is included in the calculation of the penalty.

See *British Master Tax Guide* 4300, 4303, 4980.

Law: CTA 2010, s. 455

21-080   Effect of a director's loan on penalty and interest

Example

Muscari Ltd had no corporation tax liability for the year ended 31 March 2009 due to trading losses brought forward. On 1 February 2009, the company made a £200,000 loan to its controlling shareholder, Mr Muscari, which was repaid on 31 March 2010. The company did not account for the director's loan tax liability of £50,000 (25% × £200,000).

Muscari Ltd submitted its return late on 31 October 2010 (seven months after the 31 March 2010 filing date).

Muscari Ltd is liable to the following penalties:

	£
Fixed penalties (more than three months late)	200
Tax-geared penalty	
ICTA 1988, s. 419 (now CTA 2010, s. 455) liability	
outstanding at 1/10/10	
(18 months and 1 day after 31/3/09)	
£50,000 × 20%	10,000
	10,200

Note that while the tax became due on 1 January 2010, no account is taken of the fact that the s. 419 (now CTA 2010, s. 455) tax is due nine months after the accounting period in which the loan is repaid.

If the loan had been repaid within nine months after the end of the accounting period (1 January 2010), there would have been no unpaid tax at that date and no tax-related penalty.

Interest would also accrue on the s. 419 liability of £50,000 from 1 January 2010 (nine months and one day after 31 March 2009) to 1 January 2011 (nine months and one day after 31 March 2010 – the repayment date of the loan).

See *British Master Tax Guide* 4306, 4980.

Law: FA 1998, Sch. 18; CTA 2010, s. 455

21-090   Buy-back of shares

> **Q.**   My client is disposing of shares through a buy-back of shares by the company. The shares were initially subscribed for four years ago by a venture capitalist at a premium price of £17 each. Subsequently they were sold to my client at the market price at the

time of £15 each. The current market value is £16 per share. How is the buy-back to be taxed?

A.   The share buy-back is a capital disposal for your client. However, because the shares have not been owned for five years, CTA 2010, s. 1033 does not prevent the disposal also being taxed as a distribution according to s. 1000 of the same Act. Often shares are disposed of for more than the subscription price resulting in an income distribution and because TCGA 1992, s. 37 excludes from the sale proceeds for the purpose of calculating the capital gain any amounts that have been subject to income tax, the matter becomes purely an income tax issue not a capital gains matter. In this instance, there is no liability under s. 1000 because the amount distributed is less than the consideration for which the shares were subscribed. Therefore, the disposal is simply a capital gain based on the current market value of £16 less the cost to the individual, i.e. £15 per share.

See *British Master Tax Guide* 3230.

21-100   Selling the company assets and my liabilities

Q.   I am a director of a small trading company in which I own all of the issued shares. In recent years business has not been good and I have injected funds into the company reflected by my director's loan account showing a sizeable credit balance. I wish to retire and have been negotiating a sale of the business with an interested party. I want to sell the shares in the company as my accountant has advised me that this is the most tax-efficient method to enable me to receive more of the sale proceeds. The potential buyer has agreed to buy the shares providing that the loan is written-off and the sale proceeds are reduced to reflect the corporation tax arising on the write-off. I am willing to structure the deal in this way but it seems inequitable for me to lose both the loan balance and to have to suffer tax on the loss. Is there any way to avoid this?

A.   By you writing off the loan, the company has made a loan relationship profit because it no longer has to repay the loan debt to you. Such profits are chargeable to corporation tax. You cannot claim a capital loss on the loan as the loan is not irrecoverable, you have simply decided to write it off.

For small owner-managed companies HMRC would normally only agree to capital loss treatment being available where the company was wound up and there was a shortfall in funds available to repay the loan. I assume that if the company simply sold the business, paying corporation tax on the resulting profits, there would be sufficient funds to repay the loan on a winding up.

If your accountant is correct in his calculations that a share sale is the best deal for you, it may be possible to avoid this problem by you selling both your shares and your loan. The new owner would then own the shares and the director's loan account balance. The sale of the loan account would be an exempt transaction for you. Whatever price is agreed between you and the buyer for the loan will be the buyer's base cost of the loan for capital gains tax purposes since it will not be an exempt asset in their hands.

As far as the company is concerned, it still owes the loan debt but now to the buyer rather than to you. As a result, no loan relationship profit arises to the company and no extra corporation tax will be due.

See *British Master Tax Guide* 4312, 6183.

Law: ITTOIA 2005, s. 415; TCGA 1992, s. 253

21-120   Life company taxation

Example

In March 2007, a life company received a contingent loan of £60m and accounted for it as other income. At the end of the period, the £60m remains outstanding. The £60m receipt is a taxable receipt but, as there have been no transfers to shareholders before the end of 2007, the company is allowed a deduction for the unpaid liability outstanding at the end of 2007, which is also £60m. Overall, the company has not, therefore, been taxed on the receipt of the loan. This addresses one of the industry's concerns by ensuring that 'normal' contingent loans do not lead to an inappropriate tax charge.

In July 2008, £50m of the contingent loan is repaid. In the absence of any transfers to shareholders, the tax analysis for the year is:

	£
Brought forward	60m
Closing figure	(10m)
Charge to tax	50m

A deduction of £50m is allowed, meaning that overall, there is no increase to the taxable profit of the company. Again, as the loan has not been used to avoid tax, the tax position is the same as it would have been before this legislation was enacted, albeit by means of a different tax analysis.

If in 2009, there is a transfer of £8m to shareholders, HMRC would view this as giving rise to an unacceptable tax result, and the contingent loan legislation would apply as follows:

	£
Opening figure	10m
Closing figure	(2m)
Charge to tax	8m

The £8m is brought into charge to tax as a taxable receipt.

In 2010, the contingent loan is repaid.

	£
Opening figure	2m
Closing figure	Nil
Charge to tax	2m

A deduction of £10m (the actual repayment) is allowed in 2010.

There is therefore a net deduction from taxable profit of £8m in 2010.

Over the term of the contingent loan, there is no overall difference in the taxable profits of the company. Legislation is simply accelerating the recognition of the taxable profit to reflect the timing transfers out of the long-term fund.

See *British Master Tax Guide* 4603.

Law: FA 1989, s. 83ZA

21-130   R&D claims

> **Q.** A limited company has carried out research and development (R&D) work in connection with a new product. The research has been undertaken during the period 1 April 2005 to 31 March 2009 and qualifies for the R&D tax relief. However the company has failed to make such claims for each of the accounting periods concerned. Is it possible to submit claims for these earlier years?

A. After 31 March 2008, the ability to go back six years to make a claim for R&D has been curtailed. Companies undertaking R&D work over the last six years that have not submitted claims will have missed out on savings for the earliest five of those six years. After 31 March 2008 companies will only have two years from the end of the accounting period in question to submit a claim and the six-year window is closed.

Finance Act 2006, s. 29 aligned the time-limit for claims for the enhanced deduction (for both large and small or medium enterprises (SMEs) with the time-limit for claims for payable tax credits. The time-limit is now the first anniversary of the filing date for the company tax return of the claimant company for the accounting period for which the claim is made.

The time-limit for claims for accounting periods ending after 31 March 2002 but before 31 March 2006 was 31 March 2008.

See *British Master Tax Guide* 4915.

21-140   R&D group

> **Q.**   Gordon Ltd is a company that is engaged in research and development (R&D). However, the payroll is in the name of the holding company. Will that invalidate the company's tax credit claim?

A.   HMRC's *Corporate Intangibles Research and Development Manual* confirms that, as long as the employment costs are those of the claimant company, the fact that the payroll is operated by another member of the group does not matter for purposes of calculating the PAYE/NIC cap.

See *British Master Tax Guide* 4915.

21-160   Pension contributions and R&D

> **Q.**   A company which is a categorised as a small or medium enterprise (SME) is carrying out qualifying research and development (R&D) and wishes to make a claim for expenditure it has incurred on staffing costs. A decision was made to transfer the property occupied for trading purposes into the directors' pension scheme. A deduction was made in the accounts for the contribution and corporation tax relief given accordingly. Can a claim be made to include the pension scheme contribution as staffing costs as part of the R&D claim?

A.   Only staffing costs attributable to relevant R&D can be qualifying expenditure. The directors or employees must be directly and actively involved in relevant R&D. Staffing costs in respect of clerical or administrative staff engaged in those activities are not qualifying expenditure.

Allowable staffing costs include emoluments paid to the directors and employees of the company including all salaries, wages, perquisites and profits whatsoever other than benefits in kind together with the secondary class 1 NIC paid by the company. Contributions paid by the company to any pension fund operated for the benefit of directors and employees are allowable.

HMRC also state in their guidance that where the underlying legislation requires not only that there be expenditure, but also payment.

In this case therefore no claim can be made in respect of the property transfer to the pension contribution as no payment is involved.

See *British Master Tax Guide* 4915.

21-180   Enhanced SME relief for R&D subcontracted to fellow group company

Example

Piccadilly Ltd subcontracts a new R&D project to Bonn Ltd (a fellow 100% subsidiary) during the accounting period for the 12 months ended 31 December 2009 (both are small or medium enterprises (SMEs)).

The contract for the R&D project (which was completed in 2004) was worth £200,000. During the period, Bonn Ltd's total costs were:

	£
Apportioned staff costs	120,000
Consumable items	8,000
Direct costs	128,000
Attributable overhead costs	35,000
Total project cost	163,000

Bonn Ltd's profit on the R&D contract is therefore £37,000 (£200,000 less £163,000).

Piccadilly Ltd can claim the following R&D tax reliefs:

	£
Enhanced R&D relief (175% × £128,000)	224,000
Balance – normal trading deduction	
£200,000 less £128,000	72,000
Total relief	296,000

See *British Master Tax Guide* 4915.

21-200   Tell HMRC when you start

> **Q.**   I hear that there is a requirement for a company to give notice of coming within the charge to corporation tax. I do not understand the reason for this because after incorporation a form CT41G comes from HMRC automatically.

A.   Section 55 of *Finance Act* 2004 includes a requirement for a company to notify HMRC within three months of coming within the charge to corporation tax. This duty applies to companies that have started activities after being dormant as well as newly incorporated companies.

Previous rules put the deadline to notify at 12 months after the end of the accounting period and, as you say, this was not a problem as HMRC, after being contacted by Companies House, issued a form CT41G to the company.

The earlier notification date means that the officers of the company must take the initiative. The information required is as the CT41G so it is suggested that a blank one is used with the words 'New Case' inserted instead of the tax reference number and sent to the appropriate HMRC office.

See *British Master Tax Guide* 4952.

Law: FA 2004, s. 55

21-220 Paying by instalments

> **Q.** McCarthy Ltd is in a group with 12 other companies but this is the first period of its trading. It has made profits of £1.4m. Should it be making payments on account of corporation tax in the year?

A. A company that satisfies the definition of large is required to pay tax by instalments for an accounting period. Generally a company is large if it pays corporation tax at the full rate of 28% without a reduction for marginal relief.

However, a large company is not required to make instalment payments if it has chargeable profits of £10m or less for the accounting period and was not large in the 12 months preceding that period or it has a tax liability of less than £10,000 for the period.

It would appear that your company will not be caught in its first year of trading but there are further complications. The £10m figure must be reduced if the accounting period is less than one year or if the company has associated companies. As there are 13 companies in your group the £10m upper limit must be divided by 13, which means that your companies' profit of £1.4m exceeds the upper limit.

Your company should be making payments on account of corporation tax for this, its first year of trading.

See *British Master Tax Guide* 4964.

21-240 Changing the quarters

> **Q.** Our company has to pay quarterly on account. We are shortening our period of account from 31 December 2010 to 30 September 2010. On what dates should we make the quarterly payments?

A.   When paying on account the first payment is due six months and 13 days after the beginning of the accounting period; the last is due three months and 14 days after the end of the accounting period, with payments between on a three-monthly basis. So in your case the instalment dates would be 14 July 2010 and 14 October 2010 with a final instalment on 14 January 2011. There would only be three instalment dates for the short period. If your company continues to use 30 September as its year-end after 2010, it would revert to a pattern of four instalments for each accounting period thereafter.

See *British Master Tax Guide* 4964.

Law: *Corporation Tax (Instalment Payments) Regulations* 1998 (SI 1998/3175)

21-260   Interest on unpaid tax

Example

Genista Ltd paid £1,380,000 on 1 October 2009 (the normal due date) in respect of its estimated corporation tax liability for the year ended 31 December 2008.

The company submitted its return and computations on 1 December 2009 indicating a liability of £1,650,000. At the same time, it made a further payment of £270,000, bringing the total tax paid up to the liability shown by the return. HMRC agreed the return and liability without adjustment on 15 December 2009.

HMRC will raise an interest demand for £1,128 in respect of the £270,000 which was unpaid at 1 October 2009, computed as follows:

£270,000 $\times$ 2.5% $\times$ (61 days/365 days) = £1,128

On 10 March 2010, Genista Ltd submitted an amended return indicating a reduction in its 2008 tax liability to £1,490,000 (following a roll-over relief claim on a capital gain).

HMRC agreed the revised liability of £1,490,000 and repaid £160,000 (£1,650,000 − £1,490,000). The repayment was made on 31 March 2010.

The original interest charge would be recalculated on the £110,000 (being the revised amount underpaid at the normal due date) as follows:

110,000 $\times$ 2.5% $\times$ 61 days/365 days = £459

As £1,128 had already been paid by the company, a repayment is due of £669.

See *British Master Tax Guide* 4967.

Law: TMA 1970, s. 86–90

Corporation Tax

21-280   Interest on tax repaid

Example

Iberis Ltd computes its corporation tax liability for the year ended 31 May 2009 at £460,000. It pays this amount on 28 February 2010. The return form and computations are submitted and agreed by HMRC in May 2010.

An additional group relief claim is made on an amended return on 1 August 2010, which reduces the company's liability to £350,000. HMRC agree the return and repay £110,000 on 1 September 2010, together with interest of £1,109, computed as follows:

£110,000 × (say) 2% × (184 days/365 days) = £1,109

Note: If Iberis Ltd paid its tax late, say on 1 June 2010, interest would only run from the later date, for example:

£110,000 × (say) 2% × (92 days/365 days) = £555

See *British Master Tax Guide* 4968.

Law: ICTA 1998, s. 826

21-300   Computation of penalties and interest

Example

Cosmos Ltd, a small company, finally filed its return form CT600 for the period 1 July 2006 to 30 June 2007 on 16 April 2009. HMRC had issued the notice to file in October 2007. The company paid its estimated tax liability of £560,000 on 27 March 2008.

HMRC initiated an enquiry into the return, specifically examining the capital allowance claim on a new office building. On completion of the enquiry, the company agreed to amend its return by reducing its capital allowances claim. This resulted in an additional tax liability of £40,000, which was paid by the company on 1 July 2009.

The company will be liable to the following penalties and interest:

	£	£
Penalties		
Fixed (more than three months late)		200
Tax-geared based on amount unpaid at 18 months		
Final liability	600,000	
Paid on account	(560,000)	
	40,000 × 10%	4,000
		4,200
Interest		
£40,000 × (say) 6.5% × (456 days/365 days)		3,248
Total		7,448

See *British Master Tax Guide* 4980.

21-310   Late filing penalty

Q. My company was incorporated on 15 September 2008. Accounts were prepared to 31 March 2009 and annually thereafter. I have just submitted the return for 31 March 2009 and 31 March 2010. Hence the 2010 return was a few days late. I was expecting a late filing penalty but was surprised to find that it was £500 instead of £100.

A. The late-filing penalty has become £500 because of a third successive failure to file on time. This is only the second return to be filed on time. However, what is being counted is not the number of returns filed late but the number of accounting periods covered by those late returns (FA 1998, Sch. 18, para 17(3)(a)). Therefore, if either of the returns includes more than one accounting period, as would be the case if the company had begun to trade during the time covered by the first set of accounts then the submission of the second return late would trigger a £500 penalty.

See *British Master Tax Guide* 4980.

21-320   Stock or fixed assets

Example

A capital asset which cost £60,000 is transferred from Brown Ltd to Yellow Ltd when its value is £80,000. Brown Ltd holds the asset as a fixed asset but it will be trading stock in Yellow Ltd which sells it for £85,000. For Brown Ltd, the transfer took place at no gain/no loss, i.e. £60,000 but Yellow Ltd will realise a capital gain of £20,000 plus a trading profit of £5,000. If Yellow Ltd elected, it is viewed as having neither a gain nor allowable loss but instead it realises a trading profit of £25,000 on the sale of the asset.

See *British Master Tax Guide* 5145.

Law: TCGA 1992, s. 161(3)

21-340   Construction industry company

> **Q.** My client is a limited company operating within the construction industry and has gross payment status under the Construction Industry Scheme (CIS). The limited company is a subsidiary within a group and is wholly owned by another limited company. The parent company is now going to start operations within CIS and I understand that they will automatically qualify for gross payment status where they act as subcontractors within CIS operations. Could you please confirm this.

A. Unfortunately this is not correct. If the holding company which wholly owns the subsidiary were already registered for gross payment under CIS and the wholly owned subsidiary started to operate within CIS then the subsidiary would not be required to pass the turnover test.

In this instance it is the holding company which has started to trade within CIS operations and the status of its wholly owned subsidiary has no impact on its status for trading within CIS. The holding company is required to pass the turnover test in its own right to qualify for gross payment status.

See *British Master Tax Guide* 2787.

21-360   UITF 40 adjustment

> **Q.** My client company had a UITF 40 adjustment of £250,000 for the year ended 31 August 2005. The overall trading position for 2005 was a loss of £190,000 after claiming capital allowances of £230,000 so the company elected to accelerate the charge. An amount of £200,000 was charged in the August 2005 return. What is the minimum amount of the adjustment that must be charged for subsequent years?

A. The basic rule is that for the first three years (including the year of the UITF 40 adjustment), the amount of the adjustment taxed must be at least equal to the lesser of one-third of the total adjustment income and one-sixth of the profit of the business before any adjustment for capital allowances. Therefore, the amount which would have been taxed in 2005, if there had not been an election, is £6,667 (one-sixth of £40,000). The effect on subsequent periods is that the adjustment being spread is reduced by additional amounts taxed as a result of the election. In this instance, the additional amount is £193,333 (£200,000 − £6,667). Therefore, the adjustment to be spread over later periods is £56,667 (£250,000 − £193,333). In 2006 and 2007, the minimum amount to be taxed is the lesser of £18,889 and one-sixth of the business profit before capital allowances. The making of an election to accelerate in the first year does not prevent further elections being made for later years.

See *British Master Tax Guide* 3027.

21-380   Company loans to family members

> **Q.**   My client is the sole director and shareholder of a small trading company. His sister is employed full-time in the business and has been advanced a loan during the year of £7,200. The loan is to be repaid in three years' time and no interest has been charged. What are the tax consequences for his sister?

A.   The employee will have a benefit in kind based on notional interest charged at the official rate while the loan is outstanding. Although she is not a participator in the company because she doesn't hold any shares in the company, the 25% corporation tax charge levied under CTA 2010, s. 455 catches loans or advances to an individual who is an associate of a participator. Clearly, a sister is an associate (CTA 2010, s. 448). However, she does appear to fall within the exception from charge provided by CTA 2010, s. 456 because she ('the borrower') has loans of less than £15,000, works full-time for the company and doesn't have a material (at least 5%) interest in the company's share capital. This applies where the sister is the borrower. However, if the money had been borrowed in the name of the sister to be used by her brother for his purposes then he might be considered to be the borrower and the conditions at s. 420 would therefore not be satisfied because of his interest in the company.

See *British Master Tax Guide* 4300.

21-400   Rationalising associated company's structure

> **Q.**   My client is the sole director and shareholder of a small trading company. His sister is employed full-time in the business and has been advanced a loan during the year of £7,200; the loan is to be repaid in three years' time and no interest has been charged. What are the tax consequences for the company?

A.   This will depend on whether or not the company is solvent. If the company is insolvent the association will cease from the time the liquidator is appointed, the shareholders will not have any control of the company, and they will have no rights to a distribution of any of the assets. If the company is solvent the association will continue until the liquidation is complete. While it is true that the shareholders will have no control over the company they will still be entitled to the surplus on distribution, so the company will remain associated.

See *British Master Tax Guide* 4740.

Corporation Tax

21-420   Who's associated with who?

> **Q.**   Mr A is a partner in the A partnership. He also controls two limited companies. The companies would normally be taxed at the small profits rate of corporation tax however his fellow partners of the A partnership also have interests in their own companies and this has resulted in each company concerned having association with each other and therefore must be included in the count of associates for corporation tax purposes. Mr A's companies have therefore been subject to 28% corporation tax. Mr A would like to know what the position will be following the *Finance Act* 2008 changes.

A.   Section 24 of CTA 2010 sets out the upper and lower maximum relevant amounts, reducing the relevant amounts if the company has one or more associated companies.

'Associated company' is defined in CTA 2010, s. 25 as one company controlling another or two companies being under common control. Section 449 defines control for this purpose.

When looking at who controls a company, account must be taken of associates. Under the current legislation an associate includes a business partner within that definition.

Finance Act 2008 introduced legislation whereby companies which are treated as associated because they are under the control of persons who are members of a partnership will no longer be regarded as associated by virtue of this connection. The change took effect from 1 April 2008.

This change will not apply if there have been 'relevant tax planning arrangements' put in place in relation to the taxpayer company. 'Relevant tax planning arrangements' will be defined as arrangements which involve the shareholder or director and the partner and which secure a tax advantage.

In this instance Mr A will be able to discount the companies of which his fellow partners are involved.

See *British Master Tax Guide* 4740.

21-440   Purchasing energy-saving equipment

> **Q.**   A limited company is proposing to purchase energy-saving equipment in its year ended 31 March 2010. A claim will be made to take advantage of the 100% enhanced capital allowances (ECAs) available on the purchase of such equipment; however, the claim will create a corporation tax loss. The loss will amount to £120,000, of which £100,000 will arise from the ECAs. As there is no scope to carry the loss back, the company wishes to know if there are any further reliefs available in respect of the loss.

A.   From April 2008 relief is available to companies (but not other businesses) in the form of a payable tax credit in respect of ECA allowances. Companies will gain immediate cash repayment rather than carrying losses forward indefinitely in the hope of obtaining relief when profits are realised in the future. The payable ECAs will have the following features:

(1)   Relief will be given for expenditure incurred qualifying for 100% allowances, i.e. energy saving plant or machinery and environmentally beneficial plant or machinery.

(2)   The scheme will cover only expenditure incurred from 1 April 2008.

(3)   The scheme will be available to companies of all sizes but not to other entities.

(4)   Companies can surrender the loss, to the extent that they are attributable to qualifying expenditure, so as to receive a percentage of the surrendered loss as a cash payment from HMRC.

(5)   The cash payment will not be treated as company income for tax purposes.

(6)   Companies incorporated outside the UK will be entitled to claim the relief provided they are within the charge to UK corporation tax because they are trading through a permanent UK establishment.

(7)   Companies can claim relief in any of their qualifying activities, thus including not only trades but also property businesses and investment management activities.

In order to claim the tax credit the loss must first be set against other income in the accounting period, and group relief must also be claimed if it is available. The balance will be an unrelieved loss and may be surrendered in return for a payable tax credit at a rate of 19%. The payment will be capped to the greater of:

- the total PAYE and NIC liabilities for the period of which the loss is surrendered, or
- £250,000.

Where assets that have been the subject of a claim are sold within four years of the end of the period for which the tax credit was paid, the tax credit will be clawed back. The amount repayable will be linked to the disposal proceeds recovered. Losses that had been surrendered will then be restored to the same extent.

Claims will be made on the corporation tax return. The time-limit for the claim is therefore two years from the end of the accounting period. Before making any repayment to the company, HMRC will check whether there is any tax overdue and the repayment generated will be used to settle any outstanding liabilities.

In this instance the company's loss of £100,000 arising for qualifying expenditure can be surrendered (leaving the £20,000 loss intact) and receive a cash repayment of £19,000.

See *British Master Tax Guide* 2373.

21-460   Capital allowances under the new regime

> **Q.** S Ltd, a small company, had a tax written down value (TWDV) in respect of its plant and machinery, at the beginning of the accounting period, of £2,500. The accounting period was nine months ending on 30 June 2008. The company had additions of qualifying plant of £1,000 on 1 January 2008 and £2,000 on 1 May 2008. There were disposals from the pool of £2,000 during the period. What capital allowances are available to the company?

A. Because the accounting period straddles the introduction of the capital allowances reform, we need to apply transitional rules to calculate the annual investment allowance (AIA) and also the rate of writing down applicable to the pool.

The rate of writing down the pool is calculated as the number of days in the period before 1 April 2008 at 25% plus the number of days on or after 1 April at 20%, divided by the total number of days in the period (and rounded up to two decimal places). In this case, the number of days before is 183, the number of days on or after is 91 and the total number of days is 274. Therefore the writing down rate is 23.34%.

The maximum available as AIA is calculated as if the period beginning on 1 April 2008 and ending with the end of the accounting period were the chargeable period. Therefore, the period is effectively 91 days long and the AIA is reduced proportionately to £12,466 (91/365 × £50,000).

The allowances that S Ltd can claim are: first-year allowances of £500 (50% of £1,000) plus £2,000 AIA. The writing down allowance at the hybrid rate is £117 (23.34% of £2,500 TWDV less £2,000 disposal proceeds).

See *British Master Tax Guide* 3029.

21-480   How does the family company claim AIAs?

> **Q.** Mr and Mrs B own 50% each of a company X Ltd, which retails clothes. They are also running a similar business in partnership with Mr B's father and Y Ltd.
>
> Mr and Mrs B also own 50% each of Y Ltd. What entitlement to annual investment allowance (AIA) will these parties have? Would X Ltd be able to claim AIA on assets it acquired because the partnership closed a shop and sold the equipment and fixtures to X Ltd?

A. In answer to your first question, X Ltd and Y Ltd are companies that are under the control of Mr and Mrs B and they are engaged in similar activities. Therefore, the two companies would need to share a single entitlement to AIA (CAA 2001, s. 51E). However, because the partnership has a corporate member as well as individuals, it will not qualify for AIA because it is not a 'qualifying person' (CAA 2001, s. 38A). Therefore, Y Ltd will not have any entitlement to AIA (unless it has another qualifying activity apart from its share of the partnership's trade); only X Ltd has entitlement to AIA.

The sale of assets to X Ltd by the partnership is likely to fall foul of the general exclusion 4 of CAA 2001, s. 38B. The explanatory notes accompanying Finance Bill 2008, clarify the purpose of the exclusion as follows:

> 'General exclusion 4 mirrors general exclusion 7 in section 46(2) of CAA and is an anti-avoidance provision intended to stop a business that is not entitled to, or has exhausted its entitlement to, AIA getting round the AIA restrictions by transferring an asset to another business which has not used up its entitlement.'

See *British Master Tax Guide* 3029.

21-500 How does the family company share capital allowances on long-life plant?

Q. My clients are a family of farmers. Each of the three farms they own is operated through its own limited company. The husband owns the shares of A Ltd. The wife owns the shares of B Ltd. The shares of C Ltd are owned 50% by the husband, 30% by the wife and 20% by their son. A, B and C are each operated at quite distinct places. C Ltd spent £150,000 in the year on long-life plant during the year. What capital allowances are available to C in respect of that addition?

A. Long-life assets are eligible for annual investment allowance (AIA) so the availability of AIA to C Ltd should be considered. The companies do not form a group so C will only be required to share AIA with the other two companies if it is subject to CAA 2001, s. 51E (Fourth restriction: other companies under common control). C will have to share an AIA with any company with which it is controlled by the same person and to which it is related.

In order to be related, the companies must either be engaged in similar activities or carry on activities from the same premises. All three companies are engaged in similar activities so are clearly related. If they are also controlled by the same person then they will need to share an AIA. The meaning of control for these purposes is defined by CAA 2001, s. 574(2) and is a different definition to the one used for determining associated companies. In determining associated companies, it would be necessary to attribute the voting rights of the wife to the husband so that he is found to have control of all three companies. There is no requirement to attribute the voting rights of connected persons for the purpose of s. 574 so the husband controls A and C but not B. Therefore, A and C would need to share a single AIA. The two companies can do that as they see fit. Given that any expenditure on a long-life asset that has not been relieved by AIA will be written down at 10%, it may be preferable to use the AIA in C Ltd in priority to using it in A Ltd against any plant additions.

See *British Master Tax Guide* 3029.

301

21-520   How is a VAT repayment dealt with for corporation tax purposes?

Q. A trader has received a repayment of VAT, together with an amount of interest. How should the amount received be taxed to corporation tax?

A. There are two elements to this repayment, the repayment of the VAT and the supplement received. The repayment of VAT will be taxed according to what the original supply referred to. For instance, if it is input tax on a fixed asset it would adjust the carrying value of that asset, and would not give rise to an immediate liability; if it is wrongly charged output tax it would adjust the sales, and would thus be taxable. The taxability of the interest will depend on which section of the *Value Added Tax Act* 1994 the amount is paid under. If it is a supplement paid under s. 79 the repayment supplement is exempt; if, on the other hand, it is interest paid due to an official error, it is taxable under s. 78.

See BIM31610 for further details.

See *British Master Tax Guide* 3026.

21-540   Claim for double tax relief

Q. Our client is a Spanish building company which has obtained a lucrative contract in the UK for construction work related to the 2012 London Olympic site, and which is expected to take between 18 and 24 months. Our client has undertaken other small-scale, short-term building works in the UK in recent years, but does not have any permanent office, branch or base here. All directors and shareholders are non-UK resident. Can you please confirm whether our client will be liable to UK corporation tax as a non-resident company, and, if so, whether any relief or exemption is available under the terms of the relevant double tax agreement?

A. Under the terms of the double tax agreement between Spain and the UK, a non-resident trading in the UK is taxable here on the profits attributable to that permanent establishment, calculated as though it were a distinct and separate business (art. 7). Article 5 defines a permanent establishment for this purpose and includes a building site or construction or assembly project which lasts for more than 12 months. Your client will therefore have to declare and pay corporation tax on the profits from this operation.

See *British Master Tax Guide* 3097.

21-560   Tax on foreign company dividends

Q.   A UK company prepared accounts for the year ended 31 August 2009. The company holds the shares of two trading subsidiaries. One of the subsidiaries is resident in Kenya and the other is resident in Tanzania. Together the three companies comprise a small enterprise (on the grounds that no more than 50 people are employed in the business and the group's turnover is less than €10m and/or its total assets before liabilities is less than €10m). The UK company received two dividends from the Kenyan company on 31 January 2009 and 31 July 2009; it also received a dividend from the Tanzanian company on 31 July 2009. How will the dividends be taxed?

A.   The dividend received from the Kenyan company on 31 January will be treated as a taxable distribution and subject to corporation tax. However, the dividend received on 31 July from the Kenyan company should be exempt income for the UK company because it falls within CTA 2009, s. 931B which has effect in respect of dividends paid on or after 1 July 2009. To come within the exemption the payer must be resident in a qualifying territory, i.e. one with which the UK has a double taxation agreement containing a non-discrimination clause (INTM432112). The UK has such an agreement with Kenya but not with Tanzania so the dividend received from Tanzania continues to be taxable income of the UK company even though it was paid after 1 July.

See *British Master Tax Guide* 3097.

21-580   Bad debts on cessation of business

Q.   The sole director and shareholder of B Ltd has decided after many years that the company will cease to trade. Unfortunately, the company has suffered several bad debts in the last two years and the director is of the opinion that the company will not recover these amounts in the future and, as such, bad debt relief is claimed in the final trading period. An agreement is made between the company and the director that the right to receive any recoveries is transferred to him at cessation of trade. What is the tax position of the limited company and the director?

A.   Where a trader ceases to trade and rights are transferred to a non-trading third party the legislation at CTA 2009, s. 194 treats the former trader as having a post-cessation receipt of:

- the amount (or value) given for the transfer, if it was at arm's length; or
- the amount (or value) that would have been given for the transfer, if it had been at arm's length.

Any sums subsequently received by the third party are not taxed as post-cessation receipts. However, once a debt has been assigned to some other person either by way of sale or assignment, the receipt of any proceeds will be a chargeable gain.

303

Therefore if the value of such rights at the point of transfer are nil there is no charge in the cessation computations of the limited company.

Where the business is transferred as a going concern the trade debts are generally taken over by the new proprietor and, in this case, any recoveries are to be brought into account in computing the profits of the successor.

See *British Master Tax Guide* 3028.

Law: CTA 2009, s. 194

21-600   Capital allowances on leased vehicles

Example

A company prepares its return for the year ended 31 December 2009. It has a tax written down value (TWDV) on its general pool at the beginning of the year of £15,000. It owns various cars at different times during the year as follows:

(1)   A car purchased in an earlier year for £20,000 with an emissions level of 170g/km. Its TWDV at the beginning of the year was £17,000. The vehicle was sold in November for £13,000.

(2)   A car it purchased in February for £19,000 with an emissions level of 130g/km.

(3)   A car it purchased in June for £18,000 with an emissions level of 156g/km.

(4)   A car it purchased in July for £17,000 with an emissions level of 166g/km.

The transitional provisions of the changes to capital allowances introduced by *Finance Act* 2009 classify expenditure on cars between 'new expenditure' and 'old expenditure'. The approach of the legislation is to define 'new expenditure' and then anything falling outside that definition is 'old expenditure'. New expenditure includes any unconditional obligation to pay for a car on or after 1 April 2009 and also any unconditional obligation to pay before that date if it was under an agreement that the company entered into after 8 December 2008 which didn't require the car to be made available to the company until 1 August 2009 or later. Therefore expenditure on cars (3) and (4) is new expenditure. Expenditure on car (2) will not be new expenditure unless the agreement to purchase it was entered into after 8 December and didn't require the car to be available to the company until 1 August. Car (1) was acquired as a result of old expenditure.

The capital allowances available in respect of car (1) are unaffected by the change. It is in a single asset pool because it cost more that £12,000 when purchased. This year is the final chargeable period for this pool (CAA 2001, s. 65(2)) so there is no writing down allowance for the period but instead the company can claim a balancing allowance of £4,000 (CAA 2001, s. 55(4)).

Car (2) is old expenditure on a vehicle costing more than £12,000 so this goes into a single asset pool. The emissions level is irrelevant for capital allowances purposes except that it establishes that the expenditure is not on a car with low carbon dioxide emissions and thus it does not entitle the company to a 100% first-year allowance. The company is entitled to a 20% writing down allowance subject to a cap of £3,000 in respect of this car. The car will continue to be treated in this way for capital allowances because it is old expenditure. However, if the company continues to prepare accounts to 31 December and it still has the vehicle at 31 December 2014 then the TWDV on the single asset pool at the end of the period is transferred to the main plant and machinery pool with effect from 1 January 2015 and the company will no longer be able to obtain a balancing allowance in respect of the vehicle while it carries on the business the car was bought for.

Car (3) is new expenditure and so must be pooled. Because its emissions level does not exceed 160g/km, this car will go into the main rate (20%) pool with the other plant and machinery. Because of the pooling, the company will not be able to claim a balancing allowance if the car is sold. Instead, the disposal proceeds would simply be deducted from the pool in exactly the same way as the proceeds for any other piece of plant would be.

Car (4) is new expenditure so this also must be pooled. Because the emissions level exceeds 160g/km the expenditure needs to go into a special rate pool with a writing down allowance of 10%. Since the company didn't have a special rate previously, the only expenditure in the pool is that on the car. However, it is different from the single asset pool such a car would have gone into previously: there is no £3,000 limit on the writing down allowance and there would be no balancing allowance if the vehicle is sold.

Therefore the company is entitled to writing down allowances of £11,300 (£6,600 on the main pool, £3,000 on car (2) and £1,700 on car (4)). It is also entitled to a balancing allowance of £4,000 in respect of car (1).

See *British Master Tax Guide* 3026.

Capital Gains Tax

Insurance proceeds	309
Payment in lieu of view	309
Insurance claims – minor	310
Insurance claims – far from minor	310
Share sale not at arm's length	312
How definite is probate?	312
Including costs in the computation	313
Allowable legal costs	314
Part-disposals	315
Receipts by instalment	315
Tax in instalments	316
Deferred consideration – the purchaser's view	317
Deferred (lack of) income	317
Date of disposal	318
Losses brought forward	319
Rental business losses	319
Losses and former taper relief	320
Utilising company losses	321
Mixed-use assets and former taper relief	321
Taper ownership periods for spouses (for disposals before 6 April 2008)	322
Private residence relief	324
Lost deposit when the house fell through	325
Multiple properties	325
Time apportioned gain	326
Restricting indexation	326
Agreeing valuations on probate and March 1982	327
March 1982 valuation and enhancement expenditure	328
Amount of gain charged to corporation tax	328
100-year-old wasting chattel	329
Lease dilapidations	330
Leases	330
Should I use the 1982 value?	332
Joint ownership of shares	332
Same day transactions	333
Alternative identification rules	333
What's mine is yours	334
Hold-over relief in discretionary trusts	335
Trusting in shares	336
Estate CGT	336
CGT paid by personal representatives	337
Using losses on death	338
Non-resident with UK assets	339
Use of the remittance basis	339

Capital Gains Tax

Allocation of partnership gains and losses	340
Do my wife's qualifying bonds still qualify?	341
Giving worthless QCBs away to a good cause	341
Shares for QCBs	342
Bonus issues	342
All premiums great and small	343
Goodwill, EIS and entrepreneurs' relief	344
Enterprise Investment Scheme relief	344
EIS and entrepreneurs' relief	344
Negligible value claim	345
Gift at a price	346
Planning on incorporation	347
Parts of small chattels	347
Chattels	347
Lots of life assurance	350
Build a house and then pay tax on it	350
Demolish a house then pay tax on it	351
Half a hectare	352
Principal private residence on separation	352
Dependent relatives allowances	353
Job-related accommodation	354
Deemed residence	354
Letting relief	355
Emigrating with a gift (former taper relief)	356
Rolling over a non-business asset	356
Incorporation relief	357
Disapplying incorporation relief	358
Relief on sale of business	359
Rolling over goodwill	360
Roll-over against the same asset	360
Rolling over company assets against personal assets	361
Partial roll-over	361
Roll-over relief on furnished holiday lets	362
Transfer and then roll over	363
Selling fixed assets	364
Hold-over relief on agricultural property	364
Buying a freehold	365
EMI shares and entrepreneurs' relief	365
Indemnity against future sale	366
Entrepreneurs' relief on company property	366
Entrepreneurs' relief on non-voting shares	367
Rollover and entrepreneurs' relief	368
Entrepreneurs' relief on business property	368
Shares in Northern Rock	369

CAPITAL GAINS TAX

30-000 Insurance proceeds

> **Q.** Niall bought a machine in May 2001; a flood at his premises in May 2010 damaged it severely. In June 2010 he spent £40,000 on restoring the machine and his insurance company reimbursed this amount to him in July 2010. How is the receipt of £40,000 from the insurance company treated?

A. The receipt of a capital sum in respect of an asset is a part-disposal for capital gains tax (CGT) purposes.

However, where any of the following circumstances apply it is possible to make a claim so that the receipt is not treated as a capital disposal. Instead, the part-disposal proceeds (i.e. £40,000) are rolled-over by deducting them from the original base cost on a subsequent disposal of the asset.

The receipt of the capital sum is not treated as a part-disposal if the taxpayer claims that the capital sum is either wholly applied in restoring the asset, or partly applied in restoring the asset, and the remaining part which is not required for the restoration is small compared with the whole sum or small compared with the value of the asset.

So as Niall has used the full £40,000 insurance proceeds to repair the asset he could make a claim to avoid an immediate CGT charge.

It is important to note that the roll-over cannot apply if the capital sum received is larger than the original allowable expenditure. In these cases the taxpayer can claim that the capital sum is treated as a disposal against the whole allowable expenditure, reducing the allowable expenditure to be carried forward for a future disposal to nil.

See *British Master Tax Guide* 5080, 5083.

Law: TCGA 1992, s. 22, 23

30-020 Payment in lieu of view

> **Q.** Directly behind Danny's home and garden is an area of green open space, which is owned by Mrs A. Mrs A is planning to build a house on the land. Given that there will no longer be open space beyond Danny's garden it is likely to affect the value of his home. By way of compensation Mrs A has offered Danny a one-off payment of £50,000. What are the tax implications?

A. For CGT purposes, there is deemed to be a disposal (or part-disposal) of an asset where any capital payment is derived from that asset, regardless of whether the person making the payment is acquiring the asset.

In these circumstances the £50,000 payment is being made to compensate for the potential loss of value to the individual's home. The payment is deemed to be derived from Danny's home.

As a result, a proportion of the original cost of his home, determined in accordance with the part-disposal rules will be deducted in a capital gain. However, these rules interact with the normal capital gains reliefs and accordingly any principal private residence relief available will reduce the gain arising.

See *British Master Tax Guide* 5080, 6164.

Other guidance: ESC D33

30-040 Insurance claims – minor

Example

Anthony acquired a painting for £50,000. Five years later the painting was damaged as a result of a burst pipe. Anthony received £15,000 compensation from his insurance company and paid £14,000 to have the picture restored.

The amount not used to restore the picture is small in relation to the capital sum. Anthony may therefore claim to ignore the disposal (it is less than 5% of the value of the asset). The capital gains cost of the painting will then be £50,000 + £14,000 − £15,000 = £49,000.

See *British Master Tax Guide* 5083.

Law: TCGA 1992, s. 23

30-060 Insurance claims – far from minor

Example

Alice owns a rare antique vase valued and insured at £200,000 (its estimated market value in perfect condition). She bought the vase on 6 April 1995 for £100,000. It has been cracked and the cost to restore it amounts to £25,000, but its estimated value after restoration (expenditure incurred in June 2006) amounts to only £180,000. Alice claims and recovers from the insurance company £45,000 (received in January 2007), being the restoration cost plus the reduction in value.

The sum received is not small in relation to the value of the vase. If no claim is made, Alice's gain is £18,180, calculated as follows:

	£	£
Compensation money received		45,000
Allowable expenditure:		
Cost	100,000	
Indexation		
Apr. 1995 to Apr. 1998 (0.091)	9,100	
Restoration expenditure	25,000	
	134,100	
Expenditure allowable on part-disposal:		
45,000/(45,000 + 180,000) × (£134,100) =		(26,820)
Gain before taper relief		18,180

The base cost carried forward (indexed to April 1998) of the vase is £107,280 (£109,100 + £25,000 − £26,820).

However, Alice may claim partial relief as £25,000 of the proceeds have been spent on restoration. If Alice makes a claim, then her gain becomes £6,590, calculated as follows:

	£	£
Compensation money received		45,000
Less: applied in restoration		(25,000)
Disposal proceeds		20,000
Allowable expenditure:		
Cost	100,000	
Indexation (0.091)	9,100	
Restoration expenditure applied	25,000	
	134,100	
Expenditure allowable on part-disposal:		
20,000/(20,000 + 180,000) × (£134,100)		(13,410)
Gain before taper relief		6,590

The base cost carried forward (indexed to April 1998) of the vase is £95,690 (£109,100 + £25,000 − £13,410 − £25,000).

See *British Master Tax Guide* 5083.

Law: TCGA 1992, s. 23

30-080   Share sale not at arm's length

> **Q.** I presently own all the shares in a trading company, which has been running for many years. I would like to sell the shares and retire, and my nephew and his wife who work in the company have expressed an interest in buying the shares. I am willing to sell them the shares for less than full market value as my nephew is my closest relative and I would prefer to leave the future of the company in the hands of people I know and trust. My nephew cannot afford to pay the amount I require immediately and so I propose to transfer shares piecemeal over the next few years. I understand that as we are not connected persons for CGT purposes, I can transfer the shares in this way without any tax problems. Is this correct?

A. Unfortunately not. You are correct that you are not connected with your nephew or his wife for CGT purposes and so the market value will not be substituted for the actual proceeds for that reason. However, you are clearly transferring the shares for less than they are worth and so a market value rule for the shares will apply. This is because the transaction is not at arm's length.

The value of a 100% shareholding in a trading company is more than the aggregate value of separate transfers of shares, which total 100% over time. Therefore, transferring shares over time would result in the total deemed market value you are assessed on being less than a transfer of the total 100% shareholding.

HMRC maintain that an agreement to sell, even verbally, is the relevant disposal date even though the shares are being transferred in separate tranches. Therefore, in HMRC's view you will be treated as having sold all of the shares at the date of the agreement. This can be overridden if a formal contract is entered into. The date of an unconditional contract is the date of disposal for CGT purposes. Therefore, you may wish to take legal advice regarding the contracts if the tax at stake is material.

Alternatively, you could sell all of the shares in one transaction with the proceeds being paid to you over time. Where the proceeds are being received over a period exceeding 18 months it is possible to pay by instalments. However, as explained above, a 100% shareholding will have a higher value than the aggregate values of selling such a shareholding in tranches.

See *British Master Tax Guide* 5130, 5142, 5235.

Law: TCGA 1992, s. 18, 280, 286

30-100   How definite is probate?

> **Q.** My grandmother recently died leaving me her house in her will. The solicitor dealing with the estate advises me that a probate value of £175,000 was declared as being the market value of the house for inheritance tax purposes. The house was the only real

asset my grandmother owned apart from a few hundred pounds in savings and some personal effects of small value. I am now planning to sell the house and the estate agent has advised me that I should be able to obtain over £200,000 for the house. I am concerned about the CGT liability that may arise and wonder whether I should ask the solicitor to revise the inheritance tax return.

A.   First, ensure that the property has been transferred from the estate into your name prior to sale or that the estate administration period has ended. Unless this has been done, any sale will arise to the personal representatives of the estate not to you. Although personal representatives have the same personal annual capital gains exemption that you do for the year of death and the following two years, any excess is charged at the higher rate of 40% within the estate rather than at your personal tax rates which may be lower depending on your other income and gains.

Secondly, as your grandmother's estate was well below the inheritance tax nil rate band it is likely that the Inheritance Tax Office simply accepted the declared house value rather than formally agreed it. Quite often, where small estates are concerned or where there are exemptions or reliefs available, HMRC will not waste time and resources checking valuations where there is little or no tax at stake. As no inheritance was due, the value of the house doesn't affect the amount of the liability and so the house value has not been ascertained for inheritance tax purposes. Therefore the declared value of £175,000 is not binding for CGT purposes. This means that you can obtain a new valuation figure as your acquisition cost.

When declaring the gain, you must tell HMRC that you have used a valuation and you should be prepared for the valuation to be queried, usually by the HMRC Valuation Office becoming involved to give an opinion. Providing the house is sold within a short time of your grandmother's death, HMRC may accept that any gain would be relatively small and covered by your annual capital gains exemption and so this may not be enquired into for the reason mentioned above, i.e. not to waste time and resources.

See *British Master Tax Guide* 5223.

30-120   Including costs in the computation

Example

In November 1990, Albert purchased a one-third shareholding in an unquoted trading company for £20,000. He sold it in May 2007 for £166,000, with allowable costs of sale of £1,138. The shareholding has qualified as a business asset throughout the period of ownership. The gain is calculated as follows:

Capital Gains Tax

	£
Sale proceeds	166,000
Less: costs of sale	(1,138)
	164,862
Cost	(20,000)
Indexation allowance to April 1998	
20,000 × 0.251	(5,020)
Indexed gain	139,842
Gain after taper relief	
£139,842 × 25%	34,960

Note that taper relief was abolished with from 6 April 2008 but is shown in the above calculation for reference purposes.

See *British Master Tax Guide* 5223.

30-140   Allowable legal costs

> **Q.**   An individual has disposed of shares in an unquoted trading company. Significant legal and accountancy costs have been incurred in negotiating the sale and also establishing a valuation of the shares. Can any of the costs be deducted in the capital gain computation?

A.   A taxpayer can deduct incidental costs incurred in connection with the acquisition or disposal of an asset. Specific expenditure incurred wholly and exclusively by the taxpayer for the purpose of the acquisition or for the purposes of the disposal are allowable. The specific expenditure includes fees, commission or remuneration paid for the professional services of a surveyor or valuer, auctioneer, accountant, agent or legal adviser and costs of transfer or conveyance.

The legislation also provides that in the case of a disposal, the costs of advertising to find a buyer and costs reasonably incurred in making any valuation or apportionment required for the purposes of the computation of the gain, including, in particular, expenses reasonably incurred in ascertaining market value are allowable.

However, specific professional advice relating to the prospects of a particular asset or investment are not allowable, therefore the costs of negotiating a sale will not be allowable.

See *British Master Tax Guide* 5223.

Law: TCGA 1992, s. 38

30-160   Part-disposals

Example

James bought an asset in 1975 for £10,000. Its value in March 1982 was £18,000. Part was sold in May 1987 for £14,000 when the part remaining was worth £12,000. The remainder was sold in November 2006 for £36,000. (Remember that the rebasing rules were introduced in 1988.)

The chargeable gains are computed as follows:

	£
Disposal proceeds (May 1987)	14,000
Cost (allowable expenditure)	
$\quad$ 10,000 × A/(A + B)	
$\quad$ 10,000 × 14,000/26,000	(5,385)
Indexation	
$\quad$ 5,385 × 0.283	(1,524)
Indexed gain May 1987	7,091

	£
Disposal proceeds (November 2006)	36,000
Cost (allowable expenditure)	
$\quad$ 18,000 − (18,000 × A/(A + B))	
$\quad$ 18,000 − (18,000 × 14,000/26,000)	(8,308)
Indexation	
$\quad$ 8,308 × 1.047	(8,698)
Indexed gain November 2006	18,994

See *British Master Tax Guide* 5229, 5300.

Law: TCGA 1992, s. 35, 42

30-180   Receipts by instalment

Q. I have sold an investment property I owned personally to a property development company.

We have negotiated for them to pay 25% of the sale price up-front with the remaining consideration spread over four years. I know that CGT will be due on the full amount but when will I have to pay it? It does not seem fair that it will have to be paid all at once when the money will not be received for a long time.

Capital Gains Tax

A. Where consideration is wholly or partly deferred on the disposal of a capital asset, this does not change the capital gains computation or due date and the full consideration is chargeable in the tax year in which the gain arises, the tax being payable on the following 31 January. However, in certain circumstances you may be able to defer part of the CGT which then becomes payable in instalments, linked to the deferred consideration as it is received. The conditions are as follows:

- The instalments of consideration must be received over a period of more than 18 months.
- Tax must be paid equivalent to 50% of each instalment of consideration as it is received and on that date until the tax is all paid.
- If the consideration payments are to be made over more than eight years, the tax instalments will be restricted to eight years.

If you meet the above conditions you will need to make a claim on your tax return, giving details of the amounts and dates of consideration payable under the sale agreement together with a schedule of the corresponding CGT liabilities payable at each due date.

See *British Master Tax Guide* 5235.

Law: TCGA 1992, s. 48

30-200   Tax in instalments

> **Q.**   My limited company has sold an asset to a third party and the payment for the asset is to be spread over a period of three years. As we will be receiving the amount over a period of 18 months or more but paying the chargeable gain through corporation tax in one go can we pay by instalments for CGT?

A.   HMRC manuals state that a taxpayer can apply in writing to pay CGT by instalments by arranging yearly or half-yearly instalments, and where these dates are accepted, as long as the instalment dates are abided by, no interest is charged.

As the relief specifically mentions CGT, one would assume that it is only individuals that are eligible for this arrangement. However, following an amendment passed in FA 1996, s. 134, the provisions were extended to include chargeable gains arising on companies.

See *British Master Tax Guide* 6470.

Law: TCGA 1992, s. 281

30-220   Deferred consideration – the purchaser's view

> **Q.** I understand that where a property is sold with some or all of the proceeds being paid later, CGT is charged as though all of the proceeds are due at the time of the sale. However, what is the position as regards the purchaser?

A. The CGT rules you refer to relate to deferred consideration and contingent consideration respectively. These rules affect the vendor only and broadly result in tax being due at the time of the sale, as you describe, not when the proceeds are actually received. This is subject to later adjustment if less money is received than anticipated and to the possibility of paying the tax in instalments in certain circumstances. In addition, these rules affect all assets chargeable to CGT, not just property.

For CGT purposes the purchaser's cost is based on consideration given in money or money's worth. It would be extremely unlikely that the property would be sold before the additional amount due to the original vendor had been paid. However, in such a case no deduction would be given for the amount due but unpaid and the assumption of the debt by the vendor would result in this amount being added to the actual proceeds. Assuming that the property was sold after the additional amount had been paid, this would be an allowable cost. If the property was sold by a company, indexation allowance would be given on this additional amount from the date the property was acquired, not from the later date it was actually paid.

See *British Master Tax Guide* 5235.

Law: TCGA 1992, s. 48, 280

30-240   Deferred (lack of) income

> **Q.** Karren sold her sole-trader business to an unconnected party. The arrangement was that the consideration would be an initial amount of £150,000 when the business was sold followed by a further sum of £50,000 two years later. It transpired that the buyer did not pay the second instalment and is not going to pay it because of bankruptcy. What is Karren's CGT position regarding the disposal?

A. Karren was required to calculate the gain using the full disposal proceeds in the year the business was disposed of including the expected £50,000.

If part of the consideration brought into the calculation proves to be irrecoverable, as has occurred here, then the taxpayer can claim to adjust the capital gain calculation to exclude the irrecoverable amount. There is no specific time-limit for this claim.

Note that it would have required a different approach if the arrangement had been to pay an initial £150,000 followed by a further amount expected to be around £50,000 that would be calculated by reference to the subsequent performance of the business. The right to receive further consideration valued at £50,000 would be included in the proceeds for the disposal of the business. When the actual consideration was determined, that right would be disposed of at a loss.

See *British Master Tax Guide* 5235.

Law: TCGA 1992, s. 48

30-260   Date of disposal

> **Q.**   My client entered into a contract to sell his former trading premises. The sale agreement was unconditional, with a deposit being paid by the purchaser of £25,000 and the balance of consideration payable in two equal annual instalments. After payment of the deposit, the buyer has fallen on hard times and is unable to complete the purchase. Under the terms of the agreement, the buyer has forfeited the deposit, which is retained by my client. However, the sale agreement was unconditional, although completion and possession of the property was never taken.
>
> Can you please confirm the capital gains consequences of this and in particular whether my client has, for tax purposes, disposed of, and re-acquired this property?

A.   For disposals under a contract, you are right in that the date of unconditional agreement is the disposal date for CGT purposes. For land and property in England and Wales, this is usually the date of exchange of contracts as opposed to the completion date. However, where the disposal (completion) does not in fact occur following the sale agreement, then no disposal takes place for capital gains purposes.

The forfeited deposit kept by your client is treated in the same way as a capital sum received under an Option which is subsequently abandoned, i.e. it is a stand-alone receipt in the year. Unfortunately, no base cost can be drawn upon in respect of the property which is retained. This is in contrast to the position where the vendor receives compensation from the would-be purchaser, as distinct from retention of a forfeited deposit, which can be treated as a part-disposal of the property (CG12024). Of course, under the part disposal rules a proportion of original base cost would be taken against the sale proceeds to reduce the chargeable gain.

See *British Master Tax Guide* 5235.

Law: TCGA 1992, s. 28

Other guidance: HMRC *Capital Gains Manual*, CG14261

30-280 Losses brought forward

> **Q.** I have capital losses brought forward. Do these have to be set against the next capital gain arising or can I choose not to use the loss and continue to carry it forward?

A. There is a CGT annual exemption for each year, if the capital gain is below this figure then no tax is chargeable and the loss carried forward is not used to cover the gain. If the gain is above the exemption, the losses carried forward are used to the extent necessary to reduce the gain to the amount of the exemption. The loss must be used in the first available year.

For example:

A has gains of £12,000 and losses of £4,500 brought forward from earlier years.

The taxable amount is:

	£
Gain	12,000
Losses	(1,900)
Annual exemption	(10,100)
	Nil

	£
Losses c/f are:	
Losses b/f	4,500
Less: Losses used 2010–11	(1,900)
Losses available to carry forward	2,600

See *British Master Tax Guide* 5265.

Law: TCGA 1992, s. 3

30-300 Rental business losses

> **Q.** Roy owns a rental property in his own right, which has made a substantial profit in the tax year. He is also a member of a partnership, and has a part-share in a property that the partnership lets. A loss has been made on this property during the same tax year. Can Roy's share of the loss in the partnership property be set against the profit from his own property?

A. The main method of relieving a loss on property is to carry it forward and deduct it from future rental business profits. The loss must be used against the first available rental business profits in full. However the HMRC manual states that losses made in one rental business cannot be carried across to any other rental business that the taxpayer carries on at the same time in a different legal capacity.

See *British Master Tax Guide* 5265.

Law: TCGA 1992, s. 3

30-320 Losses and former taper relief

Example

Two assets, both acquired just over eight years previously, were sold in the same fiscal year (before 6 April 2008). One was a business asset, the other was not. A loss of £65,000 arose in the same year and was deducted first from the gain on the disposal of the non-business asset.

	Business asset £	**Non-business asset** £
Sale proceeds	100,000	100,000
Cost	(20,000)	(20,000)
	80,000	80,000
Loss relieved	–	(65,000)
	80,000	15,000
Gain after taper relief 25%/70%	£20,000	£10,500

Gain subject to tax £30,500.

By setting off the loss in this way, substantial savings are made because of the availability of greater taper relief rates on the business asset.

Note that taper relief was abolished with effect from 6 April 2008 and replaced with entrepreneurs' relief.

See *British Master Tax Guide* 5269.

Law: Former TCGA 1992, Sch. A1

30-340   Utilising company losses

> **Q.**   My client has recently bought a company. At the time of the sale, the company owed its former shareholder £64,000. The debt was assigned to the new shareholder for a payment of £40,000 to the outgoing shareholder. If the company becomes able to honour the debt, how would the repayment of £64,000 be taxed in the hands of the new shareholder?

A.   Debts are generally assets chargeable to CGT in the hands of individuals. There is provision to exclude debts being disposed of by the original creditor but clearly that does not apply now that the debt has been assigned to a new owner. If the company repays the loan, the new shareholder would be making a disposal of his asset. The gain is simply the difference between the proceeds and the cost, i.e. £24,000. It will be taxed at the appropriate CGT rate (18% or 28%) and will be subject to any unused annual CGT exemptions available.

See *British Master Tax Guide* 5265.

Law: TCGA 1992, s. 251(2)

30-360   Mixed-use assets and former taper relief

Example 1

George is a sole trader who owned a warehouse which he used for his trade from its acquisition in 1997 until 5 July 1999, when he ceased trading and granted a five-year lease on the warehouse to a third party. On 6 July 2004, the expiry of the lease, he recommenced trading and once again used the warehouse for business purposes until 6 September 2007, when the warehouse was sold realising a chargeable gain of £150,000.

The qualifying holding period and the relevant period of ownership runs from 6 April 1998 to 6 September 2007 and is nine years, five months (113 months).

That part for which the asset was a business asset was:

6/4/98 to 5/7/99 = 1 year 3 months
6/7/04 to 6/9/07 = 3 years 2 months
          Total = 4 years 5 months (53 months)

The gain regarded as arising on a business asset is therefore £150,000 × 53/113 = £70,354. The asset has been held for nine complete years, which is greater than the minimum two-year period required to achieve the maximum taper relief of 75%.

Thus the gain is reduced to 25%, £17,589.

The balance of the gain, £79,646, arises on a non-business asset. As the asset was held at 17 March 1998 the qualifying holding period is increased from nine to ten complete years and the gain is reduced to 60%, £47,788.

If George had allowable losses available for relief, these would be set against the non-business gain first.

The operation of this rule can sometimes give anomalous results, as in the following example:

Example 2

On 21 April 2004, Bill and Ben each sell a 20% holding in Flowerpots Ltd, an unlisted trading company.

Bill bought his shares on 20 April 1998 for £2,000. Ben bought his shares on 20 April 2000, also for £2,000. They each receive £20,000 for the sale of their shares. Neither has ever worked for the company.

The CGT computation 2004–05 for Bill and Ben is as follows:

	£	£
Sale proceeds	20,000	20,000
Cost	(2,000)	(2,000)
Untapered gain	18,000	18,000
Taper relief for Ben (75%)	(4,500)	
Taper relief for Bill		
business asset £18,000 × 4/6 = £12,000		
non-bus asset £18,000 × 2/6 = £6,000		
£12,000 × 75%		(9,000)
£6,000 × 20%		(1,200)
Gain after taper relief	13,500	7,800

See *British Master Tax Guide* 5271.

Law: TCGA 1992, Sch. A1

30-380   Taper ownership periods for spouses (for disposals before 6 April 2008)

Example 1

Mr and Mrs S are both full-time working employees of a trading company and each can exercise 3% of the voting rights in the company.

On 1 January 2000 Mrs S transfers her 3% interest in the company to Mr S.

Following the no gain/no loss transfer Mr S can exercise 6% of the voting rights in the company and all of this holding will qualify as a business asset from the date of the transfer. In the period from the date of acquisition of a 3% holding by each spouse to the date of transfer neither Mr nor Mrs S held more than 5% of the voting rights in the company so only the non-business asset taper will be available to Mr S for this period.

Example 2

Mr and Mrs T are both full-time working employees of a trading company where Mr T can exercise 3% and Mrs T 6% of the voting rights in the company.

On 1 January 2000 Mr T transfers his 3% interest in the company to Mrs T.

A transfer from Mr T to Mrs T at no gain/no loss in this instance secures business asset status for all of the shares from the time at which Mrs T, as a full-time working employee, held more than 5% of the voting rights in the company. This is because the company was already a qualifying company for Mrs T due to her existing 6% holding. Therefore any disposal of shares in the company by her will be a disposal of a business asset from the time she had the necessary holding.

Example 3

The initial holdings of Mr and Mrs T are the same as in Example 2 except that it is Mrs T this time who transfers her 6% interest to Mr T.

A transfer from Mrs T to Mr T at no gain/no loss in this instance has significant consequences in terms of any entitlement to the business asset taper. This is because when Mr T disposes of his 9% holding only the period from the date of transfer by Mrs T, when he acquired greater than 5% of the voting rights in the company, will qualify for the business asset taper.

The benefit of Mrs T's pre-transfer holding of greater than 5% will be lost. So for the period prior to transfer Mr T will only qualify for the non-business asset taper.

Example 4

Mrs H has owned 3% of the ordinary shares of an unlisted trading company since 1 May 1998. Neither Mrs H nor Mr H are employees of the company. On 1 February 1999 Mrs H transfers all her shares to Mr H.

The shares become business assets in relation to Mr H on 6 April 2000 (shares in an unlisted trading company) and remain business assets until their disposal on 1 September 2002. Mr H's qualifying holding period is therefore 1 May 1998 to 1 September 2002. Any gain will be apportioned for taper relief purposes in relation to the period to 5 April 2000 when they were not business assets in relation to Mr H and the period after then when they became business assets.

See *British Master Tax Guide* 5270, 5272, 5274, 5500.

Law: TCGA 1992, Sch. A1

30-400   Private residence relief

> **Q.**   Ann owns two houses a few miles apart: a cottage which she purchased for her own use several years ago and which she has lived in since purchase, and a second property which she acquired for use by her elderly mother. He elderly mother has become poorly and Ann has decided that she will stay with her mother every weekend. No private residence election has been made. What is the position regarding Ann's private residence?

A.   Where an individual has two residences and where no election has been made it is necessary to establish which property is the factual main residence. HMRC will usually start by considering where the taxpayer spends the majority of his time. This can take the form of counting the number of nights spent in each residence. HMRC will possibly contend that unless more than 183 nights a year, on average, were spent at a property, that property cannot have been the factual main residence.

However, in some cases this approach may not reflect the taxpayer's personal circumstances. Family or business situations may dictate the position and this may not be of the taxpayers' choosing. In the tax case of *Frost (HMIT) v Feltham* the taxpayer was obliged by his brewery tenancy to spend most of the year in Essex but his home was in Wales. The taxpayer retreated to Wales whenever he could. The case focused on a claim for mortgage interest relief. However the objective test of time spent in each property was held to be insufficient.

Although Ann may spend most of her time at the property acquired for her mother, following the above case, the time test alone will be insufficient to determine which property is the factual main residence. Other factors will be taken into account relating to Ann's personal circumstances and it is likely that the cottage purchased for her own use will be Ann's factual main residence

See *British Master Tax Guide* 6220.

Law: TCGA 1992, s. 222; *Frost (HMIT) v Feltham* (1980) 55 TC 10

30-420   Lost deposit when the house fell through

> **Q.**   Kathy has been trying to sell her home. A deposit was paid by a prospective buyer but the sale fell through and the client retained the deposit. How is that deposit taxed?

A.   HMRC's *Capital Gains Manual* confirms that a deposit forfeited is treated just the same as an abandoned option. Elsewhere in that manual it is confirmed that principal private residence (PPR) relief applies to the option to the extent that it would apply to the property itself.

In this case, as the gain on the house would be fully covered by PPR, the gain on the option is effectively also covered.

As the effect of PPR relief is to make the gain on a property not a chargeable gain, there is no requirement to report the disposal on the capital gains pages of the individual's tax return.

See *British Master Tax Guide* 5980, 6244.

Law: TCGA 1992, s. 144, 223

30-440   Multiple properties

> **Q.**   My client has a portfolio of properties which he rents out. In the past it has been his practice to acquire new properties periodically and, with a view to doing that, he put down a deposit to purchase a new property. Following the downturn in the market he decided not to proceed with the purchase and therefore forfeited the deposit. Will he be able to set the cost against his other rental income or will it be a capital loss?

A.   The forfeit of a deposit will not be allowed against the other property income as it is properly a capital payment. However, nor will it be allowed as a loss for capital gains purposes. TCGA 1992, s. 144 refers to options not taken up and forfeited deposits and in subs. (4) it states that the abandonment of an option shall not constitute the disposal of an asset and subs. (7) says that the forfeit of a deposit shall be treated in the same way.

The forfeit of a deposit is a tax nothing and is not allowed for the purposes of any tax.

See *British Master Tax Guide* 5080.

Law: TCGA 1992, s. 144

30-460 Time apportioned gain

> **Q.** Mr Parker bought a garage for £12,000 on 1 July 1975. The property has been extended twice. The first extension in 1980 cost £5,000 and the other extension took place in 1987–88 and cost £30,000. The market value of the property was £31,000 at 31 March 1982. He operated as a sole trader until he incorporated the business at 31 August 2005. He then charged a market rent to his personal company for the rest of the time that the garage belonged to him. On 30 September 2009, the company sold its trade and assets for £150,000 to a company set up by one of Mr Parker's former employees. The business premises were sold to the former employee immediately afterwards. The sale proceeds of the property were £250,000. The gain on the shares (after claiming entrepreneurs' relief was £400,000. What CGT will Mr Parker pay in respect of the disposals?

A. The chargeable gain on the premises is £189,000, namely the disposal proceeds less the March 1982 value and the enhancement expenditure incurred in 1987. Assuming that Mr Parker disposes of the shares in his company within three years of its ceasing to trade, the disposal of the premises will be an associated disposal for the purpose of entrepreneurs' relief. Because rent has been charged during Mr Parker's period of ownership of the property after 5 April 2008, there will be a restriction in entrepreneurs' relief. The restriction is applied using a time apportionment being the period from 6 April 2008 to the disposal divided by the total period of ownership. The part of the gain eligible for entrepreneurs' relief is 95.66%. Entrepreneurs' relief will therefore be $^4/_9$ of 95.66% of £189,000, i.e. £80,350.

Therefore, the gain on the premises after entrepreneurs' relief is £108,650. Mr Parker's annual exemption for 2009–10 is £10,100. Assuming he has no other gains in 2009–10, he will have to pay CGT of £89,739 on the shares and premises.

See *British Master Tax Guide* 5297.

Law: TCGA 1992, s. 169K

30-480 Restricting indexation

Example

Stephanie bought an antique vase for £15,000 and later sold it for (i) £25,000, (ii) £20,000, (iii) £10,000. Assume an indexation allowance of £7,000 accrued between the date of acquisition and April 1998. Stephanie's chargeable gain (before taper relief, where appropriate) in each case is:

	(i)	(ii)	(iii)
	£	£	£
Proceeds	25,000	20,000	10,000
Less: cost	(15,000)	(15,000)	(15,000)
Unindexed gain/(loss)	10,000	5,000	(5,000)
Less: indexation	(7,000)	(5,000)	Nil
Chargeable gain/allowable loss	3,000	Nil	(5,000)

See *British Master Tax Guide* 5280, 5286.

Law: TCGA 1992, s. 54

30-500   Agreeing valuations on probate and March 1982

> **Q.**   Last year I sold two plots of farmland and incurred a capital gain. One plot was owned jointly with my wife and the other owned jointly with my brother. The land owned with my wife was bought before March 1982 and so was revalued at that date to arrive at my base cost. The second plot was inherited from my father's estate a few years ago and my share of the probate value was used as my cost. HMRC have enquired into my tax return and, following protracted correspondence, have accepted the March 1982 value subject to a 10% deduction being made but have accepted the probate value as reported. I am confused as to why one value is to be discounted and not the other. Also, why 10% as a deduction?

A.   The different treatment is due to the way the tax legislation is worded.

The tax rules regarding the March 1982 value state that what is to be valued is what is held at that date, i.e. in your case, a half-share of the property. Owing to valuation procedures, not tax law, a part-share is usually discounted and, more often than not, a discount of 10% is usually applied in such cases.

Regarding the inherited property, the tax law states that the assets of a deceased person first pass to the personal representatives at their market value at death and are then passed to the beneficiary at the same value. Where there is more than one beneficiary sharing in the asset, such as you and your brother, the market value is apportioned accordingly. No discount is applied as the tax law overrides normal valuation procedure here. If your father had owned only a part share of land, rather than all of it, then his share would have been valued subject to the discount, owing to the rule mentioned above, and this discounted value would have been apportioned between you and your brother.

See *British Master Tax Guide* 5300.

Law: TCGA 1992, s. 35

30-520   March 1982 valuation and enhancement expenditure

Brian bought a chargeable asset in 1980 for £50,000, and on 31 March 1982 it had a value of £65,000. In June 1992 he spent £10,000 in improvements to the asset. In September 2002, the asset was sold for £200,000.

The appropriate indexation factors are:

March 1982 to April 1998 – 1.047

June 1992 to April 1998 – 0.167

The indexed gain is calculated as follows:

	£	£
Disposal proceeds		200,000
Less:		
March 1982 value (higher than cost)	65,000	
Enhancement expenditure (June 1992)	10,000	(75,000)
Unindexed gain		125,000
Less: indexation allowance		
March 1982 value (1.047 × £65,000)	68,055	
Enhancement cost (0.167 × £10,000)	1,670	(69,725)
Indexed gain (before taper relief)		55,275

See *British Master Tax Guide* 5223, 5300.

Law: TCGA 1992, s. 35

30-540   Amount of gain charged to corporation tax

Example

A company had the following chargeable gains/(allowable losses):

Accounting period ended	Chargeable gain £	Allowable loss £
31 December Year 1	Nil	(20,000)
30 September Year 2	30,000	(11,400)
30 September Year 3	70,000	(10,000)
30 September Year 4	Nil	(5,000)

The allowable losses are offset against chargeable gains as follows:

Accounting period ended	Chargeable gain £	Allowable loss £	Allowable loss brought forward £	Allowable loss carried forward £	Net chargeable gain £
31 December Year 1	Nil	(20,000)	Nil	(20,000)	Nil
30 September Year 2	30,000	(11,400)	(20,000)	(1,400)	Nil
30 September Year 3	70,000	(10,000)	(1,400)	Nil	58,600
30 September Year 4	Nil	(5,000)	Nil	(5,000)	Nil

See *British Master Tax Guide* 5010, 5300.

Law: TCGA 1992, s. 8

30-560   100-year-old wasting chattel

> **Q.**   Barry purchased a vintage traction engine in 1970 for £500. The traction engine was manufactured in 1905 and has recently been sold for £250,000 with restoration expenditure of £50,000 during the last three years of ownership. What is the CGT position with regard to the disposal? The traction engine has not been used for business purposes.

A.   Railway locomotives, tramway engines and similar items are chattels and are also considered to be machinery for CGT purposes. This applies whatever the size or gauge of the locomotive or engine and whatever method of propulsion (steam, diesel or electricity) it uses. Plant and machinery is always regarded as having a predictable life of 50 years or less and is therefore a wasting chattel.

No chargeable gain (or allowable loss) shall accrue on the disposal of an asset which is tangible moveable property, and is a wasting asset, and which has never qualified for capital allowances. The gain on the disposal of the traction engine in this instance is therefore exempt.

See *British Master Tax Guide* 5330.

Law: TCGA 1992, s. 44

30-580　Lease dilapidations

> **Q.**　Tony is entering into a ten-year lease which he is acquiring from the current lessee who is 15 years into a 25-year lease. The current lessee is liable for dilapidations amounting to £30,000. Rather than make good the dilapidations, the current lessee will be making a payment of £30,000 to Tony to compensate him for becoming liable for the dilapidations. Is this receipt treated as income or capital for Tony?

A.　Assuming the current tenant and the ultimate landlord are unconnected, the sum paid to Tony is neither assessable as income nor is it taxed as a capital sum derived from an asset – it is received as an inducement to acquire the asset.

Where an inducement is received on the grant of a lease, it is a reverse premium. However the reverse premium rules only apply on the grant of a lease, whereas this is an assignment of a lease so there is no tax charge.

Looking to the other side of this transaction, the lessee assigning the lease will not be entitled to a deduction for the payment of £30,000 made to Tony.

See *British Master Tax Guide* 5333.

Law: TCGA 1992, s. 240

30-600　Leases

Example 1

Burt bought a freehold factory for £180,000 in May 1998. He subsequently granted a 60-year lease for a premium of £160,000 when the value of the remainder was agreed to be £50,000.

	£
Consideration:	160,000
Allowable expenditure	
(180,000 × 160,000/(160,000 + 50,000))	(137,143)
Gain before taper relief (on disposals prior to 6 April 2008)	22,857

Example 2

Alice (the freeholder) granted a lease of land to Basil for 20 years, demanding (in addition to the rent) a premium of £20,000. There will be an amount assessable for income tax purposes, as additional rent (as calculated using the standard formula):

$$20,000 - (20,000 \times (20 - 1))/50 = £12,400$$

The consideration to be taken into account for CGT purposes on the disposal by way of grant is therefore (£20,000 − £12,400) = £7,600.

The freehold cost £200,000 and the value of the reversion after the grant of the lease (including the right to receive rents) is £250,000.

The CGT computation on the grant will be as follows:

	£
Consideration (as above)	7,600
Less: cost	
7,600 × 20,000/(20,000 + 250,000)	(563)
Unindexed gain	7,037

Example 3

Alan acquired a 12-year lease for £10,000. Seven years later he assigned the lease to Ben for a premium of £7,000.

The chargeable gain (before indexation and taper relief) is calculated:

	£	£
Consideration on assignment		7,000
Less: cost	10,000	
Reduced by indexation:		
(53.191 − 26.722)/53.191 × 10,000	(4,976)	(5,024)
Chargeable gain		1,976

Example 4

Alan acquired a 12-year lease for £10,000. After two years, he granted a sublease of it for five years, at a premium of £7,000. His headlease still had ten years to run. The amount deductible from the consideration paid for the sublease is calculated as follows:

Allowable expenditure (indexed) = 10,000 × (46.695 − 26.722)/53.191 = £3,755

	£
Premium	7,000
Less: allowable amount	(3,755)
Unindexed gain	3,245

See *British Master Tax Guide* 5333.

Law: TCGA 1992, s. 240, Sch. 8

Capital Gains Tax

30-620   Should I use the 1982 value?

Example 1

Henry bought a chargeable asset in 1975 for £10,000. He sells it in November 2006 for £25,000. The March 1982 value was £5,000.

	£	£
Proceeds	25,000	25,000
Cost/March 1982 valuation	(10,000)	(5,000)
Indexation		
10,000 × 1.047	(10,470)	(10,470)
Indexed gain	4,530	9,530

The smaller gain (£4,530) will be charged to CGT.

Example 2

Sally bought a chargeable asset in 1975 for £20,000. She sells it in November 2006 for £18,000. The March 1982 value was £25,000.

	£	£
Proceeds	18,000	18,000
Cost/March 1982 valuation	(20,000)	(25,000)
No indexation as loss		
Loss	(2,000)	(7,000)

The smaller loss (£2,000) will be allowed.

If one calculation showed a gain and the other a loss, a £nil gain is included.

See *British Master Tax Guide* 5300.

Law: TCGA 1992, s. 35

30-640   Joint ownership of shares

Example

Michael acquired 2,000 shares in Pink Ltd on 1 June 1980 for £6,500. The 2,000 shares represented a 20% holding. On the same day, his wife, Helen, acquired 4,000 shares (a 40% holding) in Pink Ltd for £20,000. On 1 July 1988, she transferred her entire holding to Michael. On 1 May 2010, he sold 3,000 shares.

Values of the various holdings at 31 March 1982 were as follows:

	£
20%	8,000
40%	30,000
60%	75,000

For the purpose of the re-basing provisions and the indexation provisions, the market value at 31 March 1982 of the shares sold by Michael in May 2010 will be computed as:

3,000/6,000 × £75,000 = £37,500

See *British Master Tax Guide* 5142, 5300.

Law: TCGA 1992, s. 35, 286

30-660   Same day transactions

Example

David carried out the following transactions in £ ordinary shares of Priodot Ltd

	No. of shares	Value £
Acquired 1/6/Year 1	1,000	3,200
Acquired 31/7/Year 3	400	1,600
Disposal 8/9/Year 9	(230)	(970)
Acquisition 8/9/Year 9	300	1,300
Disposal 8/9/Year 9	(475)	(1,535)
Acquisition 8/9/Year 9	100	410

A single disposal of 705 shares for £2,505 on 8 September Year 9 is matched with a single acquisition of 400 shares costing £1,710 on that date. The balance of 305 shares is matched in accordance with the normal rules.

See *British Master Tax Guide* 5300, 5826.

Law: TCGA 1992, s. 105

30-680   Alternative identification rules

Example

On 1 December Year 1, Billy acquires 1,500 shares by exercising an HMRC-approved share option at a cost of £5 per share. On the same day, he acquires a further 1,000 shares at their market value on that date of £10 per share. The approved-scheme shares have a base cost of £7,500 (1,500 shares at £5 per share) and the other shares have a base cost of £10,000 (1,000 shares at £10 per share). On 20 May Year 2, Billy disposes of 500 shares at £14, realising consideration of £7,000. If Billy does not make an election, the gain is as follows:

	£
Consideration	7,000
Less: cost of shares (500/2,500 × (£7,500 + £10,000))	(3,500)
Chargeable gain	3,500

However, if Billy makes an election under TCGA 1992, s. 105A, he is treated as disposing of the other shares before the approved scheme shares. The gain on the first disposal is:

	£
Consideration	7,000
Less: cost of shares (500 shares at £10 per share)	(5,000)
Chargeable gain	2,000

Thus the gain on the first disposal is reduced if Billy makes the election. He must make it by 31 January Year 5.

See *British Master Tax Guide* 5300, 5826.

Law: TCGA 1992, s. 105A

30-700   What's mine is yours

Example

Husband and wife are retired, having been married for many years. Their tax adviser feels comfortable that assets can be passed between them to the best tax advantage. The husband's assets and his income can be summarised:

	Value	Income therefrom
	£	£ p.a.
Shares in family company	500,000	1,000
Portfolio of quoted equities	300,000	6,000
Fixed interest securities	200,000	12,000
Pension		30,000
	1,000,000	49,000

The wife's assets and her income can be summarised:

	Value	Income therefrom
	£	£ p.a.
Shares in family company	500,000	1,000
Pension		5,000
	500,000	6,000

The husband can purchase his wife's shareholding in the family company for £500,000, the consideration being satisfied by him passing to his wife his portfolios of quoted equities and of fixed interest securities. Each has made a CGT disposal but, by virtue of the inter-spouse rule, each has made a disposal with no gain/no loss and no CGT is payable. After the exchange, neither husband nor wife is a higher-rate taxpayer, giving a potential income tax saving of several thousand pounds p.a.

See *British Master Tax Guide* 5500.

Law: TCGA 1992, s. 58

30-720 Hold-over relief in discretionary trusts

> **Q.** I am aware that CGT hold-over relief is not available for transfers into a discretionary trust where the settlor or his wife can benefit. Is it possible to claim the hold-over relief if the settlor's minor children can benefit?

A. A change in this area was brought about by FA 2006 and has applied from 6 April 2006. From that date it is no longer possible to hold over the gain arising on the transfer of an asset to a trust where a beneficiary is a dependent child of the settlor.

A dependent child means a child who is under the age of 18 years, unmarried and does not have a civil partner.

Where a dependent child is a beneficiary of a trust, the changed legislation treats it as a trust where the settlor has an interest. As well as the denial of hold-over relief, a further consequence is that a settlor will be taxed on any gains made by the settlement.

If the trust was created before 6 April 2006 with a dependent child as a beneficiary and a gain is made after 6 April 2006, the gain will be taxed on the settlor.

Hold-over relief may be claimed if the provision exists for a dependent child to be a beneficiary but there is no dependent child. However, if within six years a dependent child becomes a beneficiary, then there will be a claw-back of the relief. This is a potential trap if the settlor remarries and his new spouse has young children.

Capital Gains Tax

335

See *British Master Tax Guide* 5590.

Law: FA 2006, Sch. 12

30-740   Trusting in shares

> **Q.**   I am acting as executor for a deceased person's estate. Estate assets consist of shares, some of which were left by the deceased and some have been purchased by the executors. These shares are going to be transferred into a discretionary will trust by the executors. Will there be CGT to pay when the shares are put into the trust and how will the trust be taxed when the shares are eventually sold by the trustees?

A.   If a trust is created by the will or intestacy then the trustees of that trust are legatees in precisely the same way as, for example, an individual taking an absolute interest in an asset. This is confirmed by TCGA 1992, s. 64(2). The personal representatives are not liable to CGT for disposals of assets which become vested in the trustees as legatees.

All assets acquired by a legatee following a death, and which were assets owned by the deceased at the date of death, are treated as though acquired by the legatee at the date of death and at their market value on the date of death.

Assets acquired by the personal representatives during the course of the administration are treated as though they had been acquired by the legatee at the date of acquisition by the personal representatives and at the cost to the personal representatives or the value at which they were acquired by the personal representatives. So that if the trustees of the will trust subsequently sell those assets, the normal rules of CGT will apply. They will pay CGT on the difference between the acquisition cost given by the above and their sales proceeds.

They will be entitled to an annual exemption which is normally half the annual exemption of an individual. This may be reduced if the deceased, who is normally treated as the settlor, has created other settlements. This settlement and the other settlements made by the settlor form a group. The annual exempt amount for each settlement is divided by the number in the group (up to five). The unused annual exemption of one settlement cannot be transferred to another.

See *British Master Tax Guide* 5550.

30-760   Estate CGT

> **Q.**   I am one of the executors of an estate where the residuary beneficiary is a charity. The estate consists of a property and we have received an offer for the property which is much higher than the probate value. Will the estate be exempt from CGT?

A.   If the executors sell the property their base cost will be probate value so that CGT will be due at the appropriate rate (18% or 28% after 22 June 2010). As the residuary beneficiary is a charity, consider obtaining the consent of the charity to appropriate the property to them before sale. The executors could then sell the property as bare trustees for the charity. It is essential that there is proper documentation to prove the appropriation. The charity should be exempt from CGT.

See *British Master Tax Guide* 5680.

Law: F(No. 2)A 2010, s. 2; FA 2008, s. 8; TCGA 1992, s. 62

30-780   CGT paid by personal representatives

> **Q.**   I am acting as personal representative in the administration of the estate of Miss A. She died 18 months ago and the main asset of the estate is a piece of land. The beneficiaries are her three nephews. Fortunately the land has increased in value since she bought it and the beneficiaries want it to be sold. Will there be CGT to pay and, if so, who will be responsible for paying the tax?

A.   When a person dies and their assets are passed to others then for CGT purposes, beneficiaries or personal representatives acquire the assets at probate value. You can see that this is a great help and in effect gives a tax-free uplift to market value at the date of death. Thus if the land has not increased in value since Miss A's death then there will be no CGT to pay at all.

If you are in the position that the increase in value has occurred in the 18 months since the death then there are two options available.

The land could be sold by you as personal representative. Personal representatives benefit during the period of administration of an estate from the full individual annual exemption from CGT for the year of death and the two following tax years (TCGA 1992, s. 3(7)). Any gain remaining after the deduction of the annual exemption is taxable at the appropriate CGT rate.

Alternatively, if each beneficiary can set their annual exemption against their share of the gain, there may be a lower overall tax liability if the land is transferred to the beneficiaries before the onward sale. If this is done then you, as personal representative, must ensure that the appropriation or assent is properly documented as HMRC may require evidence that the asset has been transferred. If the beneficiaries give instructions to you, as personal representative, to make the sale on their behalf then there will need to be a declaration of a bare trust with you as trustee.

Capital Gains Tax

There will be no stamp duty land tax on the assent or appropriation or declaration of a bare trust as there is an exemption when land passes to a beneficiary under a will or by virtue of the law on intestacy.

See *British Master Tax Guide* 5680.

Law: FA 2003, Sch. 3, para. 3A; TCGA 1992, s. 62(1)

30-800   Using losses on death

Example 1

John died in 2009–10 having made a capital gain of £9,000 and a capital loss of £24,000 during the year. His gains and losses for earlier years are:

- 2006–07 – gain £16,000;
- 2007–08 – loss £5,000;
- 2008–09 – gain £18,000.

The loss arising in 2009–10 will first be set against chargeable gains of the same year. The balance of £15,000 will be carried back and set against 2008–09 first but within the limits of preserving the annual exempt amount.

2008–09	£	
Chargeable gains		18,000
Losses		
brought forward 2007–08	(5,000)	
carried back 2009–10	(3,400)	
Gain		9,600

2006–07	£	
Chargeable gains		16,000
Losses		
carried back 2009–10	(7,200)	
Gain		8,800

The balance of the loss of £4,400 is wasted.

See *British Master Tax Guide* 5685.

Law: TCGA 1992, s. 62

30-820   Non-resident with UK assets

> **Q.**   I run a trade in the UK but am non-resident. Do I escape UK CGT on disposal of my trade?

A.   If you are a resident of another country for the purposes of the double taxation agreement, you will be liable to tax on gains from disposing of assets in that country only, therefore being exempt from capital gains in the UK. However, according to HMRC booklet HMRC6, if you are carrying on a trade or running a business through a permanent establishment in the UK, any gains you make from disposing of assets connected with the permanent establishment will continue to be chargeable to capital gains in the UK.

See *British Master Tax Guide* 5700.

Law: TCGA 1992, s. 10

30-840   Use of the remittance basis

> **Q.**   My client is not domiciled in the UK and has overseas capital gains and losses. In a previous year I set his overseas losses against the overseas gains but it was pointed out by HMRC that I had made a mistake and that the losses could not be used. In view of this it is important that I understand the new regime.
>
> My client will not be claiming the remittance basis every year but will make a decision each year. For 2009–10 he is likely to have foreign gains of £90,000, losses of £20,000, UK gains of £30,000 and UK losses of £40,000. He never remits the gain to the UK and will be claiming the remittance basis for 2009–10.

A.   As you imply, up to and including 2007–08 there was no relief for any overseas capital losses made by foreign domiciliaries. Before 2008–09 the remittance basis for capital gains was automatic and not subject to a claim.

Finance Act 2008 introduced a form of loss relief for overseas losses from 6 April 2008. For a foreign domiciliary taxed on the remittance basis it will be possible to make an election. The election must be made for the first year in which the remittance basis is claimed. If an election is not made then overseas losses of that tax year and all future years will not be allowable losses. They will be disallowed even if the taxpayer in a later year opts to be taxed on an arising basis rather than remittance basis unless he accepts that he is domiciled in the UK for all purposes.

You must think carefully before an election is made because it can cause surprising results. The order of set-off can cause problems. If the remittance basis is claimed for the tax year in which overseas capital gains are made, the total allowable losses (overseas and UK) are

Capital Gains Tax

deducted first from foreign gains arising and remitted in the year, then against unremitted foreign gains and lastly against UK gains.

For your client, who does not remit overseas gains 2009–10:

With election to use foreign losses

Total losses foreign £20,000 + UK £40,000 = £60,000

Set off against foreign gains of £90,000

Leave foreign gains of £30,000 – not taxed as not remitted

UK gains £30,000 subject to tax

With no election to use foreign losses

Total losses foreign £20,000 + UK £40,000 = £60,000

Foreign gains of £90,000 not subject to tax

UK gains £30,000 less UK losses £40,000 leave no gain taxable and £10,000 loss to carry forward.

It can be seen that in this case an election to take advantage of foreign losses will lead to a higher tax charge.

See *British Master Tax Guide* 5698.

30-860   Allocation of partnership gains and losses

Example

Antonia, Bruce and Colin are partners, each having a one-third fractional share in asset surpluses. Antonia and Bruce plan to retire soon and Colin agrees to take a heavier burden in the partnership business. The partnership premises, with a current market value of £70,000, are transferred to Colin. The indexed cost of the premises is £64,000. At the time of distribution, a chargeable gain of £2,000, after indexation, arises to each of Antonia and Bruce.

Colin is not regarded as making a chargeable gain. Instead, his base value for CGT purposes is reduced from £70,000 to £68,000.

If, instead of a gain, there had been an overall loss of, say £6,000, Colin's share (£2,000) would have been added to the current market value to give a carry-forward value of £72,000.

See *British Master Tax Guide* 5775.

Other guidance: SP D12

30-880   Do my wife's qualifying bonds still qualify?

> **Q.** Jack has held shares in ABC plc for many years. ABC plc was recently taken over and Jack received qualifying corporate bonds (QCBs) in return for part of his shareholding. For tax planning reasons Jack is considering transferring some of the QCBs to his wife Jill. If Jack transfers half of his QCBs to Jill, will the frozen gain on half of the original shares crystallise at the date of the transfer?

A. The general rule is that when shares are exchanged for QCBs, the gain or loss on the disposal of the shares is calculated at the time of the exchange, but only comes into the charge to tax when the QCBs are disposed of.

Transfers between husband and wife are treated as being for a consideration which creates neither a gain nor a loss on disposal. It would seem unreasonable that a frozen gain comes into charge (or loss arises) as a result of a no gain no loss transfer. The legislation recognises this and provides that where QCBs which have a frozen gain or loss attached are transferred between spouses, the gain (or loss) will not crystallise as a result of the no gain/no loss transfer.

See *British Master Tax Guide* 5500, 5865.

Law: TCGA 1992, s. 58, 116

30-900   Giving worthless QCBs away to a good cause

> **Q.** I sold my trading company two years ago to another company for part cash and part loan notes which I could cash after two years. Only the gain relating to the cash element was taxed at that time and the gain relating to the loan notes was deferred until the loan notes are cashed. Unfortunately the company is struggling and I have to face the possibility that my QCBs are probably worthless. Surely I will not have to pay the CGT that has been deferred from the original sale of the shares?

A. Unfortunately, in your case, as the QCB is exempt, any gain or loss on the QCB is outside the scope of CGT so that the gain held over will be taxable without the benefit of any loss relief from the QCBs. HMRC have suggested that if the disposal of the QCBs is to a charity there will be no charge on the deferred gain either on the donor or on the charity on a subsequent disposal of the bonds. Your only problem now is to find a charity that will accept worthless QCBs!

See *British Master Tax Guide* 5865.

Law: TCGA 1992, s. 116

30-920 Shares for QCBs

Example

John owns preference shares in Holdover plc which he acquired in 2000. On a reorganisation of Holdover Ltd he receives £10,000 worth of qualifying corporate bonds (QCBs) and £5,000 in cash. The preference shares were worth £15,000 at the time (representing a notional gain of £6,000 after taper relief). John sells the bonds within six months for £20,000.

The proportion of gain chargeable relates to the cash sum:

$5,000/15,000 \times 6,000 = £2,000$

Subsequent disposal of QCBs:

	£
Disposal proceeds	20,000
Acquisition cost	(15,000)
Gain (exempt as QCB)	5,000

	£
Carried-over gain	6,000
Less: gain taxed (see above)	(2,000)
Amount taxable	4,000

See *British Master Tax Guide* 5865.

Law: TCGA 1992, s. 116

30-940 Bonus issues

Example

Henry acquired 1,000 ordinary shares in WJ Ltd for £3,000. Later there is a bonus issue of one for five. Henry receives 200 extra ordinary shares.

The new holding is to be taken as the same asset as the original shares. Consequently, the new holding will have the same base cost and date of acquisition as the original shares. If Henry later sells 600 shares for £2,000 the calculation would be as follows:

	£
Disposal proceeds	2,000
Total acquisition cost: £3,000	
Apportioned acquisition cost:	
£3,000 × 600/(1000 + 200)	(1,500)
Unindexed gain	500

See *British Master Tax Guide* 5905.

30-960   All premiums great and small

Example 1

Henry purchased loan stock in WJ plc for £8,000. Subsequently there was a conversion of securities, in which Henry received:

- preference shares then worth £10,000;
- a premium on conversion of £500.

Henry later sold the preference shares for £12,500. The premium on conversion is small and so requires no immediate action.

The gain on the subsequent disposal (ignoring indexation and taper relief) will be calculated as follows:

	£	£
Disposal proceeds		12,500
Less: acquisition cost	8,000	
Less: conversion premium	(500)	(7,500)
Chargeable gain		5,000

Example 2

Henry owns 1,000 units of loan stock in WJ plc which cost him £1,000. The loan stock is converted into preference shares when it is worth £10,000 and a premium of £2 per unit is paid on conversion. The premium is not small and so the following assessment must be made:

	£	£
Premium £2 × 1,000		2,000
Less: allowable expenditure	1,000	
indexation (say)	500	(1,500)
Chargeable gain		500

Capital Gains Tax

See *British Master Tax Guide* 5913.

30-980 Goodwill, EIS and entrepreneurs' relief

> **Q.** I am disposing of my business in 2009–10. The business was established four years ago and its only chargeable asset is goodwill that I have generated. The goodwill has a value of £70,000. I have capital losses brought forward of £5,000. I want to defer any gain remaining chargeable by subscribing for Enterprise Investment Scheme (EIS) shares. How much do I need to invest to ensure that I have no chargeable gains in 2009–10?

A. The disposal of your business in this way is a material disposal of a business asset and so will qualify for entrepreneurs' relief. Consequently, the chargeable gain is reduced by four-ninths to £38,889. Assuming that this is your only gain this year, the amount to defer is £23,789 (£38,889 less losses brought forward and an annual exemption of £10,100 for 2009–10). Therefore, the required subscription in EIS shares is £23,789. When the EIS shares are eventually sold, the gain of £23,289 comes into charge. There won't be any reliefs applicable to the gain but you will be able to set that year's annual exemption against it.

See *British Master Tax Guide* 5923

Law: FA 2008, s. 9, Sch. 3

31-000 Enterprise Investment Scheme relief

Example

Ann invests £100,000 in shares qualifying for Enterprise Investment Scheme (EIS) relief and obtains tax relief of £20,000 (£100,000 × 20%) in respect of the investment. Ann sells the shares for £65,000, seven years later.

Assuming that no withdrawal of EIS relief occurs on the disposal of the shares, the allowable loss arising for CGT purposes is £15,000 (£65,000 − (£100,000 − £20,000)).

See *British Master Tax Guide* 5923

Law: TCGA 1992, s. 150A

31-020 EIS and entrepreneurs' relief

> **Q.** In June 2007, my company ceased trading; it had been trading since its incorporation on 21 December 2002. I am the sole shareholder and director, having subscribed for a £1 share at incorporation. I applied to HMRC to make a capital

distribution on informal winding up under the terms of Extra-statutory Concession C16. The distribution of £120,000 took place on 31 December 2007. In February 2008, I subscribed for £20,000 worth of EIS shares to defer some of the gain. How will my gain on disposal of my company be taxed and what will happen when the EIS shares are sold?

A. The £20,000 of the gain of £120,000 is deferred by the subscription for EIS shares. The remaining £100,000 is subject to taper relief. A time apportionment is required to determine which part of that gain is subject to taper relief at the business rate and which part at the non-business rate. The total period of ownership of the shares was five years. Assuming that the company did not have substantial assets for non-trading purposes during the time it was trading, nine-tenths (all but six months out of five years) of the gain will be at the business rate and one-tenth will be at the non-business rate. Therefore, £90,000 is subject to relief at 75% because the asset has been held for more than two complete years. An amount of £10,000 is subject to relief at 15% because the asset has been held for five complete years. Therefore the amount of gain remaining after taper relief is £31,000. Against this, the annual exemption of £9,200 is set. Therefore, gains of £21,800 will be taxed at 40% if you are a higher rate taxpayer, i.e. tax of £8,720 is due.

When the EIS shares are sold, the deferred gain comes back into charge. Because the gain is deferred from a year prior to 2008–09, the transitional rules included in *Finance Act* 2008 apply. The £20,000 deferred gain qualifies for entrepreneurs' relief because the original asset would have qualified for the relief but for the fact that entrepreneurs' relief did not exist in 2007–08. The gain is therefore reduced by four-ninths to £11,111. It is then subject to the annual exemption applying in the year that the EIS shares are disposed of and the gain remaining chargeable is subject to CGT at 18%. Using the annual exemption for 2008–09 (i.e. £9,600) for illustration, the amount of CGT would be £272.

See *British Master Tax Guide* 5923

Law: FA 2008, s. 9, Sch. 3

31-040 Negligible value claim

Q. I have some shares in my father's engineering company but unfortunately, as he suffered a large bad debt, the company is unable to recover. My shares now have negligible value. Can I get relief for the loss on the shares against my income for the year?

A. It is possible in certain circumstances to turn a capital loss into an income tax loss. Relief can be claimed in the year of the loss or the previous year. However, there are conditions, all of which must be satisfied.

The company itself must have been an eligible trading company and, here, the rules are generally in line with the definition of 'eligible trading company' necessary to claim EIS relief. Your family's engineering company should have no difficulty in qualifying here.

According to HMRC's own manuals, the company will be in liquidation and insolvent, or have ceased trading and have no assets at the date of the claim.

The relief only applies where the holder subscribed for the shares in money or money's worth or where his spouse or civil partner subscribed for the shares and later made a lifetime gift to him of the shares. You do not say how you acquired the shares but, for example, you will not be able to claim the relief if you bought the shares from your father or you inherited them from a grandparent.

If you did subscribe for the shares, the amount of the loss that you can claim is restricted to the actual value of your subscription. If the shares peaked at a higher value at some time then, I am afraid, this value has to be ignored in the calculation of the loss available for relief.

See *British Master Tax Guide* 5940.

Law: CTA 2010, s. 68

31-060   Gift at a price

Example

Erik sells the goodwill of his business to his son for £30,000 on 31 March 2008 when it has a value of £100,000. Erik purchased the goodwill in July 1982 for £10,000. The following computation is required:

	£
Market value	100,000
Cost	(10,000)
Unindexed gain	90,000
Indexation allowance	
(£10,000 × 0.986)	(9,860)
Indexed gain	80,140
Held over gain	
£80,140 − (£30,000 − £10,000)	(60,140)
Gain before taper relief	20,000
Gain after taper relief	
£20,000 × 25%	5,000

See *British Master Tax Guide* 6144.

31-080 Planning on incorporation

Example

Liz set up as a sole trader in. The business has made a good start and the goodwill is estimated to be worth £40,000 when it is subsequently decided to incorporate. Liz could give the goodwill to the company and hold over the gain. An alternative would be to sell it to the company for its full value of £40,000. Even if the company cannot afford to pay her out immediately, it can credit her director loan account with the £40,000 value. Liz can then draw against that loan account which may prove to be a very tax- and NIC-efficient way of withdrawing funds from the new company.

See *British Master Tax Guide* 6147.

Law: TCGA 1992, s. 165

31-100 Parts of small chattels

Q. Jody jointly owns a piece of art with a friend. The art is worth more than £6,000 but each person's share is not. Does the £6,000 limit for exempting gains on chattels apply to the asset as a whole or the individual's share?

A. HMRC's *Capital Gains Manual* states that it is necessary to compare each person's share of the disposal consideration with their own separate limit. Therefore a chattel valued at up to £12,000 could qualify in this way.

See *British Master Tax Guide* 6155.

Law: TCGA 1992, s. 262

31-120 Chattels

Example 1

Jemima acquires an antique chair. Its useful life is expected to exceed 50 years. She pays £3,710 for the chair on 6 September Year 1. She sells the chair for £8,000 on 6 September Year 2.

Her chargeable gain is as follows:

	£
Disposal consideration	8,000
Less: allowable expenditure:	(3,710)
Gain before chattels exemption	4,290
Less: chattels exemption	
(excess over 5/3 × (£8,000 − £6,000))	(957)
Chargeable gain	3,333

Example 2

Fred acquires a painting for investment purposes. Its expected useful life is in excess of 50 years. He pays £6,697 for the painting on 1 September Year 1. He sells it for £8,200 on 18 September Year 2.

His chargeable gain is as follows:

	£
Disposal consideration	8,200
Less: allowable expenditure:	(6,697)
Gain before chattels exemption	1,503
Less: chattels exemption	
(excess of gain over 5/3 × (£8,200 − £6,000), i.e. £3,666)	Nil
Chargeable gain	1,503

Example 3

Karen disposes of a set of rare books in September Year 4 (they have an expected useful life well in excess of 50 years). She sells part of the collection to an unconnected person, Larry, for £5,100 and the other part to his brother, Leroy, for £3,100 (the total market value being £8,200). Karen had acquired the books for £2,400 in August Year 1.

For the purposes of determining the applicable exemption, the sales are considered as a single transaction for consideration of £8,200. The reduction in chargeable gains is therefore as follows:

	£
Notional disposal consideration	8,200
Less: notional expenditure	(2,400)
Notional gain before chattels exemption	5,800
5/3 × (£8,200 × £6,000)	(3,667)
Reduction	2,133

If the reduction is apportioned between the assets on the basis of the disposal considerations in point, the gain on each part will be as follows:

	£
Disposal to Larry	
Disposal consideration	5,100
Less: allowable expenditure	
$\dfrac{5,100}{8,200} \times 2,400$	(1,493)
Gain before chattels exemption	3,607
Less: chattels exemption (51/82 × £2,133)	(1,327)
Chargeable gain	2,280

	£
Disposal to Leroy	
Disposal consideration	3,100
Less: allowable expenditure	
$\dfrac{3,100}{8,200} \times 2,400$	(907)
Gain before chattels exemption	2,193
Less: chattels exemption (31/82 × £2,133)	(806)
Chargeable gain	1,387

Example 4

Alison acquires a painting in May Year 1 for £2,100. She sells a part-share in the painting in September Year 4 for £4,000, when the market value of the remaining share is £3,900.

	£
Disposal consideration	4,000
Less: cost (2,100 × 4,000/7,900)	1,063
	2,937
	2,830
Less: reduction	1,227
Chargeable gain (see note)	1,603

Note
Gain not to exceed 5/3 × (7,900 − 600) × 4,000/7,900

See *British Master Tax Guide* 6155.

Law: TCGA 1992, s. 262

31-140   Lots of life assurance

Q. Freddie has made life assurance policy gains in respect of a cluster of identical policies taken out on the same date from the same provider. Should the gains be reported separately or jointly?

A. If the insurer has issued a number of identical policies on the same date, the gains arising on such policies are often reported on the same chargeable event certificate. In this case, the gains should be reported jointly. If the insurer has issued separate certificates for each policy but the policies are all identical, the gains should still be reported jointly with the details on each certificate for gains and tax treated as paid being totalled.

See *British Master Tax Guide* 6170.

Law: TCGA 1992, s. 210

31-160   Build a house and then pay tax on it

Q. Nyron inherited a piece of land from his grandfather in 1995, when the land was valued at £15,000. He spent £40,000 in 2001 building a house on the land. At that time the value of the land was £30,000.

He is considering selling the house next year for approximately £250,000. As this is his private residence and the rest of the land is his garden (less than half a hectare) presumably his CGT will be calculated based only on the increase in value of the land before he built his home?

A. One might reasonably make a case for splitting the capital gain into two parts:

(1)   the non-exempt gain which relates to the increase in the value of the land before the house was built;

(2)   the exempt gain which relates to the period when it was his principle private residence.

The chargeable capital gain before reliefs using this method would be £15,000 (£30,000 − £15,000 ignoring indexation).

However, it seems clear from HMRC's manual that the Revenue reject this method of calculation of the gain under these circumstances. It is their view that a time-based apportionment (which can be adjusted in a manner which is just and reasonable where there is a change in what is occupied as the individual's residence, whether on account of reconstruction or conversion of a building or for any other reason) does not apply to a property which was not occupied at all previously. HMRC regard time apportionment as the only method of calculating the gain when a dwelling house comes into existence.

In this situation the gain becomes:

	£
Sale proceeds	250,000
Less: cost (15,000 + 40,000)	(55,000)
	195,000
Less: PPR relief for 6 years out of 12	(97,500)
Gain before reliefs	97,500

See *British Master Tax Guide* 6220, 6247.

Law: TCGA 1992, s. 223–224

31-180   Demolish a house then pay tax on it

> **Q.**   We are selling an investment property that we own to a developer. He has said that if we knock down the building before we sell, he will give us an extra £25,000 for the bare land. We believe that the cost of demolishing the building will be about £10,000, which will presumably be an allowable cost, in addition to the original cost of the land and buildings. This seems too good to be true, is there any down side we should be aware of?

A.   There is indeed a down side in this situation. The allowable cost for you will not include the original cost of the building. Section 38(1)(b) of TCGA 1992 states that the expenditure must be reflected in the state or nature of the asset at the time of disposal. This means that the cost of demolition, £10,000, will be allowed, but the original cost of the building, including all the enhancements, will not be allowed.

You will need to do the arithmetic to decide if you would get a benefit. On the information you have given you will be better off if the original expenditure you incurred on the building was less than about £68,500.

		With building £		Without building £
Proceeds		300,000		325,000
Less: cost of land	100,000		100,000	
Add: cost of building	68,500			
Add: cost of demolition			10,000	
Less: allowable costs		(168,500)		(110,000)
Gross gain		131,500		215,000
Less: annual exemption	9,600 × 2	(19,200)	9,600 × 2	(19,200)
Net gain		112,300		195,800

Capital Gains Tax

351

	With building £	Without building £
Tax payable	20,214	35,244
Proceeds after tax	279,786	289,756
Payment for demolition	–	(10,000)
Cash in hand	279,786	279,756

Difference between the two options = £30

See *British Master Tax Guide* 5220, 6247.

Law: TCGA 1992 s. 38(1)(b)

31-200   Half a hectare

> **Q.**   I am aware that the permitted maximum area to which the only or main residence relief on disposal applies is half a hectare. Does this include the land on which the house stands?

A.   Yes!

See *British Master Tax Guide* 6222.

Law: TCGA 1992, s. 222

31-220   Principal private residence on separation

> **Q.**   Niall and Kevin, who had entered a civil partnership, have decided to separate. Currently Kevin owns two houses, one which is their principal private residence (PPR) and the other which Niall uses during the week as he is employed some 100 miles from their home. Kevin has agreed to give this second house to Niall as part of the agreed split. What will be the CGT consequences of the transfer?

A.   The tax consequences will depend on what stage in the tax year they actually separated and how efficient they can be in getting the transfer organised.

Nil gain/nil loss transfers are available to spouses and civil partners as long as they have been living together at some time in the year of assessment. This means that Niall will take over the original base cost of the property from Kevin, and there will be no capital gains for Kevin to pay.

As they are not actually living together at the date of the transfer, Niall will be treated as only owning the property from the date of the transfer, and will, consequently, be able to benefit from exemption under the PPR relief on the whole gain.

See *British Master Tax Guide* 6233.

Law: TCGA 1992, s. 222

31-240   Dependent relatives allowances

> **Q.**   My client's father died in 1979 and the will left the family home, which had been in father's name, to my client but in trust allowing mother to live there for her lifetime. Mother died in 1994 and since then the property has been rented out.
>
> The property is now being sold (2010) and we need to know what figure to take as the base cost. Will it be the market value in March 1982 or in 1994 when mother died?
>
> Also, will my client be able to claim dependent relative relief?

A.   When father died a trust was created by his will. Mother had a right to live in the property for her life and this is called a life interest trust. At her death the trust came to an end so that the house was treated as leaving the trust.

The relevant legislation is in TCGA 1992, Pt. III. Section 71 states that when property leaves a trust under any circumstances then that property is deemed to have been disposed of by the trustees and reacquired by them at market value. This means that normally the beneficiary will acquire the asset at its market value at that date and trustees will have a capital gain.

However, s. 73 says that in the circumstances that the trust ends due to the death of the life tenant the trustees are not taxed on the capital gain and as long as the property does not go back to the original settlor, the beneficiary still benefits from the uplift to market value.

Therefore the value that you can use as the base cost for the sale in 2010 is the market value in 1994, i.e. the date of mother's death. As we are calculating the gain from the period after mother's death a claim for dependent relative relief would not be appropriate.

See *British Master Tax Guide* 6238.

Law: TCGA 1992, s. 226

Capital Gains Tax

31-260 Job-related accommodation

> **Q.** Ian owns his own home in North London where he lived until 2009. In September 2009 he accepted an appointment as head-teacher of a school also located in the North London area.
>
> As the head-teacher, he is required to live on the school site where he is provided with a home. He is taxed on the benefit in kind accordingly. Having now been in the job for a few years Ian has decided he is likely to stay at the school until he retires. As he is provided with a home at the school, he sees no point in keeping his own home and has decided to sell it. What is the position with regard to principal private residence (PPR) relief, and is there a special concession for people who are required to reside elsewhere by their employer?

A. Ian will be entitled to PPR relief for the periods during which he has lived in the house, and as the house has been his only or main residence at some time during the period of ownership, then the final 36 months will also qualify for relief. Relief is allowed for any periods of absence up to a maximum of four years during which the individual could not live in the house because of any condition reasonably imposed by his or her employer requiring him or her to live elsewhere for the purpose of his or her employment provided that both before and after the period of absence there is a time during which the dwelling house is the individual's only or main residence.

So, if Ian moves back into the house using it as his main residence before disposing of it, PPR will apply for a maximum of four years whilst he has been absent. However, if he sells the house without moving back in, the total period of absence (excluding the final 36 months) will be chargeable to CGT.

See *British Master Tax Guide* 6241.

Law: TCGA 1992, s. 222

31-280 Deemed residence

Example

Robert purchased a house on Merseyside on 1 January 1987, which is his only or main residence. He occupied the property until 31 March 1990, when he left to travel around the world, returning on 31 March 1994. He immediately took up a new employment, as a condition of which he was obliged to occupy a property in Southend provided by his employer until 31 March 1999. He then re-occupied the Merseyside property until 30 June 2006, on which date he moved in to his girlfriend's house some distance away. On 31 December 2009, the property was sold, realising a gain of £130,000.

The proportion of the gain which is eligible for PPR exemption is calculated as follows:

31/03/89–31/03/90	actual occupation (1 year)
01/04/90–31/03/93	deemed occupation (3 years)
01/04/93–31/03/94	absence (1 year)
01/04/94–31/03/98	deemed occupation (4 years)
01/04/98–31/03/99	absence (1 year)
01/04/99–30/06/06	actual occupation (7 years, 3 months)
01/07/06–31/12/06	absence (6 months)
01/01/07–31/12/09	last 36 months

Thus, the exempt proportion of the gain is:

18 years 3 months/20 years 9 months $\times$ £130,000 = £114,337.

See *British Master Tax Guide* 6247.

Law: TCGA 1992, s. 223

31-300 Letting relief

Example

Sally buys a house in May 1998. She occupies one of the four floors as her main residence but lets out the other three floors to students at the local university. She later sells the house and realises a gain of £86,000.

Ignoring the lettings relief, £21,500 is exempt on a reasonable apportionment of the gain as relating to Sally's own occupation.

Letting relief is available up to the lower of:

- £21,500 exempt by reason of owner-occupation; and
- £40,000.

Consequently, of the gain of £86,000, an amount of £43,000 (i.e. the main £21,500 relief plus £21,500 letting relief) is exempt and £43,000 is chargeable (and subject to taper relief based on non-business asset rates, where applicable).

See *British Master Tax Guide* 6250.

Law: TCGA 1992, s. 223

31-320   Emigrating with a gift (former taper relief)

Example

Tricia gives shares to her son Mark. They are worth £250,000 and give rise to a gain of £240,000. If the gain is not held over, Tricia will obtain maximum taper relief and will pay tax on a gain of £60,000 (less any unused annual exemption).

Tricia and Mark may agree to hold the gain over. The amount held over is calculated before taper relief and so is £240,000, effectively giving Mark a base cost of £10,000 for the shares.

Three years later, Mark decides to emigrate. This brings the gain into charge in the full amount of £240,000. It appears that no taper relief is due so the full gain remains chargeable.

If Mark decides that in his new life he has better things to do than to pay UK CGT, his mother can be held liable for the full amount of tax on the increased gain.

See *British Master Tax Guide* 6289.

Law: TCGA 1992, s. 67, 168

31-340   Rolling over a non-business asset

> **Q.** Is roll-over relief available on non-business assets if the sale is forced by a compulsory purchase order?

A.   The gain arising on a non-business asset is not eligible for relief under the replacement of business assets and as such cannot receive roll-over relief.

There are circumstances in which the taxpayer is not given the choice to dispose of an asset but is forced to by local authorities under a compulsory purchase order and in these circumstances roll-over may be due.

If the compensation has arisen for the land itself it is treated as a disposal in the normal way and a gain arises.

If the compensation has arisen for an asset derived from the main asset such as a right over land, then the compensation received is rolled into the existing asset.

When the land itself, which is subject to a compulsory purchase order, is disposed of, the landowner may shield the gain by acquiring new land and rolling the gain over into the new land.

See *British Master Tax Guide* 6300.

Law: TCGA 1992, s. 245–248

31-360 Incorporation relief

Example

Barry decided to incorporate his business, which he had previously run as a sole trader. At the date of the transfer the assets of the business were:

	Market value	**Indexed gain/(loss)**
	£	£
Freehold	100,000	30,000
Leasehold	50,000	(10,000)
Goodwill	40,000	40,000
Net current assets	20,000	–
	210,000	60,000

If the consideration is taken wholly in the form of shares, the shares will be valued at £210,000.

Their base cost will be £150,000 (£210,000 – 60,000).

If the consideration consists of shares and a loan account with the company of £90,000 the value of the shares will be £120,000 (£210,000 – £90,000). The amount of the gain that is rolled over is consequently:

120,000 × 60,000/210,000 = £34,286

and the base cost of the shares would be £85,714 (£120,000 – £34,286).

Barry's capital gains computation in respect of the incorporation would be:

	£
Net gains	60,000
Less: rolled-over	(34,286)
	25,714
Less: taper relief (75%, say)	(19,286)
Chargeable gain	6,428
Less: exempt amount (restricted)	(6,428)
Taxable gain	Nil

See *British Master Tax Guide* 6302–6303.

Law: TCGA 1992, s. 162

31-380   Disapplying incorporation relief

Example

Emma has run her unincorporated business for many years. She now plans to retire and sell the business. The purchaser offers to pay £900,000 to buy a company but does not wish to buy an unincorporated business. Emma now sets about incorporating. The indexed base cost of assets in Emma's business at that time is £100,000.

If incorporation relief applies

	£
MV of business on incorporation, say	800,000
Indexed base cost of assets	(100,000)
	700,000
Gain rolled over into shares	(700,000)
Gain arising on incorporation	Nil

	£	£
Sale proceeds of shares		900,000
Base cost of shares	800,000	
Less: gain rolled over	(700,000)	(100,000)
Gain on sale of shares		800,000

No taper relief on shares held for less than 12 months

CGT payable ignoring annual exempt amount = £320,000

If election is made to disapply incorporation relief

	£
MV of business on incorporation, say	800,000
Indexed base cost of assets	(100,000)
	700,000

Gain after taper relief	
£700,000 × 25%	175,000

CGT payable ignoring annual exempt amount = £70,000

	£
Sale proceeds of shares	900,000
Base cost of shares	(800,000)
Gain on sale of shares	100,000

No taper relief on shares held for less than 12 months

CGT payable ignoring annual exempt amount = £40,000

Total CGT payable = £110,000

See *British Master Tax Guide* 6303.

Law: TCGA 1992, s. 162

31-400   Relief on sale of business

> **Q.**   Mr Smith has decided that the time has come to retire and he will sell his building business. He has various assets including a workshop, builders yard and goodwill. The goodwill is sold at profit as Mr Smith has an excellent client base; however, the workshop and builders yard will be sold at a loss due to their dilapidated state. Mr Smith has heard that he can claim entrepreneurs' relief but has been told that the capital losses will affect the claim. What is the position regarding entrepreneurs' relief and losses?

A.   Entrepreneurs' relief is due, subject to certain conditions on the disposal of business assets. Mr Smith would qualify for relief as he is selling the whole of his business which he has carried on as a sole trader. Mr Smith must meet the conditions for a period of one year before date of cessation of the business and has three years to dispose of the assets used by that business. Where there is a mixture of gains and losses, the legislation at TCGA 1992, s. 169N restricts the availability of entrepreneurs' relief on the assets realising gains.

Any loss arising on assets that would have qualified for entrepreneurs' relief had a gain resulted must first be set against assets that produce a gain which is subject to entrepreneurs' relief. Therefore the loss must be used first before entrepreneurs' relief is applied. If no entrepreneurs' relief would have been given on the assets disposed of, the losses can be claimed after entrepreneurs' relief has been given.

Mr Smith must use his losses on the workshop and builders yard against the gain on goodwill before entrepreneurs' relief is given against the remaining gains.

See *British Master Tax Guide* 5293.

Law: TCGA 1992 s. 169N

31-420   Rolling over goodwill

> **Q.** My company has sold part of its business resulting in a capital gain arising. The business was established in the early 1990s and the gain arises mostly on the goodwill as this was self-generated and has no cost. I understand that the company can roll over the gain into new assets so that no immediate tax liability arises. However, I am advised that it may no longer be possible to roll over the gain against the cost of goodwill acquired in a new business, but instead a relief is due on the new goodwill itself. Is this correct?

A. With effect from 1 April 2002 a new intangibles relief was introduced for companies which treats the commercial amortisation of an intangible asset (which includes certain types of goodwill) charged to the profit and loss account of the business as an allowable deduction for tax purposes. Prior to this change, such amortisation was not an allowable deduction. As a consequence, goodwill, which qualifies as an intangible asset under these new rules, is no longer a qualifying asset for CGT roll-over relief. However, a different type of reinvestment relief is permitted under the FA 2002 rules. This is effectively a roll-over relief for intangible fixed assets.

See *British Master Tax Guide* 6305.

Law: TCGA 1992, s. 152(1)

31-440   Roll-over against the same asset

> **Q.** Bobby purchased a warehouse for use as his trading premises. Having traded from the warehouse for nine months, he has now realised that the building is too big for his business requirements and he intends splitting the warehouse into two. He will then dispose of the freehold on the half that is not required for his business. As you are able to roll over gains against acquisitions within the previous 12 months, can the gain on the disposal of this part of the warehouse be rolled over against the cost of the remaining part of the warehouse, which is still used in the trade?

A. The concept of matching the proceeds from a part-disposal against the acquisition of that same asset was considered in *Watton (HMIT) v Tippett*. In this case the taxpayer acquired land and buildings known as Unit 1. The whole building was initially brought into use for a trade purpose, but it was later divided into two units, Unit 1 and Unit 1A, which were both used in the trade. Unit 1A was later sold and the taxpayer claimed roll-over relief by setting the gain on the disposal of Unit 1A against the remaining apportioned cost of acquiring the retained part of Unit 1.

HMRC argued that before the part-disposal the whole building was one single asset. For that reason the proceeds from the part-disposal could not be matched with the acquisition of the same asset because in order to meet the conditions of roll-over relief the proceeds had to be used to acquire other assets.

The High Court agreed emphasising that Unit 1 had been acquired as a single asset and for an unapportioned consideration. Therefore the disposal of Unit 1A was incapable of being matched with other assets. The Court of Appeal also upheld this decision. Based on the findings of the *Watton v Tippett* case, Bobby cannot roll over the gain in these circumstances.

See *British Master Tax Guide* 6305.

Law: TCGA 1992, s. 152(1); *Watton (HMIT) v Tippett* [1997] BTC 338

31-460   Rolling over company assets against personal assets

> **Q.**   Paul has sold his nursing home trade and freehold property, realising a substantial gain. His intention is to purchase a new property personally, which he will let to a new company, wholly owned by him. Can you please confirm whether he will be able to benefit from capital gains roll-over relief and deduct the gain on the old building from the capital gains base cost of the new asset?

A.   Capital gains roll-over relief is available in relation to assets owned personally and used by the owner's personal company (in which 5% or more of the voting rights are held by the individual concerned) for the purpose of its trade. However, it is clear from the legislation that both the old and new assets must be used by the same company. Therefore, disposal of an asset used by an individual for the purpose of his own trade, or by a partnership of which he is a member, cannot be rolled over into the cost of an asset bought for use by a personal company.

See *British Master Tax Guide* 6308.

Law: TCGA 1992, s. 157

31-480   Partial roll-over

> **Q.**   Peter has sold his business premises for £3.6m realising a gain of £0.5m. Out of the proceeds he has immediately bought new business premises for £1.5m. Can roll-over relief be claimed following the purchase of the new building?

Capital Gains Tax

A. You must consider if the assets qualify for the relief. Provided the old building was used for the purposes of the trade throughout the period of ownership and the consideration is applied in acquiring the new building, the assets are qualifying assets.

Relief on partial replacement is available. This will apply where the gain is less than the disposal proceeds less the amount re-invested. So in this situation, the gain is as follows:

	£m
Disposal proceeds	3.6
Less: cost of new asset	(1.5)
Difference	2.1

As the gain was £0.5m, no roll over relief will be available and the gain is immediately chargeable.

See *British Master Tax Guide* 6308.

Law: TCGA 1992, s. 152–153

31-500   Roll-over relief on furnished holiday lets

> **Q.** Russell has a residential property that has been let for some time. Now his is intending to let it in accordance with the requirements for a qualifying furnished holiday letting. How will the capital gain roll-over provisions apply when the property is sold?

A. HMRC's *Capital Gains Manual* (CG61450) confirms that the replacement of business assets roll-over relief do apply to furnished holiday lettings. However, the following part of the main provision at TCGA 1992, s. 152 applies in this case:

> '152(7)   If the old assets were not used for the purposes of the trade throughout the period of ownership this section shall apply as if a part of the asset representing its use for the purposes of the trade having regard to the time and extent to which it was, and was not, used for those purposes, were a separate asset which had been wholly used for the purposes of the trade, and this subsection shall apply in relation to that part subject to any necessary apportionment of consideration for an acquisition or disposal of, or of the interest in, the asset.'

Therefore, relief for reinvestment must be calculated with respect to the proceeds and gain time-apportioned to the use as a qualifying furnished holiday letting. This is illustrated below.

Example

Suppose the property is held for a total of ten years and was a furnished holiday letting for only the final three years. The property was disposed of for £200,000 at a gain of £90,000. The proceeds and gain apportioned to the furnished holiday letting are £60,000 and £27,000, respectively. Therefore, if proceeds of £60,000 or more are invested in a replacement asset, the gain rolled over will be £27,000. If proceeds of £33,000 or less are reinvested, there will be no roll-over relief. Between those limits, roll-over relief of £1 will be available for every £1 invested in excess of £33,000.

See *British Master Tax Guide* 6308.

Law: TCGA 1992, s. 152–153

31-520   Transfer and then roll over

Example

Victor has a hotel with an indexed cost of £550,000. He wishes to sell it and spend £525,000 on buying a small nursing home. Victor brings his wife, Vera, into partnership, giving her a one-half undivided interest in the hotel. Victor and Vera together sell the hotel for £1m. Victor alone buys the nursing home.

Victor's CGT computation is:

	£
Sale proceeds (1/2)	500,000
Indexed cost (1/2)	(275,000)
Gain	225,000
Less: roll-over relief	(225,000)
Chargeable gain	Nil

Vera's CGT computation is:

	£
Sale proceeds (1/2)	500,000
Indexed cost (1/2)	(275,000)
Chargeable gain	225,000

Base cost of nursing home for Victor:

£500,000 − £225,000 = £275,000

Victor's decision is both shrewd and careless at the same time. He decided to transfer half of the property because, if he had owned all of the hotel on disposal, he would have been reinvesting less than he was receiving from the sale into the nursing home to such an extent that he would have lost the availability of roll-over relief.

See *British Master Tax Guide* 6309.

Law: TCGA 1992, s. 152

31-540 Selling fixed assets

> **Q.** My client has appropriated some of her fixed assets to stock through her accounts in order to sell as a trade items, as opposed to an investment which it was previously. HMRC have informed her that she now has a capital gain under TCGA 1992, s. 161 as she is intent on purchasing further fixed assets for use in her business. Can she use this capital gain and roll it into other assets in order to claim TCGA 1992, s. 152 rollover relief on that potential capital gain.

A. HMRC *Capital Gains Manual* suggests (CG60792) that the gain which your client is faced with is a deemed capital gain, as she hasn't actually sold an asset to a third party, but rather transferred an asset within the business.

It permits the use of rollover relief where there is a deemed disposal or acquisition and specifically permits the use of TCGA 1992, s. 152 where an asset is appropriated to trading stock.

See *British Master Tax Guide* 6308.

31-560 Hold-over relief on agricultural property

> **Q.** Kevin owns a farm, which he farms himself. Many years ago he purchased adjacent farmland with a farmhouse. He has used only part of the acquired farmland within his own farming activities. The other part of the land together with the farmhouse (which is derelict) has never been used within his farm. He would now like to gift the farmhouse to his son to renovate for use as a private residence. Can capital gains hold-over relief be claimed on the gift of the asset to the son?

A. Hold-over relief for business assets is normally only available if the asset was used in a trade, profession or vocation carried on by the donor. However legislation has extended this to agricultural property which qualifies for IHT agricultural relief. The relief is available whether or not the donee himself uses the property.

To qualify for agricultural property relief from inheritance tax, property must be both agricultural property, and occupied for agricultural purposes. As far as the farmhouse is concerned actual occupation is a condition. Thus, in this case, capital gains hold-over relief is not available to the father on the gift of the derelict farmhouse to his son.

See *British Master Tax Guide* 6325.

Law: TCGA 1992, Sch. 7

31-580 Buying a freehold

> **Q.** I currently live in a leasehold flat in a property in which there are another six leasehold flats. Recently the opportunity has arisen to buy the freehold reversion from the landlord and all of the leaseholders have agreed to contribute equally towards the purchase. Our solicitor has advised a limited company should be set up to buy the freehold. Are there any tax consequences involved here?

A. The *Law of Property Act* 1925 stipulates that only a maximum of four persons can be the legal owners of land and property, hence the suggestion of a company by the solicitor.

However, the above restriction is for the legal ownership only. The named persons could hold the ownership as trustees for other persons too. Tax is usually based on beneficial ownership, not legal ownership. Therefore, a bare trust is often used in such cases whereby one or more persons would hold the freehold reversion as bare trustee for all seven leaseholders. For tax purposes, the tenants would be deemed to own their share of the freehold absolutely. A similar arrangement can exist in a company providing the company is a nominee company which is the corporate equivalent of a bare trust. This too would have the same consequences as a bare trust.

If it is not made clear that the company is a nominee company then strictly any transactions with the company could create tax charges. For example, if the lease periods were extended, this would give rise to a capital gains charge on the company under TCGA 1992, s. 44 and a deemed income distribution to the shareholders under TCGA 1992, s. 209. In addition, when a leaseholder sold his or her flat and, as a consequence, the shares in the company, no private residence relief would be due on the gain relating to the company shares.

See *British Master Tax Guide* 5330.

31-600 EMI shares and entrepreneurs' relief

> **Q.** Just over three years ago we allocated EMI share options to an employee, and he will be exercising them shortly before the company is sold this year. Under the pre-6 April 2008 CGT regime, EMI options started accruing business asset taper relief from the date of issue. Is this true for entrepreneurs' relief purposes?

A. No. In order to qualify for entrepreneurs' relief, the disposal must relate to the 'personal company' of the individual. In this context, 'personal company' means a company:

- at least 5% of the ordinary share capital of which is held by the individual, and
- at least 5% of the voting rights in which are exercisable by the individual by virtue of that holding.

Clearly, share options do not meet either of these two conditions and there is no concession in respect of EMI schemes. Your employee will therefore not qualify for the relief.

See *British Master Tax Guide* 6316.

31-620   Indemnity against future sale

> **Q.**   My client sold the shares in his engineering company three years ago and received a mixture of cash, shares and loan notes from the purchaser. Included in the sale agreement was an indemnity that, should the purchaser sell the business at arm's length within the next five years for a value below a certain amount, my client would pay a fixed percentage of the shortfall. The sale has occurred and my client has to pay a sum of £150,000. Is there any tax relief for this payment?

A.   TCGA 1992, s. 49 allows a measure of relief in respect of warranties and representations but, according to HMRC, this does not include indemnities. The relief is given by deducting the sum paid from the original sale proceeds. Fortunately, ESC D33 recognises this and allows relief for indemnity payments in the same way. This means revisiting the original CGT computation and claiming a refund from HMRC.

The above relief is fine for recalculating the gain on the cash received and any deferred gain on the loan notes if they were qualifying corporate bonds (QCBs). However, the sum paid can only reduce the sale proceeds to nil. It is hoped that the sale proceeds for the cash and QCBs exceeded £150,000.

As regards the shares and any non-QCBs received on the original disposal, normally a share for share treatment is obtained, whereby part of the cost of the shares sold becomes the cost of the new shares and loan notes. This part of the transaction is not treated as a disposal for CGT purposes which therefore precludes relief under s. 49

Extra-statutory Concession D52 resolves this problem for contingent liabilities arising from warranties or representations by allowing the sum paid to be added to the base cost of these assets. It is unclear whether the two concessions interact allowing similar relief for indemnity payments.

See *British Master Tax Guide* 5232.

31-640   Entrepreneurs' relief on company property

> **Q.**   My client is the director and majority shareholder of his trading company. All the shares of the company are to be sold, together with the property used for the company's trade, which my client has owned personally for ten years. The property has been used by the company for ten years but during the final two years only, my client has received a

moderate rent, which is likely to have been significantly below market value. The company has no substantial investment activity. We have had conflicting advice as to whether the gain on the building will qualify for the new entrepreneurs' relief. Can you clarify the matter for us?

A. The issue of the rental income and the availability of entrepreneurs' relief has been the cause of considerable confusion. I confirm that your client will receive a measure of entrepreneurs' relief for the building on a time-apportionment basis for any periods where the asset was not let for a full market value rent.

To qualify in principle, the disposal of the building must be associated with a 'material disposal'. New sections 169I(2)(c), (5) and (6) of TCGA 1992 confirm the disposal of the shares as meeting the definition of a material disposal. For the disposal of the building to qualify, it must meet the definition of a disposal 'associated with a relevant material disposal' under s. 169K. This includes the disposal of assets which (or interests in which) were used for business purposes. The legislation also requires that this business use must have occurred throughout the year ending with the date of the material disposal (TCGA 1992, s. 169K(4)). Your client appears to satisfy these conditions. However, the legislation at s. 169P requires 'just and reasonable' adjustments to the relief, including to the extent that the property is only partly used for business purposes over the period of ownership, or where the 'availability is dependent on the payment of rent'. In the latter case, the restriction is inversely proportionate to the extent to which the property is rented at market value. The following simple example illustrates this specific point.

Example

Property rented for 70% of the market value over the entire period of ownership.

Full entrepreneurs' relief available would be, say, £5m.

Entrepreneurs' relief due 30% × £5m = £1.5m.

In your client's case, an apportionment first needs to be made on a time basis, as full relief will be due proportionally for the initial eight years out of ten when the property was used for company business with no rent being paid. Thus, 80% of the maximum entrepreneurs' relief will be available. The remaining 20% relief will then need to be restricted along the lines of the above example.

See *British Master Tax Guide* 6311.

31-660 Entrepreneurs' relief on non-voting shares

Q. My client recently sold his non-voting preference shares in his employer's unquoted trading company for a moderate gain. He has held these for more than 12 months and was an officer/employee of the company throughout that time. He has also held 15% of the company's ordinary voting shares for several years. We have provisionally taken the view that, for capital gains purposes, preference shares will not qualify for entrepreneurs' relief as they do not carry voting rights, but we are advised that the situation may be affected by the ownership of his ordinary shares.

A. You are correct that, in themselves, non-voting preference shares would not attract entrepreneurs' relief. However, on a disposal of any shares, the relief is due provided that the company meets the definition of 'personal company' for the person disposing of the shares. A personal company for this purpose is defined as a company in which an individual holds at least 5% of the ordinary share capital and at least 5% of the voting rights. Your client meets both of these conditions and therefore the disposal of preference shares will qualify by virtue of the holding of ordinary shares.

See *British Master Tax Guide* 6311.

31-680   Rollover and entrepreneurs' relief

Q. Frank has been a sole trader plumber for several years and is now planning to withdraw from that business altogether and invest £150,000 in a shop from which to operate an off-licence. His plumbing business has chargeable assets of goodwill worth £20,000 and a yard worth £285,000. The yard stands at a gain of £170,000 and the goodwill is a gain of £20,000. What is Frank's capital gains position if he sells the business in June 2008?

A. The reliefs operating in respect of these transactions are 'rollover' relief (replacement of business assets) and entrepreneurs' relief. Rollover is the first relief to apply as it reduces the disposal proceeds and therefore the chargeable gains on the assets being disposed of. When the investment in trading premises is deducted from the total market value of the assets, the amount not reinvested falls short of the gains by £35,000; this amount is therefore the rollover relief. The chargeable gains after rollover relief total £155,000 and are subject to entrepreneurs' relief of four-ninths so the gain after the relief is £86,111. Frank can then use his annual exempt amount of £9,600 against the gain to give £76,511 which is then subject to CGT at 18%, i.e. tax of £13,772 is due.

See *British Master Tax Guide* 6305.

31-700   Entrepreneurs' relief on business property

Q. Several years ago I incorporated my newsagent business and have been running this successfully as a one-man company. I retained the premises in my personal ownership, the ground floor being the retail premises and the first floor being my private residence. I have now received an offer for my company shares and the property. I understand I can claim private residence relief on the residential part of the premises which will exempt this part of the gain. I can then claim entrepreneurs' relief on the balance of the property gain and on the gain from the share sale meaning I only pay a 10% CGT rate. Is this correct?

A.   You are selling two assets, your shareholding and the property. Entrepreneurs' relief is given on qualifying disposals which are either 'material disposals' or 'associated disposals'.

Providing the company meets the qualifying definition of a trading company and you meet the relevant conditions for entrepreneurs' relief (which it seems you do) then the relief can be claimed.

The sale of the shares will be a 'material disposal'. If the disposal took place before 23 June 2010 only $^5/_9$ of the gain will be chargeable which, after deducting your annual exemption, is taxed at 18%. This reduction equates to an effective 10% CGT rate. If the disposal took place on or after 23 June 2010 the gain will be taxed at a flat rate of 10%.

In the circumstances you have described the disposal of the property is an 'associated disposal'. Part of the gain will be covered by private residence relief as you state. The balance of the gain will be charged to CGT subject to a claim being made for entrepreneurs' relief which will reduce the qualifying gain as above. However, the amount of an associated disposal gain that qualifies for relief is reduced where:

(1)   rent is received from the company (but this rule only applies to rent from 6 April 2008); or

(2)   the property was not used in the business throughout its ownership; or

(3)   not all of the property was used in the business.

Therefore, as point (3) above is certainly valid (and possibly point (1)) there will be a restriction to the post-private residence relief gain which will attract entrepreneurs' relief. A 'fair and reasonable' apportionment of the gain based on the facts will be required to arrive at the adjustment.

See *British Master Tax Guide* 5293.

Law: TCGA 1992, Pt. V, Ch. 3

31-720   Shares in Northern Rock

Q.   My client held shares in Northern Rock plc. Can he now claim a capital loss in respect of that shareholding?

A.   HM Revenue and Customs have recently published guidance in relation to the tax position of the former shareholders of Northern Rock plc and consider that following the transfer of Northern Rock plc into temporary public ownership that this constitutes a disposal for capital gains purposes.

The disposal is within TCGA 1992, s. 24, i.e. disposals where assets are lost or destroyed, or become of negligible value. The date of disposal is 22 February 2008, the date the transfer order came into force. As no consideration has been received for the shares, any allowable costs give rise to a capital loss.

Some shareholders may be entitled to receive a payment under the Compensation Scheme Order and any such payment received will be chargeable under TCGA 1992, s. 24 as a capital sum derived from the former shareholding. The charge will arise in the tax year the compensation sum is received.

See *British Master Tax Guide* 5080.

Inheritance Tax

Lifetime tax on chargeable transfers	373
Domicile dangers	373
Can the overseas assets of a non-UK domiciled person be charged to UK tax?	374
Share valuations – various points	375
Differing charges on gifts of shares	377
Diminution in value of the family home	378
The seven-year rule	378
The seven-year rule including gifts to discretionary trusts	379
Associated loans	380
Associated assets	381
Associated leases	381
Associated assets – subvaluations	382
Periodic charges	383
Using the annual exemption – chargeable lifetime transfer or potentially exempt transfer first?	383
Allowable deductions	384
Farmhouse or Mum's house?	385
Gift with reservation	386
Was it really a gift?	386
Estate rates	387
Estate rates – exempt residuals	388
Estate rates – taxable residuals	389
PETs and estates – using up the nil band	391
The seven-year rule on death	392
Tapering potentially exempt transfers	393
Taper relief	394
The seven-year charge – extra tax due	394
Disposals after death	395
Quick succession relief	397
Double IHT charge	397
Lifetime transfer or death estate	398
Income or capital paid out with discretion	399
Ten-yearly charges	400
Exit charges	401
Late additions to a settlement	401
Exit after more than ten years	402
Pre-owned asset examples	404
Property leaving a charitable trust	405
Gifts to your spouse	406
Non-domiciled spouse	406

Transfer of unused nil-rate band (post-9 October 2007)   407
Carry-forward of annual exemption   408
Small gift and an annual exemption?   408
Reporting normal gifts out of income   409
Furnished holiday letting and business property relief   409
50% business property relief availability   409
Business property relief on quoted shares   410
Owning property through a company   410
Business property relief on replacement property   411
Non-availability of business property relief – use at death   411
Calculation of restriction of business property relief – company   412
Gift of interest in partnership   412
Calculation of restriction of business property relief – partnership   413
Business property relief on incorporation   414
Agricultural property relief on company shares   415
Agricultural property relief on a concrete yard   415
Woodland interests   416
Woodland values   416
Domicile and premium bonds   418
Estates with business property relief and exempt legacies   418
Discounted gift trust   419
Loans made during a lifetime   420
National Heritage Property   421
Use of pilot trusts   422
Who owes the tax?   422

INHERITANCE TAX

40-000   Lifetime tax on chargeable transfers

Example

In May 2010, Robin created a trust, the assets of which amounted to £150,000, under which the income was payable to his daughter, Jenny, for life, with remainder to Jenny's daughter, Emma. Chargeable transfers in the previous seven years amounted to £100,000 and he has used his annual exemptions.

As the value of the gift to the trust and the chargeable transfers made in the previous seven years is below the nil-rate band, no tax is payable on the transfer to the trust.

If Robin had made chargeable transfers of £200,000 in the previous seven years, an immediate tax charge would arise on the gift to the trust of:

£350,000 − £325,000 = £25,000 × 20% = £5,000

See *British Master Tax Guide* 6525.

Law: IHTA 1984, s. 3A

40-020   Domicile dangers

Example 1

Adam, who had lived in England all his life, emigrated to Australia, intending never to return.

Adam died two years later in Australia.

Under the general law, Adam is domiciled in Australia at the date of his death. For the purposes of UK inheritance tax (IHT), Adam is treated as deemed domiciled in the UK. Accordingly, Adam's estate will suffer tax in Britain.

Example 2

Bob is an American citizen who has been living and working in Britain for the past 18 years, during which time he has made frequent visits to the USA and reiterated his desire to return there permanently. Bob makes a gift of £100,000 to his daughter.

Under general law, Bob is domiciled in Florida. For the purposes of UK IHT, Bob is treated as domiciled in the UK. Accordingly, if Bob dies within seven years, the gift will be liable to tax regardless of where the property gifted is located.

See *British Master Tax Guide* 6540.

Law: IHTA 1984, s. 267

40-030 Can the overseas assets of a non-UK domiciled person be charged to UK tax?

Q. I had a client who was Swedish. Unfortunately she passed away in May 2008. She had a house in England worth £300,000, but no other UK assets. The solicitor is concerned that her Swedish home may be brought into account for liability to UK inheritance tax (IHT).

There is no doubt that under general law she was domiciled in Sweden as she had always maintained that her 'home' was in Sweden but her work in London meant that she had been resident in the UK since March 1992. I am aware of the 'deemed domicile' rules but am unsure exactly how these rules work.

A. The concept of domicile is crucial to the IHT charging regime. An individual domiciled in one of the countries which comprise the UK is liable to IHT on their worldwide assets. A non-UK domiciliary is only liable to IHT on assets situated in the UK. An individual is resident where he lives but domiciled in the country (or state) which is his permanent home colloquially described as 'where his heart is'.

The IHT legislation adds to the general law concerning domicile the 'deemed domicile' rules, IHTA 1984, s. 267. Section 267 provides that an individual is deemed domiciled in either of the two following circumstances:

(1) A UK domicile leaves the UK and attempts to claim that they have severed all ties and wish to become domiciled elsewhere. The individual must wait three calendar years as for those three years they are 'deemed domiciled' in the UK.

(2) If he or she has been resident (for income tax purposes) for 17 out of the previous 20 tax years ending with the tax year of assessment.

It is the second rule above which may catch your client as 'deemed domiciled'. A year will be included in the 17 years as a resident if the individual is resident for any part of the year, even one day! This could happen if someone comes to the UK on a three-year secondment and arrives on 5 April. In fact it is possible to become deemed domiciled after only 15 years and a couple of days' residence in the UK, under the 17-year rule.

Your client's first year of residence was the year to 5 April 1992 so that she entered her seventeenth year of residence on 6 April 2007. Thus your client was deemed domiciled in the UK when she died so that the solicitor's fears are justified and her worldwide assets will be charged to IHT in the UK subject to double tax relief.

There are special rules for countries with pre-1975 double tax agreements, these are France, Italy, India and Pakistan so that the above deemed domicile rules cannot always be applied to domiciliaries of these four countries.

See *British Master Tax Guide* 6540.

40-040   Share valuations – various points

Example 1

Neil makes four annual chargeable gifts to Paul, each of 10% of the shares in XYZ Ltd. The value transferred by each gift is £5,000, but the total value transferred by Neil is £40,000 (40% of XYZ Ltd is worth more than four lots of 10%).

Neil is treated as making a transfer of value at the date of the last gift of £40,000 less 3 × £5,000, i.e. £25,000.

If Neil had made three gifts of 10% holdings to his wife (conditional upon her giving them in turn to Paul) and then a further gift of a 10% holding to Paul himself, this would be treated as a transfer of value at the date of the last gift of £40,000.

Example 2

Ann makes a gift of 5% of the shares she holds in a property company to James. Before the gift Ann owned the majority share of 52%, James owned no shares in the company. This gift reduces her majority holding of 52% to a minority of 47% holding. As a majority holding her shares were worth £500,000. But now that the holding has reduced, the holding is worth £350,000. The gift has reduced her estate by £150,000 even though the 5% holding is worth little, say £10,000 to James. The transfer value is therefore £150,000.

Example 3

Andrew owns 10,000 out of 100,000 shares in a company, and his wife owns 80,000 shares in the same company. The value of Andrew's shares is £1 per share (£10,000) and the value of a share from a 90% holding is £5 per share (£450,000). When Andrew dies his 10,000 shares will be valued at:

$$£450,000 \times \frac{10,000}{90,000} = £50,000$$

To express this more simply, Andrew's 10,000 shares are valued as if part of a 90% holding (10,000 × £5 = £50,000).

See *British Master Tax Guide* 6575.

Law: IHTA 1984, s. 161

Example 4

Joan died on 3 May 2010. Her estate on death included 12,000 £1 ordinary shares in ABC plc, a company which is listed on the London Stock Exchange. The closing prices at the date of death showed 989p bid price and 993p offer price at the end of that day. The value per share is calculated as:

$$989 + (\tfrac{1}{4} \times (993 - 989)) = 990p$$

Therefore, the value of the estate is £118,800 (12,000 shares × £9.90).

An alternative, if it produces a lower valuation, is to take the price halfway between the highest and lowest sales of the day.

In this example, recorded sale bargains were 970p, 980p, 983p, 989p, 993p, and 996p. The valuation is $(970 + 996)/2 = 983p$.

The value of the shares for IHT purposes is reduced to £117,960 (i.e. 12,000 shares × £9.83).

Example 5

An unquoted property investment company (UPIC) with dividend cover similar to quoted real estate companies is valued as follows:

Dividend per share of UPIC	= 50p
Average dividend yield for quoted real estate companies	= 2.5%
2 times quoted yield	= 5%
3 times quoted yield	= 7.5%

The value of UPIC shares between £6.666 and £10 is calculated as follows:

$$\text{dividend} \times \frac{100}{\text{yield}}$$

$$0.5 \times \frac{100}{5} = £10$$

or

$$0.5 \times \frac{100}{7.5} = £6,666$$

The dividend yield chosen by the valuer may have regard to the size of holding, how the other shares are held, the dividend payment record, the gearing of the company, any issues relating to the property, etc.

See *British Master Tax Guide* 6571.

Law: IHTA 1984, s. 160

40-060   Differing charges on gifts of shares

Example

A company has 1,000 shares in issue. Dave owns 70 shares and his wife, Sheila, owns 480 shares. They have two children who own 225 shares each. The parents wish to give their children all the shares they hold.

Share values are:

   55% holding: £1,000 per share
   48% holding: £550 per share
   7% holding: £300 per share

Sheila gives the children her 480 shares, then Dave gives the children his 70 shares:

£

Shelia's transfer
Value of Sheila's estate before transfer
480 × £1,000   480,000 (value as combined 55% holding)
Value of Sheila's estate after transfer   Nil
Diminution of estate   480,000

Dave's transfer
Value of Dave's estate before transfer
70 × £300   21,000 (valued as 7% holding)
Value of Dave's estate after transfer   Nil
Diminution in estate   21,000
Aggregate of transfers   501,000

Alternatively, Dave gives the children his 70 shares, then Sheila gives the children her 480 shares.

£

Dave's transfer
Value of Dave's estate before transfer
70 × £1,000   70,000 (55% valuation)
Value of Dave's estate after transfer   Nil
Diminution in estate   70,000

Sheila's tranfer
Value of Sheila's estate after transfer
480 × £550   264,000
Value of Sheila's estate after transfer   Nil
Diminution in estate   264,000
Aggregate of transfers   334,000

This example clearly demonstrates the importance of considering the order of transfers.

See *British Master Tax Guide* 6575.

Law: IHTA 1984, s. 161

40-080   Diminution in value of the family home

Example

Adrian owns a dwelling-house worth £100,000. He transfers three one-quarter shares in the house to his three adult children, reserving the right to occupy the house from time to time, whenever he chooses. In consideration of the transfers, each child pays Adrian £15,000, representing the full value of a one-quarter share subject to Adrian's right of occupation. The value of Adrian's remaining one-quarter share, plus the reserved right, is £30,000. Adrian's estate after the transaction is worth £75,000 (30,000 + (3 × 15,000)) and hence Adrian's estate has been diminished by £25,000.

Since there is no element of bounty in the transaction, Adrian's children having given full value for what they received, this is not a disposal 'by way of gift', and, despite Adrian's reservation of benefit, and the loss to Adrian's estate, the gift with reservation rules do not apply.

See *British Master Tax Guide* 6612.

Law: IHTA 1984, s. 3

40-100   The seven-year rule

Example

Paul makes the following chargeable lifetime transfers into separate discretionary trusts over a period of 12 years (assume 2009–10 rates apply throughout and that Paul had used his annual exemption on smaller gifts every year):

Gift	*Year*	*Value transferred*
		£
1	1	250,000
2	6	160,000
3	8	50,000

Tax on gift 1	£
Cumulative total after gift 1	250,000
Less: nil band	(325,000)
Chargeable to tax	Nil

Tax on gift 2	£
Cumulative total b/fwd	250,000
Gift 2	160,000
	410,000
Less: nil band	(325,000)
Chargeable to tax	85,000
£85,000 × 20%	17,000

Tax on gift 3	£
Chargeable transfers within 7 years	160,000
Gift 3	50,000
	210,000
Less: nil band	(325,000)
Chargeable to tax	Nil

See *British Master Tax Guide* 6616.

Law: IHTA 1984, s. 7

40-120 The seven-year rule including gifts to discretionary trusts

Example

On 15 April 2009, Edward transferred £300,000 into a discretionary trust for his wife and children. He agrees to pay any IHT chargeable thereon. He had made two previous transfers: a gift of £100,000 to Freda in October 2002 and a transfer to a discretionary trust (gross) of £323,000 in October 2003. Edward used his annual exemption every year prior to the gifts listed here.

Tax is chargeable on the transfer into trust as follows:

		£
(1)	Cumulative total	
	Gift to Freda is a PET therefore ignore	
	Gift to trust Oct. 2003	323,000
(2)	Tax thereon	
	£312,000 × 0% (2008–09 nil band)	Nil
	£11,000 × 20%	2,200
	Note: Trustees pay the tax so no grossing up is required.	
(3)	Net cumulative total	£
	£323,000 − £2,200	320,800

Inheritance Tax

(4)	New net cumulative total	£
	Previous net cumulative total	320,800
	Gift to trust	300,000
		620,800

(5)	Tax thereon	£
		620,800
	Less: nil band available	(325,000)
		295,800

£295,800 × 20/80		73,950
Tax on gift into trust payable by Edward £73,950 − £2,200		71,750

See *British Master Tax Guide* 6620.

Law: IHTA 1984, s. 3

40-140 Associated loans

> **Q.** I have recently bought a holiday home in Spain in the names of my adult children. I believe that this escapes IHT but I am confused regarding the pre-owned asset tax (POAT) rules. Does this tax apply to me?

A. The transaction may not escape IHT. It seems likely that this will be a gift with reservation (GWR) and so the property will be treated as if owned by you and still part of your chargeable estate. This will follow the facts of the matter. If you simply bought the property in your children's names but use it yourself rent-free, or at less than a full market rent, then it will be caught by the GWR rule.

If you gifted cash to your children and later the property was bought in your children's names then the associated operations rule will apply if this was part of an arrangement or scheme and will then be caught under the above GWR rule. The shorter the period between the gift of cash and the purchase of the property, the more likely the associated operations rule will catch this transaction.

If, for some reason, the transaction bypasses the IHT rules mentioned above, then the POAT rules need to be considered. If you never owned the property, then the POAT will apply under the contribution rule (as you provided the consideration for the purchase) if you occupy the property rent-free or for less than a market rent and the value (i.e. rental equivalent) of your occupation is £5,000 or more. There are exceptions for gifts of cash used to buy the house but only when the gift is made at least seven years prior to the purchase.

With hindsight, it may have been better for you to make a loan to your children to enable them to buy the property. Providing the loan was either repayable on demand or subject to a formal loan agreement, this would escape the main GWR rule and POAT could not apply. The associated operations rule mentioned above could apply but the counter argument would be that your children are simply permitting you to use the property from time to time. However, any waiver of the loan would risk bringing the POAT rules into play, as you would be deemed to have indirectly contributed to the purchase of the property.

See *British Master Tax Guide* 6670.

Law: FA 2004, Sch. 15; IHTA 1984, s. 268

40-160   Associated assets

Example

Adam owns a set of stamps which, kept together as a set, is valued at £50,000. However, if the set is split up then each stamp has a value of £4,000. Every year a stamp is sold to Adam's grandson for £4,000. If Adam dies within seven years of the last of these transactions taking place, HMRC may claim IHT as an associated operation on a transfer value of the difference between £50,000 (the value of the set) and the aggregate of the prices paid by the grandson for the individual stamps. The transfer of value would be deemed to have taken place when the last of the stamps has been sold.

See *British Master Tax Guide* 6670.

Law: IHTA 1984, s. 268

40-180   Associated leases

Example

A father owns a freehold house which he wishes to give to his daughter. He grants a 15-year lease to an independent third party, the rent and premium being at the market rate. A few months later the father gifts the freehold reversion to the daughter. With a tenant in place, the value of the freehold reversion will be significantly less than the market value of the property with vacant possession. In these circumstances, the associated operation rule is relevant. However, if the gift had taken place more than three years after the grant of the lease, the two events would then be deemed not to be associated operations thus the operations of granting the lease and transferring the reversionary interest would not be considered to be a single transfer of value.

See *British Master Tax Guide* 6670.

Law: IHTA 1984, s. 268

40-200   Associated assets – subvaluations

Example

Harry owns a set of four chairs, valued, as a set, at £6,000. Individually they would be valued at only £1,000. A pair would be valued at £2,500 and three at £4,000. On 1 January of each year, Harry gives a chair to his son. The above values have increased by 10% at the end of year 1, by 20% after year 2 and so on. In the fifth year Harry dies.

Year 1	£
Value of 4 chairs	6,000
Less: value of 3	(4,000)
Value transferred	2,000

Year 2	£
Current value of 4 chairs (6,000 + 10%)	6,600
Less: value of 2 (2,500 + 10%)	(2,750)
Less: value transferred in year 1	(2,000)
Value transferred	1,850

Year 3	£
Current value of 4 chairs (6,000 + 20%)	7,200
Less: value of 1 (1,000 + 20%)	(1,200)
Less: value transferred previously (2,000 + 1,850)	(3,850)
Value transferred	2,150

Year 4	£
Current value of 4 chairs (6,000 + 30%)	7,800
Less: value transferred in years above	(6,000)
Value transferred	1,800

Total values transferred	7,800

See *British Master Tax Guide* 6670.

Law: IHTA 1984, s. 268

40-220 Periodic charges

> **Q.** In the late 1990s I set up two trusts, an interest in possession trust for my son and a discretionary trust for the rest of the family. I was advised to set these up on the same day. The discretionary trust is about to reach a ten-year anniversary charge, will the tax due be affected by the other trust?

Inheritance Tax

A. The calculation of the principal charge is very complicated but the details can be found in the HMRC's *Inheritance Tax Manual* beginning at IHTM42081. The tax charge can never be higher than 6% of the value of the assets in the trust and on many occasions will be much lower.

You set up an interest in possession trust on the same day as setting up the discretionary trust so that, in the calculation of IHT due on each ten-year anniversary, the initial value of the interest in possession trust must be taken into account in the calculation of the rate at which IHT is charged on the value of assets in the discretionary trust at the ten-year anniversary.

The effect is that the initial value of the assets settled on the interest in possession trust can have the effect of using a pro rata proportion of the nil-rate band. This will come into effect on each ten-year anniversary throughout the potential 80 years that the trust could be in existence.

See *British Master Tax Guide* 6720, 6946–6954

Law: IHTA 1984, s. 63, 85, 266

40-240 Using the annual exemption – chargeable lifetime transfer or potentially exempt transfer first?

Example

Ann makes a gift of £10,000 in May 2009. In October 2009 she makes a gift into a discretionary trust. The annual exemption for 2009–10 is set against the first £3,000 of the May gift, leaving a potentially exempt transfer (PET) of £7,000. The whole of the October gift into the discretionary trust is immediately chargeable. Any relief carried forward from 2008–09 is also available to be set against the May gift. Therefore, if Ann had made no transfers in 2008–09, there will be a total of £6,000 to be set against the May gift, leaving a PET of £4,000.

See *British Master Tax Guide* 6720.

Law: IHTA 1984, s. 266

40-260   Allowable deductions

> **Q.**   Robbie died in Portugal on 1 February 2009. His estate comprised an apartment in Portugal with a probate value of £60,000 and personal chattels located in the UK with a probate value of £40,000. The following fees have been incurred in administering the estate:
>
> - solicitor's fee for administering the estate – £4,000;
> - additional solicitor's fees for dealing with the Portuguese apartment – £3,900;
> - accountant's fees for calculating the tax liability to the date of death – £500;
> - funeral expenses including fees for transporting Robbie's body from his place of death in Portugal back to the UK – £3,000.
>
> Which, if any, are deductible from the value of the estate for IHT purposes?

A.   Generally any debts incurred by the personal representatives are not allowed as a deduction, so solicitor's fees for administering the estate and the accountant's fee for establishing the tax liability to the date of death will not be deductible.

However, legislation provides that reasonable funeral expenses will be allowable. In practice this would include the cost of transporting the body from abroad where the deceased died overseas.

A special deduction is also allowed where additional costs are incurred in administering or realising property situated overseas. These expenses can be deducted from the value of the foreign property, but the deduction is restricted to a maximum of 5% of the value of all the foreign property in the estate.

The value of the estate would therefore be calculated as follows:

	£	£
Personal chattels		40,000
Apartment in Portugal	60,000	
Additional costs (60,000 × 5% max)	(3,000)	57,000
Value of estate before expenses		97,000
Funeral costs		(3,000)
Value of estate		94,000

See *British Master Tax Guide* 6782.

Law: IHTA 1984, s. 172–173

40-280 Farmhouse or Mum's house?

> **Q.** I presently farm land in partnership with my mother. My mother inherited the land, buildings and farmhouse from my late father some years ago. My mother wants to retire and proposes to transfer the land and farm buildings to me but to retain the farmhouse as her home. My mother also owns a second house which is rented out and so has a separate source of income to maintain her. What are the IHT implications of these proposals?

A. The transfer is a potentially exempt transfer (PET) for IHT purposes and so providing that your mother survives the transfer by seven years, no IHT will be due. If your mother dies within seven years, 100% agricultural property relief (APR) should be available to cover the transfer value providing you still own the property at that time and are still using it for farming purposes. The retention of the farmhouse means that this will still be part of your mother's estate and so, depending on the value of your mother's other assets (which include the rental property), tax is likely be due on your mother's death. If this is a problem, then steps need to be taken to try and reduce the value of the estate by transferring further assets or by establishing further reliefs.

Your mother could gift you the farmhouse but would have to pay you a full market rent for her occupation to avoid the gift with reservation rules which would still treat your mother as owning the property. I assume it would be unacceptable for your mother to lose the rental income by transferring the rental property to you (this would also create a capital gains tax liability). Therefore, it may be advisable to transfer the farmland and property, including the farmhouse, into the partnership, not to you, and for your mother to remain a partner. A formal partnership agreement should be entered into which could stipulate which partner owns what capital share of the underlying partnership assets, i.e. you would have a 100% interest in the land and buildings, and your mother a 100% interest in the farmhouse. The profit shares do not have to be in the same proportions, and so a small share of the profits can be allocated to your mother. As the farmhouse is a partnership asset, it could qualify for 100% APR as a partner of a farming business is occupying it.

There is no need for your mother to draw her share of the profit, although it will still be charged to income tax, and it can be left in the partnership in her capital account. The capital account balance will qualify for 100% business property relief for IHT purposes, providing this is reflected by business assets and not simply an accumulation of large amounts of cash. The capital account balance could also be transferred to your capital account from time to time if your mother so wished. Until recently, this was generally considered to be a PET for IHT purposes. However, it is understood that HMRC may now consider this to be a gift with reservation as the funds have not left the partnership and so are still being enjoyed by the donor partner. This would mean the capital account remains in your mother's estate. Interestingly, the HMRC guidance on the pre-owned assets tax states:

> 'we do not regard the partnership interest as transparent, and the disposal of a share is unlikely to give rise to a pre-owned asset charge in any circumstances.'

See *British Master Tax Guide* 6785, 6983, 7253, 7259, 7292

Law: IHTA 1984, s. 103–109, 115

40-300 Gift with reservation

> **Q.** David's mother has given him her house because she wanted to make things easier on her death. His mother continues to live in the house rent-free and David has his own house and family which is quite separate. I know that the mother will be caught by the pre-owned asset tax (POAT) but can you give advice about the election to avoid the tax?

A. David is in a very common situation and when the gift was made there was probably no thought of IHT or any tax at all. For IHT, if David's mother were to die while still living in the property, the gift would be caught by the gifts with reservation rules. The property would be included in the calculation of her estate for IHT even though she may have physically transferred it to her son more than seven years before her death.

The mother will not be subject to POAT as there is an exemption in FA 2004, Sch. 15, para. 11(3) and (5) which exempts property which is subject to a reservation of benefit and thus will be liable to IHT on death in any event.

If the family consider that they want to escape the IHT charge the mother will need to pay a market rent for her occupation of the house and she will need to continue to pay rent until she dies or moves out. The gift will then drop out of her estate for IHT seven years after she starts to pay market rent. Paying a market rent is giving full consideration so the mother would still not be caught by POAT.

See *British Master Tax Guide* 6785.

Law: FA 1986, s. 102

40-310 Was it really a gift?

> **Q.** In 1999, while he was still working, a grandfather gave his grandson, Tommy, his violin. Tommy took it home and it was kept in a cabinet in his parents' house. It was valued at £15,000 at the date of the gift. After his retirement the grandfather was at a loose end and he 'borrowed' the violin back and took up his hobby again. He made it clear to the family that the violin was still Tommy's. The grandfather died in June 2009. The violin is now worth nearer £90,000. How is it treated for tax?

A. At first it is necessary to establish whether a valid gift of the violin has been made to Tommy at all, or if the violin remains in Grandfather's estate to be passed to his beneficiaries according to the will, or intestacy rules. A gift of a chattel (tangible, moveable property) must be perfected by gift or delivery. Grandfather did make a valid gift as he allowed Tommy to take the violin home thereby making effective delivery.

However, in asking for the violin to be returned, Grandfather did not exclude himself from benefit. This gift is caught by the 'Gifts with Reservation of Benefit' rules in FA 1986, s. 102.

These anti-avoidance rules give Grandfather's beneficiaries the worst of both worlds for tax purposes. The value of the violin at the date of death (£90,000) must be included in the grandfather's estate for IHT, but there was a valid gift to Tommy when the violin was worth £15,000 so that Tommy's base cost for CGT is only £15,000.

Had the grandfather not asked for the violin to be returned, it would have been outside his estate for IHT purposes. He had made a valid gift which was a potentially exempt transfer and had survived the gift by seven years.

Alternately, if Grandfather had just kept the violin and gifted it to Tommy in his will, then the violin would have been included in his estate for IHT purposes but for capital gains Tommy would have acquired it at the market value at the date of death, i.e. £90,000.

It can be seen that families should seek tax advice before valuable assets are gifted between generations.

See *British Master Tax Guide* 6785.

Law: FA 1986, s. 102

40-320 Estate rates

Example

Alan dies on 31 March 2009, having made no chargeable lifetime gifts. In his will he leaves £90,000 to his son Brian, subject to payment of tax thereon. The residue, worth £450,000 is shared equally between his wife Wendy and his daughter Carol.

	£
Value of estate	540,000
Less: spouse's share exempt	(225,000)
	315,000
Less: nil band available	(312,000)
	3,000
Tax thereon £3,000 × 40%	1,200

The 'estate rate' is calculated as follows:
1,200/315,000 × 100 = 0.38%

	£
Value attributed to Brian's legacy	90,000
Tax thereon at 0.38%	(344)
	89,656

	£
Value attributed to Carol's share of residue	225,000
Tax thereon at 0.38%	(856)
	224,144

Alan's estate is distributed as follows:

	£
Brian	89,656
Carol	224,144
Wendy	225,000
Tax	1,200
	540,000

See *British Master Tax Guide* 6800.

Law: IHTA 1984, s. 7–9

40-340   Estate rates – exempt residuals

Example

David dies on 31 March 2010, having made no chargeable lifetime gifts. In his will he leaves £172,500 free of tax to each of his two nephews, and the residue to Cancer Research (a charity). His estate is valued at £500,000.

	£
Value of specific gifts	345,000
Less: nil-rate band	(325,000)
	20,000

Grossed up value of gifts	
£345,000 + (£20,000 × 40/60)	358,333
Residue £500,000 − £358,333	141,667

The estate is distributed as follows:

	£
Nephew 1	172,500
Nephew 2	172,500
Cancer Research	141,667
Tax	13,333
	500,000

See *British Master Tax Guide* 6800.

Law: IHTA 1984, s. 7–9

40-360   Estate rates – taxable residuals

Example

Alan dies on 1 April 2009 having made no lifetime chargeable gifts. In his will he leaves a house valued at £317,000 to his daughter Barbara, free of tax. The residue is to be divided equally between Alan's son Charles and Alan's wife Dorothy. Thus, the residue is partly chargeable and partly exempt. Alan's estate is valued at £500,000.

Step 1

	£
House value	317,000
Less: nil band available (2008–09)	(312,000)
	5,000

The tax on the £5,000 needs to be included in the gross value of the gift. The gross value is therefore calculated as follows:

£317,000 + (£5,000 × 40/60) = £320,333

Step 2

	Exempt £	Chargeable £	Total £
Gift to Barbara		320,333	320,333
Residue:			
Charles		89,833	89,833
Dorothy	89,834		89,834
	89,834	410,166	500,000

Step 3

Tax on estate

(£410,166 − £312,000) × 40% = £39,266

Step 4

Estate rate: 39,266/410,166 = 9.57%

Step 5

Specific gift regrossed

£317,000 × 100/(100 − 9.57) = £350,547

Step 6

	Exempt £	Chargeable £	Total £
Gift to Barbara		350,547	350,547
Residue:			
Charles		74,726	74,726
Dorothy	74,727		74,727
	74,727	425,273	500,000

Step 7

Tax on estate

(£425,273 − 312,000) × 40% = £45,309

The total amount of tax payable on Alan's estate is £45,309.

Step 8

Recalculated estate rate: 45,309/425,273 = 10.65%

Step 9

Tax on £350,547 at 10.65% = £37,333

Step 10

Tax on £74,726 at 10.65% = £7,958

Step 11

The estate is distributed as follows:

	Estate £	Tax £
Barbara:	317,000	
Tax on Barbara's gift	37,333	37,333
	354,333	
Charles:		
1/2 (£500,000 − £354,333) − £7,958	64,876	
Tax on Charles's share of residue	7,958	7,958
Dorothy:		
1/2 (£500,000 − £354,333)	72,833	
	500,050	45,291

See *British Master Tax Guide* 6800.

Law: IHTA 1984, s. 7–9

40-380 PETs and estates – using up the nil band

Q.   Leighton's elderly mother went into a home in October 2006, having occupied her home under the terms of her second husband's will. The house was then sold and the proceeds of £180,000 distributed to his children. In January 2007 she terminated an interest in possession trust set up by her first husband's will and the proceeds of £160,000 were distributed to Leighton and his sister. What is the position for IHT if she dies before October 2013 (i.e. within seven years), assuming that she has assets of £120,000 on death?

A.   As Leighton's mother had an interest in possession in both trusts, the termination of each of these constitutes a potentially exempt transfer (PET) for IHT. This means that they will be brought into her estate for IHT purposes if she dies within seven years. The nil-rate band is applied against the gifts in the order in which they are made and appropriate taper relief is applied to any part of the gifts which are above the nil-rate band.

Assuming that she died in May 2010 (nil-rate band = £325,000) the position is as follows:

	£
Transfer Oct. 2006	180,000
Transfer Jan. 2007	160,000
Nil-rate band	(325,000)
Chargeable on death	15,000

May 2010

Chargeable on death	15,000 @ 40% = 6,000	@ 80%	4,800
Estate on death	120,000 @ 40%		48,000
Total IHT due			52,800

See *British Master Tax Guide* 6800–6802.

Law: IHTA 1984, s. 7–9

40-400   The seven-year rule on death

Example

In March 2004 Arthur gave £100,000 to his daughter Beatrice. He had made two previous transfers, a gift of £80,000 to Charles in June 2002 and a gross transfer of £335,000 into a discretionary trust in October 2003. Arthur died on 10 April 2010. Arthur used his annual exemption every year prior to these gifts.

How much tax becomes chargeable on the gift to Beatrice (which was originally a PET) as a result of the death?

The calculation is as follows:

(1) Gift to Charles
    Gift to Charles is a PET made more than 7 years prior to death – ignore

	£
Chargeable gift into trust (gross) – October 2003	335,000

(2) Gift to the trust

Transfer	335,000
Less: nil band available	(325,000)
	10,000

(3) Gift to Beatrice

Gift to Beatrice	100,000
Cumulative transfers within 7 years of death	335,000
	435,000
Less: nil band available	(325,000)
	110,000

	£
Tax on Beatrice's gift	
Total tax (110,000 @ 40%)	44,000
Less: tax on gift to trust	(4,000)
	40,000

(4) Less taper relief
More than 6 but not more than 7 years before death charged
£40,000 at 20% = £8,000

See *British Master Tax Guide* 6800–6802.

Law: IHTA 1984, s. 7–9

40-420 Tapering potentially exempt transfers

> **Q.** I am trying to plan for IHT and I think that the best advice would be to start making gifts now because if I survive for at least three years the gift will start to get the benefit of taper relief. However I am not quite sure that this is correct or how the taper relief works, please can you explain the details?

A. Potentially exempt transfers (PETs) become totally exempt if the donor survives for seven years, otherwise they become chargeable. When more than three years have passed since making the gift, tapering relief applies which reduces the IHT payable. The point is that taper relief only applies to reduce the tax payable on the gift and does not actually reduce the value of the gift to be brought into consideration. In fact because lifetime gifts are brought into the calculation first, many PETs merely start to use the available nil-rate band so that no IHT is payable on the gift and taper relief does not apply.

See *British Master Tax Guide* 6801.

Law: IHTA 1984, s. 7

40-440   Taper relief

Example

Jane made a gift of £450,000 to her nephew in March 2006 and used her annual exemption each year but made no other gifts. She died in April 2010. On Jane's death £125,000 will be chargeable to IHT (£450,000 less the nil-rate band of £325,000). Without taper, the nephew would need to pay £50,000 (125,000 × 40%) but as more than four years have elapsed between the gift and Jane's death, taper relief is available at 40%. Her nephew will be due to pay only £30,000 being 60% of the £50,000.

See *British Master Tax Guide* 6801.

Law: IHTA 1984, s. 7

40-460   The seven-year charge – extra tax due

Example

David has made the following transfers before his death on 10 April 2010 (along with gifts of £3,000 every year to various non-exempt organisations):

- a gift of £225,000 in May 2003 into a discretionary trust for his mother – the trust was named the 'Esther' trust, the trustees paid the tax due;
- a gift of £135,000 to Felix, his brother, in February 2004; and
- a gift of £300,000 into a separate discretionary trust for his wife and children in October 2004. The trustees pay the tax, amounting to £60,000, on David's gift into this trust.

On David's death extra tax is chargeable on the transfer into the discretionary trust set up for his wife and children, as follows:

		£
(1)	Cumulative total	
	Gift to Esther trust	225,000
	Gift to Felix chargeable as a result of David's death within 7 years	135,000
		360,000
(2)	Tax thereon	
	£325,000 × 0%	Nil
	£35,000 × 40%	14,000
(3)	New cumulative total	£
	Previous cumulative total	360,000
	Gift to trust	300,000
		660,000

(4)	Tax thereon	£
	Cumulative transfers	660,000
	Less: nil band available	(325,000)
		335,000
	£335,000 × 40%	134,000

(5) Tax on gift into trust
£134,000 − £14,000 = £120,000

(6) Taper relief:
Gift more than 4 years but less than 5 years before death
Tax chargeable £120,000 × 60%   72,000

The tax paid on the gift made in October 2004 (viz £60,000) is less than the tax computed in (6) above (£72,000). Therefore, the extra tax payable on the gift made in October 2004 is £12,000. If the tax paid at the time of the gift had been more than the tax computed in (6), then there would not be any repayment of tax.

See *British Master Tax Guide* 6803.

Law: IHTA 1984, s. 7

40-480   Disposals after death

Example 1

Albert's estate includes a 30% shareholding in XYZ Ltd, an unquoted company. Albert's spouse also holds 30% of the shares. At the date of Albert's death, a 30% holding is worth £40,000, and a 60% holding is worth £120,000. Thus Albert's holding is valued on death at:

30/60 × £120,000 = £60,000

Within the three-year period the holding owned by Albert at death is sold at arm's length for £35,000, i.e. at less than the £60,000. Relief is available, so that the shares are given the value on death of a 30% holding rather than the 60% holding under the related property rules.

The shares are thus given a value on death of £40,000.

Example 2

Elaine died leaving Whiteacre, valued at £100,000, and Blackacre, valued at £110,000. Two years later her personal representatives sold Whiteacre for £80,000, and Blackacre for £120,000. The position is:

Plot	Valuation at death £	Sale price £
Whiteacre	100,000	80,000
Blackacre	110,000	120,000
Totals	210,000	200,000

If Elaine's personal representatives wish to substitute the sale price for the valuation at death, they must take the aggregate, £200,000, in respect of both plots – they cannot single out Whiteacre on the ground that that is the only plot which has been sold at a loss.

Example 3

Edward died on 30 June 2006. Included in his estate were various holdings of land, valued for probate as follows:

	£
Plot 1	25,200
Plot 2	27,800
Plot 3	6,500
Plot 4	13,200

Land was sold by the personal representatives as follows:

On 1 December 2007, Plot 1 was sold for £24,000. On 1 August 2009, Plot 2 was sold for £30,000 and on 1 October 2009, Plot 4 was sold for £11,000.

A loss on sale claim may be made in respect of the disposal of Plot 1 shares, since it takes place within three years of death. Extended relief may be claimed in respect of Plot 4, sold in the fourth year after death, but a claim does not apply to Plot 2, as it was sold at a profit.

Therefore the total loss on sale amounts to £3,400, being £1,200 in respect of Plot 1 and £2,200 in respect of Plot 4.

Example 4

Mary dies leaving an estate which includes the following qualifying investments. The first column shows their value at the date of death. The second column shows their value 11 months later. The Kappa plc shares have been cancelled.

	£	£
1,000 shares in Theta plc	3,000	2,500
5,000 shares in Iota plc	20,000	10,000
3,000 shares in Lambda plc	5,000	7,500
10,000 shares in Kappa plc	2,000	Nil
	30,000	20,000

If the shares in Theta plc, Iota plc and Lambda plc are sold before the expiry of 12 months following the date of death, the cancelled shares in Kappa plc may be treated as sold for one pound, thus maximising the loss on sale.

The general requirement, that the investments sold within 12 months of death are valued by reference to the best consideration reasonably obtainable where that is higher than the sale price, does not apply in relation to cancelled investments, to which is attributed a nominal consideration of one pound.

See *British Master Tax Guide* 6815.

Law: IHTA 1984, s. 178–198

40-500 Quick succession relief

Example

Alan dies and leaves £135,000 to Barry. Assume that £15,000 tax is payable by Barry on the transfer.

Two years and two months later, Barry dies. In calculating the tax payable on Barry's estate, quick succession relief is available in respect of the bequest by Alan as follows:

£15,000 × 120,000/135,000 × 60% = £8,000

This figure of £8,000 will be deducted from the tax chargeable on Barry's estate.

See *British Master Tax Guide* 6820.

Law: IHTA 1984, s. 141

40-520 Double IHT charge

> **Q.** Five years ago my uncle gifted me, as his only close relative, some assets to minimise his potential IHT liability. It soon became apparent that my uncle did not have sufficient means to support himself and so I transferred these assets back to him. My

uncle recently died and I have been told that my uncle will be charged to IHT twice on these assets. Surely this is incorrect?

A. Strictly no, but there is a relief available. The transfer to you was a potentially exempt transfer and as your uncle died within seven years of making the transfer it becomes a chargeable transfer. As the assets were owned by your uncle at the time of his death they form part of his estate and so are chargeable also.

Relief is given by the *Inheritance Tax (Double Charges Relief) Regulations* 1987 (SI 1987/1130). Broadly the relief operates by making two computations, one with the chargeable transfer and excluding the same assets on death, and the second computation is the opposite, i.e. excluding the chargeable transfer but including the assets in the death estate. Whichever computation gives the higher amount of tax is the one to be used in the IHT calculation of the estate.

See *British Master Tax Guide* 6830.

Law: IHTA 1984, s. 104

40-540 Lifetime transfer or death estate

Example

On 1 March 2010 Edwina settled property on Gavin for life, with the remainder to Edwina's discretionary trustees. The property settled by Edwina was worth £330,000, and at this time Edwina had made transfers of £500,000 during the previous seven years. At Gavin's death six months later the property was still worth £330,000. Gavin's free estate amounts to £45,000.

	£
Value of Gavin's estate (including settled property)	345,000
Less: nil band	(325,000)
Chargeable	20,000
Tax at 40%	8,000
Estate rate: 8,000/345,000	2.3%
Tax due on lifetime transfer calculation	
Amount of transfer attributable to Edwina's transfer	300,000

	£
Tax on lifetime transfer from Edwina	
£300,000 × 20%	60,000
Tax attributable to Gavin's free estate	
£45,000 × 2.3%	1,035
Total	61,035

Because £61,035 is more than £8,000 then the charge on the larger figure will be the one included for IHT purposes.

See *British Master Tax Guide* 6910.

Law: IHTA 1984, s. 54A, 54B

40-560　Income or capital paid out with discretion

> **Q.**　I have recently taken over the tax affairs of a discretionary trust and have received a copy of the previous year's Trust Tax Return from the former agent. I note that this return shows discretionary payments of income amounting to £10,000 were paid to beneficiaries in the year, although the gross income shown on the tax return only amounted to interest of £3,500. As the income payments are deemed to be net of 40% tax at the trust rate, this meant that the year's self-assessment liability was much higher than the tax on just the income arising. HMRC have seemingly accepted this without adjustment, but is this correct?

A.　No. For income tax purposes, the maximum amount of trust income that can be paid to a beneficiary is the income arising in the year net of tax and allowable trust management expenses. This is confirmed each year in the HMRC *Self Assessment Trust Tax Return Guide* which also mentions the rare exception to this rule when the trust deed specifies a defined level of income for a beneficiary and capital payments made to top up this income figure are deemed to be income.

Therefore, the maximum income that could have been paid to the beneficiaries in the year is £2,100 (£3,500 less 40% tax) assuming that there are no allowable trust management expenses for the year.

The balance of the payments, £7,900, must therefore be payments from capital for tax purposes and should not have been shown in the income payment section of the return. Trust law may allow income payments to be made from accumulated income but, for tax purposes, accumulated income is capital. The capital payments are exit charges for IHT purposes under IHTA 1984, s. 65 which may result in an IHT liability depending on the circumstances of this particular trust.

The above also has a knock-on effect for the beneficiaries who may have declared the wrong amount of income to HMRC and claimed a tax refund to which they were not entitled. Therefore, the beneficiaries should be advised accordingly.

See *British Master Tax Guide* 6943.

Law: IHTA 1984, s. 65

40-580   Ten-yearly charges

Example

Colin, who had made a chargeable gift of £30,000 in 1998, creates a settlement on 8 May 2000, transferring property worth £300,000. Half of the fund is held on discretionary trusts, and an interest in possession subsists in the other half. The trustees pay the tax on this transfer, amounting to £30,000. Note that annual exemptions have been ignored. No chargeable event occurs before 8 May 2010, when the value of the whole fund is £600,000.

The ten-year charge is calculated as follows:

	£
Step 1: the special cumulation	
(a) chargeable transfers by settler	30,000
(b) amounts on which exit charges have arisen	–
	30,000

	£
Step 2: the hypothetical transfer	
(a) value of relevant property at anniversary	300,000
(b) value of other property at date when it entered fund (after deduction of tax of 1/2 × £30,000)	135,000
(c) value of property in related settlements	–
	435,000

	£
Step 3: IHT chargeable	
Special cumulation	30,000
Hypothetical transfer	435,000
Less: nil band available	(325,000)
	140,000

Tax at 40%	56,000
Of which half is relevant here to the discretionary trust	28,000

Step 4: effective rate	
Effective rate (28,000/435,000) × 100	6.436%

Step 5: rate of ten-year charge	
Rate = 6.436% × 30%	1.931%
Tax payable = £300,000 × 1.931%	£5,793

See *British Master Tax Guide* 6950–6954.

Law: IHTA 1984, s. 64, 66

40-600   Exit charges

Example

On 1 February 2002 Paul, who had already made a chargeable transfer of £40,000 on 1 May 1999, transferred £400,000 into a new discretionary trust, paying IHT of £64,400 out of the £400,000. (Annual exemptions have been ignored.) Eight and three-quarter years later, on 1 November 2010, the trustees make a capital payment to Hugh of £220,000. Hugh pays the tax due, which is calculated as follows:

	£
Chargeable transfers made by settlor in the seven years before commencement of settlement	40,000
Value of property at commencement of settlement (£400,000 − £64,400)	335,600
	375,600

Notional tax on a transfer of £335,600 by a person with a cumulative total of £40,000:

$(375,600 − 325,000) × 20\% = 10,120$

Effective rate $(10,120/335,600) × 100 = 3.016\%$

Rate $30\% × 3.016\% = 0.901\%$

35 of 40 quarters have passed between commencement and the next ten-yearly charge so:

Rate at which tax payable: $35/40 × 0.901\% = 0.788\%$

Tax payable by Hugh is therefore £220,000 $× 0.788\% =$ £1,733.60

Note: If the trustees had paid the tax, the capital payment would have had to be grossed up when working out the tax due.

See *British Master Tax Guide* 6962.

Law: IHTA 1984, s. 68

40-620   Late additions to a settlement

Example

A discretionary settlement is created on 10 March 2002. The value of the property transferred into the settlement is £120,000. On 10 March 2004, property valued at £35,000

401

was added to the settlement. On 10 September 2009, a distribution of £80,000 is made of which £15,000 is attributable to the property added in 2004.

The settlor had made chargeable transfers of £200,000 in the seven years before the creation of the settlement.

Tax due on the distribution (assuming the beneficiary pays the tax) at 2010–11 rates:

	£
Chargeable transfers by settler in the seven years before commencement of settlement	200,000
Value of property at creation of settlement	120,000
Property added to settlement	35,000
	155,000

Notional tax at half-rates on a transfer of £155,000 made by a person with a cumulative total of £200,000:

(355,000 − 325,000 (nil band)) × 20%	6,000
Effective rate (6,000/155,000) × 100	3.87%
Rate applicable = 30% × 3.87%	1.16%

Tax due:	£
on £65,000 × 1.16% × 30/40	565.50
on £15,000 × 1.16% × 22/40	195.70
	661.20

Note: If the trustees had paid the tax, the amount would have had to be grossed up.

See *British Master Tax Guide* 6964.

Law: IHTA 1984, s. 68–69

40-640   Exit after more than ten years

Example

On 1 October 1987 Adam settles property on discretionary trusts, having previously made chargeable transfers amounting to £80,000. The trustees make no distributions until 10 April 2006, when they make a capital payment of £150,000, free of tax, to Ben (i.e. the trustees are going to pay the tax so the amount needs to be grossed up).

On 1 October 1997 the trust fund was valued at £350,000.

The ten-year charge calculation (1 October 1997)
Step 1
Chargeable transfers by settlor   £80,000

Step 2
Value of relevant property at anniversary   £350,000

Step 3	£
Special cumulation	80,000
Hypothetical transfer	350,000
	430,000
Less: nil band	(215,000)
	215,000

Tax at 1997–98 lifetime rates (20%)   £43,000

Step 4
Effective rate (43,000/350,000) × 100   12.29%

Step 5
Rate of ten-year charge = 12,29% × 30%   3.69%
Tax payable (£350,000 × 3.69%)   £12,915

The exit charge (10 April 2006)

Step 1	£
Re-calculation of rate of ten-year charge:	
Special cumulation	80,000
Hypothetical transfer	350,000
	430,000
Less: nil band	(285,000)
	145,000

Tax at 2006–07 life time rates (20%)   £29,000
Effective rate (29,000/350,000) × 100   8.29%
Notional rate of ten-year charge (8.29% × 30%)   2.49%

Step 2
Multiplication by appropriate fraction (34 quarters completed)
Rate of exit charge = 2.49% × 34/40   2.116%

Step 3
Calculation of tax payable:
Gross equivalent of £150,000
Tax payable £150,000 × 2.116/(100 − 2.116)   £3,242.61

See *British Master Tax Guide* 6964.

Inheritance Tax

Law: IHTA 1984, s. 68–69

40-660 Pre-owned asset examples

Example 1

Dolores owns a small shareholding in XYZ plc, an oil company. In 1995, she gave these shares to her daughter, Keisha. At the time, the shareholding was worth £10,000.

XYZ plc, however, stumbles across a new product which it patents. The directors of the company decide that it is in the shareholders' interests for the company to be sold so that the patent can be fully exploited. Keisha's shares are subsequently sold for £150,000.

Keisha purchases a new flat with the proceeds of the sale and invites her mother to move in with her.

Since Keisha has used the proceeds of the subsequent share sale to fund the purchase of Dolores' new flat, Dolores will be subject to an income tax charge under the pre-owned assets legislation.

Example 2

Bruce, a multi-millionaire, is wooing his childhood sweetheart, Sheila. On 14 February Bruce gives Sheila £200,000. Two years later, Sheila finally caves in and suggests that she and Bruce move in together. They jointly purchase a £2m home with Sheila using some of Bruce's original gift to fund the purchase.

Consequently, Bruce would be living in (and therefore certainly occupying) a house, the purchase consideration for which had been partly given by another person (Sheila), but where Bruce had partly provided some of the consideration.

As a result, Bruce will be subject to a pre-owned asset charge.

Example 3

In 2006 Aman gives his son, Kuldip, £100,000 which Kuldip uses to purchase a flat. In 2008 Kuldip sells the flat for £500,000 and buys a new house. In 2010 Aman moves into the house as he wishes to be nearer his grandchildren.

Aman funded the purchase of Kuldip's flat. The flat was then sold and its disposal proceeds were applied towards the purchase of a house which Aman subsequently occupies. Consequently, Aman will be subject to an income tax charge under the pre-owned assets legislation.

Example 4

Erica gives £100,000 to her daughter, Vanessa, which Vanessa uses to purchase the freehold of a cottage, Les Papillons. Vanessa subsequently grants a 999-year lease in respect of Les Papillons to a third party and uses the proceeds towards the purchase of a new home, The Heathers. Several years later, Erica moves into The Heathers with her daughter.

The grant of a lease is treated as a disposal for these purposes. Hence, Vanessa has made a disposal of part of her interest in Les Papillons. Vanessa has used the proceeds of this disposal to acquire The Heathers, which Erica subsequently occupies. Provided that Erica's gift to Vanessa was made after 17 March 1986, Erica is caught by the pre-owned assets legislation.

Example 5

Robin and Rose give their daughter, Karen, £30,000 as a wedding present. Three years later Karen buys a sculpture which she places in her parents' garden as it is more suited there than in Karen's home. (It is assumed for the purposes of this example that the sculpture does not become so installed in the garden as to become a fixture.)

Robin and Rose will have the use (and possession) of the sculpture, the purchase consideration for which had been partly provided by them.

As a result, Robin and Rose will be subject to an income tax charge under the pre-owned asset tax legislation.

See *British Master Tax Guide* 6983–6991.

Law: FA 2004, Sch. 15

40-680   Property leaving a charitable trust

Example

Betty makes a settlement on 1 January 1974 under which the property is to be held for charitable purposes until 20 June 2010. The property in the settlement is valued at £200,000 on 20 June 2010. There are 125 quarters between 13 March 1979 and 20 June 2010.

Tax payable is at 0.25% for each of the first 40 complete successive quarters, at 0.20% for the next 40 quarters, at 0.15% for the next 40 and 0.10% for the remaining 5 quarters. Therefore:

	£
0.25% × 40 × £200,000	20,000
0.20% × 40 × £200,000	16,000
0.15% × 40 × £200,000	12,000
0.10% × 5 × £200,000	1,000
Total tax payable	49,000

See *British Master Tax Guide* 6998.

Law: IHTA 1984, s. 70

40-700 Gifts to your spouse

> **Q.** Is there any limit to the amount I can give to my wife without worrying about IHT?

A. As a general rule you can give what you like to your spouse and there is no danger of any tax arising. However, in rare circumstances the gift is not wholly exempt. If your spouse is non-domiciled then there is a limit of £55,000 that can be given without tax. Any amount in excess of £55,000 will be a potentially exempt transfer, and if you die within seven years it will become taxable. This amount has not changed since 1982, at which time the nil-rate band was also £55,000.

See *British Master Tax Guide* 7192.

Law: IHTA 1984, s. 18

40-720 Non-domiciled spouse

Example

Alfred marries Artemis, who has a Greek domicile, on 13 July 2003. He immediately gives her a half-share in his fortune, which amounts to £200,000. If he dies after six months, having made no other gifts, Alfred's estate at death will include not only his own half-share of £200,000 but also the non-exempt part of his gift to Artemis, £145,000. If, however, he lives until 14 July 2010 (seven years later), the problem disappears.

See *British Master Tax Guide* 7192.

Law: IHTA 1984, s. 18

40-740   Transfer of unused nil-rate band (post-9 October 2007)

Example 1

If on the first death none of the original nil-rate band was used because the entire estate was left to a surviving spouse, then if the nil-rate band when the surviving spouse dies is £300,000, that would be increased 100 per cent to £600,000.

Example 2

If, on the first death, the chargeable estate is £150,000 and the nil-rate band is £300,000, then 50% of the original nil-rate band would be unused and is available for transfer. If the nil-rate band when the surviving spouse dies is £325,000, then the amount available for transfer would be 50% of £325,000 or £162,500, giving the surviving spouse's estate a nil-rate band of £325,000 + £162,500 = £487,500 in total.

Example 3

Anna and Adam had been domiciled for many years in Spain. However, on Adam's death Anna returned to the UK, resuming her domicile of origin. She died in 2008. Adam's unused nil-rate band is available for transfer.

Example 4

Mr Jones died in 2000, having made no lifetime gifts, and leaving everything to his wife, Mrs Jones. Mrs Jones died at the beginning of 2008 and shortly before her death gave £600,000 to her son which qualified as a potentially exempt transfer (PET). As Mrs Jones died within seven years of making the gift, it is a failed PET which becomes chargeable on her death. Her remaining estate is worth £500,000.

There will be no inheritance tax (IHT) to pay on the lifetime gift as two nil-rate bands of £300,000 are allocated against it. The £500,000 left in her estate at death is fully chargeable at 40%.

Example 5

If, in the above example, Mrs Jones has settled property on her daughter instead of making an outright gift, this would have been an immediately chargeable transfer. Her nil-rate band of £300,000 would have been allocated against the £600,000 gift to the settlement which would have left a tax charge of £300,000 at 20% = £60,000.

On her death within seven years of making the settlement, additional IHT is payable. However, Mr Jones's unused nil-rate band is available to allocate against it and no additional IHT is charged. It should be noted that there is no refund of the tax charged when the settlement was created.

See *British Master Tax Guide* 7192.

Law: FA 2008, Sch. 4, para. 2 inserting IHTA 1984, s. 8A–8C; IHTA 1984, s. 18

40-760   Carry-forward of annual exemption

Example

In one tax year, Harold made transfers of value amounting in total to £1,600. The £1,400 remaining of the annual exemption may be carried forward, so that in the following tax year Harold may make gifts of up to £4,400 before anything is chargeable.

If Harold makes gifts amounting to £2,500 in the second tax year, these are treated as using up the first part of the annual exemption for that year. Thus, only the balance of £500 is available to carry forward to the third tax year. The £1,400 brought forward from the first tax year is lost.

If, alternatively, Harold makes gifts amounting to £4,000 in the second tax year, none is chargeable because of the current year's £3,000 and the previous year's £1,400. However there is now no balance to carry forward to the third tax year.

See *British Master Tax Guide* 7220.

Law: IHTA 1984, s. 19

40-780   Small gift and an annual exemption?

Q.   Mr X, who normally uses his annual exemption, gifts £3,000 to his grandson James on his birthday in September and then makes his usual Christmas gifts of £250 to his three grandchildren James, Jacob and Lucy. Mr X dies the following March. Do all the gifts qualify for exemptions?

A.   The £3,000 gift in September will be covered by the annual exemption but the £250 gift at Christmas to James would be a potentially exempt transfer (PET), which would be totally exempt provided that the donor survives for seven years. Unfortunately the death in March means that the PET has failed and the £250 will be included in the death estate for IHT purposes.

An individual may make any number of gifts of less than £250, small gifts allowance, to different recipients in each tax year, which will be free of IHT. This allowance may not be used to reduce the value of a larger gift and cannot be added to an annual allowance gift. The Christmas gifts to Jacob and Lucy will fall into the small gifts exemption.

See *British Master Tax Guide* 7220–7223.

Law: IHTA 1984, s. 19–20

40-800   Reporting normal gifts out of income

> **Q.**   Gabby makes regular gifts to his son in order to fund his grandsons' education. He considers these gifts are 'normal expenditure out of income' and therefore exempt from IHT. Do these exempt transfers need to be reported to HMRC during his lifetime? Gabby has found a form called 'Gifts made as part of normal expenditure out of income' (form D3a) on their website. Is this relevant?

A.   Provided Gabby has sufficient net income available to maintain his usual standard of living after these gifts they will be exempt as normal expenditure out of income. Exempt gifts are not reportable to HMRC during the taxpayer's lifetime but, following the death of the taxpayer, you must be able to demonstrate that the gifts were out of income. The form D3a forms part of the Inheritance Tax Account (IHT200) and, ultimately, this will need to be completed on the death of the taxpayer. Therefore, a schedule showing income and expenditure, including the relevant gifts, should be prepared annually during Gabby's lifetime, to enable completion of form D3a after the taxpayer's death.

See *British Master Tax Guide* 7226.

Law: IHTA 1984, s. 21

40-820   Furnished holiday letting and business property relief

> **Q.**   I own a holiday cottage in Devon which is let out as holiday accommodation and meets the definition of a furnished holiday let for income and capital gains tax purposes. For IHT purposes, can you please confirm whether I can benefit from business property relief (BPR) at 100% on the basis that the letting is deemed to be a trade?

A.   Business property relief may apply to a furnished holiday letting, however, there is a higher standard of test to meet for the IHT relief than for the income and capital gains reliefs. In addition to the conditions for income and capital gains relief, there must be some local involvement with the holidaymakers' plans by the owner, his agent or housekeeper. The relief will not therefore be due if the holidaymakers merely collect and drop off the keys at the beginning and end of their stay, with little or no other services provided to them beyond the provision of towels, bed linen, etc.

See *British Master Tax Guide* 7253–7255.

40-840   50% business property relief availability

Edward (who has made no other transfers of value) gifts his 14% shareholding in an unquoted company to his son. The shares are valued at £23,466 at the date of the gift.

Edward dies in the following year and tax on the gift must be computed. The amount of the chargeable transfer for these purposes will be:

	£
Value of shares tranferred	23,466
Less: business property relief at 50%	(11,733)
Reduced value transferred	11,733
Less: annual exemption	(3,000)
Chargeable transfer	8,733

See *British Master Tax Guide* 7253.

Law: IHTA 1984, s. 105

40-860   Business property relief on quoted shares

Q.   I have had an offer for my unquoted company from a plc. My company owns and runs a hotel. I have already suffered two heart attacks so I am forced to consider IHT. The plc is paying me partly cash and part shares. Will business property relief (BPR) be available on the plc shares or have I effectively lost all BPR by selling my company?

A. If you were to die while you own the shares in an unquoted trading company, full BPR is available so that, in effect, the value of the hotel can pass to the next generation with no charge to IHT.

If you sell the shares for cash plus shares in the plc the BPR will be lost. Quoted shares only qualify for BPR if they are a controlling shareholding and even then only give 50% relief.

See *British Master Tax Guide* 7253–7255.

Law: IHTA 1984, s. 105

40-880   Owning property through a company

Q.   I am presently reviewing my IHT position in an attempt to reduce the potential liability arising. I own a trading company but personally own the premises from which the company trades. I understand that as I have a controlling interest in the company, the property will qualify for business property relief but only at the 50% rate, not at the 100% rate for the shares. If I were to transfer the property to the company and hold over the capital gain arising, this would seem to mean that I now own only shares which qualify for the full 100% relief. Are there any problems with this transaction?

A. The transaction is effective for the IHT purpose mentioned. The shares have to be owned for two years, not the underlying assets. Although the transfer can be worthwhile if IHT saving is the overriding objective, CGT and SDLT implications should be fully considered as well.

See *British Master Tax Guide* 7253–7255.

Law: IHTA 1984, s. 105

40-900   Business property relief on replacement property

Example

Richard buys a confectioner's shop in 2004. In January 2009 he sells this and buys a newsagency. In January 2010 he transfers the business to his daughter. The property comes within the first category of relevant business property since it consists of a business. The newsagency has not been owned for two years immediately preceding the transfer but it does come within the replacement provisions having replaced the confectioner's shop owned by the transferor for at least two out of the last five years before the transfer. Thus the transfer will qualify for business property relief and the whole of the total open market value of the assets less the business liabilities will be reduced by 100%.

See *British Master Tax Guide* 7259.

Law: IHTA 1984, s. 106–109

40-920   Non-availability of business property relief – use at death

Example

Jack makes a lifetime gift of his haulage business to his son Kevin. The transfer is potentially exempt and so no tax is payable at this time.

Five years later Kevin sells the business and invests the proceeds of sale. One more year later, Jack dies. Tax becomes chargeable on Jack's gift within seven years before death. Business property relief (BPR) is not available in respect of this transfer because the business was not owed by Kevin throughout the period between the gift and Jack's death.

If Kevin's investment was in, for example, a manufacturing business which he ran and still ran it on the event of his father's death, then the whole amount would qualify for BPR.

See *British Master Tax Guide* 7260.

Law: IHTA 1984, s. 113

40-940   Calculation of restriction of business property relief – company

Example

A trading company has the following balance sheet:

	£
Quoted securities – MV	1,000,000
Trading assets	1,500,000
	2,500,000

A 25% shareholding is valued at £450,000 after applying a 40% discount.

Step 1: Calculate the value of the whole company, before any discount:

£450,000 × (100/25) × (100/60) = £3,000,000

The difference between the £3,000,000 value of the company and the £2,500,000 balance sheet total is goodwill.

Step 2: Calculate the value of the excepted assets as a percentage of the total value

$$\frac{1,000,000}{3,000,000} = 33.33\%$$

(Hence, BPR is available on 66.67% of the value.)

Step 3: Calculate BPR

£450,000 × 100% × 66.67% = £300,000

Hence the transfer potentially subject to IHT is:

£450,000 − £300,000 = £150,000.

See *British Master Tax Guide* 7265.

Law: IHTA 1984, s. 112

40-950   Gift of interest in partnership

Q. My client gifted an interest in a partnership to a relative in December 2002 and also gifted shares in an unquoted trading company to a discretionary trust in November 2004 and claimed business property relief (BPR) on both transfers at that time. He has since died within seven years of each of the original transfers, in October 2009, and I have the task of calculating the inheritance tax liability on his life transfers and the death estate. In the time between my client's original gift of interest and transfer of shares and his death, the shares have been distributed to a beneficiary and no longer attract BPR at the time of his death, and the partnership interest has been sold and reinvested in gilts also not now having the benefit of BPR. He also gave a cash gift to a relative after both transfers just before his death in June 2008 in order to reduce his estate on death.

When calculating the cash gift to the relative, how is the nil-rate band remaining calculated with regards to the withdrawn BPR given in life?

A.   The rules say that where a transferor dies within seven years of making either a potentially exempt transfer (PET) or a chargeable lifetime transfer (CLT) which attracted BPR in life, unless the property is still owned by the donee at the date of the donor's death and still qualifies as an asset, then no BPR will be due. However, the value of the transfer differs for calculating cumulative totals dependent on whether it was a PET or CLT in life.

If the PET becomes chargeable, the full value of the transfer minus the BPR originally given is used to calculate the cumulative totals when reducing the nil-rate band on the subsequent cash gift.

If the CLT becomes chargeable, the full value of the transfer including the BPR originally given is taken into account to calculate the cumulative totals when reducing the nil-rate band on the subsequent cash gift.

The client therefore will reduce his nil-rate band on death for the gift made in June 2008 by any failed PETs in life within seven years of the death, which had attracted BPR, but will not reduce the same nil-rate band for any CLT made in life within seven years of the death, as the original gross transfer complete with BPR remains intact for the death calculation.

See *British Master Tax Guide* 7265.

Law: IHTA 1984, s. 112

40-960   Calculation of restriction of business property relief – partnership

Example

Bert owns a freehold shop with a value of £800,000.

Bert, his son Claude and his daughter-in-law Dora run the retail trade from the shop, in partnership, sharing profits 3:1:1.

Bert wishes to pass the shop and the trade to Claude and Dora as he is in poor health, but he requires an income of £20,000 a year from the business.

Step 1
The partnership agreement is amended so that capital profits are henceforth divided 99%: 0.5%: 0.5%. Bert passes the freehold shop to the partnership.

Step 2
The partnership agreement is amended so that the first £20,000 of profit is given to Bert and the profit in excess of £20,000 is divided 1%: 49.5%: 49.5%

Step 3
Bert gifts his partnership capital account to Claude.

If Bert dies within seven years of the gift, the IHT liability is:

Transfer of value at Step 1:	£
£800,000 × 1%	8,000
Less: 50% BPR	(4,000)
	4,000
Annual exemption year of transfer	(3,000)
previous years	(1,000)
Chargeable transfer	Nil

Transfer of value at Step 3:	£
£800,000 × 99%	792,000
Less: 100% BPR	(792,000)
Chargeable transfer	Nil

If Bert had simply given the property to Claude, IHT would have been payable on £400,000 (£800,000 × 50%) less the annual exemption.

See *British Master Tax Guide* 7265.

Law: IHTA 1984, s. 112

40-970   Business property relief on incorporation

Q. My client incorporated his sole trader consultancy business last year but has kept the property from which he trades and owns personally outside of the company. We understand that this results in a reduction of the rate of business property relief (BPR) for

IHT purposes from 100% to 50%. Our client has owned the property for over ten years. Given this change in circumstances and the rate of relief, can you please confirm whether he will have to wait a further two years from the incorporation before he will qualify again for BPR?

A. I am happy to confirm that your client's ownership period for BPR is unbroken despite the incorporation and change in circumstances. IHTA 1984, s. 106 merely requires the property to have been owned by your client for two years up to a date of transfer, and for it to have been 'relevant business property' for those two years. Although the category of 'relevant business property' has changed with the incorporation, BPR will still be available in the event of a transfer, albeit at the lower rate of 50% which is determined by the conditions at the date of transfer.

See *British Master Tax Guide* 7265.

Law: IHTA 1984, s. 106

40-980   Agricultural property relief on company shares

Q. Lionel owns 80% of the shares in a limited company, whose main asset is a farm. The company does not farm the land itself and the farming tenant is not connected to him. On Lionel's death, will the shares in the company benefit from agricultural property relief (APR)?

A. There may be a claim for APR on the value of the shares provided that two conditions are satisfied. The *Inheritance Tax Act* 1984, s. 123(1) provides that relief is given where the company has owned the property throughout the period of seven years ending with the date of the death, and the property was occupied for agricultural purposes (by the company or by someone else) during that period and the shares or securities were owned by Lionel throughout that period.

See *British Master Tax Guide* 7292–7295.

Law: IHTA 1984, s. 115, 123

41-000   Agricultural property relief on a concrete yard

Q. A farmer is having extensive work carried out. He is having a milking parlour built, and a concrete yard is also being constructed outside the parlour for safety reasons. Obviously the milking parlour will qualify for agricultural buildings allowances (ABAs) but what can be claimed for the concrete yard?

A. Your client can claim ABAs on the construction costs of the yard. The expenditure on which allowances can be claimed includes a building (such as a farmhouse, farm building or cottage) or on the construction of fences or other works. The expression 'other works' includes drainage and sewage works, water and electricity installations, walls, shelter belts of trees, silos, farm roads, land reclamation and hedge demolition so will include a concrete yard as you have here.

See *British Master Tax Guide* 7295.

Law: IHTA 1984, s. 115

41-020   Woodland interests

Example

Roy has an interest in possession in settled property which consists of woodlands worth £400,000 of which £200,000 is specifically attributable to the timber and £100,000 to the land. The woodlands were not run on a commercial basis and therefore business property relief does not apply. Roy dies on 30 November 2009. The trustees elect to have the value of the timber left out of account. On death Roy had other assets worth £200,000. He had made no previous chargeable transfers.

	£
Value of settled property	400,000
Less: woodlands relief	(200,000)
Value of other assets	200,000
Chargeable estate	400,000
Less: nil band available	(325,000)
	75,000
Tax at 40%	30,000

See *British Master Tax Guide* 7320–7323.

Law: IHTA 1984, s. 125

41-040   Woodland values

Example

Andrew, who has made lifetime transfers amounting to £80,000, dies on 1 March 2005, leaving a chargeable estate valued at £300,000, plus woodlands which are left out of account. The woodlands are left to Graham and Craig.

In July 2007 Graham fells the trees on his land and sells the timber for £45,000. Allowable expenses amount to £10,000.

In January 2010 Craig makes a gift of his woodlands to David at a time when they are worth £80,000 (including £25,000 attributable to the underlying land). There are no allowable expenses.

Sale by Graham	£
Andrew's cumulative total at death	380,000
Proceeds of sale	45,000
Less: allowable expenses	(10,000)
	415,000

	£
Tax thereon (2007–08) rates	46,000
Less: tax on Andrew's cumulative total (2007–08 rates)	(32,000)
Tax payable	14,000

Gift by Craig	£
Andrew's cumulative total (including previously chargeable amounts)	415,000
Value at date disposal	80,000
Less: value of land (which would not be left out of account on A's death	(25,000)
	470,000

	£
Tax thereon (2009–10 rates)	58,000
Less: tax on £415,000 (2009–10 rates)	(36,000)
Tax payable	22,000

If the woodlands were, on Andrew's death, relevant business property, and met all other conditions for business property relief, the net proceeds of sale on Graham's disposal, and the net value at the date of Craig's disposal, will each be reduced by the appropriate percentage (100% in each case).

See *British Master Tax Guide* 7326.

Law: IHTA 1984, s. 126–130

41-060   Domicile and premium bonds

> **Q.** Jean is domiciled in Jersey but was resident in the UK for income tax purposes for eight years until her death in January 2010. She had various assets in the UK and in Jersey and we have the task of calculating to what extent her estate is liable to UK tax. Most assets are easily defined as they are either situated in the UK or Jersey, or bank accounts held in the same manner, but Jean had a holding of premium bonds. Will these be included in her estate for IHT?

A.   No account should be taken of the value of excluded property which diminishes a person's estate as a result of a disposition. Excluded property is partly defined by reference to the domicile to the person to whom it belongs. Premium bonds owned by persons domiciled in the Channel Islands or the Isle of Man are included in the definition of excluded property, and are therefore outside the scope of IHT.

See *British Master Tax Guide* 7397.

Law: IHTA 1984, s. 6

41-080   Estates with business property relief and exempt legacies

Example

Alan's estate is valued at £900,000 on his death in May 2010. An amount of £300,000 qualifies for business property relief (BPR) at 100%; £400,000 is bequeathed to Alan's spouse and the residue to his son. The estate's IHT will be calculated as follows:

	£
Value transferred on death	900,000
Less: relief at 100% (on £300,000)	(300,000)
Reduced value transferred	600,000
Less: exempt specific gift	(400,000)
Chargeable estate	200,000
Nil band available	(325,000)
Chargeable to tax	Nil

Suppose instead that Alan bequeaths one-half of his business property to his son Brian, a specific gift of £400,000 cash to his spouse and residue to his daughter Carol.

	£
Value transferred	900,000
Less: relief at 100% (on £300,000)	(300,000)
Reduced value transferred	600,000
Less: value attributed to exempt specific gift	
£400,000 × (600,000/(900,000 − 150,000)	(320,000)
Chargeable estate	280,000
Less: nil band available	(325,000)
Chargeable to tax	Nil

See *British Master Tax Guide* 7410.

Law: IHTA 1984, s. 39, 39A

41-100   Discounted gift trust

> **Q.** My client attended a free seminar at the invitation of his bank. At the seminar there was mentioned a possible investment into a 'discounted gift trust' which would save IHT. Can you explain how these trusts work, please?

A. The term 'discounted gift trust' can be explained by using the example of transferring a single premium life assurance policy (a bond) to a trust.

An individual could transfer a bond with a premium of say £100,000 to a trust for the benefit of his family but excluding himself. The transfer would be on condition that he will take a stream of payments from the trust to supplement his income. These payments would normally be set at 5% and would be payable to him, annually, for the rest of his life. It is understood that this scheme is not suitable for an individual who is expected to survive for more than 20 years.

The gift is an immediate chargeable transfer for IHT purposes, unless the trust is for the benefit of a disabled person. The value of the gift, however, can be discounted from £100,000 because the individual has given £100,000 subject to payments out being made to him annually.

These trusts can be useful for very elderly clients who may not expect to survive a potentially exempt transfer (PET) by seven years but are sufficiently sprightly for the open market value of the retained rights to the income stream to substantially reduce the value of the chargeable transfer. The value of the payment stream is called 'the discount'.

Before the 2006 changes to the IHT treatment of trusts, the transfer to the trust was a PET so that any arguments over the value of the discount only arose after a death within seven years. However, now that a transfer is immediately chargeable it is necessary to accurately establish the value of the discount so that the value of the transfer can be accurately reported. Herein lies the problem as HMRC's view of the value of the discount is likely to be much lower than the client would wish.

In a test case, *Bower & Anor v R & C Commrs*, the special commissioner, ignored the Revenue's suggested value of £250 and settled on £4,200, being two-thirds of the figure provided by the executors. HMRC have appealed this decision to the High Court.

It can be seen that the concept of 'discounted gift trusts' as a valid scheme to mitigate IIIT, is accepted by HMRC. However the scheme is not free from difficulties as shown above.

See *British Master Tax Guide* 6880.

Law: *Bower & Anor v R & C Commrs* (2008) Sp C 665

41-120 Loans made during a lifetime

> **Q.** I am assisting my client, who has been appointed executor after the death of his father. There were five siblings and the father was in the habit of making loans to his children to enable them to get onto the property ladder. There does not appear to be much paperwork. How should we proceed with evaluating the estate for IHT purposes?

A. Gathering together all the information for the IHT forms after a death can be a daunting task. The full value of any outstanding loan plus any interest due will form part of the estate and it must be disclosed on the form IHT 200.

Your client has a head start because he does, at least, know that some loans have been made. It is very important that, as well as examining the bank account records of the deceased for loans going out, he discusses with his siblings their major purchases, e.g. houses, cars, etc. to ensure that no loans are accidentally omitted. He will need to explain that this is a requirement by law as relatives will find it difficult to reveal such sensitive information.

It is quite likely that any loans will not be on commercial terms.

If a fixed-term interest-free loan is made by an individual then he is treated as making a gift at that time. As an example, father lends Johnny £25,000 interest-free to be repaid in five years' time. Father has exchanged £25,000 in cash for the right to receive £25,000 in five years' time. The interest foregone is treated as a gift at that time of, say, £9,000. The gift of £9,000 is a potentially exempt transfer (PET) and if the father fails to survive for seven years it must be taken into account for IHT purposes on his death.

If, instead, the loan is repayable on demand, there is no immediate gift as there is no loss in value of the father's estate as he has the immediate right of repayment of the full £25,000.

If any of the siblings claim that the father released the loan, then they must be able to provide the paperwork for the release to be accepted by HMRC. The release of a loan must be done by deed for this to be binding in law and in equity (*Pinnell's case*). HMRC will want to be certain that the full amount of any outstanding loan is included in the value of the estate declared on death.

See *British Master Tax Guide* 6526.

Law: *Pinnell's case* (1602) 5 Co Rep 117a

41-140   National Heritage Property

> **Q.** My client has inherited a painting from his father which in the past has been accepted as National Heritage Property and has received conditional exemption from inheritance tax (IHT). My client is not interested in art and is unwilling to comply with the conditions, thus he is unable to claim the conditional exemption himself. How can he extricate himself from this situation without undue cost?

A. There is a conditional exemption from IHT for works of art, historic buildings, etc. which are designated by the Revenue & Customs Commissioners as being of outstanding national interest. However it is merely a deferment of tax, which will become due on the occurrence of a chargeable event. The death of your father without a new undertaking being made by yourself is a chargeable event.

Your question hints that your client would be prepared or even pleased to sell the painting. There would be a substantial tax advantage if he could arrange to sell the painting by private treaty to a heritage body instead of in the open market. The sale price is calculated by HMRC in such a way that the seller keeps 25% of the benefit of the exemption (10% for land and property) and the remaining 75% (or 90%) of the tax goes to the heritage body. The seller's 25% is called the 'douceur'. There is a list of heritage bodies in IHTA 1984, Sch. 3.

Private treaty sales to heritage bodies are free not only from IHT but also from capital gains tax (CGT) and value added tax (VAT) and this is taken into account when calculating the 'douceur'.

Example

If the market value of the painting is £100,000 and it is to be sold by private treaty to, say, 'The National Art Collections Fund':

- CGT that would be payable is, say, £10,000.
- IHT exemption granted on a previous transfer and now recoverable, say 40% of £90,000 (i.e. market value less CGT) is £36,000.
- Total tax of £46,000 (is a virtual figure and actually given up by HMRC).

Net value after tax £54,000 plus 'douceur' £11,500 (£46,000 × 25%) totalling £65,500 is paid by the heritage body to your client.

Thus the heritage body obtains the painting at less than market value and your client is paid £65,500 and all deferred and current IHT and CGT liabilities are cleared.

See *British Master Tax Guide* 7346.

Law: IHTA 1984, Sch. 3

41-160 Use of pilot trusts

> **Q.** My client has five grandchildren and an estate of approximately £1.25m. His children are wealthy in their own right and as he is a widower he wants to leave his estate to his grandchildren. Another adviser has told him that setting up pilot trusts would be a good idea and he has come to me for an explanation. Can you help please?

A. Your client has in excess of the nil rate band for inheritance tax (IHT) in his estate so there will be IHT to pay on his death. The creation of pilot trusts will not affect this IHT but they can mitigate the future IHT due on the ten-year charges and exit charges that will arise on any discretionary trusts set up for the grandchildren.

The actual calculation of the ten-year charge is very complicated but it is increased if other trusts are set up by the same settlor on the same day. These other trusts are called related settlements. Thus if one large trust or three smaller trusts were set up by your client's will, unless the nil rate band increases significantly, there are likely to be substantial ten-year charges.

To avoid the trap of related settlements your client simply sets up, say, five trusts, one for each grandchild, during his lifetime. It is important that they are set up on different days, e.g. Monday trust, Tuesday trust, etc. Pilot trusts are normally set up with a nominal figure, probably £10, but this must not be forgotten as the trust will not exist without an asset.

Don't worry that this is not a scheme. Pilot trusts are accepted by HMRC and are very useful when setting up trusts for grandchildren where trustees may wish to leave the assets in the trust to accumulate to substantial sums for when beneficiaries reach a mature age.

See *British Master Tax Guide* 6880.

41-180 Who owes the tax?

> **Q.** My client's father has died and there are arguments in the family about whose legacies should bear the IHT liability. We will call my client 'A', his brother 'B', and his

sister 'C'. His widow is still alive and only the residue of the estate passed to her. She is not the mother of the children (his first wife died ten years ago) and father wanted to ensure that the family assets would pass to his children. As his estate was complicated I have simplified the main ones into a table:

Asset	Beneficiary	Approximate value £000s
Spanish villa	A	120
London investment property	B	1,250
Family jewellery	C	350
Land in Scotland	A	750
Cash	C	500
Home jointly owned with widow	Widow by survivorship	600
Residue	Widow	700

Father was also the beneficiary of a life interest trust set up by his father. The assets (value approximately £1,000,000) of the trust will be distributed to the children after any IHT has been paid.

The total IHT due on the estate is £1.450m.

The will does not state that any gifts will bear their own tax, or indeed if any are free of tax. What are the normal rules for allocation of the £1.450m IHT?

A. The tax rules governing your query are given in IHTA 1984, s. 211:

'Where personal representatives are liable for tax on the value transferred by a chargeable transfer made on death, the tax shall be treated as part of the general testamentary and administration expenses of the estate, but only so far as it is attributable to the value of property in the United Kingdom which–

(a) vests in the deceased's personal representatives, and
(b) was not immediately before the death comprised in a settlement.

This has effect subject to any contrary intention shown by the deceased in his will.'

The words 'the tax shall be treated as part of the general and testamentary and administration expenses of the estate' mean that the tax must be paid out of the residue of the estate for all legacies except those specified. This is subject to any contrary instructions that have been written in the will.

The first step is to follow the instructions in the will and allocate tax proportionately to any gifts which 'bear their own tax'. From your question none of the gifts fall into this category.

Next we notice that s. 211 only applies to UK property. Property of any nature which is situated outside the UK bears its own tax. Beneficiary A will pay tax of approximately £44,000 on the Spanish villa. This figure is in proportion to the value of the legacy.

Section 221 only applies to assets that 'vest in the deceased's personal representatives'. The family home which was owned as joint tenants with the widow passed to her by survivorship thus also bears its own tax. Fortunately, this is exempt as it has passed to his spouse so the widow has no tax to pay on this.

From s. 221(1)(b) the life interest trust will bear its own tax. The trustees must find tax of approximately £367,000 which is again proportionate to the value in the trust fund. The balance could then be paid out to beneficiaries.

We have gone through the legacies that bear their own tax so the remainder of the tax should be paid from the residue. It can be seen that the residue of £700,000 is insufficient to pay the remaining IHT of £1,039,000. In any event all of the residue will be lost to the widow as it will go towards paying the IHT. Where will the remaining £339,000 be taken from?

Under English law, the order of application of assets is laid down in the *Administration of Estates Act* 1925, s. 34(3) and Sch. 1, Pt. II. Where the estate is solvent, the order of application is as follows:

(1) property undisposed of by will, subject to retention of a fund sufficient to meet any pecuniary legacies;

(2) property not specifically devised or bequeathed but included (whether specifically or by general description) in a gift of residue, subject again to provision for any pecuniary legacies if necessary;

(3) property specifically appropriated or devised or bequeathed (whether specifically or by general description) for the payment of debts;

(4) property charged with, or devised or bequeathed subject to a charge for, the payment of debts;

(5) the fund, if any, retained to meet pecuniary legacies;

(6) property specifically devised or bequeathed, rateably according to value;

(7) property appointed by will under a general power, including entails, rateably according to value.

This gives us the order for payment of the debts therefore we attempt to pay out of pot (1) then if there are still debts we go to pot (2) etc. The effect of this is that in the vast majority of estates, the burden of payment of testamentary expenses (including, as we have already pointed out, IHT so classified) will fall upon residue, point (2). This reinforces the point that shares in residue (including exempt shares) will bear a share of the tax on other parts of the estate as well.

Going down the list the next relevant point is (5), i.e. the pecuniary legacy. Unfortunately C will find that her bequest will mostly be used to pay the IHT leaving her with cash of £161,000 instead of £500,000. The brothers will take their property free of tax.

It can be seen that it is very important for the testator to specify who should pay the tax due if he does not want his beneficiaries to suffer unintended effects.

See *British Master Tax Guide* 7590.

Law: IHTA 1984, s. 211

Value Added Tax

Samples	429
Cost of making asset available	429
Reverse charge for exempt businesses	429
Invoicing procedure and disbursements	430
Compensation	432
Stolen stock	432
Limited partnership VAT	433
Mixed supplies	433
Place of supply	434
Tools to manufacture for export	435
Place of supply of installed goods	436
Goods on sale or return	437
Tax point and invoice date	437
Contract implicitly includes VAT	438
Accounting for part payments	438
Periodical VAT return	439
Input tax relating to a third party	440
Post cessation rent	440
Partially exempt fuel	441
Partial exemption override	442
Partially exempt business	442
Partial exemption provisional and final calculations	443
Sale of capital item under the capital goods scheme	444
DIY barn conversion	445
Finishing a barn conversion	446
Building work for the disabled	447
Installing a stair lift	448
Disabled transport	448
Charity exemptions	449
Donation or taxable income?	450
Option to tax	451
Historic registration	451
Registering ahead of future sales	452
Voluntary registration into the flat-rate scheme	453
Giving up an exemption	453
Late registration	454
Can I deregister?	454
New partner, same VAT number	455
Flat-rate profit	455
Flat-rate – more than one business	455
IR35 and the flat-rate scheme	456

Different margins on goods	456
Second-hand goods scheme	457
Global margins in the second-hand goods scheme	458
Tour operators margin scheme and cash accounting eligibility	459
Correction of errors	459
Late filing penalties	460
Misdeclaration penalty	461
Fuel scale charge	461
Auctioneer's fees and commissions	462
Book royalties	462
Repossessed items	463
Second-hand vehicles	463
Housing development and multiple supplies	464
Mixing business with pleasure	465
Ending a car lease	465
Change of use of property	466
Multi-tasking doctors	467
Converting residential properties	467
Renting residential property	468
Invoicing in euros	469
EU Sales Lists	469
Transportation of goods	470

VALUE ADDED TAX

50-000 Samples

Example

Sorensen Ltd has introduced a new hand washing machine that it sells to retail outlets throughout the country for £200 plus VAT. A deal is agreed with one of the outlets that they are given a free machine each week to use as a sample and to sell it if they are able. In this case, no VAT is due on the first supply, but a VAT charge of £35 (£200 $\times$ 17.5%) should be made for future samples. This should be done by issuing a VAT only invoice. In reality, this should not prove a problem because the retailer should be able to reclaim the amount back as input tax.

See *British Master Tax Guide* 7762.

Law: VATA 1994, Sch. 4

50-020 Cost of making asset available

Example

Turner Ltd owns a company plane, which is used for business purposes. It is also used for non-business purposes by the owners of the company. Standing costs which accrue by reference to time rather than use, such as depreciation, licensing fees, etc., amount to £4,000 p.a. The usage of the plane (per annum) is as follows:

Business use	30 days
Non-business use	35 days
Not in use	300 days

On the formula historically preferred by HMRC, the amount of the standing costs attributable to non-business use would be £2,154 p.a. (£4,000 $\times$ 35/65). However, following recent court cases HMRC will now accept the answer to be £384 (£4,000 $\times$ 35/365). A substantial saving!

See *British Master Tax Guide* 7762.

50-040 Reverse charge for exempt businesses

Q. My client is an insurance broker making supplies that are exempt from VAT. Recently he has been receiving invoices from Google in Eire for advertising and no Irish VAT has been charged. I am aware of the reverse charge and how to account for it on a

> VAT return, but my client is not VAT-registered. Are there any VAT issues here, or has my client found a way to save VAT costs in his exempt business?

A. Supplies of advertising are covered by VATA 1994, Sch. 5 (services supplied where received). This means that if the supply is to a customer in business in a member state different from that of the supplier, whether the customer is VAT-registered or not, the customer is responsible for accounting for the VAT.

If the customer is already VAT-registered it must do this by applying 17.5% to the invoice figure and accounting for the VAT in box 1 of its VAT return. If the business is entitled to recover input tax then it also puts the same figure into box 4. However, if the business is wholly exempt, then it will not be entitled to recover the VAT as input tax.

The value of the received supply counts towards the taxable turnover of the customer and if a business is not VAT-registered and the value of these received supplies takes it over the VAT registration limit then it may have to register for VAT.

See *British Master Tax Guide* 7768.

Law: *Value Added Tax (Reverse Charge) Order* 1993 (SI 1993/2328)

50-060   Invoicing procedure and disbursements

Example

A registered person supplies standard-rated services to a client for a basic fee of £80. In addition, the supplier incurs £20 expenses which are passed on to the client, but which do not qualify for treatment as disbursements for VAT purposes. The supplier also pays £50 on behalf of the client in circumstances which qualify that payment to be treated as a disbursement.

The supplier must issue a VAT invoice to the client, showing:

	£
Services	80.00
Expenses	20.00
Value for VAT	100.00
17.5% VAT	17.50
Disbursements	50.00
Total	167.50

Examples of supplies which cannot be treated as VAT disbursements include the following:

Example 1

A solicitor pays a fee to a bank for the transfer of funds telegraphically or electronically to, or from, the solicitor's own business or client account. The service for which the charge is made is supplied by the bank to the solicitor rather than to the client. Although the bank's supply may be exempt from VAT, the fee when re-charged, even though at cost, is part of the value of the solicitor's own supply of legal services to the client and VAT is due on the full amount.

Example 2

A solicitor pays a fee for a personal search of official records such as a Land Registry, in order to extract information needed to advise a client. The solicitor cannot treat the search fee as a disbursement for VAT purposes. The fee is charged for the supply of access to the official record and it is the solicitor, rather than the client, who receives that supply. The solicitor uses the information in order to give advice to the client and the recovery of this outlay represents part of the overall value of the solicitor's supply. The solicitor must account for output tax on the full value of the supply.

Example 3

A consultant is instructed by the client to fly to Scotland to perform some work. The consultant cannot treat the air fare as a disbursement for VAT purposes. The supply by the airline is a supply to the consultant, not to the client. The recovery of outlay by the consultant represents part of the overall value of the consultant's supply of services to the client. The consultant must account for output tax on the full value of this supply.

Example 4

A private function is held at a restaurant. The customer pays for the food, drink and other facilities provided, and also agrees to meet the costs of any overtime payments to the staff. The restaurant cannot treat the overtime payments as disbursements for VAT purposes. The supply by the staff is made to the restaurant, not to the customer. The staff costs are part of the value of the supply by the restaurant and VAT is due on the full amount.

Example 5

A manufacturer makes a separate charge to a customer for royalty or licence fees, which were incurred in making a supply to the customer. The manufacturer cannot treat the royalty or licence fees as disbursements for VAT purposes. The recovery of these fees is part of the manufacturer's costs in making the supply to the customer. The manufacturer must account for output tax on the full value of the supply, including the royalty or licence fees.

See *British Master Tax Guide* 7776.

50-080   Compensation

Example 1

Mrs Davis lives in a detached house in Surrey, and has just bought a very expensive garage door for £2,000 plus VAT. After two weeks, she notices that some of the paint is peeling off the garage door. She takes the matter up with the manufacturer, who compensates her with £500 for the poor quality of the product.

The payment by the manufacturer is related to the original supply of the goods, so the manufacturer can treat the £500 payment as a VAT-inclusive refund, and reduce his output tax liability by £74.46 (£500 × 7/47).

Example 2

Mrs Carter lives next door to Mrs Davis and decides to buy the same garage door. After two weeks, she suffers an accident while opening the door, caused by a loose fitting. The door falls on her head and she has to have hospital treatment to deal with her injuries. The garage door company compensates her with £500 for the stress she has suffered.

This time the payment is made to reflect the injuries suffered by Mrs Carter. It is not a specific problem with the goods supplied. Compensation payments of this nature are outside the scope of VAT, so the manufacturer cannot reduce his output tax liability for the payment made.

See *British Master Tax Guide* 7776.

50-100   Stolen stock

> **Q.**   My client has lost a large amount of expensive stock. He discovered recently that employees were selling goods out of sight of the security cameras and have been pocketing the cash. As the money has never gone into the till, does he have to account for VAT on it?

A.   The liability to account for output tax depends on whether a supply has been made. Where goods are stolen, no supply is made by the business, and so no output tax is due. Where goods have been sold and cash is stolen, the goods have been supplied and so output tax remains due on the sales.

In your client's situation, where goods have been sold by his employees from the business premises, supplies would be seen to have been made so he would have to account for VAT on those supplies.

If the employee sold the goods at a lower price and put that amount in the till, that would be the consideration on which VAT is due. An exception to this would be if your client could satisfy HMRC that there has been collusion between the employee and the customer with the intention of depriving the business of the consideration. In that case HMRC will accept that there has been a theft of goods.

See *British Master Tax Guide* 7792–7798.

Law: VATA 1994, s. 3–5

50-120   Limited partnership VAT

> **Q.** I am a director of a VAT-registered limited company. I have recently formed a limited partnership with my limited company being the only general partner and another business being a limited partner. I have received correspondence from HMRC telling me that I am unable to VAT-register the limited partnership as my limited company is already VAT-registered. Is this correct?

A. Yes. A limited partnership is a partnership which consists of one or more general partners who are liable for all of the debts and obligations of the firm and one or more limited partners who, at the time of entering the partnership, contribute a sum as capital and are not liable for debts and obligations of the firm beyond the amount contributed.

If a limited partnership is registered (per s. 5 of the *Limited Partnership Act* 1907) with the Registrar of Companies then HMRC will only raise the registration in respect of the general partners, not any of the limited ones. This is because they cannot hold a limited partner liable for any debts or obligations of the limited partnership. If the limited partnership goes into debt the limited partner is liable to lose only the contribution he made to the partnership, the remaining debt will fall to the general partners.

In this case, because the limited company is already VAT-registered and is the only general partner of the limited partnership, you would be treated as the same legal entity for VAT registration purposes and would not be able to procure separate VAT registrations.

See *British Master Tax Guide* 767, 7792.

Law: FA 2004, s. 124; VATA 1994, s. 3

50-140   Mixed supplies

Example

Item A sells for a VAT-inclusive price of £200 and includes a standard-rated element and a zero-rated element. It has been confirmed that each of the supplies represents an aim in itself, rather than one of the supplies being ancillary to the main supply.

The cost of producing the standard-rated part of the supply is £80 (excluding VAT), and the zero-rated supply, £40. The VAT will be calculated as follows:

The ratio of standard-rated costs compared to total costs needs to include VAT in this example because the selling price is also VAT-inclusive.

$$\frac{£80 + \text{VAT}}{(£80 + \text{VAT}) + £40} = \frac{94}{134}$$

$$\frac{94}{134} \times £200 \times \frac{7}{47} = £20.89 \text{ output tax to pay}$$

In effect, the total selling price can be split:

	£
Standard-rated goods	119.41
Zero-rated goods	59.70
VAT	20.89
Total	200.00

See *British Master Tax Guide* 7806.

Other guidance: VAT Information Sheet 02/01

50-160   Place of supply

Example 1

Gordon is a UK business selling magic wands. It has a retail and wholesale customer base. It is also developing internet selling.

An order is received from a German VAT-registered business. Gordon dispatches the required number of wands to Germany quoting the German VAT registration number on the invoice. The place of supply is where the journey ends – Germany.

A French holiday maker visits Gordon's shop in Scotland and buys a wand. The place of supply is Scotland because this is where the goods are when the supply takes place.

Via the internet Gordon received an order from a private individual in Holland. The wand is posted to Holland by Gordon. The place of supply is Scotland unless Gordon's sales to Holland have exceeded the relevant limit in Holland and Gordon is already registered there for VAT.

Example 2

Macho plc sell furniture. They supply goods to the value of £3,000 to each of certain customers in France and Germany. Their supplies to France and Germany have not exceeded the distance selling threshold and therefore they have not registered and do not have to register for VAT in either of these member states.

Jean in France has a VAT-registered business. He orders several sofas and supplies Macho with his VAT number. The furniture is sent to him and correct documentation is obtained to show that the sofas have left the UK. The invoice sent shows Jean's VAT number and the goods are zero-rated. Jean deals with the VAT implications in France.

Hans in Germany has a business registered for VAT. He orders some tables but he does not supply Macho with his VAT registration number. The correct documentation is obtained showing that the furniture has left the UK. However, because Macho cannot endorse the invoice with Hans's VAT number, the goods are standard-rated.

Macho receive their first order for goods from Slovenia. Renata places an order for some chairs. She is not registered for VAT. Since no VAT number is available the invoice cannot be endorsed with a Slovenian VAT number and the furniture must be standard-rated although proof of the goods leaving the UK is available.

Example 3

Charleen is an Australian wine factor, based in Brisbane. She sells wine to Pat and to Harry, both based in London, and ships the wine to London. The consignment of wine for Pat is imported into the UK in Pat's name. The consignment for Harry is imported in the name of Charleen.

Under the basic rules, both of these supplies are treated as made outside of the UK, since the goods are allocated to the contracts in Australia and this is where transportation commences. However, the place of the supply by Charleen for Harry's consignment, having been imported in Charleen's name, is deemed (under EC law) to be the UK.

See *British Master Tax Guide* 7816.

Law: VATA 1994, s. 7, 14

50-180   Tools to manufacture for export

> **Q.**   We manufacture goods for an Irish company and the goods are then sent to their warehouse near Dublin. As we have their Irish VAT number, we zero-rate the goods. They have now asked us to have a mould manufactured for them, to be used with our machinery in the UK factory. As this will stay in the UK we are unsure as to whether we should charge VAT?

Value Added Tax

A. If this is a machine tool to be used in the manufacture of goods that are to be despatched to another member state or exported outside the EU, you may be able to zero-rate it. The conditions to be met are set out in VAT Notice 701/22 *Tools for the manufacture of goods for export.*

The conditions for zero-rating machine tools used to manufacture goods that will be despatched to other member states are that:

- the tool is an integral part of a contract to supply goods to a VAT-registered customer in another member state and title in the tool passes to the customer;
- you obtain and show on your VAT sales invoice your customer's VAT registration number with its two-digit country code prefix;
- the manufactured goods are sent or transported out of the UK to a destination in another member state;
- you hold commercial documentary evidence that the goods have been removed from the UK.

See *British Master Tax Guide* 7816–7824.

Law: VATA 1994, s. 7, 14

50-200 Place of supply of installed goods

Example

Sidall is a US supplier of computer hardware. It agrees to supply a mainframe computer to Retail Ltd, a company based in Billericay. The contract specifies that the computer is to be installed at Retail Ltd's Billericay head office.

The computer is shipped from Sidall Inc's Seattle factory to Billericay, and installation of it is carried out by Sidall (UK) Ltd, a subsidiary of Sidall Inc, acting as subcontractor to Sidall Inc.

The computer is regarded as supplied in the UK, since that is where it is installed on behalf of the supplier. It will be seen that this rule overrides the basic rule (which would have seen the supply as taking place outside of the UK, as the computer was outside the UK when allocated to the supply).

See *British Master Tax Guide* 7818.

Law: VATA 1994, s. 7, 14

50-220   Goods on sale or return

Example

Perez Ltd delivers 200 bags of fertiliser to Giles Farms Ltd, on sale or return terms, on 1 January 2009. On 1 July 2009 Giles Farms Ltd appropriates 100 bags of fertiliser, and returns 50 bags to Perez Ltd. No decision is taken whether to appropriate the remaining 50 bags until some time in 2010. The basic tax point for 100 bags of fertiliser arises on 1 July 2009. The 50 bags returned will clearly never be supplied. The basic tax point for the 50 bags still held by Giles Farms Ltd arises on 1 January 2010, and Perez Ltd must account for the tax on this supply by including it on its VAT return for the period in which that date falls.

See *British Master Tax Guide* 7832.

Law: VATA 1994, s. 6(2), (3)

50-240   Tax point and invoice date

Example

A Ltd makes VAT returns for quarters ending on 31 March, etc. B Ltd makes returns for quarters ending on 30 April, etc.

On 25 March, A and B exchange contracts for A to supply a taxable building to B for £5m plus VAT of £875,000. The deposit is held by A's solicitor as stakeholder. Completion is to take place on 5 May.

In the normal course of events the tax point for the supply would arise on 5 May. A would be obliged to account for the tax on its June return, making payment by 31 July. B would recover the input tax on its July return.

However, if A issues a tax invoice for the supply during April, this will create a tax point and enable B to recover the input tax on its April return, while A would still account for the output tax on its June return.

The kind of cash-flow benefit illustrated is frequently missed in practice simply because the parties are unaware of each other's VAT periods. In the case of substantial transactions, it can be well worth asking the other side for this information which can be used to the benefit of both parties. The provisions concerning disclosure of schemes must, however, now be taken into account in such situations.

See *British Master Tax Guide* 7832–7834.

Law: VATA 1994, s. 6

437

50-260   Contract implicitly includes VAT

Example

Harry contracts to sell goods to Agnes for £8,000. The contract does not mention VAT. Legislation provides that, where a supply is made for a consideration in money, the price includes VAT. Thus, Harry must account for VAT out of the £8,000 which he receives from Agnes. This will cost him £1,191.48 (being $^7/_{47}$ of £8,000).

If Harry had thought about VAT he might have contracted to supply the goods for £8,000 plus VAT. Then he would have received £9,400 from Agnes and would have had £8,000 left after paying £1,400 of VAT.

See *British Master Tax Guide* 7846.

Law: VATA 1994, s. 19(2)

50-280   Accounting for part payments

Example 1

Accounting for VAT when a part payment is made against one invoice:

Invoice A	£
Standard-rated goods	1,000
VAT	175
Total	1,175

Step 1   If a payment of £750 is made against invoice A, determine what percentage of that payment represents VAT as follows:

$$\frac{750}{1,175} \times 100 = 64\%$$

Step 2   Multiply the amount of VAT charged by the percentage calculated at Step 1.

£175 × 64% = £112

In this example £112 of the £750 payment received should be accounted for as VAT.

The remaining £63 VAT still due to HMRC should be accounted for when further payment is received.

Example 2

Accounting for VAT on a single payment made against more than one invoice, or against invoices for supplies at different rates of tax.

	Invoice B	Invoice C
Date	1/5/10	26/5/10
	£	£
Standard-rated goods	1,000	2,000
Zero-rated goods		1,000
VAT	175	350
Total	1,175	3,350

If a payment of £2,500 is made against invoices B and C which does not relate to any particular supply you should allocate it as follows:

Step 1   Allocate £1,175 of the £2,500 to the earliest supply, i.e. invoice B and account for VAT of £175.

Step 2   The balance of the payment of £1,325 should then be allocated against the later supply as in Example 1 above.

$$\frac{1,325}{3,350} \times 100 = 39\%$$

£350 × 39% = £136.50

In this example £311.50 (£175 + £136.50 = £311.50) of the £2,500 payment should be accounted for as VAT against the £525 VAT due.

See *British Master Tax Guide* 7846–7850.

Law: VATA 1994, s. 19

50-300   Periodical VAT return

Example

Henrietta is a consultant and makes quarterly VAT returns. Her records for the last three months show that she has made supplies with a value of £8,000 plus VAT (at 17.5%) of £1,400. She has incurred VAT of £175 on various expenses, and has also purchased a computer for £2,500 plus £437.50 VAT.

Her VAT return for the quarter will show:

	£
VAT due on supplies made	1,400.00
Less: VAT suffered on supplies obtained (£175 + £437.50)	(612.50)
Net amount due to HMRC	787.50

See *British Master Tax Guide* 8040.

Law: VATA 1994, s. 1, 3, 24

50-320   Input tax relating to a third party

> **Q.**   My limited company obtained a business development loan to buy a new computer system. The bank has agreed this loan but has requested that the company reimburse them for the legal fees in setting up the loan. Can the company recover this VAT?

A.   No. The supply of the legal services has been made to the bank. The bank have not supplied legal services to the company, they have merely used those services in order to provide the business development loan. The input tax was not incurred by your business and does not relate to your business and is therefore not recoverable.

See *British Master Tax Guide* 8040.

Law: VATA 1994, s. 1, 3

50-340   Post cessation rent

> **Q.**   I am a director of a manufacturing company that is ceasing to trade. The property we were trading from is leased and the lease has two years left to run. The lease contains a non-termination clause and we will be required to pay rent and service charges until the end of the term of the original lease. We will cancel the VAT registration as we will be making no more taxable supplies but would we be entitled to recover the VAT on the ongoing rent and service charges?

A.   Yes, if you have a lease that contains a non-termination clause and you cease to trade but are still required to pay any rents and service charges under the terms of the lease then you may recover the VAT.

In *I/S Fini H v Skatteministeriet* the ECJ ruled that art. 4(1)–(3) of the sixth directive is interpreted so that a person who had ceased an economic activity but who continued to pay the rent and charges on the premises used for that activity, because the lease contained a non-termination clause, is a taxable person entitled to deduct the VAT on the amounts paid, provided that there was a direct and immediate link between the payments made and the commercial activity and that there was no fraudulent or abusive intent.

The VAT registration would be cancelled in the normal way and then the ongoing input tax claims would be submitted as VAT 427 claims.

See *British Master Tax Guide* 8074.

Law: *I/S Fini H v Skatteministeriet* (Case C-32/03) [2007] BVC 415

Other guidance: HMRC Notice 700/11

50-360   Partially exempt fuel

> **Q.**   I am the director of a limited company letting out commercial properties that have been opted to tax. The company has recently purchased another commercial property which cannot be opted as it is let to charity for its non-business activities and we understand that an option to tax will not apply in those circumstances. We are therefore caught under partial exemption. We are doing our first quarterly partial exemption calculation and are happy with the partial exemption workings, apart from the fact that we recover all of the VAT on our petrol for company cars and pay a scale charge back to HMRC. Are we entitled to continue to recover all of our petrol?

A.   HMRC internal guidance V1-15 section 19 19.9 confirms that where a partly exempt business uses a vehicle for private motoring, the input tax incurred on the petrol can be recovered provided the petrol scale charge is declared in the same way as a fully taxable business. In order to recover this input tax, the business and private motoring petrol expenses must be separated. The input tax in respect of any private motoring is fully recoverable while the input tax in respect of business motoring is recoverable to the extent that the vehicle involved is used to make taxable supplies.

For businesses that are unable to separate business and private motoring, the scale charge may be reduced to equal the percentage of input tax recoverable under the partial exemption method. This means, for example, that where only 80% of the input tax is recovered, only 80% of the appropriate scale charge will be declared. When the annual adjustment is carried out, the scale charge must also be adjusted.

When using an outputs-based method, a business is entitled to include the net value of the scale charge within the partial exemption top line calculation to work out the percentage to apply to the non-attributable input tax.

See *British Master Tax Guide* 106, 8110–8128, 8230.

Law: VATA 1994, s. 26, 56, Sch. 9

50-380 Partial exemption override

Example

ABC Estate Agents Ltd incurs a lot of input tax on building costs and the directors feel that the standard method does not give a fair recovery of residual input tax. They apply to HMRC for a special method to recover input tax on building costs based on the number of employees who work in the taxable part of the business (ten) and the number of staff who work in the exempt part of the business (six). The proposed method will mean that ten-sixteenths of input tax on building costs will be reclaimed.

Having applied on 1 May 2010, the method was approved by HMRC on 1 June 2010 and became effective from 1 July 2010.

Two years later, an alert VAT officer identifies that all of the employees working in the taxable part of the business work from home, and that the building used by the business is only the base for staff employed for the mortgage activity.

The officer is likely to challenge the 'fair and reasonable' certification of the application back in May 2010 and use his powers to retrospectively assess any overclaim of residual input tax since the method was introduced.

See *British Master Tax Guide* 8144–8150.

Law: *Value Added Tax Regulations* 1995 (SI 1995/2518), reg. 102

50-390 Partially exempt business

> **Q.** My client runs a small dress shop. She also owns two flats above the shop which she rents out and this means that her business is partially exempt. My client maintains the books and records of the business manually and finds partial exemption calculations both complicated and time-consuming. Are there any simplification measures that I can advise my client of to make partial exemption less burdensome for her?

A. HMRC recently announced four changes to the partial exemption standard calculation method. Two of the changes, which are optional, may be of interest to your client as they are intended as simplification measures.

The first change is that a business can now use its previous year's recovery percentage to determine the provisional recovery of residual input tax in each VAT return in the following tax year. An annual adjustment is done at the year-end, using the figures for the full year as normal, with the resulting percentage used as the recovery rate for the following year. By using a provisional recovery rate, a business will have simpler VAT accounting for certain periods in the year.

The second change is that for tax years ending on or after 30 April 2009, businesses can now choose to include their annual adjustment in the last VAT return of the tax year, instead of the first VAT return following the end of the tax year. This reduces the number of calculations that your client has to carry out from five to four.

See *British Master Tax Guide* 8144–8150.

Other guidance: HMRC Brief 19/09; VAT Information Sheet 04/09

50-400   Partial exemption provisional and final calculations

Example

A trader's input tax analysis for the VAT year to 31 March 2009 is as follows:

	Taxable input tax	Exempt input tax	Below de minimis?	Deductible input tax
	£	£		£
30/06/08	6,200	1,900	No	6,200
30/09/08	6,100	1,450	Yes	7,550
31/12/08	8,450	1,600	Yes	10,050
31/03/09	4,200	1,850	Yes	4,200
	24,950	6,800		28,000

The annual adjustment is as follows:

	£
Taxable input tax	24,950
Exempt input tax	6,800
Total	31,750

Exempt input tax is no more than both £625 per month and 50% of all the input tax   £7,500

	£
Therefore tax recoverable	31,750
Tax previously recovered	(28,000)
Giving a further deduction of	3,750

This further deduction of £3,750 should be entered on the trader's VAT return for the quarter to 30 June 2009.

See *British Master Tax Guide* 8152.

Law: *Value Added Tax Regulations* 1995 (SI 1995/2518), reg. 99(1)(a)

50-420 Sale of capital item under the capital goods scheme

Example

Anne, a partially-exempt trader, purchases computer equipment on 25 August 2008 at a cost of £100,000 plus £17,500 VAT. The VAT periods end on 30 June, 30 September, 31 December and 31 March.

Two years later the computer is sold for £15,000 plus £2,625 VAT.

The recoverable proportion of the input tax, from the partial-exemption calculations, which is attributable to taxable and exempt supplies is as follows:

Year to 31 March during which the computer was bought	60%
Year to following 31 March	50%
Year to following 31 March during which the computer is sold	65%

The 'adjustment intervals' are as follows:

(1)   25 August 2008 to the following 31 March

(2)   Year to 31 March 2009

(3)   Year to 31 March 2010

(4)   Year to 31 March 2011

(5)   Year to 31 March 2012

There are still five intervals to be adjusted even though the computer is sold during the third one.

Initial interval
Recoverable input tax £17,500 × 60% = £10,500

Interval 2
The adjustment percentage is 50% − 60% = −10%

As this is negative, some input tax must be refunded to HMRC as follows:

10% × (£17,500/5) = £350

Interval 3

The adjustment percentage is 65% − 60% = +5%

The adjustment is 5% × (£17,500/5) = £175

This is reclaimable from HMRC.

Intervals 4 and 5

The taxable use in intervals 4 and 5 is 100% because the disposal was standard-rated.

The adjustment percentage for both years is therefore: 100% − 60% = +40%

With the adjustments for both years = 40% × (£17,500/5) = 1,400

Overall the business recovered (repaid to HMRC) the following input tax:

Interval	Recovered/(repaid)
	£
1	10,500
2	(350)
3	175
4	1,400
5	1,400
	13,125
Less: output tax	(2,625)
Balance	10,500

The balance of £10,500 is repayable to HMRC, unless HMRC use their discretion to treat the above as a genuine case.

(*Note*: The temporary reduction in the standard rate of VAT from 17.5% to 15% between 1 December 2008 and 31 December 2009 has been ignored for the purposes of this example.)

See *British Master Tax Guide* 8186–8188.

Other guidance: HMRC Notice 706/2

50-430   DIY barn conversion

> **Q.**   My wife and I converted a barn to a dwelling for us to live in personally, which was completed a year ago. We engaged contractors to do the work who charged us 5% VAT and, once the conversion was completed, we submitted our DIY VAT claim to HMRC. We included all of our invoices from the contractors, submitted the claim within the

three-month time-limit and the claim was repaid by HMRC. Now, nine months later, we have received a late invoice with 5% VAT on from a contractor who should have been VAT-registered at the time and the invoice relates to the supply and installation of a very expensive stained glass window in the house. Can we put in another claim for VAT to HMRC or are we outside the time-limit?

A. There are a few particular circumstances where a further claim for VAT on a DIY build or conversion can be made outside the three-month period. A supplementary payment may be allowed for invoices:

- relating to retentions;
- erroneously omitted from the original claim; or
- issued late by contractors.

So therefore, in your case, you may submit a further claim to claim back the input tax on this invoice. This is confirmed in HMRC Manual V1-8A section 22, para. 22.12.

See *British Master Tax Guide* 8222.

50-440   Finishing a barn conversion

Q. I am purchasing a barn that has been partly converted into a house by another developer who ran out of funds and was unable to complete the conversion. He is selling it to me with no VAT as he tells me the sale is zero-rated because it is the first grant of a major interest. When I sell it on, after completing the conversion, will my supply be exempt and does that mean I will be prevented from recovering input tax on the remaining work that needs to be carried out to finish the conversion?

A. In certain circumstances more than one person can zero-rate the grant of a major interest in a dwelling.

The *Value Added Tax Act* 1994, Sch. 8, Grp. 5, Item 1(a) zero-rates the first grant by a person constructing a building designed as a dwelling and item 1(b) zero-rates the first grant by a person converting a non-residential building into a building designed as a dwelling. HMRC guidance manuals state that there are circumstances where more than one person can have 'person constructing' status and can zero-rate the respective grants of a major interest.

Therefore if a developer who partly constructs a dwelling past foundation stage then sells it when it is partly constructed to a second developer who then completes and sells it then the grant of the major interest in each case will qualify for zero-rating.

In addition to 'person constructing', the above also applies to a person converting a building from non-residential use into a house, flats or relevant residential building. The guidance manual indicates that where planning permission has been given for an acceptable conversion and the work in accordance with that planning permission has commenced, more than one person throughout the conversion may have 'person converting' status and grant a zero-rated major interest in that property.

See *British Master Tax Guide* 8222.

Law: VATA 1994, Sch. 8

50-460   Building work for the disabled

Q. My client is a builders' merchant and has been asked by a disabled person to zero-rate the sale of materials that will be used in works to his house that would not ordinarily qualify for zero-rating. He has been told that the works are to be carried out by a local builder who is not VAT-registered. I always thought that materials had to be supplied and fitted by the same person in order to be zero-rated with the building works. Is this different because of the disability aspect?

A. There are various factors here. First, you are correct that, in the case of the zero-rating of construction services of new-build dwellings, relevant residential and relevant charitable buildings, and approved alterations to listed buildings, the building materials are only zero-rated when they are supplied by the person supplying the zero-rated building services.

However, the wording in VATA 1994, Sch. 8, Grp. 12 (drugs, medicines, aids for the handicapped, etc.), which covers the zero-rating of goods and materials for qualifying works for the handicapped, is different. Item 13 zero-rates the supply of materials but only refers to 'the supply of goods *in connection with a supply* described in items 8, 9, 10 or 11' (the qualifying building works) and it does not specify that the supply of the materials must be by the person supplying the services.

There is a tribunal case (*Flather*) in which this issue was considered. The services, to be carried out by unregistered builders, were of building ramps and widening passageways, and the tribunal decided that the supply of materials by a different supplier (a builders' merchant) was clearly *in connection with* those supplies, and qualified for zero-rating by the builders' merchant.

On a practical level, your client needs to be sure that the labour for the building works is to be supplied by way of business, and not done free of charge by a friend or relative or in a DIY capacity, and that the works would qualify to be zero-rated if supplied by a VAT-registered builder.

See *British Master Tax Guide* 8222.

Law: VATA 1994, Sch. 8; *Flather* [1995] BVC 780

50-470   Installing a stair lift

Q. I am a VAT-registered builder and I have been asked to install a stair lift and handrail in an elderly person's house. I quoted for the work including VAT at 17.5% as normal but my customer has challenged this and advised me that I should only be charging 5% reduced rate on the supply and installation. I have never heard of any of this except for zero-rating certain things for disabled people but my customer is not disabled, just over 60, is he correct?

A. Yes, with effect from 1 July 2007 the supply and installation of certain mobility aids are eligible for VAT at the 5% reduced rate. This reduced rate applies to supplies to people over the age of 60 where the work is in their personal domestic accommodation. It applies to:

- grab rails;
- ramps;
- stair lifts;
- bath lifts;
- built-in shower seats or showers containing built in shower seats; and
- walk-in baths with sealable doors.

The reduced rate applies to the supply and installation of these items, but not if it is the supply of the goods alone and it does not apply to any repairs or replacements of those goods. *Revenue & Customs Brief* 47/07 provides guidance on this subject.

See *British Master Tax Guide* 8210.

50-480   Disabled transport

Q. I run a taxi firm. I have recently decided to expand my business and so I purchased a mini bus with ten seats. I then had work carried out to accommodate wheelchair users. Six of the seats have been taken out and adaptations made to the floor of the vehicle to secure the wheelchairs. I have been charging VAT on my fares to wheelchair users but a customer recently advised me that I should not be charging VAT. Is this correct?

A. The zero-rating of passenger transport generally only applies to passenger transport in a vehicle, ship or aircraft designed or adapted to carry ten or more passengers. The driver and crew are treated as passengers for the purposes of determining the carrying capacity (VATA 1994, Sch. 8, Grp. 8, item 4(a)). However, transport in a vehicle that has been modified to cater for the special needs of people with disabilities and has had its carrying capacity reduced to less than ten persons, thus disqualifying it from zero-rating under item 4(a), may be zero-rated by extra-statutory concession provided certain conditions are met.

The concession was introduced to prevent transport in vehicles with a conventional seating capacity of ten or more passengers (which would have qualified for zero-rating of passenger transport) being taxed when they carried less than that capacity after adaptation for people with disabilities. It covers private operators and local authorities, even in circumstances where that authority makes commercial charges.

The concession applies to transport in a vehicle which has:

- a nominal carrying capacity of ten or more persons conventionally seated; and
- a carrying capacity of less than ten persons when equipped with conventional seats and/ or facilities specifically designed for the use of passengers with disabilities.

If the vehicle also complies with these conditions it will be treated as if it had, at all times, a carrying capacity of not less than ten persons. To take advantage of the concession, suppliers must apply to their local VAT Business Advice Centre for approval of each qualifying vehicle. The application must be in writing and give details of the vehicle together with a declaration that it conforms with the structural criteria and conditions set out. Suppliers of transport services who buy a vehicle to which approval to operate the concession has previously been given must apply to their local VAT Business Advice Centre for approval in their own name.

See *British Master Tax Guide* 8222.

Law: VATA 1994, Sch. 8

Other guidance: HMRC Notice 744

50-500   Charity exemptions

What is the VAT effect of each of the following charity auction scenarios?

Example 1

A local fund-raising committee organises an auction for local charities. The committee is not a charity. Goods are given to it for the auction. It runs the auction and gives the proceeds to the charities. Title to the goods passed to the committee and therefore they made the sale. As a non-qualifying body, the proceeds are taxable.

Example 2

As above, except that the goods were sold by the committee acting as agent for the donors, i.e. title never passed to the committee. The sale is still by a non-qualifying body (the donors) but no VAT needs to be paid on sales unless the donors are VAT-registered.

In this example, the donors could not use the zero-rating for goods donated to charities for sale as they are not giving the goods – they are giving the sale proceeds.

Example 3

As in Example 1, except that the goods were donated to a charity and the committee sold them as agent for the charity. The conditions of the relief are met and therefore zero-rating applies.

Example 4

An artist agrees to sell a work at a charity auction. Title in the work does not pass to the charity but it is agreed that the sale proceeds will be shared equally between the artist and the charity. Providing that the bidding documentation makes it clear that the proceeds will be split, the artist is only liable to VAT on his share, with the charity's share being partly consideration for its services in promoting the auction and partly a donation by the buyer.

See *British Master Tax Guide* 8230.

Law: VATA 1994, Sch. 9

50-520   Donation or taxable income?

Example

The treasurer of Hale Football Club is keen to reduce the club's output tax liability. He has decided to change current policy so that instead of charging spectators £10 to watch the game as an admission charge (standard-rated supply), he will erect a sign at the entrance to the club saying: 'Free entry – donation of £10 recommended'. His thinking is that a donation is outside the scope of VAT (a correct conclusion), therefore avoiding any output tax liability.

The key test is to understand what happens when a spectator arrives at the entry point to the ground and decides that he is not going to pay his £10 donation but still wants to see the game. If he is allowed in without charge, then the arrangement is a genuine situation of a donation. If, however, there is pressure on him to make payment or entry is refused, then the sign at the entrance is misleading, and the reality is that the club is still making a £10 admission charge that is standard-rated.

As a final point, the analysis above highlights a very important principle of VAT that applies in many situations, namely that the actual facts of a situation are more relevant than any written agreement, notice or contract.

See *British Master Tax Guide* 8230.

Law: VATA 1994, Sch. 9

50-540   Option to tax

Example

A developer bought a freehold warehouse in a city centre in Wales. After the developer had elected to tax the building, he sold the freehold of the building to a fully-exempt person. The developer's profit is calculated as follows:

	£
Building sale proceeds	3,000,000
Less: output tax	
7/47 × £3,000,000	(446,808)
building and land cost	(1,700,000)
refurbishment cost	(200,000)
Profit (if election)	653,192

What if the developer does not opt to tax?

	£
Building sale proceeds	3,000,000
Less: output tax	
building and land cost	(1,700,000)
refurbishment cost	(200,000)
VAT not recovered	
17.5% × £200,000	(35,000)
Profit (without election)	1,065,000

See *British Master Tax Guide* 8230.

Law: VATA 1994, Sch. 10

50-560   Historic registration

Example 1

A business expects to turn over up to £45,000 per month from commencement.

At the end of month 1 its turnover has not exceeded the registration threshold but at the end of month 2 its turnover has exceeded the turnover limit, and notification of liability to register must be made within 30 days. The business is then registered from the first day of month 4.

Value Added Tax

Over the first three months of trading the business has turned over £135,000 free of VAT, saving output tax of £20,106 ($^7/_{47}$ of £135,000). Against this must be set any loss of input tax.

The deferment of registration may not be particularly valuable for businesses with high levels of input tax, such as those dealing in standard-rated goods, who may prefer to accept a slight cost for greater administrative simplicity and elimination of risk, by registering early as an intending trader.

Where a person is liable to be registered under the future turnover rule, he or she is required to notify HMRC before the end of the 30-day period. That person is then registered from the beginning of that period so, for example:

Turnover is expected to exceed the specified limit in the 30 days beginning 15 May 2010.

Liability to notify: before 14 June 2010.

Registration with effect from 15 May 2010.

Where both tests are breached simultaneously the future test will take precedent as follows.

Example 2

John commences in business in January 2010. During May 2010, his cumulative turnover exceeds £68,000, necessitating registration with effect from 1 July 2010. However, on 20 May 2010, he agrees a single order worth £70,000, to be delivered and invoiced within 30 days. This necessitates registration with effect from 20 May 2010 irrespective of the historic breach.

See *British Master Tax Guide* 8256–8262.

Law: VATA 1994, Sch. 1

50-580   Registering ahead of future sales

> **Q.** My client is a well-known entertainer who was VAT-registered in the past. Over recent years his popularity waned and he fell below the turnover threshold and so although he continued to receive royalties, he was deregistered for VAT. His record company have now decided to issue a Greatest Hits album and he will receive an advance of royalties of £75,000 in the next few weeks. Will he have to VAT-register again, what will be the effective date and will this first royalty payment attract VAT?

A. Yes. Your client will have to register for VAT on the 'forward look' as per VATA 1994, Sch. 1, para. 1(1)(b) which outlines that a person not already registered must register at any time, if there are reasonable grounds for believing that the value of his taxable supplies in the period of 30 days then beginning will exceed the registration threshold. He must notify HMRC before the end of that 30-day period and the effective date of the registration will be the date that he first formed the expectation and so the first royalty payment will be liable to VAT.

If your client were confident that the release would be unsuccessful he could argue that his taxable supplies would fall back below the registration threshold and request permission from HMRC not to register for the one payment.

See *British Master Tax Guide* 8256.

Law: VATA 1994, Sch. 1

50-600   Voluntary registration into the flat-rate scheme

Example

Jean is a self-employed secretary, earning £58,000 p.a. She has never registered for VAT. She mainly works from home, so has taken the view that because she would have negligible input tax, there would be no benefit in registering for VAT, even though all of her clients are VAT-registered and would be able to recover any VAT she charged as input tax.

If Jean becomes VAT-registered on a voluntary basis, and applies to use the flat-rate scheme, she will charge output tax of £10,150 on her sales (i.e. £58,000 $\times$ 17.5%). However, the flat-rate percentage for secretarial services is 11% of gross turnover, so she will actually pay HMRC an amount of £7,496.50 ((£58,000 plus VAT) $\times$ 11%). On the basis that Jean has negligible amounts of input tax to claim, she is gaining £2,653.50 p.a. by registering for VAT and using the flat-rate scheme.

A newly registered business also benefits from a 1% discount on the flat rates in the first 12 months, so Jean would save an additional £681.50 in her first year.

See *British Master Tax Guide* 8260, 8365.

Law: VATA 1994, s. 26B, Sch. 1

50-620   Giving up an exemption

> **Q.**   I have been trading for some time but applied for exemption from VAT registration because my supplies are all zero-rated and I had little input tax to make registration cost effective. However, I am about to refurbish my trading premises, so it would now make sense to be registered to recover the input tax. Can I change my mind and apply to become VAT-registered?

A. You can withdraw from exemption as long as you continue to make taxable supplies. The registration can only be from a current date. To withdraw from exemption you should submit a completed VAT 1 application form and return the form VAT 8 that would have been issued when you were first allowed exemption from registration.

See *British Master Tax Guide* 8264.

Law: VATA 1994, Sch. 1

50-640   Late registration

Example

Fred registers for VAT belatedly. His first return VAT period runs from 1 October 2008 to 31 July 2010. The first normal return will be for the three months to 31 October 2010. The 21-month return covers a special accounting period which must be subdivided into the following periods:

Longer period 1:   01/10/08 to 30/04/09
Longer period 2:   01/05/09 to 30/04/10
Longer period 3:   01/05/10 to 31/07/10

The breakdown will always be periods up to the end of the 'VAT year' of 30 April.

See *British Master Tax Guide* 8270.

Law: VATA 1994, s. 3(1), Sch. 1

50-660   Can I deregister?

Example

Mr A trades as an architect, working for the general public, making taxable supplies of £72,000 per year (£6,000 per month). Next year, he plans to take a six-week holiday in Australia, so his expected turnover for the year will be £65,500 and he is therefore thinking of deregistering. While Mr A meets the turnover tests, one important rule as far as the deregistration limit is concerned is that the fall in turnover must not be because a business intends to suspend trading for 30 days or more. This rule therefore prevents Mr A from applying for deregistration.

See *British Master Tax Guide* 8274.

Law: VATA 1994, Sch. 1

50-680   New partner, same VAT number

Mr Smith takes on Mr Jones as a business partner on 1 January 2010 and form VAT 68 is completed to retain the same VAT number. Six months later, a VAT inspection identifies underpaid VAT for the June 2009 period, an amount of £10,000 being due.

Mr Jones and Mr Smith are equally liable for the VAT debt, even though it was relevant to the period when the business was wholly owned by Mr Smith though it is possible that a legal agreement may be in place giving Mr Jones protection against situations like the one mentioned. However, Mr Jones's position would have been protected if he had insisted on a new VAT registration at the time when he became a partner in the business.

See *British Master Tax Guide* 8316.

50-700   Flat-rate profit

> **Q.**   I have decided to adopt the flat-rate scheme for VAT as I will make a profit on the VAT. Will the profit be taxable?

A.   Yes, the profit on the VAT should be included in the trading profits of your business. When you use the flat-rate scheme you will not calculate VAT on each individual input and output for the VAT account. Instead only the VAT calculated on the flat-rate percentage of turnover will need to be passed to the VAT account.

Expenses will probably be shown inclusive of VAT in your accounts and on the tax return and turnover can be shown net of the flat-rate VAT payment. Alternatively you may show the flat-rate VAT payment as a profit and loss expense rather than deducted from total turnover. If you have a personal service company and are caught by the IR35 rules, then for calculation of the deemed salary it is the VAT-exclusive amount (i.e. the gross amount less the amount of flat-rate VAT payable) that is used in step 1 of the calculation.

See *British Master Tax Guide* 8365.

Law: VATA 1994, s. 26B

50-720   Flat-rate – more than one business

> **Q.**   My partner and I run a gift shop and are registered for VAT. We are considering going on the flat-rate scheme, which will only be 6% for our trade sector. However, we also own a couple of houses in our joint names, which we let out residentially and treat as exempt from VAT. Does the income from these get included in our flat-rate turnover and if so which rate would be used?

A. It is a common misconception that exempt supplies are excluded from the flat-rate scheme and many people are caught out by this, particularly as residential letting is not always treated as a trading activity for direct tax purposes.

However, residential property letting is a business activity for VAT purposes, albeit an exempt one. As such it must be included in the turnover to which you apply the flat-rate percentage. You must apply the flat-rate percentage appropriate to your main business activity as measured by turnover.

This has proved particularly problematic for pubs where food is served. They must decide whether they are a pub serving food or a restaurant serving drinks.

See *British Master Tax Guide* 8365.

Law: VATA 1994, s. 26B

Other guidance: VAT Notice 733

50-740   IR35 and the flat-rate scheme

Q.   My client provides her services via her own limited company through which she invoices her clients. She has recently joined the flat-rate VAT scheme and is now unsure about the invoice value used to calculate income for the starting point for calculating the deemed payment under IR35 rules. Is it based on the figure inclusive of VAT or the figure net of VAT?

A.   The *Employment Status Manual* (ESM3160) states that where an intermediary is registered for VAT, then the net income exclusive of any VAT should be used as the starting point for the assessment of the deemed payment. As your client has joined the VAT flat-rate scheme, it will still be the VAT-exclusive amount (i.e. the gross amount less the amount of flat-rate VAT charged) that should be used. The flat-rate VAT percentage of course will vary according to the sector in which your client operates.

See *British Master Tax Guide* 265, 8365.

Law: ITEPA 2003, Pt. 2, Ch. 8; VATA 1994, s. 26B

50-760   Different margins on goods

Example

Sam's Store is a mixed retail business using the first apportionment scheme. In the year to last 31 December, Sam's purchases are:

	Cost	VAT	Total
	£	£	£
Food (all zero-rated)	170,000	–	170,000
Non-food (all standard-rated)	140,000	24,500	164,500
Total purchases	310,000	24,500	334,500

On his food purchases, Sam made an average profit on sales of 15%, so that if he had been using a point-of-sale scheme his zero-rated takings would have been £200,000. However, on his non-food purchases Sam makes 30% (excluding VAT) so that his standard-rated takings would have been £200,000 plus VAT of £35,000, i.e. £235,000. His total takings are therefore £435,000 and his VAT liability for the year would have been £35,000 (stock losses ignored and assuming all goods purchased are sold in the period).

Under the first apportionment scheme, the liability would work out as follows:

		£
Standard-rated purchases (VAT-inclusive)		164,500
Total purchases (VAT-inclusive)		334,500
Sales apportioned	$\dfrac{164,500}{334,500} \times 435,000$	213,924
Output tax	$7/47 \times 213,924$	31,861

Sam's VAT saving by using the first apportionment scheme is therefore £3,139 (being £35,000 − £31,861) for the year.

See *British Master Tax Guide* 8386.

50-780   Second-hand goods scheme

Example

Bert Cod is a freelance fisherman, and is registered for VAT. He wishes to buy a boat for use in his business. Harry Tub is prepared to sell him a second-hand boat for £20,875. Harry is selling the boat under the second-hand goods scheme for boats. He bought it for £15,000, and the sale price of £20,875 includes £875 in respect of VAT (£875 is 17.5% of (£20,000 − £15,000)). Harry therefore expects to receive £20,000 net after paying the VAT to HMRC.

The net cost to Bert of buying the boat under the second-hand goods scheme will be £20,875, as he cannot reclaim any of the VAT on the purchase. Bert would do better to buy the boat from Harry outside of the scheme, for £20,000 plus £3,500 VAT (at 17.5%). Bert would be able to reclaim the VAT, so his net cost would be £20,000, while Harry would still receive the same net price.

See *British Master Tax Guide* 8392.

Law: FA 1995, s. 24; VATA 1994, s. 32, 50A

50-800   Global margins in the second-hand goods scheme

Example

In period 03/10, Frances, a taxable person, makes purchases of £14,500, and sales of £18,260.

In period 06/10, she makes purchases of £21,400, and sales of £19,800.

In period 09/10, she makes purchases of £13,000 and sales of £19,300.

She accounts for output tax as follows:

		£
P03/10	Global margin (£18,260 − £14,500)	3,760
Output tax	£3,760 × 7/47	560
P06/10	Global margin (£19,800 − £21,400)	(1,600) – negative margin
Output tax		Nil
P09/10	Global margin (£19,300 − £13,000 − £1,600)	4,700
Output tax	£4,700 × 7/47	700

In the first period in which a person uses global accounting, they are entitled to add any stock in hand at the start of the period to purchases in that period. Similarly, in the final period in which the person uses global accounting, they must add the purchase price of closing stock to the sales figures for the final prescribed accounting period. The impact on the above example, if there was £24,000 of stock in hand, would be that the first period margin would be negative (£20,240) and no VAT would be charged.

If £11,560 of closing stock was added to the above final period the global margin would rise to £17,860 (ignoring prior period negative margins).

See *British Master Tax Guide* 8392.

Law: VATA 1994, s. 50A

50-820   Tour operators margin scheme and cash accounting eligibility

Example

Andrea arranges UK holidays using a third-party coach operator and third-party hotels. The total cost in the year for transport is £800,000 and for accommodation is £1,600,000. Her total income is £2,600,000.

The amount of VAT due is calculated as follows:

$(£2,600,000 - £1,600,000 - £800,000) \times 7/47 = £29,787$.

The value of her margin scheme supplies is calculated as follows:

$£2,600,000 - £1,600,000 - £800,000 - £29,787 = £170,213$.

Thus, although the cash throughput of her business is £2.6m, Andrea's taxable turnover is around £170,000. She is therefore eligible to use the cash accounting scheme.

See *British Master Tax Guide* 8404–8410.

Law: VATA 1994, s. 53

Other guidance: VAT Notice 731

50-840   Correction of errors

> **Q.**   I have discovered an underdeclaration of £8,000 in my client's VAT records. How should this be disclosed? I am aware that there were some changes to the rules for reporting VAT errors but am not familiar with the details.

A.   The thresholds at which errors must be notified in writing to HMRC, rather than corrected on later returns have been revised by the *Value Added Tax, etc (Correction of Errors etc) Regulations* 2008 (SI 2008/1482).

The amended rules apply to the correction of errors in earlier accounting periods where the error is discovered on or after 1 July 2008. Previously, VAT errors not exceeding £2,000 could be corrected on the VAT return for the period in which the error was discovered without notifying HMRC. This limit is now increased to the greater of £10,000 VAT, or an amount of VAT equal to 1% of 'turnover', subject to a maximum of £50,000. 'Turnover' is the correct figure to be entered in Box 6 of the VAT return for the period in which the error is discovered. For errors exceeding £50,000, separate notification will always be required.

See *British Master Tax Guide* 8454.

Other guidance: HMRC Notice 700/45

50-860   Late filing penalties

Example 1

ABC Ltd submitted its October 2006 return late and received a default surcharge liability notice. It then submitted its January 2007 and April 2007 returns on time, but made a late payment in July 2007. The payment due for the July 2007 period was £20,500. It was late in October 2007 as well (VAT due was £7,500) and again in January 2008 (VAT due was £3,500).

Having submitted its October 2006 return late, the company needed to be on time and fully compliant with the next four VAT returns up to and including the period ending 31 October 2007. It did not achieve this goal.

The next default in July 2007 attracts the initial 2% penalty (£410), and the next period attracts a 5% penalty (£375). However, because the total penalty is less than the £400 de minimus for a 5% period, then no penalty is issued. The penalty for January 2008 is also less than £400 (£3,500 × 10%) but this penalty is applied because we are no longer in either the 2% or 5% periods.

Example 2

DEF Ltd is in the default surcharge system and liable to a 2% penalty if it defaults in the October 2007 period. It submits the October 2007 return on time, but instead of paying the full tax due amount of £25,000 can only make a part-payment of £5,000. The company's VAT adviser suggests the part-payment be increased to £5,001.

The surcharge penalty is based on the amount of outstanding VAT for the period not paid by the due date. In this particular case, the amount is £19,999. A 2% penalty therefore equates to £399.98 which will be waived because it is less than the £400 de minimis limit. The extra pound makes all the difference!

See *British Master Tax Guide* 8516.

Law: VATA 1994, s. 59

Other guidance: HMRC Notice 700/50

50-880   Misdeclaration penalty

Example

A business has failed to submit its quarterly VAT return (owing £150,000), so HMRC issue a central assessment to estimate the bill, which they assess at £90,000. The business welcomes the £60,000 cash flow saving and pays the £90,000 estimate. It intends to submit the return with the correct figure when funds allow.

Unfortunately, there is a problem with their cunning plan mainly because of the misdeclaration penalty that the business will be liable to if it does not notify HMRC of the true position within 30 days of the assessment being issued.

A 15% misdeclaration penalty could be applied by HMRC if the assessment paid by the business means that the VAT which could have been lost exceeds the lesser of £1m and 30% of the true amount of VAT for the period being £45,000 (£150,000 × 30%).

The VAT which could have been lost is the understated liability of £60,000 and so a penalty of £9,000 could be applied (£60,000 × 15%).

See *British Master Tax Guide* 8528.

Law: VATA 1994, s. 63

50-900   Fuel scale charge

Example

During 2010, an employee uses for private mileage a motor car, which is owned by his employer who provides all the petrol used by the car. The emission figure for the car is stated in Part 4 of Form V5C (Registration certificate) as 140g/km. His employer prepares calendar quarterly VAT returns.

The VAT return for the period from 1 July 2010 to 30 September 2010, i.e. which starts after 30 April 2010, and so the fuel scale charge is based on the CO_2 rating, should declare output tax of £35.89. The gross and net outputs for the fuel scale charge are £241.00 and £205.11 respectively.

If the scale charge for output tax applies, all input tax on privately used fuel can be recovered.

See *British Master Tax Guide* 106.

Law: VATA 1994, s. 57(4A)–(4G) and 57(9)

Other guidance: Notice 700/64/2007, para. 9.1; HMRC Manual V1-12, para. 7.18; and V1-13, para. 19.2; *Revenue & Customs Brief* 13/2007 (12 February 2007)

50-920   Auctioneer's fees and commissions

Example

Mary, an auctioneer, sells an item at £2,000. Her commission is 7.5% plus VAT for the vendor and 10% plus VAT for the buyer.

		£
Vendor's commission	£2,000 × 7.5% + VAT	176.25
Purchase price	£2,000 − £176.25	1,823.75
Buyer's premium	£2,000 × 10% + VAT	235.00
Selling price	£2,000 + £235.00	2,235.00
Auctioneer's margin	£2,235 − £1,823.75	411.25
(this will also equal £176.25 + £235.00)		

Mary's output tax is £411.25 × 7/47 = £61.25.

50-960   Book royalties

> **Q.**   My client is VAT-registered as a consultant and has just finished writing a book that will be published in the UK. Unfortunately we will not know how much he has earned from book sales until the money arrives from the publishers. Where do we stand with regards to invoicing for royalties and accounting for VAT?

A.   Regulation 91 of the *Value Added Tax Regulations* 1995 (1995/2518) covers royalty payments. This states that where the whole amount of the consideration for a supply of services is not ascertainable at the time when the services were performed and subsequently the use of the benefit of those services by a person other than the supplier gives rise to any payment or consideration for that supply which is:

- in whole or in part determined or payable periodically or from time to time or the end of any period; or
- additional to the amount, if any, already payable for the supply; and
- not a payment to which the rules relating to continuous supplies of services apply.

A further supply is treated as taking place each time a payment in respect of the use of the benefit of those services is received, or a VAT invoice is issued, by the supplier, whichever is the earlier.

As the publishers will be in a better position than your client to calculate the royalties due from the book sales, it is usual for them to self-bill. This means they will raise the sales invoice to themselves on behalf of the author and they will send a copy of the invoice to him together with the payment. Your client should notify the publisher that he is VAT-registered and give them his VAT number. The invoice should show the client's VAT number and the output tax due which must be accounted for by him on the date that the payment is received.

See *British Master Tax Guide* 7838.

50-980 Repossessed items

Q. My client buys laptop computers from insurance companies who have taken possession of them in settlement of claims under insurance policies. He repairs the laptops and sells them on to both businesses and to private individuals. How should he account for the VAT on the sales?

A. The disposal of second-hand goods by an insurer who has taken possession of them in settlement of a claim under an insurance policy is outside the scope of VAT provided the goods are in the same condition at the time of disposal as when they were taken into the insurer's possession. The legal reference for this is the *Value Added Tax Special Provisions Order* 1995 (SI 1995/1268), art. 4. As no VAT is charged on the supply of the goods to your client, then they can be sold on under the second-hand margin scheme (and possibly the global accounting scheme if the purchase price of the laptops is £500 or less) provided the conditions of the scheme are satisfied. Public Notice 718: *Margin Schemes for Second-hand Goods, Works of Art, Antiques and Collectors' Items* sets out the conditions and record keeping requirements of the scheme.

See *British Master Tax Guide* 8392.

51-000 Second-hand vehicles

Q. I have a client who deals in second-hand vehicles. He has received an enquiry about one of his vans from a VAT-registered trader and he has been asked to sell it on a VAT invoice. The van was bought in from an individual who was not VAT-registered and didn't charge VAT, so normally my client would just account for VAT on the margin under the second-hand scheme. Does my client have the option of charging VAT and issuing a VAT invoice, and what is the effect?

A. Where goods are eligible for sale under the margin scheme, a business has the choice to use it or to account for VAT on the full selling price. A VAT-registered business may request a VAT invoice on the basis that by recovering the VAT element, the vehicle will cost less; however, whether this is the case will depend on how the parties negotiate the deal:

	£
Purchase price	12,000
Advertised selling price	13,500

If sold on the margin scheme, output tax due would be due on the margin

£1,500 × 7/47 = £223.40

Customer would pay £13,500 with no VAT to recover.

Seller would retain profit margin of £1,276.60 after accounting for VAT.

Clearly, treating the advertised selling price as VAT-inclusive gives the worst outcome for your client, and adding VAT to it, gives the best outcome for him but the worst outcome for the purchaser. As the customer will probably be hoping that claiming the VAT will make the van cheaper for him, your client could negotiate a price by maintaining his profit margin and then adding VAT to the final selling price (calculating it as below):

	£
Purchase price	12,000.00
Profit margin	1,276.60
Total	13,276.60
VAT on total	2,323.40
Final selling price	15,600.00

which gives your client the same income as using the margin scheme, but gives the buyer a better price, after taking into account the deduction of input tax.

See *British Master Tax Guide* 8392.

51-020 Housing development and multiple supplies

Q. My client is a new housing developer. He is buying a piece of land from another developer who has already carried out civil engineering works on the land. The civil engineering works include access to drainage, sewerage, gas and electricity. He is selling the land and civil engineering works to my client without VAT. I have always been of the understanding that the supply should be treated as consisting of two supplies – an exempt supply of land and a standard-rated supply of civil engineering. Please can you clarify the position?

A. HMRC announced a change of policy on the VAT treatment of serviced building plots on 17 October 2007. Prior to this date HMRC did consider the supply of serviced building plots as an exempt supply of land and as standard-rated supply of civil engineering. However, following a VAT tribunal decision in *Virtue & Anor t/a Lammermuir Game Services* HMRC now accept that the supply of a 'serviced building plot' is a single exempt supply of land with no separate standard-rated element. Further details can be found in HMRC *Business Brief* 64/07.

See *British Master Tax Guide* 7806.

Law: *Virtue & Anor t/a Lammermuir Game Services* [2007] BVC 2,518

51-040   Mixing business with pleasure

> **Q.** My client has a dance studio that he uses in his own business and also rents out the rooms to other dance teachers to hold classes. However, he also has the opportunity to let out the smaller studios for meetings. We know that the hiring out of a 'sports facility' is standard-rated, unless the conditions are met for exemption as a series of lets or a let of over 24 hours; however is it still standard-rated if it is let out for a different purpose?

A. You are correct that the hiring of a sports facility is standard-rated but exemption from VAT applies if the relevant conditions are met. For the benefit of readers not familiar with these conditions, they are:

(1)   a 'continuous period' of use exceeding 24 hours; or

(2)   a series of ten or more periods, whether or not exceeding 24 hours in total, where the following conditions are satisfied:

    (a)   each period is in respect of the same activity carried on at the same place;

    (b)   the interval between each period is not less than one day and not more than 14 days;

    (c)   consideration is payable by reference to the whole series and is evidenced by written agreement;

    (d)   the grantee has exclusive use of the facilities; and

    (e)   the grantee is a school, a club, an association or an organisation representing affiliated clubs or constituent associations.

A 'sports facility' is a premises designed or adapted for playing sport or taking part in physical recreation, but is only standard-rated when it is let to be used, and is used for that purpose. A specially designed room let for ballroom dancing would be standard-rated but the same room let for a meeting will be exempt unless your client has opted to tax the property.

See *British Master Tax Guide* 7712.

51-060   Ending a car lease

> **Q.** My client has been leasing a car on a monthly basis and because the vehicle has been used both for business and private purposes, the input tax recovery has been restricted to 50%. The lease agreement is coming to an end and although the client is prohibited from actually buying the car outright, the leasing company have told them that

Value Added Tax

if he finds a buyer then he will receive 95% of the sale proceeds as a 'rebate of rentals'. Please could you clarify how he should treat this for VAT purposes?

A. The correct treatment of such rebates is contained in the HMRC guidance on car leasing and early termination payments (V1-13 Input Tax s. 22.8). Therefore although you do not say whether your client is being charged an early termination sum, it would seem sensible to explain how both matters are dealt with as they often occur simultaneously.

When a finance lease is terminated early, the lessee is normally charged a termination fee. This charge may be offset by a 'rebate' based upon the residual value of the car and in some cases the rebate may exceed the termination charge and the lessee is due a net repayment.

HMRC have agreed that the lessor may choose to treat the termination charge as either:

- an outside the scope compensation payment; or
- consideration for a taxable supply of services.

Whichever treatment they choose is then applied to the countervailing rebate. Where the lessor treats the termination payment as taxable, they often offset the rebate against the termination payment and issue either a tax invoice for a net termination payment or a VAT credit note for a net rebate, as appropriate.

If the lessee is charged a net termination payment, this is not seen as consideration for the supply of the car, rather a charge for getting out of the lease, so the input tax is 100% recoverable subject to the normal rules. Where there is a net rebate, as in your client's case, the lessee who has incurred a 50% restriction on the rental charges need adjust only 50% of the VAT credit.

See *British Master Tax Guide* 7766.

51-080   Change of use of property

Q. I am considering purchasing a commercial property and I intend to apply for planning permission to convert the property to 12 flats which I intend to sell. Unfortunately, the property I am interested in has VAT on it. My accountant has advised me that because I am going to convert this property to dwellings the sale to me can be treated as exempt by the vendor even though he has opted to tax and no VAT will be charged. Is this correct and if so how do I go about it.

A. The rules changed as from 1 June 2008. Before that date you merely had to notify the seller in writing that you intended to convert the commercial property into a dwelling or a number of dwellings in order for the seller's option to tax to be disapplied and to have the property supplied to you without VAT.

From 1 June 2008 you have to provide a certificate to the seller of the property in the form of a VAT 1614D, which can be downloaded from the HMRC website. You complete the certificate when you are acquiring a building that you intend to convert into a dwelling or dwellings with a view to it being used as a dwelling. In order for the option to tax to be compulsorily disapplied, you should furnish the seller with the completed certificate before the price is legally fixed, i.e. by exchange of contracts, letters or missives or the signing of heads of agreement. If you issue a certificate after the price for the grant has been legally fixed, then the seller may choose at his discretion whether to disapply the option to tax or not. Further details may be found in VAT Notice 742A.

See *British Master Tax Guide* 7746.

51-100   Multi-tasking doctors

> **Q.**   I am a qualified doctor and pathologist and I have recently had to VAT register due to breaching the VAT registration limits. Along with my normal doctor's practice, which I understand is still exempt, I write medical reports for insurance companies which I understand is standard-rated. I have also recently been requested to carry out post mortems. I have no choice in this matter but I am paid for it. Should I charge VAT on this?

A.   No. Where a doctor is compelled by statute to perform a statutory service and charges a fee for it then the supply is outside the scope of VAT.

Under s. 19 of the *Coroners Act* 1998 a coroner can appoint a doctor (pathologist) to carry out a post mortem if necessary. As this is a statutory requirement and the doctor must provide the service, any payment received will be outside the scope.

See *British Master Tax Guide* 8230.

Law: VAT Notice 701/57 section 3.12

51-120   Converting residential properties

> **Q.**   My client is a developer who has acquired a site comprising a large house with a detached garage. He would like to convert the garage into a separate dwelling and sell it on. Please could you confirm that the sale would qualify for zero-rating as a non-residential to residential conversion and my client can recover input tax incurred on the conversion costs.

A.   You are correct in thinking that the grant of a major interest (freehold sale or lease exceeding 21 years) in a dwelling that has been converted from a non-residential building can be zero-rated, thus enabling full input tax recovery on the conversion costs.

However, a 'non-residential conversion' only qualifies where either the building being converted has never been used as a dwelling or for a relevant residential purpose; or in the ten years immediately before the sale, the building has not been used as a dwelling or for a relevant residential purpose.

The conversion of a garage, which was occupied together with a dwelling, into a building designed as a dwelling is not a non-residential conversion unless the dwelling in question has been empty for ten years or more. The legal reference is VATA 1994, Sch. 8, Grp. 5, Note 8 which states:

> 'References to a non-residential building ... do not include a reference to a garage occupied together with a dwelling.'

See *British Master Tax Guide* 7766.

Law: VATA 1994, Sch. 8, Group 5, Note 8

51-140   Renting residential property

> **Q.**   My client, a VAT-registered trading company, is currently renovating two flats, with the intention of renting one to a director and the other to a third party tenant. The builder is charging VAT at the standard rate on the work as the flats have only been vacant for a period of a few months. Can my client recover this VAT as input tax?

A.   The rental of residential property is exempt from VAT and as such any VAT incurred in relation to such an intended supply is recoverable only if it falls below the partial exemption deminimis limits.

However, there are specific rules in relation to accommodation provided to directors and connected persons. Under VATA 1994, s. 24(3) companies are not able to claim any VAT relating to the provision of accommodation to directors and their families where the use of the accommodation is purely domestic. Even if there are excellent business reasons for providing the accommodation, the VAT incurred by the company is not input tax. The definitions of 'director' and 'person connected' with a director are contained in VATA 1994, s. 24(7).

The restriction applies whether the accommodation is a main residence, a second home, a weekend retreat or a flat available when directors are visiting town for a business meeting. It does not apply to ordinary hotel accommodation. The restriction applies to tax incurred on all expenses which relate to the provision of the accommodation including repair, refurbishment, furnishing and legal and estate agents' fees.

Therefore despite the fact that the flat will be rented to the director, the VAT incurred on expenses relating to that flat is not input tax and is specifically blocked.

See *British Master Tax Guide* 8040.

Law: VATA 1994, s. 24(3)

Other guidance: VAT Notice 706

51-160   Invoicing in euros

> **Q.** I have a UK VAT-registered business that manufactures and supplies seasonal novelties. I have recently won a contract to supply a large amount of my goods to another UK company but they have asked me to invoice them in euros. I understand that I need to show the VAT amount on my invoice in sterling, using one of the agreed methods of conversion published in VAT Notice 700 section 7.7, but I am currently operating the cash accounting scheme. When I get paid, as the exchange rate may have changed and be different to the one on my invoice, do I need to recalculate the VAT?

A. VAT Notice 731 states in section 5.10 states that if you issue a VAT invoice in a foreign currency and then are paid in full you must always declare the sterling amount of the VAT due on the supply as shown on your VAT invoice. You do not need to recalculate the exchange rate when the cash is received.

See *British Master Tax Guide* 7858.

51-180   EU Sales Lists

> **Q.** My client is required to submit EC Sales Lists for both goods and services from 1 January 2010. I understand that the reporting requirement for goods will change from calendar quarters to calendar months if sales exceed certain limits. At present, my client has several large customers in other member states. Please can you clarify the limits and also, if my client exceeds these limits, whether he will have to submit data for sales of services on a monthly basis as well? My client expects his sales to customers in other member states to fall during 2010. Will my client be able to return to quarterly EC Sales Lists if his sales fall below these limits in the future?

A. From 1 January 2010 to 31 December 2011 monthly EC Sales Lists must be submitted if the total quarterly value of supplies of intra-EC goods, excluding VAT, exceeds £70,000 in the current quarter or any of the previous four quarters. From 1 January 2012 the threshold is reduced and monthly EC Sales Lists must be submitted if the total quarterly value of supplies of intra-EC goods, excluding VAT, exceeds £35,000 in the current quarter or any of the previous four quarters.

In addition, from 1 January 2010 the option to submit quarterly EC Sales Lists for goods will cease at the end of any month during which the total value, excluding VAT, of the taxable supplies of intra-EC goods exceeds the relevant quarterly thresholds, and businesses will be required to submit monthly returns from the first day of the following month in which they exceeded the threshold.

If a business supplies both goods and services and they are above the quarterly reporting threshold for goods, businesses may either report goods in month one, month two and month three and services for the whole quarter in month three or report both goods *and* services each month.

In future, if your client's sales to customers in other member states reduce, it is possible to move back to quarterly EC Sales Lists as soon as the value of goods (excluding VAT) in the current quarter and the previous four quarters falls below the specified thresholds. To apply to move back to quarterly submissions you should email: esl.helpdesk@hmrc.gsi.gov.uk

or write to:

HMRC
DMB Banking
Accounting Adjustments
3rd Floor
Queens Dock
Liverpool
L74 4ZY

See *British Master Tax Guide* 8460.

51-200   Transportation of goods

> **Q.**   My client is a director of a small freight transport company. The majority of work is done in the UK for UK companies. However, he has just won a new contract with a UK company to transport goods from Australia to America on a regular basis. Under the rules on international freight transport prior to 1 January 2010, because the transport took place outside the EC, the supply was outside the scope of UK and EC VAT. Is this still the case or have the rules now changed?

A.   The rules changed from 1 January 2010 and freight transport services now fall under the general rule when supplied to business customers. The general rule is that the place of supply of services to a person who is in business is the place where the customer belongs for the purposes of receiving the supply. Therefore, as your client's customer is based in the UK, the place of supply of the service is the UK. Where a journey is from a place within to a place outside the EC (or vice versa) the supply of the transport will be zero-rated, but where the transport is either wholly within or wholly outside the EC, as you describe in your question, the supply is standard-rated and your client should charge UK VAT.

See *British Master Tax Guide* 7816.

National Insurance Contributions

Sleeping partners	473
IR35 calculation	473
Jobseeker's allowance	474
Do I get a state pension?	474
Pension entitlement	475
Company secretary or director?	475
Tips, troncs and NIC	476
Tips paid via credit card	477
Tips through the payroll	477
PAYE settlement agreement or not?	478
Contracted-out computation	478
Contracting out, the effect on employee and employer	479
The effect of paying employees on an ad hoc basis	479
Director appointment mid-year	480
Director reaching retirement age	481
Exact percentage method, simple example	481
Using the tables	482
Does Class 1A have a lower earnings limit?	482
Class 1A benefit in kind	482
Timing of a PAYE settlement agreement	483
Class 1B calculation	483
Voluntary Class 2	484
Furnished holiday letting loss set-off	484
Carry forward losses against a different trade?	485
Class 1 deferment (directors)	485
How long does a deferment certificate last?	486
Class 1 deferment (employee)	486
Direct repayment	487
Default penalties for large businesses	487
Working in the UK for a foreign employer	488
UK duties, French residence	488
Foreign students	489
Working overseas for 12 months	490
Class 3 refunds	490
Am I trading?	491

NATIONAL INSURANCE CONTRIBUTIONS

60-000 Sleeping partners

> **Q.** My client is a partner in a partnership but only by virtue of the fact that he has made a substantial investment in the partnership. He takes no part in the running or management of the trade at all. Is he required to pay Class 2 and/or Class 4 National Insurance contribution (NIC)?

A. Every person aged 16 or over but under state pension age who is ordinarily self-employed is liable to pay Class 2 NICs unless they are excepted from liability, or they do not fulfil the residency test.

So the question becomes whether a so-called 'sleeping partner' is ordinarily self-employed? The National Insurance Commission have held that a sleeping partner falls outside the definition of self-employed on the basis that he does no work in the business. Therefore provided your client is not involved in the running of the business in any way then Class 2 contributions will not be due.

By virtue of *Social Security Contributions and Benefits Act* 1992 (SSCBA 1992), Sch. 2, para. 4, all partners (including members of a limited liability partnership), are liable for Class 4 NICs on their own share of the profits of the trade or profession carried on by the partnership. However, the HMRC *National Insurance Manual* (NIM24520) confirms that a sleeping partner is not liable for Class 4 NICs because they cannot be held to have profits which are immediately derived from the carrying on or exercise of one or more trades, professions or vocations. Therefore neither classes of NIC are due.

See *British Master Tax Guide* 8718.

Law: SSCBA 1992, s. 2

60-020 IR35 calculation

Example

Richard provides his services to clients through a limited company. During the tax year in question, services are provided under a contract that falls within the scope of IR35. The contract is Richard's only work that year. The client pays £50,000 to Richard's limited company.

Richard pays himself a salary of £30,000. The company also pays £3,000 into a registered pension scheme. Richard has a company car provided by the company, the cash equivalent value of which is £4,000.

The deemed payment is calculated as follows.

	£	£
Sum received from client under contract		50,000
Less:		
5% deduction for running costs	2,500	
Earnings paid subject to tax (salary)	30,000	
Benefits subject to tax (car)	4,000	
Contributions to pension scheme	3,000	
Employer's Class 1 NIC		
(£30,000 − 5,715) × 12.8%)	3,108	
Employer's Class 1A NIC		
(£4,000 × 12.8%)	512	(43,120)
Balance		6,880

$$\text{Deemed payment } £6,880 \times \frac{100}{(100 + 12.8)} \qquad 6,099$$

The deemed payment can be paid to the worker as salary or as dividends or it can be retained within the company. The tax and National Insurance is payable on the deemed payment irrespective of whether it is actually made to the worker.

See *British Master Tax Guide* 8732.

60-040   Jobseeker's allowance

One of the targets for jobseeker's allowance (JSA) entitlement is an earnings factor for a year of 50 times the lower earnings limit (LEL), so earnings subject to NIC or credited must reach £97 × 50 = £4,850 for 2010–11, if this year is to be a qualifying year for these purposes. An earner who earns at or above the upper earnings limit (UEL) should achieve this target after only six weeks, by which point he will have reckonable earnings of 6 × £844 = £5,064 on his record.

See *British Master Tax Guide* 8734.

60-060   Do I get a state pension?

> **Q.** A director of a small company intends to take a salary equal to the basic personal allowance in order not to incur any actual PAYE or National Insurance costs. However, as no NICs are being paid, will he still qualify for state retirement pension? Is a P14/P35 still required if no tax and NICs are due?

A. It is not necessary to have actually paid NICs for a year to qualify for state retirement pension. The qualifying condition is that the individual has recorded earnings for NICs purposes of at least 52 × LEL (for 2010–11 this will be 52 × £97 = £5,044).

To ensure that the earnings are correctly recorded and credited to the individual, a form P14 (and P35) must be completed and submitted. Where earnings have been paid at or above the LEL, completion of annual end-of-year return forms is, in any event, a legal requirement and failure to do so will result in automatic penalties being imposed by HMRC.

See *British Master Tax Guide* 8736.

Law: SSCBA 1992, s. 21

60-080 Pension entitlement

Example

Viktor reaches age 65 this year. He settled in the UK in March 1987, since when he has worked and paid contributions every year. His record shows 22 qualifying years to April 2010. He needs 30 years on the record to qualify for a full pension. His entitlement is calculated as follows:

$$\frac{22}{30} \times 100 = 73.33\%,$$ giving an entitlement to 74% of the full basic pension.

If Viktor had died below the age of 65, his widow's pension on the basis of his contributions would have been based on a shorter working life. If his contributions were not contracted-out, he will also be entitled to a SERPS and S2P pension.

See *British Master Tax Guide* 8736.

Law: SSCBA 1992, s. 21

60-100 Company secretary or director?

Q. Is a company secretary a director for NIC purposes?

A. The significance of being a company director is that an annual earnings period must be applied for NIC purposes. It is therefore important to be clear as to who the directors of a company actually are.

For example, there may be persons within the organisation who are called directors, but for whom that is just an honorary title.

The office of company secretary is not, of itself, treated as that of a director and the annual earnings period therefore does not usually apply. Of course a person fulfilling the role of company secretary may, separate from that position, also be a director.

There are also provisions for a person who is not actually registered as a director, but who in reality performs the function of a director, to be treated as such. They are referred to as shadow directors. Under *Companies Act* 2006, s. 251 this could include any person in accordance with whose directions or instructions the directors of the company are accustomed to act.

See *British Master Tax Guide* 8768.

Law: CA 2006, s. 251; *Social Security (Contributions) Regulations* 2001 (SI 2001/1004), reg. 2, 22

60-120   Tips, troncs and NIC

Example 1

Antonio runs a hairdressing business. He decides the allocation of tips, although the task of paying the tips over is undertaken by a senior employee. As Antonio has decided the allocation an NIC liability arises on the employees.

Example 2

Jamal runs a restaurant. He passes the tips paid by credit card onto his staff. As the money is initially paid to Jamal and then passed on by him to the staff an NIC liability arises.

Example 3

Julie runs a café. She agrees a minimum amount that her staff will receive in tips each month. If the actual tips left by customers fall short of the guaranteed tips, Julie makes up the shortfall. NIC will be due on the whole amount paid.

Example 4

Lilly runs a restaurant. A tronc is in place for distributing cash tips left by customers. The troncmaster collects the tips and decides how they are to be allocated amongst the staff. No NIC liability arises.

Example 5

Bob runs a barbers. A tronc is in existence for distributing tips, but Bob decides how the tips are to be allocated. A NIC liability arises and the payment must be made by Bob, rather than the troncmaster.

See *British Master Tax Guide* 8812.

60-130   Tips paid via credit card

> **Q.** We run a restaurant. Any cash tips are put into a pool and then distributed by a member of staff who is registered with HMRC as the troncmaster and basic rate tax is deducted from amounts given to staff. If a customer leaves a tip using their credit card, then we take a deduction to cover our credit card charges before passing on the money to the troncmaster. Does this affect the National Insurance position?

A. No. The employer is entitled to make a deduction in respect of any actual charge suffered. Providing the employer has no involvement in how the tips are shared out no Class 1 National Insurance liability will arise. If, however, the employer makes any other deduction or otherwise influences the amount available for distribution to staff, then National Insurance contributions (NICs) will be due.

Also, if the bill includes a compulsory service charge (as opposed to a freely given gratuity) then an NIC charge will arise no matter how the money is distributed.

See *British Master Tax Guide* 8812.

60-140   Tips through the payroll

> **Q.** Tips are paid to our restaurant staff via the payroll. However, a member of staff acts as troncmaster and decides how much of the tip fund each employee gets and advises the owner what to add to each staff member's pay as tips. We have now been told that we must deduct PAYE and NIC from these payments. Is this correct?

A. It is correct that the employer is required to recover PAYE from these payments as they are being paid directly via the employer's payroll. However, as the amounts paid are determined by a troncmaster then there is no NIC due on the payment of these tips even though paid via the employer's payroll. In this instance the employer is acting as an agent for the troncmaster in effecting payment of the tips. If your payroll software will allow it, you should set up a taxable but not NICable pay element to allow payment without the recovery of National Insurance.

See *British Master Tax Guide* 8812.

Other guidance: HMRC leaflet E24

National Insurance Contributions

60-160   PAYE settlement agreement or not?

Example

Blur Ltd rewards its top salesman, Tony, by allowing him to use the company villa and reimbursing his travel costs. The taxable benefit for the use of the villa is agreed to be £800 and the tickets cost £400. Tony is a 40% taxpayer and already pays maximum Class 1 contributions at the main primary rate.

In the absence of a PAYE settlement agreement (PSA), Tony's benefit of £1,200 would be reported on his P11D. Tony would pay tax of £480. The benefit of the villa would be subject to Class 1A contributions, but the reimbursement of the ticket costs would be within Class 1 and should be dealt with through the payroll. The primary NIC would be 1% of £400 (£4) and the secondary NIC and Class 1A for Blur would be 12.8% of £1,200 (£153.60). The total cost for Blur is therefore £1,353.60 and Tony is £484.

Blur enters into a PSA before any of the transactions take place and accounts for tax of £800 (40% × £1,200 × 100/60). Class 1B contributions are due on £2,000 at 12.8% (£256). The total cost to Blur is therefore £2,256 and the cost to Tony is £nil.

Blur could have simply given Tony enough cash to ensure he could (after tax and NIC) rent the villa. Blur would therefore have had to give him £2,033.90 gross (£1,200 × 100/59). Blur's secondary Class 1 liability would have been £2,033.90 × 12.8% (£260.34). Total cost to Blur is £2,294.24 and the cost to Tony is £nil.

See *British Master Tax Guide* 9000–9004, 9100–9110, 9140–9142.

Law: SSA 1998, s. 51, 53; SSCBA 1992, s. 10

60-180   Contracted-out computation

Example

Michael had two separate part-time jobs throughout the year. His contributions in the first job were contracted-out through a contracted-out salary-related (COSR) scheme. His liabilities for 2010–11 are as follows:

		£
Job 1 Earnings are £18,000 (£346.15 per week)		
COSR contributions	52 × 11% × (£346.15 − £110.00)	1,350.78
Less: rebate	52 × 1.6% × (£346.15 − £97.00)	(207.29)
		1,143.49
Job 2 Earnings are £17,400 (£1,450 per month)		
NCO contributions	12 × 11% × (£1,450.00 − £476.00)	1,285.68
Total Class 1 payable		2,429.17

See *British Master Tax Guide* 9006.

Law: PSA 1993, s. 41

60-200   Contracting out, the effect on employee and employer

Example

Kevin joins his employer's final salary pension scheme, which is contracted-out. He earns £113 per week part-time. The contributions due for 2010–11 are:

	Earnings £	Primary £	Rebate £	Secondary £	Rebate £
LEL	97.00	–	–	–	–
LEL to PT	13.00	–	(0.24)	–	(0.56)
Above PT	3.00	0.33	(0.05)	0.38	(0.11)
	113.00	0.33	(0.29)	0.38	(0.67)

Net employee contributions due are 4p while the employer is entitled to recover 29p net from contributions deducted from other earners' pay.

If Kevin begins to work full-time and, with commissions, is paid £850 per week the effect on NIC is as follows:

	Earnings £	Primary £	Rebate £	Secondary £	Rebate £
LEL	97.00	–	–	–	–
LEL to PT	13.00	–	(0.21)	–	(0.48)
PT to UEL	734.00	80.74	(11.75)	93.95	(27.16)
Above PT	6.00	0.06	–	0.77	–
	850.00	80.80	(11.96)	94.72	(27.64)

See *British Master Tax Guide* 9006.

Law: PSA 1993, s. 41

60-220   The effect of paying employees on an ad hoc basis

Example

During 2007–08 Arthur earns £12,000 p.a. as a basic wage, paid weekly. His employer agrees to pay him £86.99 per week, with four top-ups of extra wages of £1,869.13 at times during the year when the business cash flow is strong enough to support the payments.

National Insurance Contributions

If Arthur was paid the whole of his basic salary weekly, he and the company would pay contributions for 48 weeks on earnings of £230.77, paying extra when the four commission payments were added.

As both Arthur and his employer only begin to pay once weekly earnings reach £100, their Class 1 charge would be on £130.77 at 11% and 12.8% respectively. Over a year, £6,800.04 of the £12,000 of earnings would be liable costing Arthur £748.00 and his employer £870.41.

However, Arthur's actual earnings paid are below the LEL for 48 weeks, with no contribution liability for employer or employee. In the other four weeks, his earnings would exceed the UEL, so the NIC liable on the earnings would be:

		£
Employer:	4 × (£86.99 + £1,869.13 − £100.00) × 12.8%	950.33
Employee:	4 × (£670.00 − £100.00) × 11%	250.80
	4 × (£86.99 + £1,869.13 − £670.00) × 1%	12.86

The employer's charge thus increases by £79.92 but Arthur's charge falls by £484.34.

Note that although this looks like a great saving it will actually cost Arthur in the long term, as the year now ceases to qualify for pension entitlement purposes.

See *British Master Tax Guide* 9016.

60-240   Director appointment mid-year

Example

Chris is appointed to the board of Teachers Ltd in week 44 of the tax year. As he is a director, the primary threshold and upper earnings limit are calculated for the rest of the tax year by multiplying the weekly values by 9 (the earnings period starts with the week of appointment).

In 2010–11, Chris will pay NICs at the main rate of 11% on his director's earnings between £990 (9 × £110) and £7,596 (9 × £844) and at the additional 1% rate on all earnings above £7,596 paid up to 5 April.

See *British Master Tax Guide* 9026.

Law: SSCBA 1992, s. 3

60-250 Director reaching retirement age

> **Q.** One of our company directors has reached the age of 65. Should we calculate National Insurance liability on a pro rata basis up to the birthday?

A. A pro rata calculation is only required where a company director is appointed part way through a tax year.

Where a director reaches pension age within a tax year, National Insurance contributions (NICs) are payable by the director on all the earnings (paid or due to be paid) before pension age was reached, and the normal annual earnings period is used for this calculation.

If an election has been made to pay NICs on account using a monthly or weekly earnings period rather than using the annual earnings basis, you will need to reassess the NICs due on the director's total earnings prior to reaching pension age on the basis of the annual earnings period. No further NICs are payable by the director on any earnings paid or due to be paid on or after pension age is reached.

The company will continue to pay the employer's NICs on all earnings paid or due to be paid both before and after the attainment of pension age. However, where the director had been paying NICs at the contracted-out rate (as a member of an approved company pension scheme) then, for any earnings paid or due to be paid after pension age, employer's NICs are due at the not contracted-out rate and the director's NIC table letter should be amended to Table C, not contracted-out.

See *British Master Tax Guide* 9062.

Other guidance: HMRC leaflet E24

60-260 Exact percentage method, simple example

Example

Helen is paid weekly and in 2010–11 earns £1,000 a week. Using the exact percentage method, her primary Class 1 contributions are:

(11% (£844 − £110)) + (1% (£1,000 − £844))   £82.30

The secondary Class 1 liability is:

12.8% (£1,000 − £110)   £113.92

There are certain circumstances in which the exact percentage method must be used, for example, where the earnings from two jobs are aggregated and one is contracted out and the other is not.

National Insurance Contributions

481

See *British Master Tax Guide* 9058.

60-280 Using the tables

Example

Greg is 43 and in not contracted-out employment. He is paid weekly. For a particular week in 2010–11 his earnings are £380.

The relevant table is table A, which appears in CA38. As Greg is paid weekly, the weekly table A should be used. His weekly earnings of £380 are located in the left-hand column of the table. Reading across the column, the primary contributions payable are £29.75 and the employer contributions payable are £34.62.

See *British Master Tax Guide* 9060.

60-300 Does Class 1A have a lower earnings limit?

Q. Will Class 1A NICs apply to benefits reported on Form P11D if the individual concerned has earnings below the lower earnings limit for NICs? (A P11D has been completed because the individual is a director.)

A. Class 1A NICs will apply to benefits reported on form P11D irrespective of the individual's earnings. Class 1A is an employer-only charge which is not subject to either the lower or upper earnings limits.

See *British Master Tax Guide* 9110.

Law: SSCBA 1992, s. 10

60-320 Class 1A benefit in kind

Example

Two employees share the same car throughout the tax year 2010–11. The car has a list price of £20,000 and an 'appropriate percentage' of 23%.

Assuming each employee had sole use of the car, each would be taxed on a cash equivalent of £4,600.

Class 1A contributions payable in respect of each employee, based on the total cash equivalent of £4,600 are £588.80. This is divided by two to reflect the fact that the car is shared by two employees, giving an adjusted Class 1A liability in respect of each employee of £294.40.

See *British Master Tax Guide* 9120.

Law: SSCBA 1992, s. 10

60-340   Timing of a PAYE settlement agreement

Example

A PAYE settlement agreement (PSA) is agreed on 30 July 2010. The PSA includes items that would otherwise attract a liability to Class 1 NIC. The employer pays PAYE and NICs monthly. Payments are made electronically and are due on the 22nd of the month.

At the time of agreement of the PSA, Class 1 NIC for months 1 and 2 (ending 5 May and 5 June respectively) have already fallen due for payment. The original liabilities stand. However, the Class 1 liabilities for month 3 onwards have not yet fallen due for payment at the time that the PSA was agreed so Class 1B contributions are payable on the items included in the PSA instead of Class 1 contributions from month 3 onwards.

As the liability to Class 1 contributions is an employer and employee liability, whereas the Class 1B liability is an employer only liability, it makes sense to agree a PSA as early as possible in the tax year (and in any event before the first payment of Class 1 contributions becomes due) to save employee contributions. If the PSA is agreed later than 22 April (19 April where payments are not made electronically) after the end of the tax year, the full Class 1 liability for the year will stand.

See *British Master Tax Guide* 9140, 9339.

60-360   Class 1B calculation

Example

A company has agreed a PAYE settlement agreement (PSA) covering the provision of minor benefits. Benefits included within the PSA for 2010–11 that would otherwise have attracted a liability to Class 1 or Class 1A are valued at £4,000. Tax payable under the PSA is £10,000.

Class 1B contributions are payable at a rate of 12.8% on £14,000 (tax of £10,000 plus benefits otherwise attracting a charge to Class 1 or Class 1A of £4,000). Thus Class 1B contributions payable by 19 October 2011 (or 22 October where payment is made electronically) are £1,792.

See *British Master Tax Guide* 9142.

Law: SSCBA 1992, s. 10A

National Insurance Contributions

60-380   Voluntary Class 2

Q. My client has lived and worked in Italy for many years but pays voluntary NIC in order to maintain her entitlement in respect of a UK state retirement pension. She has always paid Class 3 contributions but I have heard that it may now be possible to pay Class 2 instead. What is the correct position?

A. Though not widely publicised, UK citizens living abroad and who are in employment or self-employment have always had the option to pay Class 2 or Class 3 NICs. Historically, Class 3 was the usual option as it was marginally cheaper. However, from 6 April 2000 the rate of Class 2 NICs was greatly reduced (from £6.55 to £2.00 per week) and has remained significantly lower than Class 3 ever since. For 2010–11 there is an annual saving of £501.80 ((£12.05 − £2.40) × 52) with no loss of benefits. This option is not open to persons who are not in employment or self-employment and for them Class 3 is still the only available method.

Payment can be made retrospectively up to the end of the sixth year following that in which the contributions were due.

See *British Master Tax Guide* 9210, 9466.

60-400   Furnished holiday letting loss set-off

Q. My client has a profitable sole trade business in addition to a source of rental income from a furnished holiday letting. This year a loss arises on the holiday lettings and I am proposing to set this off against the sole trader profits under ITA 2007, s. 64. I understand that a mirror relief to the income tax provisions is available for Class 4 National Insurance where trading losses are set against profits which have suffered Class 4 NIC. Can you confirm whether Class 4 NIC can be relieved on the sole trader profits accordingly?

A. Unfortunately, SSCBA 1992, Sch. 2, para 3(1)(a) makes it clear that the losses must arise from activities which would themselves be subject to Class 4 NIC. Furnished holiday lettings are not regarded as a trade for NIC purposes and remain outside the charge to Class 4 NIC along with rental profits generally.

See *British Master Tax Guide* 9252.

Law: SSCBA 1992, Sch. 2

60-420   Carry forward losses against a different trade?

> **Q.** An individual has trading losses in the period to cessation of his sole trade business. For income tax purposes, the losses have been relieved against other income of the year. Can the losses be carried forward for Class 4 NIC purposes and set against profits of a different trade?

A. When a trading loss is relieved against other income (i.e. employment income) relief has not been given for Class 4 purposes as required by SSCBA 1992, Sch. 2, para. 3. The loss can be carried forward and set off against the first available trading profits for subsequent years. Although the law is vague on this matter, the HMRC *National Insurance Manual* at NIM24615 states that a Class 4 NIC loss can only be carried forward against a loss of the same trade.

See *British Master Tax Guide* 9252.

Law: SSCBA 1992, Sch. 2

60-460   Class 1 deferment (directors)

Example

Margaret has three non-executive directorships, with three independent companies: A, B and C generating income of £15,000, £16,000 and £17,000 per year respectively. She will have Class 1 earnings of £48,000, which is well above the UEL, but she will be unable to apply for deferment as she will only reach up to £33,000 of income from any two of the directorships (deferment will not be available if the annual maximum can only be reached by aggregating all contributions in all jobs). She will be obliged to pay full contributions in all jobs and make a refund claim after the year-end.

She is then offered a further directorship by company D with a fee of £13,000. Taking the earnings from A, B and D together, Margaret will have total earnings above the UEL, so HMRC should grant deferment for the employment with C. Margaret will still have to apply for a refund if her total contributions exceed the annual maximum, after taking into account the fact that she will have been given the benefit of three primary thresholds when paying contributions via A, B and D.

See *British Master Tax Guide* 9062, 9310.

Law: SSCBA 1992, s. 19

National Insurance Contributions

60-480   How long does a deferment certificate last?

> **Q.** One of our client's employees had another job in which he was paying NIC at the maximum rate. As a result he produced a CA 2700 certificate of deferment and paid only 1% on earnings above the periodic threshold on his earnings from our client. He has now retired from his main job and is working only for our client. Should we still operate the deferment certificate?

A. You can continue to apply the 1% deferment rate for NIC to earnings in the employment. However, one of the conditions in applying for deferment of NIC is that the individual will notify the National Insurance Contributions Office (Deferment Section) of any changes such as a job ending or starting a new job. Once the individual has honoured his obligation to notify that office of the change, they will advise the employer to cease applying deferment and to deduct NIC at the full rate.

See *British Master Tax Guide* 9310.

Law: SSCBA 1992, s. 19

60-500   Class 1 deferment (employee)

The calculation required to decide if class 1 deferment is available is based on the following equation:

$$UEL + (E - 1)\ WET$$

where:

UEL   = upper earnings limit (£844 per week for 2010–11)
WET   = weekly earnings threshold (£110 per week for 2010–11)
E   = the number of employments from which earnings are taken into account.

Thus, deferment is possible in respect of any remaining employments, if, say, earnings from six employments are at least £1,394 (£844 + ((6 − 1) × £110)).

Example

During 2010–11 Sarah has five jobs. Her weekly earnings in respect of each job are as follows:

Job 1   £600
Job 2   £300
Job 3   £60
Job 4   £70
Job 5   £30

The earnings from jobs 1 and 2 are £900. As this exceeds £844, Sarah can apply for a deferment in respect of jobs 3, 4 and 5.

See *British Master Tax Guide* 9310.

Law: SSCBA 1992, s. 19

60-520   Direct repayment

> **Q.** We had an employee who told us she was over 60 years old. We asked her for an age exemption certificate, but she was unable to produce it, nor any other proof of her age. We therefore used letter A to calculate her NIC liability. After a couple of months she left and we supplied her with a P45 and considered the employment finalised.
>
> She later produced an exemption certificate and is now asking for a refund of her National Insurance payments. Do we have to make a refund, or should we tell her to go to HMRC for the money?

A. This will depend on whether or not you received the certificate in the same tax year as the payments. If you receive the certificate by 5 April then you must repay the employee's contributions and adjust your monthly payments and your year-end returns to account for the refund. If you receive the certificate after 5 April you can make no adjustments and it is up to the employee to make an application to HMRC for a direct refund.

See *British Master Tax Guide* 9354.

Law: SSCBA 1992, Sch. 1, para. 3

60-540   Default penalties for large businesses

Example

Megaco plc missed the e-payment deadline four times in 2004–05. Its net remittances based on form P35 for the year were £240m. The first two defaults cost nothing, but the third and fourth give a cumulative surcharge of 0.34% (0.17 + 0.17), so it received a surcharge notice demanding £816,000.

The employer had to meet its payment deadlines throughout 2005–06 to avoid a surcharge for that year. However, it failed again, five times. It had already been surcharged for four defaults in the surcharge period, so for 2005–06 the surcharge calculation was the cumulative total of defaults five to nine, which is 1.74% (0.17 + 0.33 + 0.33 + 0.33 + 0.58). As its net P35 total for the year was now £300m, the surcharge cost £5.22m.

In 2006–07, the employer defaults only once, but this alone means that the surcharge period continues, and the charge is based on a tenth default: 0.58% of the annual remittance.

In 2007–08, the company meets its payment obligations on time and restarts the clock: no surcharge is payable.

When the company defaults again, three times, in 2008–09 the surcharge for three defaults in a period is only 0.17% (0 + 0 + 0.17).

See *British Master Tax Guide* 9386.

60-560   Working in the UK for a foreign employer

> **Q.** I have been offered a position as UK Sales Director for a Finnish company. My duties will be based in the UK and I will remain resident and domiciled in the UK. What is my liability for UK PAYE and NIC? The Finnish company has suggested I set up my own company and bill them for my time via my own company. Can I do this and would my liabilities be different under one arrangement as opposed to the other?

A. First, it would not be beneficial to set up your own company to receive remuneration from employment with the Finnish company. As director (and therefore employee) of your own company, your company would be liable to account for PAYE and both Class 1 primary and secondary NIC under IR35 rules.

As an employee of the Finnish company you would need to set up a Direct PAYE (NI) Scheme with your local HMRC office and account for your own PAYE and primary Class 1 NICs. There would be no liability for Class 1 secondary NICs as the Finnish company is neither resident nor has a place of business in the UK.

This is a far better option than the expense of setting up your own company and incurring employer's NIC on your own earnings.

See *British Master Tax Guide* 9452.

60-580   UK duties, French residence

> **Q.** A director of a UK based company has moved permanently to France and is no longer domiciled or resident in the UK. She will perform all her duties at home in France. Will she be exempt from UK PAYE and NIC?

A. She will not be liable to UK PAYE for any duties of the employment, which are performed in France. However, payment for any duties of the directorship which are performed in the UK will be subject to PAYE.

The NIC treatment for certain UK duties of the directorship is different. Exemption will be granted for certain UK duties if they comprise of attendances at board meetings only, and those attendances are in one block not exceeding two weeks or, are no more than ten visits not exceeding two days each. If her UK duties amount to more than the exemption for board meetings she will be liable to UK NIC.

As the director is resident and domiciled in France, it is likely that they will be liable to French social security on her earnings. If this is the case she will not be liable to UK NIC for any duties in excess of attendance at board meetings if she produces a certificate of continuing liability (E101) from the French authorities.

See *British Master Tax Guide* 9452–9454.

Law: SSCBA 1992, s. 1(6)

60-600   Foreign students

Q. My client has decided to employ a foreign student who is from Moldova but is studying in Romania. He has proof that the work is related to his studies and the assignment will last for up to 12 months. I believe he can be paid free of tax and NIC. Is this correct?

A. PAYE is due on income arising from duties of employment performed in the UK. Generally, NIC is due on pay to employees who come from abroad to work in the UK. The liability normally arises from the date they start work in the UK.

The only exemption for NIC relating to students on courses abroad who take up temporary work in the UK which is related to their studies could not be applied in the circumstances described. To qualify for exemption for up to 52 weeks of employment the following conditions must be met:

(1)   the employee does not normally live in the UK;

(2)   the job is done during their holidays; and

(3)   the job is related to, or similar to, their studies.

Although conditions 1 and 3 are clearly met, point 2 is not and therefore both PAYE and Class 1 NIC are due on the income from the employment.

See *British Master Tax Guide* 9454.

National Insurance Contributions

60-620   Working overseas for 12 months

Example

A British national, normally resident in the UK, who is sent by his UK employer to work for up to 12 months in France may pay only UK NICs throughout his assignment. Note that the contract of employment must remain at all times with the home employer before this rule applies, since it is explicitly required that he continues to perform work for that employer. If the home contract is terminated and a host contract substituted, the individual falls immediately into the host scheme. This can be an extremely expensive matter for both employers and employees since social security contribution rates vary widely.

See *British Master Tax Guide* 9456.

60-640   Class 3 refunds

> **Q.** I have made voluntary National Insurance Class 3 contributions to maintain my contribution records so that I will have access to the full state pension when I retire. However I have recently been told that the number of qualifying years needed to qualify for a full basic state pension will be reduced so that I have paid over amounts to the Government unnecessarily. Can I apply for a refund?

A. HMRC have issued information on the refund of voluntary National Insurance Class 3 contributions following the Paymaster General's announcement on 16 January 2007. HMRC give details about the administrative arrangements for making refunds and links to the application form can be found at www.hmrc.gov.uk/nic/vc3-important.htm

Under the *Pensions Act* 2007 the number of qualifying years required to qualify for the full state pension has been reduced from 39 years for women and 44 years for men to 30 years for those reaching state pension age on or after 6 April 2010.

In order to qualify for a refund there are certain conditions that must be satisfied:

- you must reach state pension age on or after 6 April 2010;
- you have paid voluntary contributions on or after 25 May 2006 (the date the Pension White Paper was published) but before 26 July 2007; and
- you were not aware of the changes when they were paid. This means that at the time they were paid, you had not received information from HMRC about the changes.

There are also provisions to make a refund of Class 2 contributions if they have been paid voluntarily.

See *British Master Tax Guide* 9210.

60-660   Am I trading?

> **Q.** My client is renting out four properties as residential and commercial accommodation. HMRC are saying that he should be paying Class 2 National Insurance contributions (NICs) based on the income from the properties. Is this really due?

A. The answer is no! In the case of *Rashid v Garcia (Status Inspector)*, Mr Rashid tried to claim incapacity benefit based on his contributions of Class 2 NICs. Mr. Rashid was a landlord and had been paying Class 2 NICs based solely on his rental income. His right to benefits was disputed on the grounds that he should not have been paying Class 2 NICs. HMRC decided that the appellant was not entitled to pay Class 2 NICs as he was not a 'self-employed earner', and this was upheld by the commissioners. There was insufficient activity for it to constitute a business. It was an investment which by its nature required some activity to maintain it.

See *British Master Tax Guide* 9150.

Law: *Rashid v Garcia (Status Inspector)* (2002) Sp C 348

Legislation Finding List

(References are to paragraph numbers)

Provision	Paragraph
Administration of Estates Act 1925	
34(3)	41-180
Sch. 1, Pt. II	41-180
Aggregates Levy (Registration and Miscellaneous Provisions) Regulations 2001 (SI 2001/4027)	
reg. 2	2-000
Air Passenger Duty and Other Indirect Taxes (Interest Rate) Regulations 1998 (SI 1998/1461)	1-160
Capital Allowances Act 2001	
6	12-240
13	12-280
14	12-510
15	12-505
21, 22, 23	1-120
33A	1-120
38A	21-480
38B	12-510; 21-480
45A–45C	1-120
45D	1-120; 1-300
45E, 45F	1-120
45H–45J	1-120
46(2)	1-120; 11-570
51E	21-480; 21-500
51I(4), (5)	12-490
51J(3)	12-490
52	1-120
53–66	12-320; 12-330
55(4)	21-600
56	1-120
65(2)	21-600
67(3)	12-290
83–89	12-300
85	1-280; 1-520
260(3), (6)	1-520
281	1-120
298(3)	1-120
360A	1-120
360O	12-370
393A	1-120
393I	12-340
394	1-120
437	1-120
452	1-120
464	1-120
484	1-120
490	1-120
569(1)	1-520
570(5)	1-280

Provision	Paragraph
573	12-370
574(2)	21-500
574(3)	12-490
577	12-510
Companies Act 1985 (Accounts of Small and Medium-Sized Enterprises and Audit Exemption) (Amendment) Regulations 2004 (SI 2004/16)	1-120
Companies Act 2006	
251	60-100
382	1-120
392	1-120
466	1-120
Coroners Act 1998	
19	51-100
Corporation Tax Act 2009	
2–9	20-020; 20-060; 20-080
2	20-620
8–10	20-100; 20-120
50	12-280
61	20-480; 20-490
190	20-640
194	21-580
Pt. 5	20-140; 20-160; 20-180; 20-490
330	20-490
Pt. 8	20-220; 20-240; 20-720; 21-020
Sch. 1, para. 272(2)	20-980
931B	21-560
Corporation Tax Act 2010	
19	20-300
24, 25	21-420
37	20-400; 20-760
37(3)(b)	20-420
45	20-360; 20-500; 20-800
68	31-040
92	20-440
92	20-760
Pt. 5, Ch. 2	20-780; 20-800; 20-820; 20-840; 20-860
Pt. 5, Ch. 4	20-740
439	20-980
448	21-380
449	21-000; 21-020; 21-040; 21-420
455	10-960; 21-060; 21-080; 21-380
456	21-380
719	20-520; 20-540
945(1), (4), (5)	20-460
1000	21-090

Corporation Tax Act 2010 – continued

Provision	Paragraph
Pt. 23, Ch. 3	20-560
1033	21-090
1154	20-620
Sch. 2, para. 99	20-460

Corporation Tax (Instalment Payments) Regulations 1998 (SI 1998/3175) 1-160; 1-500; 21-240

Finance Act 1986

67(3)	1-700
79	1-700
87	1-700
92	1-700
99(3)	1-700
102	40-300; 40-310

Finance Act 1989

83ZA	21-120
102	1-160
102(2)	1-520
178	1-100; 1-700

Finance Act 1994

Pt. III	1-960
118(3)	1-520

Finance Act 1995

24	50-780

Finance Act 1996

Pt. III	1-980
83(6), (7)	1-520
134	30-200
Sch. 5, para. 26	1-980

Finance Act 1998

See generally	1-500
Sch. 18	20-020; 21-080
Sch. 18, para. 2	1-160
Sch. 18, para. 17(2), (3)	1-160
Sch. 18, para. 17(3)(a)	21-310
Sch. 18, para. 18	1-160
Sch. 18, para. 20, 23, 29	1-160
Sch. 18, para. 46(1)	1-520
Sch. 18, para. 74	1-520
Sch. 18, para. 82	1-520
Sch. 18, para. 89	1-160

Finance Act 1999

110	1-700
112(1)(b), (2)	1-700
Sch. 13, para. 3, 4	1-700
Sch. 13, para. 11–13	1-700
Sch. 13, para. 11	1-700
Sch. 13, para. 12(3)	1-700

Finance Act 2001

16	2-000
Sch. 4	2-000
Sch. 5, para. 5	2-000

Finance Act 2003

56	1-700

Provision	Paragraph
125	1-700
176	11-720
Sch. 3, para. 3A	30-780
Sch. 5	1-700

Finance Act 2004

55	21-200
56	11-300
59(1)(1)	12-620
124	50-120
189(1), (1)(c)	12-090
227–234	11-880
Sch. 15	40-140; 40-660

Finance Act 2005

14	11-380
92	12-360
Sch. 6	12-360

Finance Act 2006

29	21-130
Sch. 12	30-720

Finance Act 2008

See generally	1-120; 30-840
8	30-760
9	30-980; 31-020
Sch. 3	30-980; 31-020
Sch. 4, para. 2	40-740

Finance Act 2009

23	12-190
53	10-810
Sch. 28, para. 2	10-810

Finance (No. 2) Act 2010

2	30-740

Income and Corporation Taxes Act 1988

1(5)	1-040
5	1-260
10	1-500
13	1-480
100(1C)	1-280; 1-520
117–118	50-120
209	21-090
239(3)	1-520
240(1), (6)	1-520
257(1)	1-040
393(1)	1-520
393A(1), (10)	1-520
412	1-520
419	1-500
552	11-640
573(2)	1-520
590B	1-420
590C	1-420
592, 594, 599	1-420
617	1-340
640A, 646A	1-420
655	1-420
660B(2)	11-360

Provision	Paragraph
826	21-280
Sch. 17A, para. 2	1-520

Income Tax Act 2007

Provision	Paragraph
11	20-950
24(1)	1-380; 1-400
42	11-700
64	1-280; 1-580; 12-180; 60-400
71	1-280; 1-580
72	1-280; 12-180
83	1-280
86	12-160
89	1-280; 12-200
96	1-280; 1-580
132	20-510
Pt. 5	11-800
209	11-820
234	11-780
240	11-780
383	11-740
392	11-740
409(1)–(2), 410	11-780
429	11-260
498	11-400
815	20-950
825	20-950
831, 832	12-560
903	11-260

Income Tax (Construction Industry Scheme) Regulations 2005 (SI 2005/2045)

Provision	Paragraph
reg. 22(1)	12-620

Income Tax (Earnings and Pensions) Act 2003

Provision	Paragraph
3, 4	10-400
5	10-040
7	12-540
Pt. 2, Ch. 8	50-740
62	10-100; 10-620
70–72	10-440; 10-460
Pt. 3, Ch. 4	10-280; 11-930
89	12-000
90(1)	11-930
92	11-930
99–100	10-260
99	10-240
114–148	10-700; 10-800
114	10-660; 10-680
119	10-120
123	10-740
134, 139	1-300
144	10-790
147	10-690
149–153	10-820; 10-840
150	1-300
154–155	10-660
154–159	10-670
155	10-720

Provision	Paragraph
156	10-500
158	10-670
171	10-720
173–191	10-920; 10-940
175	10-900; 10-960
181	1-380
191	10-900
198–202	10-020
203–207	10-580; 10-600
204	10-500; 10-620
205	10-640
206	10-560
230	1-320
237	10-480
239	10-680
240	10-220
241	1-460
248	11-980
264	10-160; 12-400
269	10-680
270A(7)	10-990
288	1-440
Pt. 4, Ch. 7	10-200
309–310	11-040; 11-060; 11-080
314–315	10-240; 10-260
318	10-990; 11-000
319	11-020
320	10-560
321	10-180
323	10-140
336	10-640; 11-920; 11-940
337–341	11-960
356–357	12-020
414	11-660
471–487	10-300
527–531	10-420
677(1)	1-360
703–707	12-380; 12-400

Income Tax (Exemptions of Minor Benefits) (Amendment) Regulations 2007 (SI 2007/2090) 10-460

Income Tax (Pay As You Earn) Regulations 2003 (SI 2003/2682)

Provision	Paragraph
reg. 2(1)	1-040
reg. 9(8)	1-040
reg. 67	1-060
reg. 73	1-060
reg. 85–87	1-060
reg. 90	1-060

Income Tax (Trading and Other Income) Act 2005

Provision	Paragraph
33	12-140
34	11-100
35	12-600
61	12-120
72	11-280
116, 119	11-340

Income Tax (Trading and Other Income)
Act 2005 – continued

Provision	Paragraph
142	12-260
175	1-280
216	11-120
221	11-320
222	1-280
223	11-310
250	12-220
257(4)	1-280
270–272	11-560
272	11-740
277–279	11-600
323–326	11-570
349–352	12-220
360	11-760
403	11-660
415	21-100
491	11-460; 11-640
602	20-000
620	11-500
629	11-360; 11-540
631	11-360; 11-540
633	11-540
634	11-500
649–682	11-480
650, 653	11-440
731	12-740
731(2)(a)–(e)	12-740
733	12-740
784–801	11-580
850	11-200

Inheritance Tax Act 1984

3	40-080; 40-120
3A	40-000
6	41-060
7–9	40-320; 40-340; 40-360; 40-380; 40-400
7	40-100; 40-420; 40-440; 40-460
7(4)	1-760
8A–8C	40-740
18	1-760; 40-700; 40-720; 40-740
19–20	40-780
19	1-760; 40-760
20	1-760
21	40-800
22	1-760
39, 39A	41-080
54A, 54B	40-540
63	40-220
64	40-580
65	40-560
66	40-580
68–69	40-620; 40-640
68	40-600
70	40-680
85	40-220
103–109	40-280
103	1-760
104	40-520
105	40-840; 40-860; 40-880

Provision	Paragraph
106–109	40-900
106	40-970
112	40-940; 40-950; 40-960
113	40-920
115	1-760; 40-280; 40-980; 41-000
123	40-980
125	41-020
126–130	41-040
141	1-760; 40-500
151A–151C	1-780
160	40-040
161	40-040; 40-060
172–173	40-260
178–198	40-480
211	41-180
211(1)(b)	41-180
226	1-800
266	40-240
267	40-020; 40-030
268	40-140; 40-160; 40-180; 40-200
Sch. 1	1-740
Sch. 3	41-140

Inheritance Tax (Delivery of Accounts)
(Excepted Estates) (Amendment)
Regulations 2006 (SI 2006/2141) 1-780

Landfill Tax (Qualifying Material) Order
1996 (SI 1996/1528) 1-980

Law of Property Act 1925 31-580

Local Government, Planning and Land Act
1980 1-120

Partnership Act 1890
24 11-160

Partnerships (Restrictions on Contributions
to a Trade) Regulations 2005
(SI 2005/2017) 11-240

Pensions Act 2007 60-640

Pension Scheme Act 1993
41 .... 60-180; 60-200

Social Security Act 1998

51	60-160
53	60-160

Social Security Contributions and Benefits
Act 1992

1(6)	60-580
2	60-000
3	60-240
10	60-160; 60-300; 60-320
10A	60-360
19	60-460; 60-480; 60-500
22	60-060; 60-680
Sch. 1, para. 3	60-520
Sch. 1, para. 6(2), (3)	1-060; 1-160; 1-920
Sch. 2	60-400; 60-420

Provision	Paragraph
Social Security (Contributions) Regulations 2001 (SI 2001/1004)	
reg. 1	1-920
reg. 2	60-100
reg. 22	60-100
Social Security (Contributions) (Amendment) Regulations 2008 (SI 2008/133)	1-920
Stamp Act 1891	
15A, 15B	1-700
Stamp Duty (Exempt Instruments) Regulations 1987 (SI 1987/516)	1-700
Stamp Duty Reserve Tax Regulations 1986 (SI 1986/1711)	
reg. 11, 13	1-700
Taxation (International and Other Provisions) Act 2010	
42	20-320; 20-340
Taxation of Chargeable Gains Act 1992	
2A	1-610
2A(8)	1-610
3	30-280; 30-300
3(7)	30-780
7	1-560
8	30-540
9(3)	12-560
10	30-820
17	20-510
18	30-080
22	30-000
23	30-000; 30-040; 30-060
24	31-720
24(2)	1-580
28	30-260
35	30-160; 30-500; 30-520; 30-620; 30-640
35(6)	1-580
36	1-580
37	21-090
38	30-140
38(1)(b)	31-180
42	30-160
44	30-560
48	30-180; 30-220; 30-240
49	31-620
54	30-480
Pt. III	31-250
58	30-700; 30-880
62	30-760; 30-800
62(1)	30-780
62(7)	1-580
64(2)	30-740
67	31-320
73	31-250
104–110	30-900
105	30-660

Provision	Paragraph
105A	1-580; 30-680
106A	1-620
116	30-880; 30-900; 30-920
144	30-400; 30-440
150A	1-640; 31-000
152–153	31-480; 31-500
152	31-520; 31-540
152(1)	1-580; 31-420; 31-440
155	1-660
157	31-460
161	31-540
161(3)	21-320
162	31-360; 31-380
162A	1-580
164A(2)	1-580
165	31-080; 31-520
165(1)	1-580
168	31-320
Pt. V, Ch. 3	31-700
169I(2)(c), (5), (6)	31-640
169K	30-460; 31-640
169K(4)	31-640
169N	31-400
169P	31-640
170–171	20-660
171A	1-520
178–179	20-720
179	20-700
192	20-920
209	31-580
210	31-140
222	30-400; 31-200; 31-220; 31-260
222(5)	1-580
223–224	31-160
223	30-400; 31-280; 31-300
226	31-240
240	30-580; 30-600
245–248	31-340
251(2)	30-340
253	20-510; 21-100
253(3)	1-580
262	31-100; 30-120
280	30-080; 30-220
281	30-200
286	30-080; 30-640
Sch. A1	1-610; 30-300; 30-320; 30-360; 30-380
Sch. A1, para. 3, 4, 5	1-610
Sch. 4, para. 9(1)	1-580
Sch. 5B	1-640
Sch. 6, para. 5(2)	1-580
Sch. 7	31-560
Sch. 8	30-600
Tax Credits Act 2002	11-680
Tax Credits (Definition and Calculation of Income) Regulations 2002 (SI 2002/2006)	
reg. 3	11-670

Provision	Paragraph
Taxes (Interest Rate) Regulations 1989	
(SI 1989/1297)	1-100
Taxes (Interest Rate) (Amendment)	
Regulations 1993 (SI 1993/222)	1-380
Taxes (Interest Rate) (Amendment No. 4)	
Regulations 1993 (SI 1993/3171)	1-380
Taxes (Interest Rate) (Amendment No. 3)	
Regulations 1994 (SI 1994/2657)	1-380
Taxes (Interest Rate) (Amendment)	
Regulations 1995 (SI 1995/2436)	1-380
Taxes (Interest Rate) (Amendment)	
Regulations 1996 (SI 1996/54)	1-380
Taxes (Interest Rate) (Amendment No. 2)	
Regulations 1996 (SI 1996/1321)	1-380
Taxes (Interest Rate) (Amendment No. 3)	
Regulations 1996 (SI 1996/2644)	1-380
Taxes (Interest Rate) (Amendment)	
Regulations 1997 (SI 1997/1681)	1-380
Taxes (Interest Rate) (Amendment)	
Regulations 1999 (SI 1999/419)	1-380
Taxes (Interest Rate) (Amendment No. 3)	
Regulations 2001 (SI 2001/3860)	1-380
Taxes (Interest Rate) (Amendment)	
Regulations 2007 (SI 2007/684)	1-380
Taxes Management Act 1970	
7	1-160
12B	1-160
43(1)	1-580
59A	1-160
86–90	21-260
86	1-700
87	1-160
87A	1-160
89	1-100
93, 93A	1-160
95, 95A	1-160
97AA	1-160
98, 98(2)	1-060
98A	1-060
98A(4)	1-060
109	1-160
Sch. 1B	11-320
Value Added Tax Act 1994	
1	50-300; 50-320

Provision	Paragraph
3–5	50-100
3	50-120; 50-300; 50-320
3(1)	50-640
6	50-240
6(2), (3)	50-220
7	50-160; 50-180; 50-200
8	50-440; 50-460; 50-480
14	50-160; 50-180; 50-200
19(2)	50-260; 50-280
24	50-300
24(3), (7)	51-140
26	50-360
26B	50-600; 50-700; 50-720; 50-740
32	50-780
50A	50-780; 50-800
53	50-820
56	1-880; 50-360
57(4A)–(4G)	50-900
57(9)	50-900
59	50-860
63	50-880
74	1-100; 1-160; 1-960; 1-980; 2-000
74(3)	1-160
78	1-100
Sch. 1	50-560; 50-580; 50-600; 50-620; 50-640; 50-660
Sch. 2	1-840
Sch. 3A	1-840
Sch. 4	50-000
Sch. 8, Grp. 5, Note 8	51-120
Sch. 9	50-360; 50-500; 50-520
Sch. 10	50-540
Value Added Tax, etc (Correction of Errors etc) Regulations 2008	
(SI 2008/1482)	50-840
Value Added Tax Regulations 1995	
(SI 1995/2518)	
Pt. VII	1-860
reg. 91	50-960
reg. 99(1)(a)	50-400
reg. 102	50-380
Value Added Tax (Amendment) (No. 2)	
Regulations 2007 (SI 2007/768)	1-860
Value Added Tax (Reverse Charge) Order 1993 (SI 1993/2328)	50-040
Value Added Tax (Special Provisions) Order 1995 (SI 1995/1268)	
art. 4	50-980

Index

(References are to paragraph numbers)

Paragraph

A

Accommodation – see also Living accommodation
. employees seconded overseas 10-230

Accounting date
. changes 11-120

Agricultural property
. hold-over relief 31-560

Agricultural property relief
. company shares 40-980
. concrete yard 41-000
. farmhouse, partnership asset 40-280

Air miles 10-280

Animals
. capital allowances treatment 12-280

Annual exempt amount
. capital gains tax: losses brought
   forward 30-280
. inheritance tax
. . carry forward 40-760
. . chargeable lifetime transfer or potentially
   exempt transfer 40-240
. . small gifts 40-780

Annual investment allowance (AIA) – see Plant and machinery allowances

Assets held on 6 April 1965 – see Capital gains tax

Assets held on 31 March 1982 – see Capital gains tax

Associated companies
. Finance Act 2008 changes 21-420
. group or association 21-020
. limited liability partnership 21-000
. minimum controlling combinations 21-040
. structure, rationalising 21-400

Associated operations – see Inheritance tax

Auctioneers
. fees and commissions, value added tax 50-920

Paragraph

B

Bad debts
. corporation tax 20-040
. . cessation of business 21-580
. . groups of companies, loan
   relationships 20-200
. generally 12-660

Barn conversions
. value added tax
. . do-it-yourself build 50-430
. . finished conversion 50-440

Beneficial loans – see Employment-related loans

Benefits in kind – see Employee benefits

Budget Notes
. 12/08 12-500

Business entertainment 12-020

Business equipment 12-150

Business premises renovation allowances
. generally 12-360
. on retirement 12-370

Business property
. entrepreneurs' relief 31-700

Business property relief
. companies
. . owning property through 40-880
. . restriction of relief, calculation 40-940
. estates with, and exempt legacies 41-080
. 50 per cent availability 40-480
. furnished holiday lettings 40-820
. incorporation 40-970
. non-availability, use at death 40-920
. quoted shares 40-860
. replacement property 40-900
. restriction, calculation
. . companies 40-940
. . partnerships 40-960

Buy-back of shares 21-090

Paragraph

C

Capital allowances
. annual investment allowance (AIA) – see
    Plant and machinery allowances
. business premises renovation
    allowances........................ 12-360
.. on retirement 12-370
. flat conversion allowances 12-340
. furnished holiday lettings 11-570
. generally........................... 12-240
. groups of companies 20-780
. plant and machinery – see Plant and
    machinery allowances
. prizes 12-510
. property letting businesses 12-505
. when expenditure incurred 12-260
. writing down allowances 12-330

Capital assets
. stock or fixed asset 21-320

Capital expenditure
. computer 20-220

Capital gains tax
. annual exempt amount: losses brought
    forward 30-280
. assets held on 31 March 1982
.. agreeing valuations on probate 30-500
.. joint ownership of shares 30-640
.. using 1982 value 30-620
.. valuation and enhancement
    expenditure 30-520
. buying a freehold 31-580
. chattel exemption – see Chattel exemption
. consideration – see Consideration
. date of disposal 30-260
. death – see Death
. disposal where capital sums derived from
    assets – see Capital sums derived from
    assets
. enterprise investment scheme – see
    Enterprise investment scheme (EIS)
. entrepreneurs' relief – see Entrepreneurs'
    relief
. forfeited deposits
.. multiple properties................... 30-440
.. unsuccessful house sale............... 30-420
. gifts 31-060
. hold-over relief – see Hold-over relief
. husband and wife 30-700
. incorporation, planning 31-080
. indemnity against future sale 31-620
. indexation allowance, restriction 30-480
. instalment payments 30-200
. lease dilapidations 30-580
. leases 30-600
. legal costs, allowable deduction 30-140
. life assurance policy gains 31-140
. non-resident with UK assets 30-820

Paragraph

. part disposals 30-160
. partnerships, allocation of gains and
    losses 30-860
. payment by instalments................ 30-200
. personal representatives................ 30-780
. private residence relief – see Private
    residence relief
. probate valuations 30-100
.. agreeing and March 1982 30-500
. rental business losses 30-300
. roll-over relief – see Roll-over relief
. shares and securities – see Shares and
    securities
. taper relief – see Taper relief
. time apportioned gain 30-460
. use of remittance basis 30-840
. wasting asset, 100-year-old chattel 30-560

Capital goods scheme – see Value added tax

Capital sums derived from assets
. insurance claims
.. far from minor claims................. 30-060
.. minor claims 30-040
. insurance proceeds.................... 30-000
. payment in lieu of view 30-020

Cars
. benefit charges
.. classic car........................ 10-690
. company cars....................... 10-800
.. petrol with repayments 10-840
.. prices 10-740
. company fuel 10-820
. expensive 10-810
. fuel, value added tax
.. partial exemption.................... 50-360
. horsebox.......................... 10-680
. leased 10-790
.. capital allowances 10-790
.. ending lease, value added tax 51-060
. mileage allowances – see Mileage
    allowances
. pool cars.......................... 10-780
. private number plates 10-760
. scrappage scheme 12-680

Cases
. Bower v R & C Commrs (2008) Sp
    C 665 41-100
. Flather [1995] BVC 780................ 50-460
. Frost v Feltham (1980) 55 TC 10 30-400
. I/S Fini H v Skatteministeriet (Case
    C-32/03) [2007] BVC 415............. 50-340
. Mallalieu v Drummond [1983] BTC
    380............................. 12-040
. Munby v Furlong (1977) 50 TC 491 12-150
. Pinnell's Case (1602) 5 Co Rep 117a 41-120
. Rashid v Garcia (2002) Sp C 348 60-660
. Stevenson v Wishart [1987] BTC 283; 59
    TC 740 11-360

Paragraph

. Virtue (t/a Lammermuir Game Services)
  [2007] BVC 2,518 51-020
. Watton (HMIT) v Tippett [1997]
  BTC 338 31-440

Cessation of trade or business
. bad debts 21-580
. post-cessation
. . carry forward of losses 20-360
. . expenses 12-220
. . rent 50-340

Change in ownership of company
. change in trade 20-540
. control of company 20-520

Chargeable gains – see Capital gains tax

Chargeable transfers – see Inheritance tax

Charitable trusts
. property leaving, charge to
  inheritance tax 40-680

Charities
. value added tax exemption 50-500

Chattel exemption
. generally 31-120
. 100-year-old wasting chattel 30-560
. parts of small chattels 31-100

Childcare
. nursery care or family baby sitting 10-980
. vouchers 11-000
. . stockpiling whilst on maternity leave 10-990

**Civil partnerships – see Married couples
  and civil partners**

Classic cars
. benefit 10-690

Close companies
. associated companies – see Associated
  companies
. determination 20-980
. loans to participators
. . effect of directors loan on penalty and
    interest 21-080
. . participation in penalty calculation 21-060
. . selling company assets and subsequent
    liabilities 21-100

Clothing 12-040

Codes
. PAYE notice 12-460

Commencement of trade or business
. corporation tax, accounting periods 20-100
. opening year rules 10-020
. pre-trading expenditure 12-140; 20-480; 20-490

Commercial investment properties
. capital allowances 12-500

Paragraph

Commissions
. auctioneers, value added tax 50-920

Companies
. associated – see Associated companies
. business property relief
. . owning property through company 40-880
. . restriction, calculation 40-940
. close – see Close companies
. corporation tax – see Corporation tax
. interest relief 11-760
. property, entrepreneurs' relief 31-640
. residence 20-940

Company secretary
. director for National Insurance contributions
    purposes 60-100

Company vehicles – see Cars; Vans

**Compensation – see also Capital sums
  derived from assets**
. personal injury 12-740
. value added tax 50-080

Compulsory purchase
. non-business assets, roll-over relief 31-340

Computers
. private use 10-560
. revenue or capital expenditure 20-220

Congestion charge
. reimbursement 10-480

Connected persons
. ownership of shares 30-640

Consideration
. deferred
. . lack of, income 30-240
. . purchaser's view 30-220
. receipts by instalment 30-180

Consortium relief – see Group relief

Construction industry scheme (CIS)
. deemed contractor 12-620
. gross payment status 21-340

Continuing professional development 11-920

Convertible securities 10-320

Corporation tax
. accounting periods
. . company in liquidation 20-120
. . exceeding 12 months 20-080
. . newly formed company 20-100
. . straddling 31 March 20-260
. amount of gain charged to 30-540
. associated companies – see Associated
  companies
. bad debts 20-040
. . cessation of business 21-580

Corporation tax – continued   **Paragraph**
. buy-back of shares 21-090
. calculation of taxable trading profits,
     adjustments 20-020
. change in ownership of company
 . . change in trade 20-540
 . . control of company 20-520
. close companies – see Close companies
. company loans to family members 21-380
. company residence 20-940
. computation 20-060
. computer, revenue or capital
     expenditure 20-220
. construction industry company 21-340
. double taxation relief claim 21-450
. energy-saving equipment, purchasing 21-440
. foreign company dividends 21-560
. government loans...................... 20-440
. groups of companies – see Group relief;
     Groups of companies
. hive-down of trade with transferor company
     left insolvent 20-580
. intangible amortisation 20-240
. late filing penalty 21-310
. life insurance company, contingent loan 21-120
. limited liability partnership, associated
     company 21-000
. losses – see Losses
. notice of coming within charge 21-200
. overdue, interest 21-260
. payment – see Corporation tax self-
     assessment
. penalties and interest, computation........ 21-300
. pre-rental expenditure 20-480
. pre-trading expenditure 20-490
. relief
 . . income tax payments................. 20-000
 . . loan relationships – see Loan relationships
 . . marginal 20-300
. repayment of tax
 . . interest 21-280
 . . value added tax 21-520
. research and development – see Research
     and development
. small companies' rate 20-280
. stock or fixed assets 21-320
. UITF 40 adjustment 21-360
. value added tax repayment 21-520

Corporation tax self-assessment
. changing to quarterly payments 21-240
. instalment payments 21-220

Crystallisation events 11-900

D

Death
. capital gains tax
 . . estates, exemption 30-760
 . . personal representatives............... 30-780
. chargeable events..................... 11-640

                                   Paragraph
. estates
 . . capital gains tax exemption 30-760
 . . inheritance tax – see Inheritance tax
. losses, using........................ 30-800
. non-availability of business property relief,
     use at death....................... 40-920
. probate valuations 30-100
 . . agreeing and March 1982 30-500
. reasonable excuse for non-payment 12-580

Debit cards
. employers, expenses payments 11-930

Deductions
. value of estate, inheritance tax 40-260

Default surcharge
. value added tax 50-860

Dependent relatives allowances
. private resident relief 31-240

De-registration
. value added tax – see Value added tax

Diesel – see Cars

Directors
. National Insurance contributions
 . . appointment mid-year 60-240
 . . Class 1 deferment 60-460
 . . reaching retirement age 60-520
. not employee 10-040
. PAYE timings 10-100

Disabled persons
. value added tax
 . . building work...................... 50-460
 . . installation of stair lift............... 50-470
 . . transport 50-480

Disbursements
. value added tax invoices................ 50-060

Discounted gift trust.................. 41-100

Discretionary trusts
. gifts, seven-year rule 40-120
. hold-over relief 30-720
. taxation............................ 11-380

Dividends
. foreign company, corporation tax 21-560

Doctors
. fee for statutory service, value added
     tax 51-100

Domicile
. inheritance tax purposes – see Inheritance
     tax

Donations
. value added tax 50-520

Double taxation relief
. corporation tax....................... 21-450
. foreign tax 20-320

	Paragraph
. UK and foreign income	12-720
. withholding tax	20-340

Dwelling-houses
. building managing director a home	10-620
. diminution in value of family home	40-080

E

EC Sales Lists	51-180

Emigration
. gifts (former taper relief)	31-320

Employee benefits
. asset or accommodation	10-640
. building managing director a home	10-620
. cars – see Cars	
. Class 1A National Insurance contributions	60-320
. cost allocation	10-500
. cost to employer	10-520
. employee assets	
. . transfer	10-600
. . with costs	10-580
. expenses payments	
. . how much earned	10-460
. . medical check-ups and health screening	10-440
. loans – see Employment-related loans	
. overseas employment	12-540
. part-time employee, full-time wife	10-540
. vans – see Vans	

Employee-controlled companies 11-780

Employees
. meals	10-170
. . vouchers	12-000
. seconded overseas, expenses	10-230
. suggestion awards	10-180

Employee share schemes
. convertible securities	10-320
. enterprise management incentive	10-420
. forced value shares	10-340
. qualifying options to the maximum	10-380
. save as you earn	10-400
. shares at undervalue	10-300
. withdrawing share options	10-360

Employment income
. childcare vouchers	11-000
. . stockpiling whilst on maternity leave	10-990
. termination payments – see Termination payments	

Employment-related loans
. beneficial loans	10-940
. . interest	10-900
. free shares	10-920
. lending money to family	10-960

	Paragraph
Energy-saving equipment	
. purchasing	21-440

Enterprise investment scheme (EIS)
. capital gains tax	31-000
. entrepreneurs' relief	31-020
. . goodwill	30-980
. generally	11-800
. less than maximum relief	11-820

Enterprise management incentive (EMI)
. entrepreneurs' relief	31-600
. generally	10-420

Entertainment – see Business entertainment

Entrepreneurs' relief
. business property	31-700
. company property	31-640
. enterprise investment scheme	31-020
. . goodwill	30-980
. enterprise management incentive	31-600
. non-voting shares	31-660
. sale of business	31-400
. sole trader, sale of business/investment in another	31-680

Estate income
. administration of estates	11-460
. generally	11-480
. life interest income	11-440

Euros
. value added tax invoices	51-160

Exit charge – see Inheritance tax

Expenses
. allowable, dealing with	11-940
. employer debit cards	11-930
. how much earned	10-460
. incidental overnight expenses	10-220
. legal	
. . capital gain computation, allowable deduction	30-140
. . defending reputation	12-100
. medical check-ups and health screening	10-440
. post-cessation	12-220
. relocation expenses	10-200
. travel	
. . employees seconded overseas	10-230
. . home to work	10-010; 11-960

Expensive cars 10-810

Extra-statutory concessions
. A11	12-520
. A17	12-580
. A37	10-040
. A43	11-780
. C16	31-020
. D33	30-020; 31-620
. D52	31-620

Paragraph

F

Family company
. annual investment allowance (AIA) 21-480
. . long-life plant 21-500

Family members
. company loans 21-380
. employment-related loans 10-960

Farmhouses
. partnership asset, inheritance tax
   implications 40-280

Farming
. farmers averaging 11-320
. fluctuating profits, relief 11-310
. herd basis 11-340

Fees
. auctioneers, value added tax 50-920

Flat conversion allowances 12-340

Flat-rate scheme – see Value added tax

Foreign companies – see Non-resident companies

Foreign employers
. UK based workers, National Insurance
   contributions 60-560

Foreign income
. mixed up with UK income 12-720

Foreign students
. National Insurance contributions 60-600

Foreign tax
. corporation tax, credit 20-320

Foreign workers
. statutory maternity pay (SMP) 12-700

Forfeited deposits
. multiple properties 30-440
. unsuccessful house sale 30-420

Foster care 11-720

Freight transport services
. value added tax 51-200

Furnished holiday lettings
. business property relief 40-820
. capital allowances 11-570
. loss set off, National Insurance
   contributions 60-400
. roll-over relief 31-500

G

Gift aid 11-260

Gifts
. capital gains tax
. . emigration (former taper relief) 31-320
. . goodwill 31-060

Paragraph

. inheritance tax
. . discretionary trusts, seven-year rule 40-120
. . gift of interest in partnership 40-950
. . gifts to spouse 40-700
. . gifts with reservation 40-300; 40-310
. . reporting normal gifts out of income 40-800
. . small gifts and an annual exemption 40-780
. . valid gift 40-310

Goodwill
. enterprise investment scheme and
   entrepreneurs' relief 30-980
. gift 31-060
. incorporation 31-080
. roll-over relief 31-420

Government loans 20-440

Group relief
. capital allowances 20-780
. comprehensive example 20-840
. consortium claims 20-740
. newly acquired subsidiary, computation of
   relief 20-820
. profits available for, calculation 20-800
. wasting losses and double tax 20-760

Groups of companies
. degrouping charge 20-700
. degrouping goodwill 20-720
. group/consortium structure 20-860
. group or association 21-020
. loan relationships 20-180
. . bad debts 20-200
. notional group transfer 20-680
. pre-entry losses 20-660
. research and development 21-140
. . subcontracted R&D, enhanced small or
   medium-sized enterprise relief 21-180
. return period, identifying 20-600
. sale of trading stock on intra-group transfer
   of trade 20-640
. unincorporated associations 20-620

H

Handicapped persons – see Disabled persons

HMRC Briefs
. 13/07 50-900
. 47/07 50-470
. 64/07 51-020
. 19/09 50-390

HMRC Leaflets
. E24 . . . . 60-140; 60-250

Hold-over relief
. agricultural property 31-560
. discretionary trusts 30-720

Paragraph

Husband and wife – see Married couples and civil partners

I

Incidental overnight expenses – see Overnight expenses

Income tax
. accounting date, changes 11-120
. air miles 10-280
. allowable expenses, dealing with 11-940
. annual party or function 10-160
. business entertainment 12-020
. business equipment 12-150
. cars – see Cars
. chargeable events on death 11-640
. childcare
. . nursery care or family baby sitting 10-980
. . vouchers 10-990; 11-000
. clothing 12-040
. computer, private use 10-560
. continuing professional development 11-920
. crystallisation events 11-900
. death, chargeable events 11-640
. directors
. . not employee 10-040
. . PAYE timings 10-100
. employee benefits – see Employee benefits
. employee control 11-780
. employee share schemes – see Employee
    share schemes
. enterprise investment scheme relief 11-800
. . less than maximum 11-820
. estate income – see Estate income
. farming
. . farmers averaging 11-320
. . fluctuating profits, relief 11-310
. . herd basis 11-340
. foster care 11-720
. gift aid 11-260
. goods taken for own use 11-100
. incidental overnight expenses 10-220
. incorporation losses 12-160
. interest relief, companies 11-760
. IR35 10-060
. jury service 10-080
. late night transport provided for
    employees 11-980
. lease premium 12-120
. legal expenses, defending reputation 12-100
. living accommodation 10-260
. . ancillary accommodation expenses in
    exempt accommodation 10-240
. loan interest 11-740
. . relief, companies 11-760
. long service awards 10-140
. losses – see Losses
. married couples allowance and wealthy
    pensioners 11-700

Paragraph

. meal vouchers 12-000
. moving expenses 10-200
. opening year losses 12-180
. opening year rules 10-020
. overnight expenses 10-220
. overseas expenses 10-230
. partnerships – see Partnerships
. patent royalties 11-260
. PAYE – see PAYE
. payroll giving 11-280
. pensions – see Pensions
. post-cessation expenses 12-220
. pre-trading expenditure 12-140
. property – see Property income
. rates:
. . abolition of starting rate 12-600
. recharged motoring costs 10-480
. relocation allowance 10-200
. salary sacrifice
. . mobile phone 11-020
. . training costs 10-120
. self-employed users of mileage rates 10-000
. settlor's income
. . capital and income to settlor 11-500
. . settlor interested loans 11-520
. sports club 11-300
. staff meals 10-170
. . vouchers 12-000
. staff suggestions 10-180
. tax credits 11-680
. . method of calculating income 11-670
. terminal losses 12-200
. termination payments
. . after termination 11-040
. . group termination 11-060
. . termination in kind 11-080
. travel expenses 10-010; 11-960
. trivial pensions 11-840
. trust income – see Trusts
. UK and foreign income 12-720
. vans – see Vans
. working overseas 11-660

Incorporation
. losses 12-160
. planning, gifts of business assets relief 31-080
. roll-over relief
. . disapplication 31-380
. . generally 31-360

Indemnity payments
. against future sale 31-620

Inheritance tax
. agricultural property relief – see Agricultural
    property relief
. allowable deductions 40-260
. annual exemption
. . carry forward 40-760

Inheritance tax – continued   **Paragraph**
. . chargeable lifetime transfer or potentially
    exempt transfer 40-240
. . small gifts 40-780
. associated assets 40-160
. . sub valuations 40-200
. associated leases 40-180
. associated loans 40-140
. business property relief – see Business
    property relief
. chargeable transfers, lifetime tax 40-000
. diminution in value of family home 40-080
. discounted gift trust 41-100
. disposals after death 40-480
. domicile
. . dangers 40-020
. . non-UK, overseas assets 40-030
. . premium bonds 41-060
. double charge 40-520
. estate rates 40-320
. . exempt residuals 40-340
. . taxable residuals 40-360
. estates with business property relief and
    exempt legacies 41-080
. exit charges 40-600
. . after more than ten years 40-640
. gift of interest in partnership 40-950
. gifts with reservation 40-300; 40-310
. income or capital paid out with
    discretion 40-560
. liability, responsibility for 41-180
. lifetime transfer or death estate 40-540
. loans made during lifetime 41-120
. National Heritage Property 41-140
. normal gifts out of income, reporting 40-800
. overseas assets of non-UK domiciled
    person 40-030
. periodic charges 40-220
. pilot trusts, use of 41-160
. potentially exempt transfers
. . estates, using up the nil band 40-380
. . taper relief 40-420
. pre-owned assets 40-660
. property leaving charitable trust 40-680
. quick succession relief 40-500
. rates
. . estates 40-320–40-360
. settlement, late additions 40-620
. seven-year charge, extra tax due 40-460
. seven-year rule 40-100
. . death 40-400
. . gifts to discretionary trusts 40-120
. shares
. . gifts, differing charges 40-060
. . valuations 40-040
. small gift exemption 40-780
. taper relief 40-440
. . potentially exempt transfers 40-420
. ten-yearly charges 40-580
. transfers between spouses or civil partners
. . gifts to spouse 40-700

                                        Paragraph
. . non-domiciled spouse 40-720
. . transfer of unused nil-rate band (post-9
    October 2007) 40-740
. valid gift 40-310
. woodlands
. . interests 41-020
. . values 41-040

Input tax – see **Value added tax**

Insolvency
. transferor company, hive down of trade 20-580

Installed goods
. place of supply, value added tax 50-200

Instalment payments
. capital gains tax 30-200
. . consideration – see Consideration
. corporation tax 21-220

Insurance
. capital sums derived from assets 30-000;
                                          30-040; 30-060
. life assurance policy gains, reporting 31-140

Insurance companies
. contingent loans 21-120

Interest
. beneficial loans 10-900
. loans 11-740
. . companies 11-760
. corporation tax
. . overdue tax 21-260; 21-300
. . repayment of 21-280

Interest relief
. companies 11-760

Intermediaries – see **IR35**

Invoices
. value added tax – see Value added tax

IR35
. calculation, National Insurance
    contributions 60-020
. income tax 10-060
. value added tax flat-rate scheme 50-740

J

Jobseeker's allowance 60-040

Jury service 10-080

L

Large businesses
. National Insurance contributions default
    penalties 60-540

Lease dilapidations 30-580

Paragraph

Lease premiums 12-120

Leases
. cars 10-790
. . ending lease, value added tax 51-060
. property 30-600

Legal expenses
. capital gain computation, allowable
    deduction 30-140
. defending reputation 12-100

**Life insurance companies – see Insurance
companies**

Lifetime transfers – see Inheritance tax

Limited liability partnerships
. associated company 21-000
. losses 11-240

Limited partnerships
. value added tax 50-120

Liquidation
. corporation tax, accounting periods 20-120

Living accommodation
. ancillary expenses in exempt
    accommodation 10-240
. generally 10-260
. job-related, private residence relief 31-260
. non-residents 12-560

Loan relationships
. groups of companies 20-180
. . bad debts 20-200
. non-trading deficit 20-140
. related loans 20-160

Loans
. associated 40-140
. close company participators – see Close
    companies
. company loans to family members 21-380
. conversion to shares 20-510
. employees – see Employment-related loans
. government 20-440
. interest 11-740
. interest relief, companies 11-760
. made during lifetime, inheritance tax 41-120

Long service awards 10-140

Losses
. buying 20-460
. capital losses brought forward 30-280
. carry back
. . date of repayment 12-420
. . temporary extension of rules 12-190
. . trading losses 20-420
. carry forward
. . against different trade, National Insurance
    contributions 60-420
. . post-cessation 20-360
. company reconstruction 20-500

Paragraph

. conversion of loans into shares 20-510
. former taper relief 30-320
. furnished holiday lettings, National Insurance
    contributions set off 60-400
. incorporation 12-160
. opening year 12-180
. partnerships – see Partnerships
. post-cessation carry forward 20-360
. pre-entry, groups of companies 20-660
. property rental business 30-300
. terminal 12-200; 20-400
. utilising 30-340
. . on death 30-800

M

Machine tools
. manufacture of goods for export 50-180

Married couple's allowance
. wealthy pensioners 11-700

Married couples and civil partners
. capital gains tax 30-700
. . taper relief – see Taper relief
. qualifying corporate bonds, transfer from
    husband to wife 30-880
. separation, principal private residence
    relief 31-220
. transfers between – see Inheritance tax

Meal vouchers 12-000

Medical check-ups 10-440

Mileage allowances
. generally 10-860
. overstated claims 10-890
. rates
. . double 10-880
. . self-employed 10-000; 10-870

Mobile phones
. salary sacrifice 11-020

Motoring costs
. recharged 10-480

Moving expenses – see Relocation expenses

N

National Heritage Property
. inheritance tax 41-140

National Insurance contributions
. carry forward losses against different
    trade 60-420
. Class 1 deferment
. . directors 60-460
. . employees 60-500
. Class 1A
. . benefit in kind 60-320
. . lower earnings limit 60-300

National Insurance
    contributions – continued   **Paragraph**
. Class 1B calculation 60-360
. Class 2: voluntary 60-380
. Class 3 refunds 60-640
. company secretary or director 60-100
. contracting out
. . computation 60-180
. . effect on employee and employer 60-200
. default penalties for large businesses 60-540
. deferment certificate, length of time
    one lasts 60-480
. directors
. . appointment mid-year 60-240
. . reaching retirement age 60-520
. direct repayment 60-520
. exact percentage method 60-260
. foreign students 60-600
. furnished holiday letting loss set off 60-400
. IR35 calculation 60-020
. jobseeker's allowance 60-040
. overdue
. . dates from which interest runs 10-160
. PAYE settlement agreement
. . PSA or not 60-160
. . timing of 60-340
. paying employees on an ad hoc basis, effect
    of 60-220
. sleeping partners 60-000
. state pension
. . entitlement 60-080
. . qualification 60-060
. tables, using 60-280
. tips and troncs 60-120
. . payment via credit card 60-130
. . payment via payroll 60-140
. trading or not 60-660
. UK duties, French residence 60-580
. working in UK for foreign employer 60-560
. working overseas for 12 months 60-620

Non-domiciled person 12-520

Non-resident companies
. dividends, corporation tax 21-560
. tax treatment 20-950

Non-residents
. capital gains tax
. . non-residents with UK assets 30-820
. . use of remittance basis 30-840
. living accommodation 12-560

Northern Rock
. shares in, capital loss claims 31-720

O

Opening year losses 12-180

Opening year rules 10-020

Overdue tax
. interest – see Interest

                                 Paragraph
Overnight expenses
. reimbursement 10-220

Overpayment of tax
. interest – see Interest

**Overseas companies – see Non-resident
    companies**

**Overseas employment – see Working
    abroad**

P

Parking costs
. reimbursement 10-480

Part disposals
. chargeable gains computation 30-160

Partial exemption – see Value added tax

Parties or functions 10-160

Partnerships
. agreements 11-200
. allocation of gains and losses 30-860
. business property relief, restriction,
    calculation 40-960
. interest 11-180
. . gift of 40-950
. limited – see Limited partnerships
. limited liability partnerships – see Limited
    liability partnerships
. losses with profits 11-140
. new partner, same VAT number 50-680
. partner rents 11-220
. profit shares 11-160
. sleeping partners, National Insurance
    contributions 60-000

Part payments
. accounting for value added tax 50-280

Patent royalties 11-260

PAYE
. codes
. . notice 12-460
. pensions 12-440
. settlement agreements – see PAYE
    settlement agreements
. timings, directors 10-100

PAYE settlement agreements
. all employees 12-400
. generally 12-380
. PSA or not 60-160
. timing of 60-340

Payment of tax
. corporation tax – see Corporation tax self-
    assessment
. non-payment of payment on account, death a
    reasonable excuse 12-580

Paragraph

Payroll giving 11-280

Penalties
. interest on – see Interest
. National Insurance contributions: default
   penalties for large businesses........... 60-540
. returns
.. corporation tax, computation 21-300
.. value added tax 50-860
. value added tax
.. default surcharge 50-860
.. misdeclaration penalty 50-880

Pensions
. annual allowance 11-880
. effect of 11-860
. excess contributions............. 12-060; 12-080
. PAYE 12-440
. paying contributions whilst working
   abroad 12-090
. research and development 21-160
. retirement pension
.. entitlement 60-080
.. qualification where no National Insurance
   contributions paid 60-060
. trivial 11-840

Personal injury
. compensation 12-740

Personalised number plates.............. 10-760

Personal representatives
. capital gains tax..................... 30-780

Personal service companies – see IR35

Petrol – see Cars

Pilot trusts
. inheritance tax 41-160

Place of supply – see Value added tax

Plant and machinery allowances
. animals, treatment 12-280
. annual investment allowance (AIA) 12-480;
                                   21-460
.. commercial investment properties 12-500
.. family company 21-480; 21-500
.. sharing 12-490
. energy-saving equipment, purchasing 21-440
. leased vehicles 21-600
. pooling 12-320
. short-life asset election 12-300
. stolen van.......................... 12-290

**Post-cessation – see Cessation of trade or
business**

**Potentially exempt transfers – see
Inheritance tax**

Pre-entry losses – see Groups of companies

Premium bonds
. domicile, inheritance tax 41-060

Paragraph

Pre-owned assets...................... 40-660

Pre-trading expenditure.... 12-140; 20-480; 20-490

Private/non-business use of business assets
. value added tax 50-020

Private residence relief
. building house then paying tax........... 31-160
. deemed residence.................... 31-280
. demolishing house then paying tax 31-180
. dependent relatives allowances 31-240
. generally.......................... 30-400
. job-related accommodation 31-260
. lettings 31-300
. permitted area (half a hectare) 31-200
. separation 31-220

Prizes
. capital allowances 12-510

Probate valuations
. agreeing and March 1982 30-500
. generally.......................... 30-100

Property – see also Dwelling-houses
. buying a freehold 31-580
. entrepreneurs' relief
.. business property 31-700
.. company property 31-640
. lease premiums 12-120
. value added tax
.. change of use 51-080
.. converting residential properties 51-120
.. renting residential property 51-140

Property income
. multiple properties.................... 30-440
. non-resident landlord.................. 11-620
. property rental business losses 30-300
. proportion of premium really rent 11-600
. rent-a-room relief.................... 11-580
. renting in two capacities 11-560

Property rental business
. capital allowances 12-505
. losses 30-300
. pre-rental expenditure 20-480

Purchase by company of own shares....... 20-560

Q

Qualifying corporate bonds
. shares for 30-920
. transfer from husband to wife 30-880
. worthless, disposal to good cause 30-900

Quick succession relief.................. 40-500

Quoted shares
. business property relief 40-860

Paragraph

R

Rates of tax
. corporation tax: small companies'
    rate................................ 20-280
. income tax: abolition of starting rate 12-600
. inheritance tax: estates 40-320–40-360

Reasonable excuse
. death, payments on account 12-580

Reconstructions
. losses 20-500

**Redundancy payments – see Termination
    payments**

Registration
. value added tax – see Value added tax

Relocation expenses 10-200

Remittance basis
. overseas capital gains and losses 12-640;
                                              30-840

Rent
. post-cessation, value added tax............ 50-340

Rental income – see Property income

Repayment of tax
. corporation tax, interest.................. 21-280

**Replacement of business assets – see Roll-
    over relief**

Repossessed items
. value added tax 50-980

Research and development
. claims.............................. 21-130
. groups of companies 21-140
.. subcontracted R&D, enhanced small or
    medium-sized enterprise relief.......... 21-180
. pension contributions.................. 21-160

Residence
. companies 20-940
. non-domiciled person 12-520
. UK duties and French residence, National
    Insurance contributions 60-580

Residential property – see Property

Retail schemes – see Value added tax

Returns
. corporation tax, late filing............... 21-310
. value added tax, periodical 50-300

Revenue expenditure
. computer 20-220

Reverse charge
. value added tax exempt businesses 50-040

Road fuel – see Cars

Paragraph

Roll-over relief
. company assets against personal assets 31-460
. furnished holiday lettings 31-500
. goodwill 31-420
. incorporation relief 31-360
.. disapplication....................... 31-380
. non-business asset 31-340
. partial replacement 31-480
. sale of fixed assets 31-540
. same asset 31-440
. sole trader, sale of business/investment in
    another........................... 31-680
. transfer of property 31-520

Royalties
. value added tax 50-960

S

Salary sacrifice
. mobile phone........................ 11-020
. training costs 10-120

Sale or return goods
. value added tax 50-220

Samples
. value added tax 50-000

SAYE share option schemes 10-400

Scrappage scheme..................... 12-680

**Second-hand goods scheme – see Value
    added tax**

Self-employed
. mileage rates 10-000; 10-870

Separation
. principal private resident relief............ 31-220

Settlements
. late additions 40-620

Settlor's income
. capital and income to settlor.............. 11-500
. school fees from trust income 11-540
. settlor interested loans.................. 11-520

Share loss relief
. negligible value claim 31-040
.. Northern Rock shares 31-720

**Shares and securities – see also Quoted
    shares**
. agricultural property relief 40-980
. bonus issues 30-940
. buy-back of shares 21-090
. conversion of loan capital............... 20-510
. conversion of securities, premiums great and
    small 30-960
. employees – see Employee share schemes
. joint ownership 30-640

Paragraph

. loss relief – see Share loss relief

. pre-sale sales 20-960

. purchase of own shares 20-560

. qualifying corporate bonds – see Qualifying corporate bonds

. sale not at arm's length 30-080

. same day transactions 30-660

.. alternative identification rules 30-680

. substantial shareholdings 20-880

.. nil gain nil loss rules 20-900

.. substantial share for share exchange 20-920

. trusting 30-740

. valuation, inheritance tax 40-040

.. gifts, differing charges 40-060

Short-life assets 12-340

Sleeping partners

. National Insurance contributions 60-000

Small companies' rate

. corporation tax 20-280

Small gift exemption

. inheritance tax 40-780

Sports clubs 11-300

Spouses – see Married couples and civil partners

Staff meals 10-170

Staff suggestion awards 10-180

Stair lifts

. installation, value added tax 50-470

Statements of practice

. D12 30-860

. 1/90 20-940

Statutory maternity pay (SMP)

. foreign workers 12-700

Stock

. theft, value added tax 50-100

Substantial shareholdings – see Shares and securities

T

Taper relief

. emigrating with gift 31-320

. inheritance tax 40-440

.. potentially exempt transfers 40-420

. losses 30-320

. mixed use assets 30-360

. ownership periods for spouses (pre-6 April 2008 disposals) 30-380

Taxable benefits – see Employee benefits

Tax credits

. generally 11-680

. method of calculating income 11-670

Paragraph

Terminal losses 12-200; 20-400

Termination payments

. after termination 11-040

. group termination 11-060

. termination in kind 11-080

Theft

. stock, value added tax 50-100

Tips

. National Insurance contributions 60-120

.. tips via credit card 60-130

.. tips via payroll 60-140

Tour operators' margin scheme – see Value added tax

Trading losses – see Losses

Trading stock

. sale on intra-group transfer of trade 20-640

Training costs

. salary sacrifice 10-120

Transport

. late night, provided for employees 11-980

. value added tax

.. disabled persons 50-480

.. freight transport services 51-200

Travel expenses

. employees seconded overseas 10-230

. home to work 10-010; 11-960

Troncs

. National Insurance contributions 60-120

Trusts

. income 11-400

.. interest in possession trusts 11-420

.. school fees from 11-540

. inheritance tax

.. discounted gift trust 41-100

.. pilot trusts, use of 41-160

. shares 30-740

. taxation 11-360

.. discretionary trusts 11-380

U

Unincorporated associations

. group company 20-620

V

Valuation

. inheritance tax, estate on death, allowable deductions 40-260

Value added tax

. accounting for part payments 50-280

. auctioneer's fees and commissions 50-920

Value added tax – continued   **Paragraph**
. barn conversion
.. do-it-yourself 50-430
.. finishing 50-440
. book royalties 50-960
. capital goods scheme, sale of capital
    item 50-420
. car lease, ending 51-060
. change of use of property 51-080
. compensation 50-080
. contract implicitly including VAT 50-260
. converting residential properties 51-120
. correction of errors 50-840
. cost of making asset available 50-020
. default surcharge 50-860
. de-registration 50-660
. disabled persons
.. building work 50-460
.. transport 50-480
. disbursements, invoices 50-060
. doctors: fee for statutory service 51-100
. donation or taxable income 50-520
. EC Sales Lists 51-180
. exemptions
.. businesses, reverse charge 50-040
.. charities 50-500
.. giving up 50-620
. flat-rate scheme
.. IR35 50-740
.. more than one business 50-720
.. profit 50-700
.. voluntary registration 50-600
. fuel scale charge 50-900
. goods on sale or return 50-220
. input tax: third parties 50-320
. installation of stair lift 50-470
. invoices
.. disbursements 50-060
.. in euros 51-160
.. tax point and invoice date 50-240
. late filing penalties 50-860
. limited partnership 50-120
. misdeclaration penalty 50-880
. mixed supplies 50-140
.. housing development 51-020
. mixing business with pleasure 51-040
. option to tax 50-540
. partial exemption
.. override 50-380
.. partially exempt business 50-390
.. provisional and final calculations 50-400
.. road fuel 50-360
. partnerships
.. limited partnership 50-120
.. new partner, same VAT number 50-680
. periodical returns 50-300
. place of supply 50-160
.. installed goods 50-200
. post-cessation rent 50-340
. registration
.. ahead of future sales 50-580

                    Paragraph
.. historical 50-560
.. late 50-640
.. voluntary into flat-rate scheme 50-600
. renting residential property 51-140
. repayment, corporation tax 21-520
. repossessed items 50-980
. residential properties
.. converting 51-120
.. renting 51-140
. retail schemes, different margins on
    goods 50-760
. returns, periodical 50-300
. reverse charge, exempt businesses 50-040
. road fuel
.. fuel scale charge 50-900
.. partial exemption 50-360
. samples 50-000
. second-hand goods scheme 50-780
.. global margins 50-800
.. vehicles 51-000
. stolen stock 50-100
. tax point and invoice date 50-240
. third parties, input tax 50-320
. tools to manufacture for export 50-180
. tour operators' margin scheme, cash
    accounting eligibility 50-820
. transport
.. disabled persons 50-480
.. freight transport services 51-200

Vans
. capital contributions by employee 10-670
. generally 10-660
. horsebox 10-680
. private use
.. mileage allowances – see Mileage
    allowances
.. normal commuting 10-720
.. while on call 10-700
. second-hand, value added tax 51-000
. stolen, capital allowances 12-290

VAT Information Sheets
. 02/01 50-140
. 04/09 50-390

VAT Notices
. 700, para. 7.7 51-160
. 700/11 50-340
. 700/45 50-840
. 700/50 50-860
. 700/64, para. 9.1 50-900
. 700/22 50-180
. 701/57, para. 3.12 51-100
. 706 51-140
. 706/2 50-420
. 718 50-980
. 731 . . . . 50-820; 51-160
. 733 50-720
. 742A 51-080
. 744 50-480

Paragraph

Vehicles – see Cars; Vans

W

Wasting assets
. 100-year-old wasting chattel 30-560

Withholding tax 20-340

Woodlands
. inheritance tax
. . woodland interests 41-020
. . woodland values 41-040

Paragraph

Working abroad
. benefits in kind 12-540
. expenses 10-230
. income tax 11-660
. National Insurance contributions 60-620
. pension contributions 12-090

Work-related accommodation
. private residence relief 31-260

Writing-down allowances
. capital allowances 12-330